Using Japanese

D0071973

This is a guide to Japanese usage for students who have already acquired the basics of the language and wish to extend their knowledge. Unlike conventional grammars, it gives special attention to those areas of vocabulary and grammar which cause the most difficulty to English-speakers. Careful consideration is given throughout to questions of style, register, and politeness which are essential to achieving an appropriate level of formality. There are also sections dealing with a selection of common social rituals such as greetings, introductions, and apologies. Clear, readable, and easy to consult via its two indexes, is an essential reference for learners seeking access to the finer nuances of the Japanese language.

WILLIAM TSUYOSHI McCLURE is Assistant Professor at Queens College and The Graduate Center of the City University of New York. He has also taught Japanese language and linguistics at Cornell University and the University of Durham.

Companion titles to *Using Japanese*

Using French (third edition)
A guide to contemporary usage
R. E. BATCHELOR and M. H. OFFORD
(ISBN 0 521 64177 2 hardback)
(ISBN 0 521 64593 X paperback)

Using Spanish
A guide to contemporary usage
R. E. BATCHELOR and C. J. POUNTAIN
(ISBN 0 521 42123 3 hardback)
(ISBN 0 521 26987 3 paperback)

Using German
A guide to contemporary usage
MARTIN DURRELL
(ISBN 0 521 42077 6 hardback)
(ISBN 0 521 31556 5 paperback)

Using Russian
A guide to contemporary usage
DEREK OFFORD
(ISBN 0 521 45130 2 hardback)
(ISBN 0 521 45760 2 paperback)

Using French Synonyms
R. E. BATCHELOR and M. H. OFFORD
(ISBN 0 521 37277 1 hardback)
(ISBN 0 521 37878 8 paperback)

Using Spanish Synonyms
R. E. BATCHELOR
(ISBN 0 521 44160 9 hardback)
(ISBN 0 521 44694 5 paperback)

Using German Synonyms
MARTIN DURRELL
(ISBN 0 521 46552 4 hardback)
(ISBN 0 521 46954 6 paperback)

Using Italian Synonyms
HOWARD MOSS and VANNA MOTTA
(ISBN 0 521 47506 6 hardback)
(ISBN 0 521 47573 2 paperback)

Using French Vocabulary
JEAN H. DUFFY
(ISBN 0 521 57040 9 hardback)
(ISBN 0 521 57851 5 paperback)

Further titles in preparation

Using Japanese

A guide to contemporary usage

WILLIAM McCLURE

PUBLISHED BY THE PRESS SYNDICATE OF THE UNIVERSITY OF CAMBRIDGE

The Pitt Building, Trumpington Street, Cambridge, United Kingdom

CAMBRIDGE UNIVERSITY PRESS

The Edinburgh Building, Cambridge CB2 2RU, UK   www.cup.cam.ac.uk

40 West 20th Street, New York, NY 10011-4211, USA   www.cup.org

10 Stamford Road, Oakleigh, Melbourne 3166, Australia

Ruiz de Alarcón 13, 28014 Madrid, Spain

© William Tsuyoshi McClure 2000

This book is in copyright. Subject to statutory exception
and to the provisions of relevant collective licensing agreements,
no reproduction of any part may take place without
the written permission of Cambridge University Press.

First published 2000

Printed in the United Kingdom at the University Press, Cambridge

Typeface: Honmincho / Times New Roman [AU]

A catalogue record for this book is available from the British Library

Library of Congress Cataloguing in Publication data

ISBN 0 521 64155 1 hardback
ISBN 0 521 64614 6 paperback

Contents

PROPERTY OF
LIBRARY OF THE CHATHAMS
CHATHAM NJ

Acknowledgments

Writing this book has forced me to clarify much of what I have come to believe about Japanese, and it has made me think about the best way to present that information to students of the language. It has also shown me where my knowledge is still lacking, and where better and more complete explanations must still be found. In helping me through this project, I am most grateful to Miki Suzuki who has read every word and thought about every fact. Her attention to detail and willingness to explain her point of view have pushed me in the right direction time and time again. Any inaccuracies which remain are the result of my refusal to see sense.

Takako Katsuno, John Weste, and John Whitman have all read and re-read the manuscript helping me to maintain thoroughness, accuracy, and as much humor as possible. Each has spent a significant amount of time explaining their understanding of the Japanese language, and I am grateful for their insights. My students Natalya Borukhov and Ilene Tzou have also commented on the manuscript, with an eye to keeping it as accessible and clear as possible.

I am fortunate, actually, to be surrounded by Japanese who are interested in their own language and anxious to help. Those who have contributed in ways both large and small include Katsuhiko and Fumi Agatsuma, Katsushige and Izumi Akama, Mari Fujimoto, Kaori Furuya, Ariko Komiya, Atsuko Miyajima, Masaaki and Ayako Sakurai, Mamori Sugita, Kiyoko and Yasumatsu Suzuki, Toru and Yukiyo Terakawa, Keiko Uehara, and Toshiyuki Yabe. I am equally fortunate to have had excellent teachers, and in my own time to have taught so many students who have asked so many questions that I have been unable to answer the first time around.

More practical support has come from the Research Foundation of the City University of New York, Eiichi Ito of the Japan Foundation Library in Los Angeles, Kate Brett and Karl Howe of Cambridge University Press, and my brother David McClure.

I am grateful personally for the friendship and guidance of Gennaro Chierchia, Veneeta Dayal, Gita Martohardjono, and Don Starr. I am ever grateful for the companionship of William Pérez.

This book is dedicated to the memory of Charlie Tenny.

1 Register and politeness

1.1 Japan and Japanese

Japan is a country of 125.5 million people (1996) making it the eighth most populated country in the world. It has an area of 143,750 square miles (372,313 square kilometers) which is somewhat smaller than California, but somewhat larger than Germany. Tokyo and its metropolitan area is amongst the world's most populous cities. Japan has the second largest economy in the world after the United States. It is third if the European Union is treated as a single entity.

Japanese is the eighth most spoken language in the world, after Mandarin Chinese, Spanish, English, Bengali, Hindi, Portuguese, and Russian (1999). Although Japanese is spoken by communities totaling nearly 1.5 million people in South America and the United States, as well as by many smaller communities in Southeast Asia and Europe, it is unique to the degree that almost all of its speakers live in the same country. Japanese is studied around the world although it is a major activity in countries of the Pacific Rim.

1.2 Introduction

This book is really about how to be polite in Japanese, but this should be interpreted broadly to mean how to use the language appropriately in many different contexts. While anyone reading this book surely knows that Japanese has polite (行きます), honorific (いらっしゃる), humble (まいる), and familiar (行く) verb forms, there is more to speaking appropriately than just using the right words. Body language, tone of voice, even your choice of topics help to create an impression which is more or less polite, and which may as a consequence be more or less appropriate in a given situation. In addition, understanding and responding to unspoken signals is also a crucial part of speaking Japanese well. What is *not* said in a Japanese conversation may be just as important as what *is*.

To begin, I would like to talk a bit about English. While much is made of politeness in Japanese, politeness plays a role in English as well. Presumably everyone talks to their best mate differently from the way they talk to their grandparents or to their employer. Think about how you would introduce yourself to the Queen of England or to your future father-in-law. Think even about making a speech in front of a class of students. Would you be nervous? Or would it be just like talking on the phone with your brother or sister? How do you ask your friend if you can borrow a piece of paper? How do you ask the same person if they will lend you next month's rent? How do you argue? Or convey news about a death in the family? When we are nervous or when we are trying to make a specific impression, our speech changes. Perhaps we use bigger words or use longer sentences. We are more careful in what we say, and we try as hard as possible to think before we speak. In Japanese, when people are nervous or tense, they use more formal speech. They also fall back on well-worn and standardized ritual expressions.

This is not to say that formal speech is used only when you are uncomfortable. In English, it is quite likely that you are more careful when speaking to someone much older than you, or to a priest or rabbi, even to a teacher. This is not necessarily because you are uncomfortable, but may simply be a sign of respect. Similarly in Japanese.

Are there differences between the way men and women speak English? While men and women probably use more or less the same words in English, there are a great number of books written lately which focus on how men and women use their language differently. Men are supposed to order. Women to suggest. Men are supposed to exclude. Women to include. While it is impossible to say that all men speak one way while all women speak another, there may be some truth to the differences, and again, such differences can be found in Japanese. In fact, they are probably exaggerated in Japanese (and Japanese women's speech is a topic of academic study in its own right). Typically it is said that Japanese women sound softer and are more polite than men. They tend to use a higher pitch when they speak. Is any of this true of all women? No. Crude speech is not the sole domain of men. Is the opposite completely not true of men? No. Polite speech is not the sole domain of women. Nevertheless, there are real tendencies as well as stereotypes about speech and gender, and students should be aware of these tendencies and stereotypes in order to mimic or to avoid them. The stereotypes can be used (or ignored) for particular effect. I know a young American woman in her thirties who speaks Japanese like a grandmother in her sixties. Her speech is both extremely polite and slightly out of date. This had made her a star of the town where she lives and works, welcome wherever she goes. Other times, you hear young people or exchange students who speak nothing but the familiar Japanese used by their college-age peers. Such Japanese is usually inappropriate when addressing older Japanese people and almost always inappropriate when speaking at a job interview. While no one may tell you that your Japanese is impolite, it is less likely that anyone will take you very seriously, and in the long run, it is unlikely that you will get a job in a Japanese environment if you are unable to speak appropriately to your superiors. Lastly, a too common sight is the foreign man who has learned to speak by imitating his Japanese girlfriend. While communication may not be hampered, such a sight is often very amusing to people who understand that the man's speech is strange. The reverse situation also occurs, although it is generally not as startling.

Another question is to ask about the differences between how we speak and how we write. Are there obvious differences? Surely, the answer is yes. No one talks like a newspaper article. Not unsurprisingly, the same is true of Japanese. Further, there are various styles of written language, newspapers, novels, contracts, each of which has its own characteristics and conventions. Some of these will be addressed in this chapter.

It is also important to think about expressions which might be considered translations of each other. Words such as *mother, mom, mum, mommy, ma* can all be used to address the same person, your mother, but it is unlikely that you use all of them, and certainly not in the same conversation. Each expression is appropriate when spoken by a certain kind of person in a certain context. *Mommy* sounds childish; *ma* sounds very informal, less childish, probably very American. *Mom* is American while *mum* is British. *Mother* is potentially very formal, but it may also sound sarcastic when an embarrassed teenager uses it with the right intonation. Japanese also has a range of such expressions: お母さん, お母ちゃん, 母さん, 母ちゃん, 母. All of them except for the last may be used to talk to your own mother. お〜 and 〜さん mark politeness. 〜ちゃん is more intimate, perhaps more common amongst younger children. The simple 母 is usually used when talking about your mother to someone else. Interestingly, English does not have a word for *mother* like 母 which is used only to talk about your mother to someone else. (As an aside, a representation like 〜さん used here is read in Japanese as 何々さん meaning something like *blah-blah-san* with 〜, which is called a 波形 in Japanese, standing in for an appropriate word or phrase.)

To deal with mothers (your own and others') effectively, it is important to understand the differences between the various Japanese words which might all be translated into English as *mother*. Which word or expression is appropriate in which context? As much as possible, every point in this book is illustrated with a contrast, and sometimes as many as thirty different versions of the same expression are compared. Alternatively, a single Japanese expression may be contrasted with a number of English equivalents. These contrasts should make you think about this relationship between language and situation. While Japanese is often presented as a mysterious and difficult language, I wish to convince the English speaking student that Japanese is not necessarily that different from English. Similar issues often influence the choice of words in both languages.

None of this to say that there are no differences between Japanese and English. This is obviously false. The words, the sounds, the grammar, the rituals are clearly not the same, and specific difficulties for students of Japanese are addressed in this book. The topics found in the various chapters have been selected because they reflect aspects of the language which are avoided by non-native speakers or are often used either incorrectly or inappropriately for any number of reasons. As the emphasis of the book is on usage, no attempt is made to give a comprehensive grammar. All examples are written in their normal Japanese style, although a large number of Chinese characters appear with ふりがな above them or ひらがな readings after them. English translations are generally italicized.

1.3 What is neutral speech?

Neutral speech in Japanese is generally called です・ます体, where です is used instead of だ and the verbs ends in 〜ます. The choice of です over だ or 行きます over 行く indicates a degree of distance between the speaker and the listener. This may be because the speaker and the listener are not especially well known to each other, or it may indicate discomfort on the part of the speaker (perhaps because she is about to make a difficult request or to convey some bad news). It may also indicate no more than a polite speaker showing a general respect for the listener.

The first thing to realize is that similar distinctions are made in English and for the same reasons. While English does not have different verb endings, it does have a lot of different ways to say the same thing. We have already talked about words for mother: *mother, mom, mum, mommy, ma*. Of these, the word *mother* is probably the most neutral. It is somewhat formal as a term of address, but if your mother should happen to meet your friend's mother, she would probably say something like *Oh, so you are John's mother. I'm very pleased to meet you at last*. It would be quite strange for her to exclaim *Oh, so you are John's mommy* or even *Oh, so you are John's ma* (and saying so would reveal a great deal about your mother).

We can look at some different situations as well. The first is a basic greeting. While all of the following might be used to greet someone *How are you?* is surely the neutral form in American English, less so in British English.

How ya' doin? What's up? 'Sup? Yo! 'Aaright.
How are you? How are you today? Hello, John. How are you ?

All of these expressions are ritualistic, which means they do not require careful or literal responses. When two people greet each other, they are following scripts; they are not actually listening very carefully to each other (start listening carefully to people as they greet each other; more often than not they are not actually using the same script so the conversation make little or no actual sense). *How are you?* is the neutral greeting, and all of the others are less neutral for various reasons. The first set of expressions is probably used by friends when greeting each other. Such friends are probably young, and they might even be predominantly of one gender or the other. In contrast the second set of expressions is used between people whose relationship is probably constrained by some kind of social convention. Perhaps they have just met. Perhaps they have very different social positions. Perhaps they are simply old. *Hello, Mother. How are you?* sounds reasonable when a sixty year old son is greeting his eighty year old mother. It would be unexpected coming from a young child. Said by a teenager (with the right kind of intonation), it may indicate displeasure, embarrassment, sarcasm. It may also be a warning that said teenager is about to give some bad news. In some homes, it may also be completely normal, but to most people it would probably indicate a very formal household.

Neutral speech is unlikely to get you into trouble. You can greet everyone you encounter with a cheerful *How are you?* and you are unlikely to cause a great deal of insult. At worst, people will think you are a bit strange, possibly standoffish. Remember that the neutral form is somewhat impersonal. It does not sound right when speaking to friends or close colleagues. It may also be a bit impertinent or inappropriate if you are addressing someone who expects deference or if you are in a very formal situation. Would you greet the Queen of England with a rousing *How are you?* Is this an appropriate way of addressing the judge who is about to hand down your sentence?

The neutral form in Japanese has a similar range of use. It is appropriate between adults in almost all social circumstances: at work, at an interview, at a party. In some circumstances, more polite Japanese may exist and may be appropriate, but neutral forms are rarely insulting. Again, it may be inappropriate when speaking to someone who expects deference or in a highly ritualized situation. Because neutral speech reflects a distance between speaker and listener, it is strangest between friends, especially for young people. If you are a high school or college student talking to friends (or even new acquaintances), they would probably find you distant and overly polite. This is unlikely to be insulting but it is strange and in the long run is probably off-putting. Most people can deal with inappropriate politeness for only so long. Likewise, remember that non-native speakers of English may sound strange at least partially because they are using a neutral polite (possibly textbook) form of English all the time. The words are correct, but they are perceived as mildly inappropriate.

1.4 Actual speech

While everyone has a sense of what it means to speak in a neutral style, actual language is very rarely straightforward and consistent. No one uses です・ます forms all the time, and during the course of a single conversation, it is very common to move back and forth between speech levels. For example, two people who have just met may start out using honorific and humble language before moving to more neutral Japanese as they become more comfortable with each other. Friends who usually speak in familiar Japanese may switch to more polite Japanese when making a difficult request or conveying bad news. And one way to indicate displeasure or to convey anger with a family member is to use です・ます forms. The effect of polite language is to create a psychological distance between two people. This may be a sign of respect, anger, simple discomfort.

The rest of this chapter consists of language selections arranged into related sets. Usually, one example is authentic, while the others are translations. The examples have been chosen to illustrate different levels of politeness. Spoken language is compared to some written forms. Male speech is compared to female. One selection has been translated into a well-known dialect of Japanese. Specific names have been changed throughout. Most of the Japanese examples are given idiomatic English translations.

1.4.1 Keeping someone waiting

We have already looked at different ways to refer to one's mother in English and Japanese. We now look at more complex examples. In the conversations here, the first person has been kept waiting by the second. The first of these exchanges is authentic.

A. *Hey, what happened, man? I been wait'n here fer hours.*
B. *Yo, Jack, sorry man, I got stuck in some awful traffic. It was like a
total nightmare.*

A. *Well, hello. What happened to you?*
B. *I'm really sorry, Jack. I got stuck in some awful traffic, and it took me twice as
long as I expected to get here. I guess I should have left at four instead of five.
I'm really very sorry.*

A. *Finally.*
B. *I'm very sorry, sir. The traffic was very bad, and I should have left at four
instead of five. It really is inexcusable, but I assure you that it will not happen
again.*

What are the differences here? In the first exchange, a college student has kept his friend Jack waiting. The two men in question are both nineteen years old. Both use slang, and while the first man is mildly annoyed, the tone of the conversation is relaxed. In the second, the language is more neutral, and as a result the two men do not seem to be as close. They sound older. Perhaps they have a business relationship. The excuses are also much more profuse and more detailed. It is argued that a full English apology in may have as many as five parts: (i) the apology; (ii) an explanation (iii) an acknowledgement of responsibility, (iv) an offer of repair; and (v) a promise of forbearance (Olshtain and Cohen, page 22). Comparing these first two exchanges, it is clear that the second, more polite conversation has more of these elements. In addition to using the right words, more polite speech must satisfy more of the conventions of the language. A simple *I am sorry* would probably sound a bit curt even though it is the most basic and neutral apology. Presumably, also, the person making the apology must have the right expression on his face. Does he look contrite? Does he make the right kind of eye contact? Does all of this match the spoken excuses?

The final conversation actually sounds like a young chauffeur apologizing to his new boss (who is probably in a bad mood). There is no expectation of equality between the two men, in age or social status, and the more excuses the chauffeur makes, the more foolish he becomes. Presumably, there is no eye contact whatsoever between the chauffeur and his employer. Exaggerating a bit, in the end, all he can hope to do is throw himself on the mercy of his boss.

The following are Japanese translations of the above conversations:

A．おそいなあ。どうしたの？

B．ごめん、ごめん。道が込んでてさー、もっと早く出ればよかったんだけど〜

A．ああ、中山さん。

B．お待たせいたしました。すみません。

A．君、ちょっと遅いじゃないか。

B．遅くなりました。申し訳ありません。

The first apology is clearly informal, between relative equals. The words are all informal. A grammatically more polite form of おそいなあ is おそいですね; どうしたの can be translated as どうしたんですか or どうしましたか; and ごめん as ごめんなさい. The repetition of the phrase ごめん is also relatively informal, although it serves to strengthen the apology. A similar affect might be accomplished by drawing out a single ごめーん with rising intonation and emphasis on the second half of the word. Finally, the form 込んでて is a contraction of 込んでいて. This expression which ends in the て-form is not sentence final, and a phrase like *and that is why I am late* is omitted. In Japanese, especially in ritualistic situations, it is neither necessary nor particularly elegant to insist on saying the whole expression. You can stop talking as soon as your meaning is clear (which will be quite soon if you are saying the right things). A simple excuse 道が込んでて with an appropriate look of contrition is what is expected. The alert listener will easily infer the rest through a process of accommodation, asking him or herself, "What is going on here and what has not yet been said?" Stating that which should be obvious in a conversation is socially somewhat clumsy. When someone is late, accommodation is very easy. In other situations it may be more subtle, but it is almost always crucial in a Japanese interaction to note what is *not* being said as well as what *is*. Likewise, what is *actually* being said may differ from what is *normally* said in a particular situation. Such subtle variation is almost always done for a reason.

Simply translating each informal expression of the first conversation into a more neutral expression gives us the following conversation:

A．おそいですね。どうしましたか。

B．ごめんなさい。ごめんなさい。道が込んでいて。もっと早く出ればよかったん

ですけど〜

While this is clearly a more polite conversation, it is somewhat overstated, and sounds overly correct. In contrast, the second conversation above which is more neutrally polite is actually very different from the original informal exchange. The expressions are polite,

but they are all different. The facts mentioned are different. The person kept waiting actually greets Nakayama as if nothing is amiss, although more than likely there is an edge in
his voice. He uses the polite suffix 〜さん. The word おそい is not spoken. Nakayama
uses a standard, very polite apology used for keeping someone waiting. This is followed
by a slightly more intimate (but still polite) ごめんなさい. He makes no excuses, although presumably he has an appropriate expression of worry and slight dismay to match
his apology. Again, there is repetition, but the facts of the situation (which are basically
obvious) are not really mentioned at all. Nakayama is late. Presumably he made an effort
to be on time, but events conspired against him. Presumably he will try harder next time.
Accommodation is very easy here, and this overall restraint is considered more seemly
and therefore more polite. The person kept waiting may or may not be angry or annoyed,
but this can be conveyed by his facial expression and the tone of his voice. The person
who is late will respond with an appropriately contrite demeanor. In this sense, body
language is at least as important as the words actually spoken, and the lack of words
should not be interpreted as a lack of emotion or involvement.

In the final conversation, the boss grunts a complaint. Unlike the young friends in the
first exchange, the boss is not interested in why the driver is late, and the chauffeur apologizes but makes no excuses. (A gracious boss will probably ask if there has been a problem later in the car.)

Crucially for the native speaker of English, the strategies used in Japanese in this situation are very different. In English, the person who is late makes a series of excuses
before apologizing. The excuses become more extreme as the situation becomes more
difficult. At some point, *there is no excuse* is the only excuse. In contrast, in Japanese,
the more difficult the situation, the fewer words spoken aloud and excuses are not spoken
at all. Using words (even very polite words) in such a situation is unnecessary and clumsy. While the situation is universal (everyone is late some of the time, and everyone feels
to some degree embarrassed or worried depending on whom they have kept waiting), the
strategies for expressing contrition do not translate directly from one language to another.
To speak polite Japanese, it is necessary to learn not only the polite words, but also to
learn how to use these words correctly and effectively. And as we have seen here, this
may involve learning what *not* to say.

The words in a Japanese conversation might also vary based on the gender of the participants. Here we have three conversations based on an original conversation by two
teenage girls. Again, it is a situation where one person has kept another person waiting.
The second conversation would be natural for two women in their late twenties, while the
third sounds like two women perhaps in their early fifties. In all three cases, the two women sound like friends, and they are quite intimate with each other. They freely give details and explanations as well as apologies. Professional obligations do not seem to play
any role. Nevertheless, the three conversations are clearly very different, and they sound
much more feminine that the above conversations. How is this accomplished?

A.　あっ、マリちゃん、ごめーん。遅<ruby>遅<rt>おく</rt></ruby>れちゃった。

B.　ちょっとー、どうしたのー。

A.　ごめん、ごめん。<ruby>道路<rt>どうろ</rt></ruby>、めちゃ<ruby>込<rt>こ</rt></ruby>んでてサア、バス、<ruby>全然走<rt>ぜんぜんはし</rt></ruby>ンなくってェ〜

A.　あっ、マリさん、ごめんなさい。<ruby>遅<rt>おそ</rt></ruby>くなってしまって。

B.　いえ、いえ。<ruby>何<rt>なに</rt></ruby>かあったの？

A.　いえ、ちょっと<ruby>道路<rt>どうろ</rt></ruby>が<ruby>込<rt>こ</rt></ruby>んでて、バスが<ruby>全然進<rt>ぜんぜんすす</rt></ruby>まなくって〜

A.　あっ、<ruby>山本<rt>やまもと</rt></ruby>さん、どうもすみません。

B.　いいえ、どうかなさったんですか。

A.　いえ、ちょっと、<ruby>道路<rt>どうろ</rt></ruby>が<ruby>混雑<rt>こんざつ</rt></ruby>しておりまして、<ruby>途中<rt>とちゅう</rt></ruby>、バスが<ruby>全然進<rt>ぜんぜんすす</rt></ruby>まなくて〜

In general, these three conversations are both feminine and casual in tone. Expressions such as 遅<ruby>遅<rt>おく</rt></ruby>れちゃった (with 〜ちゃった) or even 遅<ruby>遅<rt>おそ</rt></ruby>くなってしまって (ending with 〜て) contrast with the blunter 遅<ruby>遅<rt>おそ</rt></ruby>くなりました. Use of 〜ちゃん or of a first name with 〜さん (マリさん) reflects intimacy. In general, the frequent use of verbs which end in the て-form is considered softer because it allows a sentence to fade away rather than coming to a definite conclusion. In addition, the written representation of the first conversation includes non-standard use of カタカナ to represent the exaggerated intonation of teenage speech. The line normally used only in カタカナ represents a lengthened vowel: ごめーん, ちょっとー, どうしたのー. This might also be used to represent emphatic stress (especially since the girl kept waiting here is somewhat upset). In the third line, the sentence final particle さ characteristic of Tokyo speech is written in カタカナ and exaggerated. <ruby>走<rt>はし</rt></ruby>らなくて is contracted to <ruby>走<rt>はし</rt></ruby>ンなくってェ with テェ used to represent a lengthened and non-standard final vowel sound probably with a raised intonation.

In contrast, the second and third conversations are both more or less standard Japanese, although their level of politeness differs significantly. The second conversation is polite but familiar. The third conversation is characterized by a number of overtly polite forms (for example, the verbs なさる and おります). The use of polite speech in an interaction between friends is one characteristic of what might be called "good breeding," although in modern Japan, the use of polite speech in intimate situations is probably limited to people beyond middle age. Further, while such a style is not limited to women, it is often interpreted as a certain kind of female speech.

Note that the two explicitly polite verbs in the third conversation are actually used in two different ways. なさる is an honorific form of する. Honorific verbs are one device used to indicate respect for other people (or their associates). In contrast いたす is the humble form of する. Humble verbs are used to indicate one's own humility or the extended humility of one's own set of associates. In Japanese, humble verbs are called 謙譲語 while honorific verbs are called 尊敬語. It is typically the case that honorific and humble verbs can only be used with respect to people (so that a sentence like 電車がいらっしゃいました is pretty strange). おります, on the other hand, is usually defined as the humble version of います, but it may also be used as no more than a very polite form. As a humble verb is must take a human being as a subject: 父はおりませんが. In the third conversation, however, おります appears in the following sentence which takes 道路 as its subject: 道路が混雑しておりまして. This is one illustration of what is generally called 丁寧語 *polite language* or *super-polite language*, language which makes a sentence sound more polite and more elegant. Such words do not show respect or humility and therefore do not require human subjects. The other common example of a super-polite verb is ござる or ございます, a very polite form of ある. Here is a complete list of the humble, honorific, and super-polite verb forms which are different from the basic 〜ます form. Note that not all positions are filled (because the subject of もらう and the object of くれる are usually the person speaking). やる is a more colloquial version of 上げる. Also, the polite form of 知る *know* is actually a noun form (which can be made more polite by using a more polite form of だ). The Japanese name for the dictionary form of a verb is either 基本形 or 辞書体. The general name for all polite language is 敬語.

英語	基本形	謙譲語	尊敬語
English	Dictionary	Humble	Honorific
be	居る・いる	おる	いらっしゃる お出でだ・おいでだ
go	行く・いく・ゆく	参る・まいる	いらっしゃる お出でになる・おいでになる
come	来る・くる	参る・まいる	いらっしゃる お出でになる・おいでになる
do	する	致す・いたす	なさる
see	見る・みる	拝見する・ はいけんする	ご覧になる・ごらんになる
know	知る・しる	存じる・ぞんじる	ご存じだ・ごぞんじだ
eat	食べる・たべる	頂く・いただく	召し上がる・めしあがる
drink	飲む・のむ	頂く・いただく	召し上がる・めしあがる
receive	もらう	頂く・いただく	--------

give	上げる・あげる やる	差し上げる・ さしあげる	--------
give	くれる	--------	下さる・くださる
say	言う・いう	申す・もうす 申し上げる・ もうしあげる	おっしゃる
visit (*go, come*)	--------	伺う・うかがう	--------
copula	だ	--------	でいらっしゃる

英語 English	基本形 Dictionary	丁寧語 Super-polite
have, exist	有る・ある	ござる
exist, be	居る・いる	居る・おる
copula	だ・である	でござる

である is the literary form of the copula, frequently encountered in written Japanese, very polite when spoken.

There are also general ways to make any verb both humble and honorific, although the humble forms are only appropriate in certain situations.

英語 English	基本形 Dictionary	謙譲語 Humble	尊敬語 Honorific
write	書く・かく	お書きする	お書きになる

The お〜になる construction is a general honorific form for verbs which do not have completely different honorific alternatives. The お〜する construction is a parallel humble form, although its use is actually most common in two kinds of situations. First, a suggestion like お書きしましょうか or the even more formal お書きいたしましょうか is a polite way of offering to do something for someone else. (See the discussion on page 150 for a comparison with suggestions like 書いて差し上げましょうか.) Secondly, the お〜する construction is very common when interrupting someone when you are about to ask a favor: ちょっとお伺いしたいんですが or ちょっとお聞きしたことがありますが. Here it almost always occurs in the 〜たい form. As a general rule, verbs like いる, 行く, or 来る which have completely different humble and honorific forms do not occur in either the お〜する or お〜になる constructions. Exceptions are 食べる and 飲む. Both お食べになる and お飲みになる are possible, although neither is as polite as 召し上がる. Turn to

page 77 in Chapter 2 for discussion and a list of verbs which occur in these two constructions.

　A further polite form is known as the *honorific passive*. The passive form is used as
if it is a regular verb (with no changes in case-marking). It is honorific without sounding
excessively polite, and may perhaps be characterized as a "professional" honorific. It is
most commonly used in job-related situations, and allows one to be succinct but polite.
Contrast the following which are all polite (with a 〜ます form).

田中さんは何時ごろ行きますか。

田中さんは何時ごろ行かれますか。

田中さんは何時ごろいらっしゃいますか。

行きます is polite without being honorific. Tanaka is not given any special kind of respect. In contrast, いっらしゃいます is both polite and honorific, indicating a great deal
of respect for Tanaka. He is of a significantly higher rank; he is much older; he is an important guest from another organization. 行かれます indicates respect with more familiar-
ity. Tanaka is higher ranking or older than the speaker, but not by a great deal. He may
also be a guest, but he is more familiar rather than less.

　Finally, while most students study honorific and humble verb forms, polite language
is not limited to verbs. Polite adjectives are all of the form: お高うございます. They are
not particularly common in everyday usage, however, and can safely be considered relatively archaic (except, of course, for the common お早うございます). Many nouns, on the
other hand, have polite and humble alternatives with the affix 御〜 pronounced お, ご, or
おん. See page 77 in Chapter 2 for lists of nouns which take such prefixes. Many polite
nouns are so common as to be taken as the normal noun: お茶 *tea*, ご飯 *rice, dinner*, お
医者 *doctor*, or お宅 *your home*. In addition, as we have already seen, the copula (the
word だ) may itself be very polite. When used with a noun or with an adjectival nominal,
the level of the entire expression is affected. Compare そうですか and そうでございます
か.

1.4.2 Construction accident

Next we look at the differences in politeness between three significantly longer passages.
One of these is written (a letter to friends or family) and two are messages left on answering machines (one-sided conversations). The answering machine message to friends
is authentic. The other two passages are translations. All three passages are about the
same event: a scaffolding collapse which killed one person in New York City in the
summer of 1998. The person speaking is a woman in her late twenties who lives in a
building just across the street from the accident. Because of the accident, she was unable
to return home or go to work for more than a week.

Answering machine message to friends

もしもし、真由美です。   Hi. It's Mayumi.

しばらく電話しなくって、ごめんね。   I'm sorry, I haven't called in a while.

アパートの近くですごい事故があって、   There was a big accident near my apartment
                      accident

いろいろ取り込んでて、全然   so it's been confusing and I haven't had a
     be busy, confused

電話できなくて～   chance.

家のまわりって高いビルばっかり   Around where I live there are nothing but

なんだけど２１日に工事中のビル   tall buildings, and on the twenty-first, the
          under construction

からのエレベーターとか器材とか   elevator and tools and materials from a
              tools and materials

落っこちてきて、すごい事故になった   construction site crashed to the ground. It
fell   accident

わけ。   was a terrible accident.

Reassuring message to a nephew (age seven)

もしもし、けんちゃん。   Hello, Ken.

おばちゃんです。しばらく電話   It's your Aunt. I'm sorry I haven't called

しなくって、ごめんね。この間   in a while. The other day

おばちゃんちのそばですごい事故が   there was a big accident near my home,
                    accident

あってね、電話全然できなかったのよ。   so I haven't been able to call.

たかーいビルから色々な物が落っこちて   *A lot of stuff fell from a tall building*
　　　　　　　　　　　　　　fell

きて大変だったんだよ。だけど、   *and it was a mess. But,*

おばちゃんちは大丈夫だからね、   *my home is okay, so*
　　　　　okay, safe

心配しないでね。じゃあね。バイバイ。   *don't worry. Ok. Bye-bye.*
worry

Both answering messages are relatively informal, with the only です form occurring in the first line (as part of the ritual beginning of a phone call). Both messages begin with a brief apology. Nevertheless, there are distinct stylistic differences which make it clear that the one message is for adults while the other is for a child. In the message to friends, Mayumi gives her name once at the beginning; she never addresses her friends. In contrast, in the message to her nephew, Mayumi refers to herself not by name, but by her relationship to Ken (おばちゃん). She does this three times, each time using the diminutive 〜ちゃん ending. She uses it when addressing Ken as well. Presumably she has spoken to Ken this way for his entire life. This style indicates a great deal of intimacy between Mayumi and her nephew which is reflected in the message content. Mayumi is calling is to reassure Ken that she is okay.

　　Other choices reflect the fact that Ken is a child while Mayumi's friends are not. The message to Ken contains many short sentences, and it contains fewer specifics about the accident. Longer expressions are broken up with repeated use of ね to offer reassurance and to check if he is listening. The ends of sentences are marked with expressions like の よ and だよ. In contrast, よ never occurs in the message to friends where almost every sentence ends with a softer 〜て, and the final sentence ends with the more adult わけ. The choice of words is also different. When speaking to her friends, Mayumi uses expressions which are arguably more adult.

Message to friends	Message to nephew
真由美	おばちゃん
アパート	おばちゃんち（おばちゃんの家）
高いビル	たかーいビル
エレベーターとか器材とか	色々な物
す……事故になった	大変だった

　　It is important to see that the overall effect in Japanese is achieved by the correct combination of a number of different elements. What forms of address and what kind of vocabulary is used? How polite are the predicates? What kinds of sentence particles are appropriate? How long are the sentences? How are the sentences linked to each other? In addition, Mayumi adjusts the amount of detail she provides. A little introspection should reveal that similar differences would be found in English as well. How do you speak with an adult? And how does that compare to the way you speak to a child?

We can now compare these two spoken passages with a written version. Differences are perhaps more striking, although again, they may not be that unexpected.

Letter home

お元気ですか。しばらく連絡しない
　　　　　　　　　　　contact

How is everyone? I'm sorry I haven't

でごめんなさい。予想もしないことが
　　　　　　　　expectation

written in a while, but something you'd

家の近くでおこったものだから、

never expect happened near my home, so it's

すっかり混乱して、書こうと
　　　　confusion

been very confusing, and the letter I've been

思っていた手紙がこんなに遅くなって

trying to write has just gotten later and

しまいました。

later.

マンハッタンは「摩天楼」の街と呼
　　　　　　　skyscraper town

As you'd think given that Manhattan is such

ばれている通り、高層ビルが密集して
　　　　　　　high　　　*crowded*

a "high" city, tall buildings are crowded

いて、家は、タイムズスクエアの

together. I live near Times Square now, but

近くなんですが、7月21日に

on the 21st, the scaffold elevator and

50階建てのビルから建設用の
story　　　　　　　*construction*

a lot of tools and materials fell from a fifty

エレベーターや器材が落ちて、大事故に
　　　　tools and materials　*big accident*

story building, causing a terrible accident.

なってしまいました。

The third passage is a relatively informal letter which begins with an informal greeting: お元気ですか. All sentences end with です・ます forms. In contrast, only the opening line of either telephone message (the short ritualistic part of these messages) contains a です form. Comparing it to the message to friends, we find longer sentences, more details, and more sophisticated vocabulary. All of these elements combine to give an effect of greater sophistication and a more regimented style, although it should be noted that this letter is in fact very informal. The differences here are typical of the way one adult might speak and write to another.

While letter and phone calls obviously begin differently (お元気ですか versus もしもし), all three of these passages do begin with some kind of an apology: しばらく連絡しないでごめんなさい versus しばらく電話しなくって、ごめんね. しなっくて and ごめんね are obviously less formal than しないで and ごめんなさい.

The short explanations which follow are also very different.

The excuse in the letter home	*In the message to friends*
予想もしないことが家の近くで	アパートの近くですごい事故があって
expectation	accident
おこったものだから、すっかり混乱	いろいろ取り込んでて、全然
confusion	be busy, confused
して、書こうと思っていた手紙が	電話できなくて〜

こんなに遅くなってしまいました。

The written sentence is longer than the spoken sentence with more polite verb forms. Specific vocabulary in the written passage, while appropriate to the letter, might be considered somewhat heavy-handed if spoken.

Letter home	*Message to friends*
予想もしないこと	すごい事故
おこった	あって
すっかり混乱して	いろいろ取り込んでて

Crucially, the structure of the written sentence is significantly more complex than in the spoken sentence. While the phrases of the spoken sentence are in linear order connected by 〜て forms (*near my apartment, there was an accident, so I've been busy, and I haven't been able to call*), the written sentence includes both more details and more modification. The accident is described in the sentence not as an accident but as *an unexpected event that occurred near my apartment*. It continues that the accident *resulted in confusion*, and concludes that *the letter I've been thinking about trying to write has been delayed.*

This pattern of increased detail, more sophisticated vocabulary, and greater modification is evident throughout the second paragraph of the letter.

The setting in the letter home

マンハッタンは「摩天楼」の街と
     skyscraper town

呼ばれている通り、高層ビルが密集
     high crowded

していて、

In the message to friends

家のまわりって高いビルばっかりなんだけど

Here it is obvious that the letter home gives a much more detailed description of the buildings in Manhattan. Likewise, words such as 高層ビル and 密集して are more characteristic of written language. This view is reinforced in the part of the sentence which describes the accident.

The event in the letter home

家は、タイムズスクエアの近く

なんですが、7月21日に

50階建てのビルから建設用の
story   construction

エレベーターや器材が落ちて、大事故に
  tools and materials big accident

なってしまいました。

In the message to friends

21日に工事中のビルからのエレベーター
   under construction

とか器材とか落っこちてきて、
tools and materials fell

すごい事故になったわけ。
  accident

The final sentence of the written passage is significantly longer than that of the spoken passage because it contains much more detail. The vocabulary is likewise more sophisticated and less conversational.

Details in the letter home

time
7月21日に〜

Details in the message to friends

time
21日に

location
５０階建てのビルから

location
工事中のビルから

what fell
建設用のエレベーターや器材が

what fell
エレベーターとか器材とか

what happened?
落ちて

what happened?
落っこちてきて

what was the outcome?
大事故になってしましました。

what was the outcome?
すごい事故になったわけ。

Expressions such as ５０階建て, 建設用, 落ちて, and 大事故 are more formal and precise than their conversational equivalents. They add a level of detail which is not really necessary and is actually not found in the spoken passage. とか is a conversation connector (implying a list with other items as well). Its written equivalent is や. なってしましました is more formal than なったわけ.

Summary

The passages so far have allowed us to compare three levels of formality within a relatively narrow range. These differences are seen most obviously in the choice of verb endings and the use of ritualistic language. Conversations and letters begin with clearly different expressions. A verb like します is more polite than the verb する. Unfortunately, other characteristics of a particular style of language are not necessarily easy to pin down. Without a context, it is hard to say that 混乱する is more formal than 取り込む or that 建設用のエレベーターや器材 is more detailed than エレベーターとか器材とか. が by itself does not look more polite than けど (although generally speaking it is). Nevertheless, the consistent use of more precise expressions (which usually means more Chinese expressions) and the consistent addition of greater detail is characteristic of more formal or written language (although it must be noted that all three passages are directed to friends or family; the differences here are really not that great).

We turn now to two more written passages related to the same incident. The first is a letter, the second a newspaper article. The letter is written to an organization in Japan. It contains many more of the conventions found in "typical" business letters, and it is more formal because Mayumi is in the position of having to explain to her superiors why she has not sent some promised documents on time.

前略<ruby>ぜんりゃく</ruby>   *Dear —*

Greetings

送付させていただくことになって   *I sincerely apologize for the delay*

send

おりました書類がこのように遅く   *in sending you the documents as*

documents   late

なってしまいましたことを深くお詫び   *promised.*

                    deeply apologize

申し上げます。

say, give

以前お電話を差し上げた通り１０日程   *As I said before on the telephone, about ten*

before   about

前にタイムズスクエアの付近で建築   *days ago there was a construction accident*

                    vicinity

事故がございまして、近辺の住人約   *near Times Square. It was a major disaster*

accident   neighborhood residents

４００世帯と商店街を巻き込む大惨事   *affecting about four hundred households as*

homes business involve disaster

となりました。その結果、付近の   *well as businesses. The roads in the area*

                    result vicinity

通行路が、閉鎖され、会社の建物への   *were closed making it impossible for me to*

roads   closed   company

通勤が一週間程不可能になり、ご依頼   *go to the office for a week, and as a result.*

commute   impossible   entrusted

うけたまわっておりました書類を   *I was unable to send you the necessary*

                    documents

予定通り送付させていただくことが   *documents as promised.*

on time send

できませんでした。

This letter is significantly more polite than the letter home. First, and most obviously, the greeting here is a standard 前略<ruby>ぜんりゃく</ruby> which sets a very different tone from お元気<ruby>げんき</ruby>ですか. At the end of the letter we expect to find 早々<ruby>そうそう</ruby> (see page 301). This particular greeting is quite common but actually relatively informal (and means that the formal greeting has been omitted). Second, nearly every word in these opening paragraphs is polite or ritual-istic. To look at one expression carefully, the first line 送付させていただくことになって おりました書類 can be reduced to a conversational 送ることになっていた書類 meaning *documents I was to send*. 送付する is a Chinese compound which is more formal than 送 る. させていただく is basically する. なっていた is humbly realized as なっておりました. The full 〜ます form おりました is used to modify 書類. Continuing to the end of the line, 深くお詫び申し上げます is a humble and abject (but nevertheless ritualistic, and in this situation appropriate) apology. This tone is carried into the second paragraph with sophisticated vocabulary, polite verb forms (事故がございましてand うけたまわっており ました書類), polite sentence connectives (閉鎖され instead of 閉鎖されて), and polite particle expressions (〜となりました instead of 〜になりました). The sentences are also extremely complex with a great deal of modification. This is most striking in the last sentence which begins with その結果 and ends with 書類を予定通り送付させていただく ことができませんでした. At this point, the apology is so explicit and so well developed, it is hard to imagine anyone begrudging Mayumi the short delay. The is exactly the desired effect. The style displayed is not actually that extraordinary, although the message is nevertheless conveyed with an elegance which is extremely difficult for a student of Japanese to master. It is in fact difficult for native speakers of Japanese as well (which is one reason that there are so many how-to-books for writing proper letters). The woman who actually wrote these paragraphs struggled to get the phrasing just right — very polite and apologetic but not too much so.

Note also what kinds of things are not mentioned when compared to the letter home. In particular, Mayumi makes no mention of herself, and there are no personal excuses. In fact, she is careful to justify her tardiness with a neutral description of the construction accident and its aftermath. To the degree possible the letter is written from the point of view of the recipients, and this is an explanation which any reasonable person would ac-cept. An English speaking observer might note that Mayumi seems to be apologizing for the fact that she did not have a contingency plan just in case of such an accident. This is not completely true, as she is apologizing for the inconvenience caused as well as for her own lack of foresight.

Finally, we compare all of these accounts with the first paragraph of a newspaper report on the accident.

Newspaper article

ＮＹタイムズスクエアで高層ビル建築事故   *Construction accident at a Times Square*
                                                              skyscraper accident

【ニューヨーク発・共同　二十一日】   *skyscraper — New York, July 21 (Kyodo)*
            from   Kyodo

二十一日午前八時半（日本時間二十一日   *At about 8:30am on July 21 (8:30pm July 21*

夜）、ニューヨーク市マンハッタンの   *JST) a part of the materials and scaffolding*

タイムズスクエア付近で、建築中の高層   *at a skyscraper construction site near Times*
      vicinity   construction   high

ビルの建築資材が一部落下、死者一名、   *Square in New York's Manhattan fell, in a*
   materials   part   fell   dead   one

負傷者十数名を出す大事故が起こった。   *serious accident which killed one and*
injured   tens   accident   occurred

場所はマンハッタンの中心部であるミッ   *injured dozens. Occurring in Midtown*
location   center

ドタウン。金曜朝の交通ラッシュと重   *Manhattan during the Friday morning rush,*
       traffic   pile on

なったこともあり、周辺は一時騒然とな   *the accident caused temporary chaos, and as*
      vicinity   chaos

り、二十二日現在は建築中のビルがある   *of today, July 22, the area around the*
     presently

区域を中心に、周辺区域は完全に封鎖   *building is completely blocked off (related*
zone   zone   completely   closed

されている。（二十六・七面に関連記事）   *stories on pages 26 and 27)*
      page   related   article

The related stories include detailed descriptions of the location and effects of the accident as well as particulars of the construction company and the building's owners. While many of the basic details are the same, there is a clear emphasis on facts, as one would expect from a newspaper. There is reference to the number dead and number injured, potentially disturbing news not relevant in any of the letters. The writing style is impersonal with no apologies to readers, no honorifics, and no ritualistic expressions. There are no ～ます forms. Newspaper Japanese also includes a number of distinct expressions and features.

Newspaper	Less formal written
ＮＹタイムズスクエア	ＮＹのタイムズスクエア
ニューヨーク市マンハッタン	ニューヨーク市のマンハッタン

いちぶ らっか
一部落下
ししゃいちめい　　ふしょうしゃじゅうすうめい
死者一名、負傷者十数名
ちゅうしんぶ
中心部であるミッドタウン。
きんようあさ
金曜朝
にじゅうににちげんざい
二十二日現在
いちじそうぜん
一時騒然となり
くいき　　ちゅうしん
ある区域を中心に

いちぶ らっか
一部落下して
ししゃいちめい　　ふしょうしゃじゅうすうめい
死者一名と負傷者十数名
ちゅうしんぶ
中心部であるミッドタウンだ。
きんよう　あさ
金曜の朝
いま　　にじゅうににち
今は or 二十二日
いちじそうぜん
一時騒然となって
くいき　　ちゅうしん
ある区域を中心にして

The sentences are extremely long with several layers of modification. For example, taking
away all modification, the first sentence reduces to 大事故が起こった "A serious accident
has occurred." The four lines which precede all modify *accident*. The vocabulary is the
most exact encountered so far with a large number of Chinese compounds: 建築事故, 建
築資材, 一部落下, 死者一名、負傷者十数名, 一時騒然となり, 区域, 完全に封鎖されてい
る. Except for verbs, there are basically no native Japanese words in this article. The
combination of specific content, vocabulary, and an impersonal direct style produce the
particular effect associated with newspapers.

1.4.3 A day in the life

The series of conversations here illustrates the speaking style of a man named 中島 as he
interacts with different people in different social situations. Nakajima is married in his
early forties with two children. He is an employee at a local office of a national newspaper. The content of each conversation is different. Crucially, Nakajima's speech varies
based on the relative social distance he feels from the person he is speaking to (and he is
more polite when he feels weaker). While the examples here are relatively straightforward,
these calculations of "appropriate social distance" may actually be quite complicated. As
one becomes friends with one's teacher, how can one express friendship and respect at the
same time? While woman are generally more polite than men, how do powerful women
interact with male subordinates? A foreign student in Japan may find him or herself in
two conflicting roles. A foreign visitor in Japan can expect the treatment shown a guest.
At the same time, however, students are not generally treated with a great deal of
deference (except by younger students). Does the foreign student act like a guest or like a
student? Again, the basic effect of formality in language is to create a psychological distance between two people. As such it can be used to show respect (by keeping your distance), but it can also be used to create or preserve distance (if, for example, you find
yourself interacting with someone who is not particularly to your liking or if you find
yourself in the middle of an actual disagreement).

　　The first situation is fairly chaotic. The family is in the kitchen, and both children are
noisy and needing attention. Kaori spends much of the time running around. Nakajima's
wife (B) is actually preparing different kinds of breakfast for six people (her mother and
father are in the kitchen as well, but they do not speak here). In response to this chaos,

Nakajima's mood actually shifts quite rapidly from one moment to the next.

In the morning with his wife and children (Kaori age 7 and Ken age 2)

(Speaking to Kaori)

A. おはよう、かおり。

    (Turning to Ken) ケンちゃん、

    おはよー。おはよー。ケンちゃんは

    よく食べるな。(Turning back to

    Kaori) 何してるの？ちゃんと

    食べなさいよ。(Turning to his wife)

    ママご飯。

    Morning, Kaori.

    Ken,

    G-o-o-d m-o-r-n-i-n-g. G-o-o-d

    m-o-r-n-i-n-g. Ken, you're eating good.

    What are you doing?

    Eat!

    Mama, can I have some rice.

B. 夕べまた遅かったの？

    You were late again last night?

A. うん、一時半ごろ。また代行

    で帰ってきちゃった。(His wife

    looks upset) ごめーん。(Turning

    to Kaori who is running around

    and fiddling with Ken) ちょっと、

    かおり、ちゃんと座りなさいよ。

    ケンちゃんほっといて。(When

    Kaori persists) だいじょうぶ。

    ケンちゃんはだーいじょうぶ

    だって。(Turning back to his wife

    as Ken begins to fuss) ママ、

    ちょっとケンちゃん見てやって。

    (Back to Kaori who is running

    around) かおり、こっち来い。

    Yeah. About 1:30. I got a driver again.

    Sorry.

    Hey,

    Kaori, sit down.

    Leave Ken alone.

    He's okay.

    I said Ken is o-k-a-y.

    Mama,

    look after Ken.

    Kaori, come here. Sit down properly

ちゃんと座って食べなさいよ。   *and eat.*

(then feeling regret for speaking

so harshly) テレビ、大きくしよう   *Shall I make the TV louder? Is this okay?*

か。これでいいかい。聞こえる？   *Can you hear it?*

(Back to his wife) 今日はまた飲み   *There is another drinking party tonight,*

会なんだけど、はやく帰ってくるよ。   *but I'll come home early.*

B. 薬飲んでるの？お医者さんもゆって   *Are you taking your medicine? The*

いるでしょう。   *doctor said so, right.*

A. うん。飲んでるよ。子供じゃないん   *Yeah, I'm taking it. I'm not a kid, you*

だからさ。うるさいですね、本当に。   *know. What a pain you are, really.*

B. (Silence)   *(Yeah, yeah)*

Stylistically, this is a very informal conversation. The only です・ます forms come at the end when Nakajima and his wife disagree over his medicine. She checks that he is taking his medicine (お医者さんもゆっているでしょう), and he replies with an inappropriately polite うるさいですね、本当に to convey his irritation ("I am not a child you know!"). In contrast, all of the following expressions would be considered reflections of intimacy: use of 〜ちゃん; a command like 食べなさい instead of 食べてください; contractions such as ほっといて; omitted particles; grunts instead of a clearer ええ or はい.

Intimate	*More neutral*
ケンちゃん	ケン
なにしてるの？	なにをしているの？
食べなさい	食べてください
ご飯	ご飯ください
うん	ええ
帰っちゃった	帰ってしまった
ケンちゃんほっといて	ケンちゃんをほっておいて。
だって	だから or と言っているでしょう
これでいいかい	これでいいか

おはようー reflects the extra clear enunciation used when talking to babies and very young children, while ごめーん reflects an exaggerated apology for a repeat offense. It actually sounds quite childish and here reflects an ongoing disagreement over the use of expensive 代行タクシー (taxis with two drivers, one to drive you home, and one to drive your car home after a night of drinking). Nakajima's wife is obviously not happy about the whole drinking thing and the expense it entails. Her husband has presumably promised to change his ways, but has nevertheless repeated his past behavior. The disagreement is mild but real. だーいじょうぶ reflects annoyance with Kaori who continues to fuss with Ken. Nakajima's commands are very direct, but he immediately regrets his anger and turns his attention to her needs ("Is the television loud enough? Shall I raise the volume?"). Throughout, the speech addressed to the children is short and often clipped. The only complete sentences are almost always commands. In contrast, except for his grunted ママご飯, communication between husband and wife is in short but nevertheless complete sentences. In addition, it should be assumed that the tone of their voices changes from the extra clear, often exasperated speech used with children, to a more normal mode of adult interaction. One can easily imagine the same thing in an English speaking household.

When Nakajima speaks with his wife and children at breakfast, he uses very familiar language which his wife reciprocates. In contrast, when Nakajima speaks to his superior at work, there is a clear asymmetry in the way his boss addresses him and his response.

At work with his boss

A. おはようございます。   *Good morning.*

B. おはよう。あのですね。   *Morning. Umm ~*

A. はい。   *Yes?*

B. 中島君は来週から出張だね。   *Nakajima, you're away on business next*
    away from the office   *week, right?*

A. はいそうです。係長と鈴木さんと   *Yes, that's right. I am going to Tokyo with*
    managing chief
    東京の方へ。   *Suzuki and the chief.*

B. そうかい～   *I see ~*

A.　なんでしょうか。

Is there something I can do?

B.　いやいや、２４日から客がくる

　　　　　にじゅうよっか　　きゃく

　　　　　visitor, guest

　　ん だけど、いないから、いい。

No, it's okay. There's a visitor coming from

the 24th, so I was thinking, but you won't

　　まちだ　　　　　き

　　町田さんに聞く。

be here, so no problem. I'll ask Machida.

A.　そうですか。おそれいります。

I see. I'm sorry.

B.　あっ、君、今日の予定は？

　　　　　きみ　きょう　よてい

　　　　　　plans

So, you, what are you doing today?

A.　今日ですか、今日は先日の件の

　　きょう　　　きょう　せんじつ　けん

　　　　　　　　matter   paperwork

　　しょるい　せいり　かかりちょう　ほう　　　ようけん

　　書類の整理と係長の方からの用件

paperwork put in order   business

　　が入っておりますが〜

Today? Well I have to take care of the

paperwork from the other day, and the

chief gave me some work to take care of.

B.　突然ですまないが、これ、ひまを

　　とつぜん

　　suddenly

　　　　み　　　　　　　　　　　　　　あした

　　見てやっててくれないかな。明日

This is sudden, but could you take a look

at this today when you get a moment? All

　　きゅう　つか

　　急に使うことになったんだよ。

of a sudden, I need it by tomorrow.

A.　こちらですか。はい、わかりました、

　　なん　　　　　　　　　　　　ゆうがたごろ

　　何とかやってみます。夕方頃まで

　　　　　　　　　　　　　　おも

　　かかると思いますが、よろしいで

　　しょうか。

This? I understand. I'll try and get it

done. It'll probably take until

evening. Is that satisfactory?

B.　ああ、じゃあ、頼^{たの}むよ。　　　　　　　　*Okay. I'm counting on you.*

　　　　ask, request

A.　はい。　　　　　　　　　　　　　　　　　*I understand.*

The difference in rank is asserted in the first line. Nakajima (A) offers a polite おはようご ざいます; his boss (B) replies with a terse おはよう. Nakajima is quick to respond with a clear はい when his boss indicates that there is something on his mind あのですね. His boss addresses Nakajima as 中島君^{なかじまくん} and later as 君^{きみ}. Throughout, Nakajima uses polite で す・ます forms while his boss uses words like だ or sentence particles like かい. At one point Nakajima apologizes with a very polite おそれいります. He appears to be apolo- gizing for the fact that he will be away from the office on business, although he is more likely apologizing for the inconvenience he is causing his superior. Note incidentally that Machida is probably a woman since the boss refers to her as 町田^{まちだ}さん. In addition to the actual words which are used, the difference in rank between Nakajima and his boss is re- flected in the ease with which the boss asks for favors. *Are you going to be here on the 24th? No, no matter. I can get someone else* (the implication being that Nakajima's role in the visit would probably not be very crucial). *What are you doing today?* Even after Nakajima explains that he is actually very busy, his boss asks him to take on an addi- tional task as well. There is no empathy, just a terse 頼^{たの}むよ. Nakajima gets as much time as possible (*it will probably take until this evening*), but he is unable to refuse.

　　Nakajima's boss also uses speech which is characteristic of men. Compare the follow- ing section of the above conversation rewritten as a female boss might speak.

Male boss   *Female boss*

B.　あっ、君^{きみ}、今日^{きょう}の予定^{よてい}は？　　　B.　あっ、そうそう。あなた今日^{きょう}の予定^{よてい}は。

　　　　　　plans　　　　　　　　　　　　　　　　　*plans*

A.　今日^{きょう}ですか〜　　　　　　　　　　A.　今日^{きょう}ですか〜

B.　突然^{とつぜん}ですまないが、これ、ひまを　B.　突然^{とつぜん}で本当^{ほんとう}に申^{もう}し訳^{わけ}ないんだけれど

　　suddenly　　　　　　　　　　　　　　　*suddenly*　　　　*apologize*

見^みてやっててくれないかな。　明日^{あした}　　これ、ちょっとひまを見^みてやってい

急^{きゅう}に使^{つか}うことになったんだよ。　　ただけないかしら。明日^{あした}急^{きゅう}に使^{つか}うこと

　　　　　　　　　　　　　　　　　　　　になったのよ。

A．こちらですか～   A．こちらですか～

B．ああ、じゃあ、頼むよ。   B．ええ、ごめんなさいね。お願いするわ。
　　　ask, request

A．はい。   A．はい。

Overall, Nakajima's female boss uses more polite vocabulary and one or two expressions which are considered overtly feminine, but she is not really any less direct. It is still obvious who is in charge.

Male speech	Female speech
あっ、	あっ、そうそう。
君	あなた
すまないが、	申し訳ないんだけれど、
ひまを	ちょっとひまを
見てやっててくれないかな。	見てやっていただけないかしら。
使うことになったんだよ。	使うことになったのよ。
じゃあ、	ごめんなさいね。
頼むよ。	お願いするわ。

Nakajima's speech becomes even more polite when he is speaking on the phone to a person who works for a separate organization. The speech here is typical of how men who are asking favors address those they need the favors from. The extraordinary politeness reflects two separate issues. First, everyone is more polite on the phone, especially in any professional context, and there is a great deal of ritualized language which is typical of business phone calls. In addition, Nakajima is asking a favor which the other person is in no way obligated to grant. His extreme politeness reflects his position of relative weakness.

On the telephone

もしもし、こちらは日々新聞の中島と申　*Hello. My name is Nakajima from the*

しますが、お世話になります。あの、教　*Nichinichi News. Hello. I'd like to speak*
　　　　　　　　　　　Superintendent

育長室の三好正弘様、いらっしゃいます　*with Mr. Masahiro Miyoshi from the*

Office

でしょうか。そうですか、会議中でいら　*Superintendent's Office. I see. He is in a*

っしゃいますか。そうですか。そうです　*meeting? I see. I see.*

か。あの、何時ごろ事務室にお戻りにな office return るでしょうかねぇ。そうですか。まあ、	*Do you know when he will return to the* *office? I see.*

わたくし、先ほど言いましたように、日
          before
々新聞の中島と申しますが。文部省が
                    for the time being
出した最近の国際問題に関するレポート
          Ministry of Education
について、コメントを聞かせて
international problem   report
いただきたいと思いまして、
	Well, as I said, my name is Nakajima from
	
	the Nichinichi News. Could you please tell
	
	him that I called and that I would like to
	
	ask him for his comment on the report from
	
	the Ministry of Education on the latest

電話を差し上げましたが。今日は、そう ですねえ、お忙しいようですので、明日 busy の朝またこちらからお電話いたしますの で、よろしくお願いいたしますように	*international problem. Today, well, since he* *seems to be busy today, I would be grateful* *if you could you please tell him that I will* *try to reach him again tomorrow morning,*
お伝えいただけますでしょうか。そう convey ですか。どうぞよろしくお願いいたしま	*and I hope I will be able to speak with him* *then. Thank you very much.*
す。ごめんください。	*Good-bye.*

While the gist of this phone call is very straightforward (Nakajima is trying to reach a man named Miyoshi, but ends up leaving a message), the conversation is filled with extremely polite ritualistic expressions and multiple polite predicates. The style is also very indirect. Nakajima is doing everything possible to make his message indirect and apologetic in an effort to make sure that Mr. Miyoshi will be as cooperative as possible.

Polite phone conversation	More neutral phone conversation
〜と申（もう）しますが	〜と言（い）いますが
〜様（さま）	〜さん
いらっしゃいますか	いますか
会議中（かいぎちゅう）でいらっしゃいますか	会議中（かいぎちゅう）ですか
お戻（もど）りになるでしょうか	戻（もど）るでしょうか
わたくし	わたし
聞（き）かせていただきたい	聞（き）きたい
電話（でんわ）を差（さ）し上（あ）げました	電話（でんわ）をしました
お電話（でんわ）いたします	電話（でんわ）します
よろしくお願（ねが）いいたしますように	よろしくお伝（つた）えください
お伝（つた）えいただけますでしょうか	
どうぞよろしくお願（ねが）いいたします	よろしくお願（ねが）いします

In addition, it is nearly obligatory to begin a job-related telephone conversation with お世話（せわ）になります, meaning something like "I will be taken care of (by you)" but really referring to the ongoing relationship between one person or organization and another. Likewise, it is necessary to end such a conversation with a string of statements which basically mean "Thank you." For more discussion of these styles see page 286 in Chapter 4.

In the final conversation, Nakajima (A) is chatting with another man named Seki (B) who is somewhat his junior.

At lunch with a friend

A．おーい、関（せき）、またカレーかい。　　　*Hey, Seki, curry again?*

B．はい、好（す）きっすからね。　　　　　　*Yeah, because I like it.*

　　中島（なかじま）さんは？　　　　　　　　*What about you, Nakajima?*

A．俺（おれ）は、またバーガーだよ。　　　　*A burger again for me.*

B．そうっすか。来週（らいしゅう）から出張（しゅっちょう）って　　*I see. I heard you're away next week.*

　　聞（き）いたんっすけど、本当（ほんとう）っすか。　　*Is it true?*

A．うん、東京（とうきょう）だよ。でも、鈴木（すずき）も来（く）る　　*Yeah, Tokyo. But Suzuki is coming too*

	から、あんまり遊べねーんだよな。	*so I won't be able to have much fun*
	真面目なやつだから。	*cuz he is so serious.*
B.	そうですね。残念ですねぇ。	*Yeah. Too bad.*
A.	いや、もったいないんだよ、	*Yeah, it's a waste.*
	東京だからさ。	*It's Tokyo after all!!*
B.	そうですね。カラオケっすか。	*Yeah, you go to karaoke?*
A.	うーん、でもそれより銀座とか	*Yeah, but also going to Ginza and*
	六本木とか	*Roppongi and places ~*
B.	そうですよね、せっかくだから。	*Yeah. Since you're going all that way.*
A.	鈴木ももう少しくだけたところ	*Too bad Suzuki doesn't have a*
	があるといいんだが～	*wild side!*

The difference in age and length of employment is reflected in the fact that Seki uses a significant number of です・ます forms as well as a style of speech which is characteristic of younger men speaking to their superiors: the full form です is realized as っす or even す. The greater the contraction, the greater the intimacy. This style is generally used first in sports clubs and other highly regimented organizations at high school or university. Such speech habits may continue for years. Other details. Seki refers to Nakajima as 中島さん. He uses the proper question particle か in contrast to Nakajima's かい. To the degree that pronouns are used, Nakajima uses 俺 in contrast to Seki's 僕. Nakajima uses the slang 遊べねーんだ (遊べないんだ) to express his unhappiness at going to Tokyo with his dull co-worker. And while there are differences between the relative rank of Nakajima and Seki, the conversation reflects a friendship not realized when Nakajima is talking to his boss.

In the final version, the conversation is transported to the Kansai region, in Western

Japan somewhere in the vicinity of Osaka. Note the lengthened vowel sounds in shorter words as well as the different verbal endings. Most obviously, だ is や, and 〜ません is 〜まへん. The 〜さん ending is 〜はん. A least one word is completely different: 本当 is pronounced ほんま.

At lunch with a friend near Tokyo	*near Osaka*
A．おーい、関、またカレーかい。	なあー、関、またカレーか。
B．はい、好きっすからね。	はい、好っきやからねえ。
中島さんは？	中島はんは？
A．俺は、またバーガーだよ。	俺は、またバーガーやで。
B．そうっすか。来週から出張って	そうでっか。来週から出張やって
聞いたんっすけど、本当っすか。	聞いたんやけど、ほんまでっか。
A．うん、東京だよ。でも、鈴木も来る	うん、東京やでえ。けど、鈴木も来はる
から、あんまり遊べねーんだよな。	から、あんまし遊ばれへんねんや。
真面目なやつだから。	真面目なやっちゃからなあ。
B．そうですね。残念ですねぇ。	そうでんなあ。残念でんなあ。
A．いや、もったいないんだよ、	いやあ、もったいないねんよ。
東京だからさ。	東京やからさ。
B．そうですね。カラオケっすか。	そうでんなあ。カラオケでっか。
A．うーん、それより銀座とか	うーん、それよか銀座とか

六本木<ruby>ろっぽんぎ</ruby>とか〜 六本木<ruby>ろっぽんぎ</ruby>とか〜

B.　そうですよね、せっかくだから。　　そうでっしゃねえ。せっかくやから。

A.　鈴木ももう少しくだけたところが　　鈴木ももう少しくだけたとこが

　　あるといいんだが〜　　　　　　　　あるとええんやけど〜

In addition to the obvious contrasts found in the written representation, there are significant (and truly enjoyable) differences in accent and intonation, and the Kansai dialect is often considered more colorful than standard Japanese.

A great many Japanese speak both a regional dialect and the standard language. Use of a dialect may reflect a sense of intimacy because the standard language is considered more formal and distancing, significantly less personal. Quite likely the amount of dialect in the above conversation would decrease if Nakajima were speaking with his boss rather than to his friend Seki. Note, in addition, that dialects of Japanese are just as complex as the standard language, and it is possible, for example, to be both polite and familiar while speaking a dialect. Looking just at negative verbs, 行かへん is the Kansai equivalent of 行かない, while 行きまへん is the equivalent of 行きません (at least for speakers from Osaka). 行かはらへん and 行かはりまへん, on the other hand, are the Kansai equivalent of the honorific いらっしゃらない and いらっしゃいません. There is a difference in usage in that 行かはらへん is much more common than its standard equivalent.

Use of a dialect may also reflect regional pride (both to advertise and to exclude). 関西弁 or Kansai Dialect (spoken around Osaka, Kobe, Kyoto) is the main competition to what is known as standard Japanese. The Kansai area is in many ways the historical and cultural center of Japan. Osaka is the country's second largest city with a much longer history than Tokyo. It may view itself as more Japanese when compared to Tokyo which is more international. Kyoto was home to the emperor for nearly one thousand years. It is very proud of its history, and is still the location of most of the country's traditional religious and cultural institutions. In fact, almost every part of Japan has its own dialect, much like in England, and as England is split north versus south, Japanese is split east versus west. Particularly famous for being difficult to understand are the dialects from the 東北 region to the north and east of Tokyo and 鹿児島 in the southernmost part of Kyushu. The only place without a strong sense of local dialect is 北海道 (in the far north) which has experienced a relatively recent influx of people from all over Japan. In order to communicate with each other, the residents of Hokkaido have had to resort to something very much like standard Japanese, in spite of their relative distance from Tokyo.

2 Words

2.1 Word meaning

Japanese is well-known for words with identical sounds but different meanings (and different written representations). The words here are divided into two types: (i) those which are completely unrelated in meaning (section 2.1.1), and (ii) those which are taken to have related meanings but are nevertheless distinct words written with different Chinese characters (section 2.1.2). Note that this book does not contain a section devoted specifically to synonyms (i.e. a group of words such as 勉強する, 学ぶ, 学習する, 研究する which might all be translated as *to study*). Cambridge University Press is producing a sister volume to this book which is devoted solely to synonyms in Japanese. Note also that Japanese has basically no *faux amis*, Japanese words which are easily confused with words of another language. Rather, Japanese borrows directly from other languages, often changing meaning and almost always changing sound in the process. Such words are of course written in カタカナ so there is no doubt as to their status. Borrowing and loan words are the topic of section 2.3 beginning on page 111.

2.1.1 Homonyms (same sound, unrelated meaning)

A cursory scan of a Japanese dictionary reveals hundreds of apparent homonyms. An extreme example is the listing かく with eighteen entries in Kenkyusha's *New Japanese-English Dictionary* (pp. 687–8). The orthography is deceptive, however, because it hides differences in what is known as *pitch accent*: the individual mora of a Japanese word may have a low pitch (L) or a high pitch (H), where high and low are defined relative to each other. Compare: 神 *god* with the falling accent pattern かみ (HL) and 紙 *paper* with the rising accent pattern かみ (LH). A comparable kind of difference is found in English not with pitch accent, but with stress. Think about the word *contrast* in the following two sentences: "There is a stark *contrast* between what he says and what he does" and "*Contrast* the personalities of the two main characters." Given the differences in stress, it is unlikely that *contrast* the noun and *contrast* the verb would be considered homonyms. Likewise in Japanese, many commonly cited homonyms actually differ in their pitch accent. (This is actually marked in Kenkyusha's dictionary.) Of course, true homonyms do exist in Japanese; 髪 *hair* is a real homonym of 紙 *paper* with the same rising accent pattern かみ (LH). While the following sets of words have the same ひらがな representation, some are true homonyms with the same pitch-accent while others are not. Note also that nouns may differ as to whether they carry their final pitch onto a following particle or not.

あつい	暑い・あつい *temperature hot*; 熱い・あつい *hot to the touch*; 厚い・あつい *thick*
いる	居る・いる *to be*; 要る・いる *to need*
うつす	写す・うつす *to copy, imitate*; 移す・うつす *to move, shift, transfer*
かい	階・かい *building floors*; 会・かい *meeting, conference*; 回・かい *revolutions, times*
かう	買う・かう *buy*; 飼う・かう *raise a pet*
かみ	神・かみ *god*; 紙・かみ *paper*; 髪・かみ *hair*
き	気が・きが *spirit, soul*; 木が・きが *tree*
きく	聞く・きく *ask, listen*; 効く・きく *be effective*; 利く・きく *do good, work, operate*; 菊・きくが *chrysanthemum*
きる	切る・きる *cut*; 着る・きる *wear*
さます	覚ます・さます *awaken*; 冷ます・さます *cool*
し	四・しが *four*; 死・しが *death*; 詩・しが *poem*; 市・しが *city*; 氏・しが *Mr., Mrs., etc.*
した	下・したが *under, down*; 舌・したが *tongue*
すむ	住む・すむ *to live, reside*; 済む・すむ *finish, be finished*
せい	性・せいが *gender, sex*; せい・せいが *blame, fault*; 姓・せいが *family name*
せん	線・せんが *line*; 千・せんが *thousand*
せんたく	洗濯・せんたくが *washing, laundry*; 選択・せんたくが *choice, selection*
だい	大・だいが *large size*; 代・だいが *generation, reign*; 代・だいが *price, fee*; 題・だいが *title, topic*; 台・だいが *stand*; 第・だいが *number, -th*
たいよう	太陽・たいようが *sun*; 大洋・たいようが *ocean*
なる	鳴る・なる *chime, ring out*; なる・なる *become*

のう	能・のうが talent, ability; 脳・のうが brain; 農・のうが farming, agriculture
は	歯・はが tooth; 葉・はが leaf
はし	橋・はしが bridge; 端・はしが edge, end, border; 箸・はしが chopsticks
はち	八・はちが eight; 蜂・はちが bee; 鉢・はちが bowl, flower pot
はな	花・はなが flower; 鼻・はなが nose
はなす	話す・はなす to speak; 離す・はなす to separate; 放す・はなす set free, loosen
ひ	日・ひが sun, sunlight, day; 火・ひが fire
ふく	服・ふくが clothing; 福・ふくが good fortune; 吹く・ふく blow, whistle; 拭く・ふく wipe, mop
ふる	降る・ふる fall (rain, snow); 振る・ふる wave, shake, swing
め	目・めが eye; 芽・めが sprout, nut
やく	役・やくが role, position; 約・やくが approximately; 焼く・やく to burn, toast
よる	夜・よるが night; 寄る・よる drop by, approach; 因る・よる be caused by; 依る・よる depend on
れい	例・れいが example; 礼・れいが bow, salute; れい・れいが zero

Learning the pitch accents of individual Japanese words is a formidable undertaking for non-native speakers. The task is complicated by the fact that the accent of a specific word may vary significantly from one part of Japan to the next, and consistent differences in accent are central to the definition of different Japanese dialects. Compare the following patterns for the phrase 橋が bridge (taken from Shibatani 1990, page 190).

橋が・はしが bridge	Aomori はしが; Akita はしが; Sendai はしが; Mito はしが; Tokyo はしが; Shizuoka はしが; Nagoya はしが; Niigata はしが; Toyama はしが; Kanazawa はしが; Kyoto はしが; Osaka はしが; Nara はしが; Okayama はしが; Hiroshima はしが; Yamaguchi はしが; Oita はしが; Fukuoka はしが; Kumamoto はしが; Miyakonojo はしが; Kagoshima はしが

There is some comfort in knowing that because of this kind of variation, an incorrect accent for a particular word rarely results in a serious misunderstanding. Across sentences and longer phrases, however, incorrect pitch accent is more distracting, in much the same way that incorrect stress can be distracting to speaker's of English. At the very least, it is important to learn the patterns for common verbs and the basic *Noun* + です phrases (Noun+です) in order to sound more Japanese.

2.1.2 Character synonyms (same sound, related meanings)

These are words which have related (and therefore easily confused) meanings. Many are actually different words which are often confused. Others are considered different "versions" of the same word, although the versions are written with different Chinese characters. In these cases, one character is often considered the default character, used whenever the particular meaning is not clear. Likewise, some words or some specific usages of particular words are usually written in ひらがな. These conventions have varied throughout Japanese history and are still not completely settled. The examples here have been edited to reflect "normal" usage. Where appropriate, idiomatic uses of the words are also included.

あう （合う・会う・遭う）

合う *meet, fit, suit, agree with*
二つの川が合って大河となる。*Two rivers meet and become one.*
体に合わない服 *clothes which do not fit my body*
その話は事実と合う。*What they said corresponds to reality.*
気が合う *get along with*
お口に合うかどうかわからないが〜 *I don't know if you will like this or not* 〜

会う *meet a person*
友だちに会う *meet with a friend*
彼女との出会い *coming upon her, an encounter or meeting with her*

遭う *meet by accident* (generally with an event)
事故に遭う *meet with an accident*
夕立ちに遭う *run into a rain shower*

あがる （上がる）   See transitive 上げる below.

上がる *go up, rise*
屋根に上がる *go up to the roof*
階段を上がる *go up the stairs*
物価が上がる *prices rise*
どうぞお上がりください *Please, come in*
高校に上がる *enter high school*

上がる *finish, complete,* 仕上がる, でき上がる
雨が上がる *the rain stops* (also 雨が止む)

あく（空く・開く）　See transitive and intransitive あける below.

空く *become empty or open*
席<small>せき</small>が空く *the seat is open, unoccupied*
電話<small>でんわ</small>が空く *the phone is no longer in use*
手<small>て</small>が空かない *to be busy, not free*
洋服<small>ようふく</small>に穴<small>あな</small>が空く *get a hole in your clothes*

開く *open,* opposite of 閉<small>し</small>まる; also read ひらく with different senses (see page 134)
窓<small>まど</small>が開いている *the window is open*
八時<small>はちじ</small>に開く *open at 8* (on a daily basis)
開いた口<small>くち</small>がふさがらなかった *to be struck speechless*
幕<small>まく</small>が開く *the curtain goes up, opens*

あける（開ける）　See intransitive あく above.

開ける *open,* opposite of 閉<small>し</small>める; also read ひらける with different senses (see page 134)
窓<small>まど</small>を開ける *open a window*
店<small>みせ</small>を開ける *open a store* (on a daily basis) (cf. 開店<small>かいてん</small>)

あける（明ける）　See intransitive あく and transitive あける above.

明ける *become bright, become easy to see, conclude*
夜<small>よる</small>が明ける *the night becomes bright*
梅雨<small>つゆ</small>が明ける *the rainy season ends*
年<small>とし</small>が明ける *the year comes to an end*

あげる（上げる・挙げる・揚げる）　See intransitive 上<small>あ</small>がる above.

上げる *raise, lift, give*
差<small>さ</small>し上げる *give to a person of higher status*
手荷物<small>てにもつ</small>をテーブルに上げる *put the hand luggage on the table*
スピードを上げる *increase the speed*
大学<small>だいがく</small>に上げる *send to college*

挙げる *arrest, round up, catch*
犯人<small>はんにん</small>を挙げる *catch a criminal*
確証<small>かくしょう</small>を挙げる *present* (conclusive) *evidence*
例<small>れい</small>を挙げる *bring up, list*

揚げる *deep fry*
天<small>てん</small>ぷらを揚げる *fry tempura*

揚げる・上げる *fly, send into the air*
タコをあげる *fly a kite*
花火<small>はなび</small>をあげる *set off fireworks*

あし（足・脚）

足 *leg* (of a person or when the leg is used to cause a movement)
長い足 *long legs*
揚げ足を取る *carp, nitpick*
足が遠のく *come and go less frequently than before*
足を洗う *wash one's hands of something*
足を引っ張る *drag someone down*

脚 *leg* (generally of an object)
机の脚 *leg of a desk*
両脚 *both legs* (animate or not)

あたたかい（温かい・暖かい）

温かい *warm* (to the touch), *warm hearted* (internal warmth)
ご飯が温かい *the rice is warm*
温かい家庭 *warm household*

暖かい *feels warm* (overall, external)
暖かい部屋 *a warm room*
暖かい風 *a warm breeze*

あつい（暑い・熱い）

暑い *hot, warm, sultry*; opposite of 寒い *cold*
冷房のきかない暑い部屋 *a hot room where the air conditioning is not effective*
暑い夏の夜 *a hot summer night*

熱い *hot, heated*; opposite of 冷たい *cold, chilled*
風呂の湯が熱い。 *The water in the bath is hot.*

熱い *passionate*
熱い思い *a passionate, strong memory*
２人は熱い仲だ。 *The two are madly in love.*

あと（後・跡）

後 *direction or order, after*; opposite of 前 *before, in front of* or 先 *before*
後になる *it will be later*
後片付け *cleaning up afterwards*

跡 *mark, print, impression, remains*
城の跡 *the remains of a castle*
足跡 *footprint*

ある （有る・在る・或る）

有る *have, possess*; opposite of 無い
リンゴがある *I have an apple*

在る *exist, occur, be located*
郵便局は駅の前にある *The post office is in front of the station.*

或る *some, one, a*
ある人 *some person, a generic person*
ある日 *one day, some day, on a given day*

いる （要る・居る）

要る *need*
金が要る *need money*

居る *exist, be*
宇宙人がいる *aliens exist*
どのぐらい日本にいますか。 *How long have you been in Japan?*

うつ （打つ・撃つ）

打つ *hit, strike, knock*
くぎを打つ *strike a nail*
太鼓を打つ *beat on a drum*

撃つ *shoot, fire*
ピストルで撃つ *fire a pistol*

おす （押す・推す）

押す *push* (with physical force)
ドアを押す *push (open) the door*
判を押す *stamp, seal* (press your name stamp)
ボタンを押す *press a button*

推す *infer, conclude, judge; recommend, support*
君の言うことから推して *From what you say, we concluded that~*
会長に推す *propose or support as chair*

おろす （下ろす・降ろす・卸す）

下ろす *move from high to low*
ベンチに腰を降ろす *sit yourself down on a bench*
棚から荷物を下ろす *get the luggage down from a shelf*

下ろす *remove from storage*
新しいバスタオルをおろす *use a new bath towel*
銀行からお金をおろす *take money out of the bank*

降ろす *get out of a means of transportation; relieve of a position*
車から荷物を降ろす *get the luggage out of the car*
低い地位に降ろされる *be demoted*

卸す *sell at wholesale*
安く卸す *sell off cheaply*

かえす（返す・帰す）　See intransitive かえる below.

返す *return something to the original location, situation, or condition*
本を図書館に返す *return a book to the library*

帰す *return someone home*
生徒を早く家に帰す *return the students home quickly*

A verb like 帰す contrasts with 戻す which means *return something to a place* (not usually home): 使った物を元に戻す *return things back to where they were.*

かえる（返る・帰る）　See transitive かえす above.

返る *return to the original location, situation, or condition*
子供に返りたいものだ。 *I wish I was a child again.*
我に返る *come to oneself*

帰る *return home*
留学生が本国に帰る。 *The exchange student is going back to his country.*
早く帰ろう。 *Let's go home quickly.*

A verb like 帰る should be contrasted with 戻る which means *return to a place* (not usually home): 会社に戻る *return to the office* or 意識が戻る *regain consciousness.*

かえる（変える・代える・替える・換える）

変える *change, alter, shift*
形を変える *change form, change shape*
色を赤から青に変える *change the color from red to blue*

代える *replace, relieve, substitute* (a position or duty)
投手を代える *relieve the pitcher*
議長を代える *change the chairman* (to a new person)

替える *replace, substitute* (with something perceived to be the same or equivalent)
池の水を替える *replace the water in the pond*
入れ替える *change places with*

換える *change or replace something* (more general)
ドルを円に換える *change dollars into yen*
バスを乗り換える *transfer buses*
言い換える *say again, rephrase*

替える seems limited to replacement of one thing by another thing of the same kind, while 換える refers to a broader range of exchanges. This is a relatively subtle distinction, and at least one dictionary lists both characters in examples such as シーツをかえる and ドルを円にかえる. Others use ひらがな in both kinds of examples. There is a sense that ひらがな is more likely to be used the more common the activity. (It is therefore more likely when talking about changing sheets than when talking about changing money).

かかる（掛かる・掛る・懸かる） See transitive かける below.

掛かる・掛る *hang on or over, be suspended from, catch*
壁に絵画がかかっている *a picture is hanging on the wall*
魚が網にかかる *catch a fish in a net* (lit. *a fish is caught in a net*)
洋服が掛かっている *be wearing Western clothes* (lit. *Western clothes are hanging*)
エンジンがかかる *an engine starts*
風邪で医者にかかる *be under the care of a doctor for a cold*
音楽がかかっている *music is playing*

懸かる *hang down from, be caught on one's heart*
電線にタコがかかる *a kite is caught in the wires*
気にかかる *weigh on one's mind*
賞金がかかっている *a prize is offered, a reward is offered*

かく（書く・描く・画く）

書く *write* (letters and words)
ローマ字で書く *write in romanization*
手紙を書く *write a letter*

描く *draw* (a picture)
絵を描く *draw a picture*

画く *draw* (a graph, design)
図を画く *draw a diagram, graph, plan*

かげ（陰・影）

陰 *places where light does not shine, places which are not visible*
山の陰 *the shadows on a mountain*
陰でうわさをする *spread a rumor secretly, from the shadows*
お陰様で *thanks to you* (thanks to your invisible support); also written お蔭さまで

影 *light, shadow, silhouette*
月の影 *moonlight*
影がうつる *cast a shadow* (lit. *a shadow is cast*)
影を落とす *cast a shadow on*

かける（掛ける・懸ける）　See intransitive かかる above.

掛ける *hang, suspend, catch*
顔にヴェールを掛ける *wear a veil over the face*
肩に手を掛ける *put your hands on someone's shoulders*
腰を掛けてください。　*Please sit down.*
メガネを掛ける *wear glasses*
5に3をかける *multiply 3 by 5*
大変ご面倒を掛けてすみません。*I am sorry to be such a burden*
時間をかける *spend time, take time*
電話をかける *make a phone call, telephone*
カギを掛ける *lock*

懸ける *hang down from, catch on one's heart*
深く心にかける *take to heart*
命をかける *risk one's like*

In practice, almost all occurrences of かかる or かける discussed here can be safely written in ひらがな.

かける（架ける・賭ける）See かかる・かける just above as well.

架ける *hang or suspend* (between two locations, in one direction)
橋を架ける *build a bridge, put up a bridge*
電線を架ける *hang electric wires*

賭ける *bet, wager*
人気馬に金を賭ける *bet money on a popular horse*

かぜ（風・風邪）

風 *wind*
強い風 *strong wind*
北風 *wind from the north*

風邪 *a cold*
風邪を引く *catch a cold*

かたい（硬い・堅い・固い）

硬い *hard* (like a rock), *stiff* ; opposite of 柔らかい *soft*
硬い石 *a hard rock*
表情の硬い人 *a person with a hard facial expression*

堅い *hardened, firm, rigid*; opposite of もろい *delicate, frail, tender*

堅いパン *hard bread, dried bread*

堅い木 *hard wood*

目標達成は堅い *the achievement of our goal is certain*

頭が堅い *strong headed, willful*

固い *outside is hard, solid, impenetrable*; opposite of ゆるい *loose, not firm*

固い地盤 *solid foundation*

固い友情 *strong friendship*

頭がかたい *dense, thick, not too bright*

かたち・かた・けい（形）かた・けい（型）

形 *shape, form, the way something looks*

その形は魚に似ている。 *That shape resembles a fish.*

本の形で *in book form, as a book*

型・かた *impression, style, mold, usage*

型を取る *make a model of*

彼の洋服の型は英国風だ。 *His clothes are British in cut.*

き（気・機・器）

気 *spirit, mind, soul*

気持ち *feeling, sense*

気分 *mood*

電気 *electricity*

機 *machine* (loom); *chance*

機械 *large, industrial machine*

機会 *chance, opportunity*

器 *container, tool*

器械 *smaller, more technical machines* like cameras, hospital equipment, VCRs, etc.

楽器 *instrument*

Contrast the following (which illustrate the above differences):

日本電気 *Nihon Power* (electricity)

三菱電機 *Mitsubishi Heavy Industries* (big machines)

松下電器 *Matsushita Electrical (Panasonic)* (appliances and small machines).

Further expressions with 気:

気が　　　気が小さい *be timid, cowardly*; 気が散る *cannot concentrate, be distract-ed*; 気が早い *be impatient, hasty*; 気が変わる *change one's mind*; 気が利く *be attentive*; 気が紛れる *be diverted or distracted*; 気が短い *be short-tempered*; 気が向く *be interested in, inclined toward*; 気が長い *be patient*;

その気がない *do not feel like*; 気が重い *be dispirited, depressed*; 気が多い *be fickle, changeable*; 〜という気がする *have the feeling that* 〜; 気が進まない *be unwilling to, hesitate to*; 気がつく *realize*; 気が強い *be strong-willed*; 気が弱い *be weak-willed*; 気が緩む *be relaxed*

気に　　　気に入る *like, be satisfied with*; 気に掛かる *weigh on one's mind*; 気に掛ける *worry*; 気に食わない *dislike, hate*; 気になる *weigh on one's mind*; 気にする *mind, care, concern oneself with*

気を　　　気を引く *attract attention*; 気を入れる *work hard, be attentive*; 気を利かせる *exercise tact, have good sense*; 気を配る *be sensitive to*; 気を揉む *worry about, be anxious*; 気をそそる *arouse one's interest in*; 気を使う *care about, worry about*; 気を付ける *take care, be careful*; 気を悪くする *become displeased*; 気を緩める *relax one's attention, take it easy*; 気を許す *trust, relax one's guard*

き（期・季）

期 *period of time* (from when to when)
期間 *period of time*
夏期講習会 *summer term lectures*
一学期 *first term*

季 *season*
季節 *season*
夏季休暇 *holiday during the summer*

きく（聞く・聴く）

聞く *listen, ask* (with the ears)
ラジオを聞く *listen to the radio*

聴く *listen closely* (where listening is the point)
音楽を聴く *listen to music*
裁判を聴く *listen to the trial*

Note that 聞く may be translated into English as *listen* or *ask*.
聞いているかどうかわからない。 *I don't know if they are listening or not.*
ご意見を聞いてもいいですか。 *May I ask your opinion?*

聞こえる means *is audible, can be heard* while 聞ける means *able to ask* or *able to listen* (because conditions are right). Contrast 何も聞こえなかった *I couldn't hear anything* and 聞けると思っていたけど時間がなかった *I thought I'd be able to ask, but there was no time.*

さす（刺す・指す・差す）

刺す *pierce, penetrate* (literally and figuratively)
くしで刺す *pierce with a stick*
身を刺すような寒さ *cold which pierces the body*

指す *point in a direction*
針が北を指す *the compass needle points north*
指を指す *point to*
傘を差す *open an umbrella*

さびしい・さみしい（寂しい・淋しい・さびしい）

寂しい *lonely, lonesome, desolate, sad*
寂しい夜道 *a desolate road at night*
寂しい顔 *a sad face*
寂しく暮らす *live a lonely life*

淋しい originally referred to the dripping of water
さびしい *sad, lonely* (poetic, especially emotional)

The usual character is 寂しい, and the usual reading for both characters is さびしい.

じき（時機・時期・時季）See き above.

時機 *a time of opportunity, chance*
時機を失う *miss an opportunity*

時期 (bounded) *period of time, season*
入学の時期 *the school entering season*
取り入れの時期 *harvest time*

時季 *season* (climate)
時季外れの長雨 *unseasonably long rain*
目に青葉の時季 *season when green leaves strike the eye*

しまる（閉まる・締まる）See transitive しめる below.

閉まる *to close, shut*
八時に店が閉まる *the shop closes at eight*

締まる *to be tight, controlled*
筋肉が締まる *be muscled, be in shape*

しめる（絞める・締める・閉める・占める）See intransitive しまる above.

絞める *strangle, wring*
首を絞める *ring someone's neck*
絞め殺す *strangle to death*

締める *tie, tighten, control strictly*
帯を締める *tie an obi*
ネクタイを締める *tie a necktie*
ねじを締める *tighten a screw*
気持ちを締める *brace oneself, pull oneself together*
締め切り *deadline*

閉める *close* (something which was opened)
戸を閉める *close a door*

占める *take for one's own*
前列に席を占める *occupy a seat in the front row*

すすめる（進める・勧める・薦める）

進める *advance, move* (troops) *forward*
時計を１時間進める *move the clock forward one hour*
車を前に進める *urge one's car forward*

勧める *encourage* (an action or use of an object)
食事を勧める *offer food and encourage to eat*
参加を勧める *encourage participation*

薦める *recommend, advise, encourage* (something you consider good)
彼女を課長に薦める *recommend her for section chief*
生徒に薦めたい本 *a book I want to recommend to my students*

たえる（耐える・絶える）

耐える *bear, stand, endure, tolerate*
痛みに耐える *endure pain*
３人の重さに耐えられる *able to bear the weight of three people*

絶える *become extinct, cease to exist*
この人類はすでに絶えてしまった。 *The race has already died out.*
通信が全く絶えた。 *All correspondence ceased.*
息が絶えてしまう *pass away, breathe one's last*

たずねる（訪ねる・尋ねる）

訪ねる *visit, pay a visit to*
知人を訪ねる *visit an acquaintance*
お訪ねください。 *Please come by and see me.*

尋ねる *ask, inquire, question,* 質問する
案内所で尋ねる *inquire at the information desk*
名前を尋ねる *ask a person's name*

たつ（立つ・建つ） See transitive たてる below

立つ *stand, rise, become vertical*
駅の前に立っていた *was standing in front of the station*
市長選に立つ *run for mayor*
人の上に立つ *lead others*
腹が立つ *become angry*

建つ *be built*
記念碑が建つ *a monument is built*

たてる（立てる・建てる） See intransitive たつ above.

立てる *stand something, put vertical*
棒を立てる *stand a rod, put a rod on end*
計画を立てる *make a plan*
人を証人に立てる *call a person to witness*

建てる *build, put up a building*
畑に家を建てる *build houses in the fields*

たま（玉・珠・球・弾）

玉 *ball, something round like a ball*
火の玉 *ball of fire*
百円玉 *¥100 coin*

珠 *the ball from an oyster, a pearl*
貝からとられた真珠の珠 *the sphere of pearl taken from the oyster*
目玉焼き *fried egg*

球 *ball* (used in sports), *light bulb*
球を投げる *throw a ball*
電気の球が切れた *the bulb is burnt out*

弾 *bullet*
弾に当たる *hit with a bullet*

たまご（玉子・卵）

玉子 *egg* (in cooking)
玉子焼き *omelette, fried egg*
玉子料理 *egg cuisine*

卵 *egg* (raw, of a living thing)
小鳥の卵 *the egg of a little bird*
アリの卵 *ant eggs*
外交官の卵 *a budding diplomat*

つく（付く・着く・就く）See transitive つける below.

付く *stick to, adhere, attach to*
ズボンに泥が付く *mud gets on your pants*
ポケットの付いていないコート *a coat with no pockets*
家具が付いている *furnished*
人に付いて行く *go following a person, go after a person*
ぜい肉が付く *put on weight*
日本語の力がつく *get better at Japanese*

着く *attain a goal, arrive*
東京に着く *arrive in Tokyo*
席に着く *take a seat*
テーブルに着く *sit at the table*

就く *settle into place, take a position*
仕事に就く *take a job*
床に就く *settle into bed, take to your sickbed*
眠りに就く *fall asleep*

つくる（作る・造る）

作る *make* (something basically small)
料理を作る *cook*
家具を作る *make furniture*
列を作る *form a line*
畑にトマトを作る *grow tomatoes in the field*
試験の問題を作る *write an examination*
子を作る *have a child*
この野菜でサラダを作る *prepare a salad with these vegetables*
資金を作る *raise the funds*
時間を作る *make some time*

造る *make, construct* (something basically big)
船を造る *build a ship*
犬小屋を造る *build a dog house*
お酒を造る *brew sake*

つける（付ける）See intransitive つく above.

付ける *attach*
名前を付ける *give a name*
ドアにカギを付ける *lock a door*
机に傷を付ける *scratch a desk*

とぶ（飛ぶ・跳ぶ）

飛ぶ *fly* (literally and figuratively)
飛べない鳥 *a flightless bird*
パリへ飛ぶ *fly to Paris*
うわさが飛ぶ *a rumor spreads afar*
空中を飛ぶ *fly across the sky*
小遣銭もすっかり飛んでしまった。 *My pocket money is all gone.*
その本は飛ぶように売れている。 *That book is a runaway seller.*
１０ページから１５ページへ飛ぶ *skip from page ten to page fifteen*

跳ぶ *jump, leap, spring, bound*
カンガルーがぴょんと跳ぶ *kangaroos hop*
このミゾが跳べるか。 *Can you jump this ditch?*

とまる（止まる・泊まる）　See transitive とめる below.

止まる *stop, come to a stop*
バスが止まった。 *The bus stopped.*
時計が止まった。 *My watch stopped.*
止まれ！ *Stop!*

泊まる *stay, lodge, stop at*
ホテルに泊まる *stay at a hotel*
船が港に泊まっている。 *The ship is in port.*

とめる（止める・泊める）See intransitive とまる above.

止める *stop, bring to a halt*
車を止める *stop the car*

泊める *put up*
客を家に泊める *put a guest up in one's home*

とる（採る・捕る・執る・撮る・取る）

採る *use, employ, gather*
卒業生３名を採る *employ three graduates*
採るべき道はただ一つだ。 *There is but one course to take.*
カブト虫を採る *gather, collect beetles*
ブドウから汁を採る *squeeze juice from grapes*

捕る *capture, catch*
ねずみを捕る *catch a mouse*
飛球を捕ろうとする *try to catch a fly ball*

執る *take hold, grasp*
筆をとる *hold the brush*
事務をとる *do business, attend to business*

撮る *take a photo*
写真を撮る *photograph, take a photo*
ビデオで子どもを撮る *take a video of a child*

取る *have, hold, take for one's own,* 持つ
手に取る *hold in one's hand, take in one's hand*
責任を取る *take responsibility*

For any occurrence of とる which does not fit obviously into one of the usages defined here, it is usual to use 取る or とる.

取る・とる   年を取る *get older*; 場所を取る *take a place, hold a place*; メモを取る *take a memo*; リズムを取る *get the rhythm*; 金を取る *steal, take money*; 帽子を取る *remove one's hat*; MBAを取る *obtain an MBA*; 休みを取る *take a holiday*; 新聞を取る *subscribe to a newspaper*; 朝食をとる *have breakfast*; 連絡を取る *contact, get in touch with*

なおす（直す・治す）See intransitive なおる below.

直す *fix, repair; redo*
間違えを直す *fix a mistake*
書き直す *rewrite*

治す *cure*
風邪を治す *cure a cold*

なおる（直る・治る）See transitive なおす above.

直る *become fixed, repaired*
機械が直る *the machine starts to work again*

治る *recover from an illness*
傷が治る *a cut heals*

ながい（長い・永い）

長い *long* (but bounded) *time or distance*; opposite of 短い *short*
髪が長い *hair is long*
長い間 *for a long time, a long time*
長い目で見る *take a long-term view of*

永い *without end, forever*
永い眠り *an endless sleep*

のぞむ （望む・臨む）

望む *want, desire, hope, wish,* 期待する
世界旅行ができることを望む。 *I wish I could travel around the world.*
彼にこれ以上何を望むのですか。 *What more do you expect from him?*

望む *view, look upon* (subject is a person)
車窓より富士を望む *view Fuji from the car window*

臨む *attend*
開会式に臨んであいさつする *attend the opening ceremony and make a speech*

臨む *overlook* (subject is a place)
湖を臨むホテル *a hotel overlooking a lake*

のびる （延びる・伸びる）

延びる *prolong, extend* (by adding or unfolding)
道路が延びる *the road becomes longer*
会議が延びる *the meeting goes on late*

伸びる *become long, stretch*; opposite of 縮む *shrink* (internally controlled)
伸び縮み *expansion and contraction, elasticity*
背が伸びる *back straightens*
売上げを伸ばす *increase sales*

のる （乗る・載る）

乗る *get on, be on* (generally of people)
飛行機に乗る *get on a plane*
屋根の上に乗る *get on the roof*

乗る *be in sync with, be in full swing, participate in*
リズムに乗る *get into the rhythm*
相談に乗る *give advice, discuss*

載る *get on* (generally of objects); *be published, appear in a book*
机の上に載っている本 *books placed on the desk* (乗る is also possible in this example)
この単語は辞書に載っていない。 *This word is not in my dictionary.*
新聞に載る *appear in a newspaper*

はかる （測る・計る・量る・図る・謀る）

測る *measure height, distance,* etc.
速度を測る *measure the speed*

測る *measure, guess* (at something vague or ill-defined); also written 量る
新入社員の能力を測る *estimate the abilities of the new employees*

計る *count numbers and time*
時間を計る *measure time* (cf. 時計)

量る *measure weight, volume, etc.*
体重を量る *weigh, measure the weight*; see 測る *above as well*

図る *try, plan, try to*
会社の発展を図る *aim to develop the company*
解決を図る *try for a settlement, attempt to resolve*

謀る *plan, devise, scheme*
暗殺を謀る *plan an assassination*

はじめ（始め・初め）

始め *beginning to do something, something begins* [a verb]
始める *begin something*; 始まる *something begins*
第一章から始める *begin with the first chapter*
泣き始める *begin to cry*

初め *the beginning* [a noun]
春の初め *the beginning of spring*
初めから *from the beginning*
生まれて初めての経験 *a first experience* (since being born)
初めまして *pleased to meet you*

はな（花・華）

花 *a flower, something beautiful*
花が咲く *flowers bloom*
生け花 *flower arranging*

華 *essence, core part* (is sometimes written 花 as well)
武士道の華 *the flower of chivalry*
人生の華 *the flower of life*

はね（羽・羽根）

羽 *feather, plume, wing* (of a bird, insect, airplane, etc.)
羽が生える *feathers grow, appear*
羽を伸ばす *spread your wings*

羽根 *feathers, things made from feathers*
羽根突き *Japanese badminton; battledore and shuttlecock*
風車の羽根 *arms of a windmill*, (赤い風車 *the Moulin Rouge*)
風車の羽根 *feathers of a pinwheel*

はやい（早い・速い）

早い *early*
早い時刻 *an early time*
朝早く起きる *wake up early in the morning*
お早うございます。 *Good morning!*

速い *fast, quick*
ピッチャーの速い球 *a pitcher's fast ball*
流れが速い *the current is fast*
足が速い *run quickly*

ひ（火・灯）

火 *fire; passion, heat*
火をつける *light a fire*
鍋に火をかける *heat a pot*
火に油を注ぐ *make things worse* (lit. *pour oil on fire*)
火を通す *cook, boil, heat thoroughly*
火の車 *be in financial straits*

灯 *lights*; 灯る *light, burn, be lit*
灯がともる *a light burns, a light is lit*
街の灯 *city lights*

In contrast to 火 and 灯, 光 refers to *light* in the sense which is the opposite of *darkness*.
光る means *shine, be bright, be brilliant*: 太陽の光 *sunlight* or 光を放つ *emit light*.

ひく（引く・弾く・挽く）

引く *pull* (closer to yourself)
子供の手を引く *take a child by the hand*
ドアを引く *pull a door open*
気を引く *get the attention of*
直線を引く *draw a straight line*
風邪を引く *catch a cold*
貴族の血を引いている *be descended from a noble family*
腫れが引く *swelling goes down*

引く *extend, install, draw off*
電話線を引く *install a phone line*
水道を引く *have water supplied*
カーテンを引く *close, draw the curtains*

引く *pick out*
くじを引く *draw lots*
辞書を引く *consult a dictionary*; 引き方 *way of using a dictionary*
5 ひく 2 *five minus two*

弾く *play* (a stringed instrument)
ピアノを弾く *play the piano* (also 琴, バイオリン, ギター, etc.)

挽く *grind*
コーヒー豆を挽く *grind coffee beans*
のこぎりを挽く *saw* (a saw)

ふ・ぶ（不）ぶ・む（無）

不 *opposite, not*
不便 *inconvenient, not convenient*
不自然 *unnatural*

無 *non-existence*; opposite of 有; contrast 有る and 無い
無理 *impossible, unreasonable*
無名 *nameless*
無害な *harmless*
無事に帰ってください。 *Please get home without incident. Take care.*

While 有る and 無い are considered translations of *have* and *not have*, they are really different words written with different Chinese characters.

ふく（吹く・噴く）

吹く *movement of wind; blowing*
風が吹く *the wind blows*
口笛を吹く *to whistle*

噴く *emit, blow out* (all at once; gradual appearance is still written 吹く or in ひらがな)
三原山が煙を噴いている。 *Mt. Mihara is smoking.*
汗が噴き出る *sweat comes poring out*

ふね（舟・船）

舟 *small boats*
小舟 *a small boat*
舟をこぐ *row a boat*

船 *large boats, boats in general*
親船 *the mother ship*
船に乗る *board a ship*

ほか（外・他）

他 *other, stranger, unfamiliar*; usually read た in compounds

他の人 or less conversationally 他人 *other people*

課長他三名 *three people in addition to the section chief*

その他 *in addition* is pronounced そのほか and sometimes written in ひらがな. More formally and in writing, その他 is pronounced そのた. ほか can be contrasted with 内 when referring to inside and outside of a well-defined group. Compare: そのほか三人が来た "Three people (in addition to those expected) came" and そのうち三人が来た "Three of the people (we invited) came."

外 *other* (particularly of locations)

外で食べよう。 *Let's eat some other place.*

外で探してください。 *Please look in other places, some other place*

This character is also read そと where it refers to the *outside* of an object. Here it is the opposite of 中.

外にいる。 *He is outside.*

家の外 *the outside of the house*

Read そと, it can also be understood as what is objective and in some sense available to everyone, as opposed to 内 which is subjective and personal.

感情をめったに外に表さない。 *He rarely shows his feelings.*

彼は胸の内を明かしてくれなかった。 *He never told me what was on his mind.*

まじる・まざる（交じる・混ざる） See transitive まぜる below.

交じる *mix, blend* (so that that the parts are still visible)

漢字仮名交じり文 *a passage with both Chinese characters and kana*

道が交じる *the roads cross*

混ざる *mix, blend* (so that parts are not visible)

水と油は混ざらない。 *Water and oil don't mix.*

まぜる（混ぜる） See intransitive まじる and まざる above.

混ぜる *mix, blend* (so that parts are not visible)

玉子に牛乳を混ぜる *mix milk into the eggs*

玉子と牛乳を混ぜる *mix milk and eggs*

まち（町・街）

町 *town, a place with lots of people and houses*

町と村 *towns and villages*

町はずれに *on the outskirts of town*

街 *noisy or busy street; area where one kind of people are concentrated*
街へ行く *go downtown*
学生の街 *student town, college town*

まるい（丸い・円い）

丸い *round, spherical, not sharp*
地球は丸い *the earth is round*
角の丸いテーブル *a table with rounded* (not sharp) *corners*
丸い人柄 *a mild personality*

円い *round, circular*; opposite of 四角い *square*
円いテーブル *a round table*

まわり（回り・周り）

回り *movement around, going around; via; effect;* 回る *go around*
左回り *going around to the left*
北極回りで *by way of the North Pole* (in an airplane)
この酒は回りが早い。 *This alcohol takes effect quickly.*

周り *circumference; surroundings, area*
湖の周りの道 *the road around a lake*
家の周りは住宅地です。 *The area around my house is residential.*

みる（見る・診る）

見る *see, sense* (using eyes)
テレビを見る *watch television*
変な夢を見る *have a strange dream*
じろじろ見る *to stare*
見る目がある *to have an eye for something*
見るに見かねる *to be unable to stand watching something*
見るからに *from just a look, at a glance*
見て見ぬ振りをする *to pretend not to see, to look the other way*

診る *medical examination by a doctor*
医者に診てもらう *be seen by a doctor*
脈を診る *take your pulse*

Other uses of みる may be written in ひらがな or with 見る. Also, contrast 見える meaning *is visible, can be seen* with 見られる meaning *able to see* or *able to look* (because
conditions are right). Contrast ここからその絵が見えた *I was able to see the picture
from here* and 美術館に行けばその絵が見られる *If you go to the museum you will be
able to see that picture.* The latter usage should not be confused with the passive:友達に
はだかを見られた *My naked body was seen by my friend.* (The passive is on page 139.)

め（目・眼）

目 *eye; number* (ordinal suffix)
目を閉じる *close your eyes*
目玉 *eyeball*
三番目 *third, third place*

眼 *eye* (medical)
眼鏡 *eye glasses*
眼科医, 眼医者 *ophthalmologist*
眼球 *eyeball* (medical sounding)

もと（元・基・下）

元 *beginning, source, cause*
元に戻る *return to the beginning*
失敗は成功の元 *failure teaches success*

元 *capital, source*
商売を始めるにはずいぶん元がかかる。*We need a lot of capital to start a business.*

元 *previous, former*
元の住所 *previous address*
元アメリカ大統領のカーター氏 *former US president Carter*

基 *foundation, base*
この小説は事実に基づいている。*This novel is based on facts.*
農業は国の基だ。*Agriculture is the foundation of a nation.*

下 *underneath, the bottom*
足下 *underfoot, step*

下 *under* (the direction of), *at the foot of*
先生の指導の下に *under the direction of a teacher*
夫のもとを去る *leave one's husband*

All other uses of もと (and some of those given here actually) may be written in ひらがな.

や（家・屋）

家 *home*
我が家 *my home, our home*
貸し家 *rented home*

屋 *store*
米屋 *rice store*
山田屋 *the Yamada store*
小屋 *cabin*

やわらかい（柔らかい・軟らかい）

柔らかい *soft, tender, pliant, weak*, opposite of かたい (see page 43)
柔らかいまくら *a soft pillow*
柔らかい声で話す *speak in a soft voice*
体が柔らかい *pliant body*

軟らかい *soft, easy to change shape, to break* (something which should be hard or rigid)
地盤が軟らかい *the foundation is weak*
軟らかい木材 *pliant lumber*

ゆく（行く・逝く）

行く *go, progress* (more commonly pronounced いく)
学校へ行く *go to school*
東京行の電車 *train bound for Tokyo*
うまく行く *go well*
駅へ行く道 *road to the train station*

逝く *die* (can also be read いく)
父が逝く *father will die*

When you are invited over to where someone is, in English you announce, *I'll be right over* or *I'll come right away*, or *I'll come in a bit*. In Japanese the verb in this situation is 行く (すぐ行くよ or 後もうすこしで行く). Japanese announce (particularly on the telephone) *I'll go to where you are* because Japanese 行く *go* actually means something like *move from where I am now*. 来る, on the other hand, means *move to where I am now*.

よい（良い・善い）

良い *good*
成績が良い *marks are good, good grades*
運が良い *good luck, is lucky*
ああ、よかった。 *What a relief. That is great.*
行っても良い *may I go, it is okay to go*
都合が良い *is convenient*

善い *good character, right, true*
善い人 *a person whose behavior is good, a well-behaved person*

良い and いい are more or less synonymous, although 良い might be seen as a little more formal or archaic. In the negative and past, of course, only 良くない and 良かった are possible.

よる（因る・寄る）

因る *depend on, be based on, result from* (usually in ひらがな)

それは君が来るかどうかによる。*It depends on whether you will come or not.*

ニュースによると〜 *According to the news 〜*

交通事故による死亡 *a death resulting from an accident*

寄る *come close to, near, stop by*

右側に寄ってください。*Please move to the right.*

ちょっとお寄りになりませんか。*Won't you come by for a bit?*

わかる（分かる・解る）

分かる *be able to analyze, understand*

解る *comprehend, understand,*

In general, わかる is written in ひらがな or with the character 分かる. It implies analysis and an understanding which comes with thought. Occurrences of 解る are significantly less frequent, although this representation can be used to imply understanding of something difficult or requiring more detailed analysis. The character is taken from the Chinese compound 理解する. In contrast, 知る is used when referring to possessed knowledge or to knowledge which is in some sense instantaneously knowable (like the present time, or the fact that you know someone or not). Compare the following: 兄の気持ちが分からない *I don't understand my older brother's feelings* and お兄さんを知らない *I don't know his old brother. I have never met his older brother.*

わかれる（別れる・分かれる）See transitive わける below.

別れる *leave, separate*

私は彼と駅で別れた。*He and I left each other at the station.*

その夫婦は別れてしまった。*The couple have divorced (split up, separated).*

分かれる *divide*

私たちは二つのグループに分かれた。*We divided into two groups.*

道が二つに分かれている *the road divides into two*

わける（分ける）See intransitive わかれる above.

分ける *divide something*

ケーキを半分に分ける *divide the cake into halves*

米を分けてください *please give a portion of rice, give me some rice*

2.2 Word formation

Japanese words are commonly classified into three groups based on origin: native Japanese words (大和言葉), words of Chinese origin (漢語), and borrowed words (foreign words of non-Chinese origin, 外来語). To some extent, each of these word categories has its own grammar. For example, words of Chinese and other foreign origin are almost all nouns. The vast majority of verbs and adjectives are native Japanese. Words can then be combined in various ways to produce new or longer words.

2.2.1 Reduplication

Reduplication is a process where one shorter word is repeated twice to create a longer word. Remember also that repetition (ごめんごめん or そうそうそうそうそう〜) is one strategy for giving emphasis to what you are saying (see page 7). A number of Japanese words are produced with reduplication. Most are adverbs or nouns, although some are adjectives, and a very few are verbs. Sometimes a reduplicated word is plural. Examples include:

荒々しい	あらあらしい	*violent*
色々な	いろいろ	*various*
正々堂々	せいせいどうどう	*fair and square*
騒々しい	そうぞうしい	*noisy*
涼々たる	そうそうたる	*be eminent, well-known*
度々	たびたび	*frequently, often*
段々	だんだん	*gradually, be degrees*
次々に	つぎつぎに	*one after another, in succession*
時々	ときどき	*sometimes*
所々	ところどころ	*here and there*
人々	ひとびと	*people*
日々	ひび	*day after day, every day*
益々	ますます	*more and more*
銘々	めいめい	*each, his or her own*
我々	われわれ	*we, ourselves*

Note that a word like 人々 is pronounced ひとびと and not ひとひと. The second occurrence of ひと begins with a び rather than a ひ. In the above list, this is true of ところどころ, ときどき, ひび, and possibly そうぞうしい as well. More generally, the same is true of all the compounds below: the first sound of the second word changes from a sound without 濁音 (the two marks in the upper right) to one which has 濁音. These two marks distinguish between *unvoiced* sounds such as か or き (spoken without the vocal chords vibrating) and *voiced* sounds such as が or ぎ (spoken with the vocal chords vibrating).

紙・かみ	*paper*	手紙・てがみ	*letter*
すし	*sushi*	巻きずし・まきずし	a kind of sushi
印・しるし	*mark, sign*	星印・ほしじるし	*asterisk*
田・た	*rice field*	高田・たかだ	surname
棚・たな	*shelf*	本棚・ほんだな	*bookshelf*
寺・てら	*temple*	尼寺・あまでら	*convent*
橋・はし	*bridge*	日本橋・にほんばし	place name
人・ひと	*person*	旅人・たびびと	*traveling person*

This voicing of the first sound of the second part of a compound is called 連濁 ^{れんだく} which is generally translated into English as *sequential voicing*. Conditions under which sequential voicing occurs are not completely understood, but it has been observed that the change is usually limited to words of Japanese origin (which is why *ice coffee* is アイスコーヒー and not アイスゴーヒー), and it only happens whenever there is no other voiced sound in the second word (which is why *frequently* 度々 is not たびだび and *strong wind* 大風 is not おおがぜ). Sequential voicing is also felt to be a property of an entire compound as distinct from its individual parts. To take a specific example, this means that び と is not considered an independent reading for the character 人, and it has no such listing in a character dictionary. Rather the びと reading occurs only when certain conditions are met in the structure of the overall compound.

2.2.2 Compounding

Japanese forms words out of other words quite productively. In the lists here, the new words are all nouns. Verbal compounds (where two verbs are combined to produce a new verb) are discussed in the next section. Note where sequential voicing does and does not occur.

Native Japanese compounds

Both elements here are native Japanese words

noun	秋空	あきぞら	*autumn sky*
+ noun	山寺	やまでら	*mountain temple*
	子犬	こいぬ	*puppy*
	網戸	あみど	*screen door*
adjective	大雨	おおあめ	*heavy rain*
+ noun	青葉	あおば	*foliage, green leaves*
	広場	ひろば	*open space*
	古本	ふるほん	*second-hand books*

verb	飲水	のみみず	*drinking water*
+ noun	見事	みごと	*wonderful, great*
	回り道	まわりみち	*detour*
	変り者	かわりもの	*eccentric person*
noun	雪解け	ゆきどけ	*snow melting*
+ verb	物語	ものがたり	*tale, story*
	人殺し	ひとごろし	*murder*
	昼寝	ひるね	*nap* (lit. *day sleeping*)
adjective	長続き	ながつづき	*long-lasting*
+verb	小走り	こばしり	*trotting*
	大笑い	おおわらい	*big laugh*
	早起き	はやおき	*early rising*
adverb	がぶ飲み	がぶのみ	*gulping down*
+ verb	横滑り	よこすべり	*sliding sideways*
	共倒れ	ともだおれ	*going under together*
	横揺れ	よこゆれ	*rolling* (back and forth)
verb	立ち読み	たちよみ	*reading while standing*
+ verb	出入り	でいり	*going in and out*
	飲みすぎ	のもすぎ	*drinking too much, over drinking*
	書き直し	かきなおし	*a rewrite*

Sino-Japanese compounds

It is estimated that as much as 40% of the modern Japanese vocabulary is of Chinese origin. The percentage increases as the vocabulary becomes more technical. Most Chinese compounds are actually from China, although the Japanese invented a large number of their own compounds as well, and even created a few of their own characters. Sino-Japanese compounds are all nouns, but many of them can be made into verbs by adding する. This is the topic of section 3.8.2 beginning on page 228.

A lot of compounds are real Chinese words but the meaning has changed (often quite dramatically) in Japanese. The most famous example is 手紙 which means *letter* in Japanese and *toilet paper* in Chinese. Such changes are paralleled in the modern era with borrowings from European languages (see section 2.3 beginning on page 111). A smaller set of compounds are original Japanese words. In particular, many of the names for Western concepts and products were invented by Japanese at the end of the nineteenth century and actually borrowed back into China (which had a much more difficult time interacting with the West).

銀行	ぎんこう	*bank*
経済	けいざい	*economics*
立場	たちば	*stand point*
鉄道	てつどう	*railroad*
電信	でんしん	*telegram*
弁護士	べんごし	*lawyer*

Some actual characters are also completely Japanese. These are called 国字^{こくじ}.

俤	おもかげ	*one's face, image*
榊	さかき	*sacred Shinto tree*
峠	とうげ	*mountain pass*
働く	はたらく	*to work*

Hybrid compounds

These words are all of Japanese origin. The elements are mixed. *Foreign* here refers to words which have been borrowed from European languages.

Chinese	台所	だいどころ	*kitchen*
+ native	半月	はんつき	*half month*
	新前	しんまえ	*novice, beginner* (carpenter)
	本物	ほんもの	*real, genuine*
native	手帳	てちょう	*notebook, memo book*
+ Chinese	荷物	にもつ	*luggage*
	小文字	こもじ	*small letters, lower case*
	御茶	おちゃ	*tea*
Chinese	石油ストーブ	せきゆストーブ	*oil stove*
+ foreign	半ドア	はんドア	(car) *door not properly closed*
	あんパン		*bun with red bean jam*
	大リーグ	だいリーグ	*major league* (baseball)
foreign	フランス語	フランスご	*French* (language)
+ Chinese	クリーン産業	クリーンさんぎょう	*clean industry*
	ギリシア文字	ギリシアもじ	*Greek alphabet*
	ミドル級	ミドルきゅう	*middle weight*
native	板チョコ	いたチョコ	*chocolate bar*
+ foreign	赤ワイン	あかワイン	*red wine*
	日ロ	にちロ	*Japanese-Russian* (relations)
	大形トラック	おおがたトラック	*very big truck*

foreign	ガラス窓	ガラスまど	*glass window*
+ native	ペトリ皿	ペトリざら	*Petri dish*
	アメリカ式	アメリカしき	*American style*
	トルコ石	トルコいし	*turquoise* (the stone, not the color)
foreign	マイカー		*personal car*
+ foreign	ビフテキ		*beef steak*
	ワイシャツ		*white shirt, collared shirt*
	ベビーサークル		*playpen*

The individual words in many longer borrowed expressions do not necessarily make sense on their own. Many Chinese characters never occur on their own. Likewise, it is not clear how many Japanese know that longer words borrowed from English are often composed of individual shorter words.

Words are also produced in Japanese by shortening longer words. This process (called *clipping*) with examples is discussed on page 117 with borrowed words.

2.2.3 Verbal compounding

Verbal compounding is very common in Japanese. Students usually learn the more common and productive compounding verbs such as:

～過ぎる・ すぎる *too, over*	食べ過ぎる・たべすぎる *over eat*; 言い過ぎる・いいすぎる *say too much*; やり過ぎる・やりすぎる *over do it*; 働き過ぎる・はたらきすぎる *over work*; 優し過ぎる・やさしすぎる *too nice*; 大き過ぎる・おおきすぎる *too big*; 長過ぎる・ながすぎる *too long* (Note that ～過ぎる combines with adjectives as well as verbs.)
～直す ・なおす *again, re-*	書き直す・かきなおす *rewrite*; 言い直す・いいなおす *say it again, re-phrase*, 作り直す・つくりなおす *fix it over*; やり直す・やりなおす *redo*; 建て直す・たてなおす *rebuild*; 読み直す・よみなおす *reread*; 考え直す・かんがえなおす *rethink*; 洗い直す・あらいなおす *rewash*
～始める ・はじめる *begin to*	話し始める・はなしはじめる *begin to speak*; 泣き始める・なきはじめる *begin to cry*; 歩き始める・あるきはじめる *begin to walk, set out*; 食べ始める・たべはじめる *begin to eat*; 書き始める・かきはじめる *begin to write*; 飲み始める・のみはじめる *begin to drink*
～続ける ・つづける *continue to*	立ち続ける・たちつづける *continue standing*; 上がり続ける・あがりつづける *continue to go up*; 話し続ける・はなしつづける *continue to speak*; 通い続ける・かよいつづける *continue to go by, commute*; 燃やし続ける・もやしつづける *continue to burn*; 降り続ける・ふりつづける *continue to rain*; 打ち続ける・うちつづける *continue to hit, strike again and again*

～にくい *difficult*	言いにくい・いいにくい *difficult to say*; 書きにくい・かきにくい *hard to write*; 答えにくい・こたえにくい *difficult to answer*; 食べにくい・たべにくい *difficult to eat*; 賛成しにくい・さんせいしにくい *difficult to agree with*; 見にくい・みにくい *hard to look at*; 読みにくい・よみにくい *difficult to read, dense, illegible*
～やすい *easy*	歩きやすい・あるきやすい (shoes that are) *easy to walk* (in); 書きやすい・かきやすい (a pen that is) *easy to write* (with); しやすい *easy to do*; 座りやすい・すわりやすい (a chair that is) *easy to sit in*; 食べやすい・たべやすい *easy to eat*; 話しやすい・はなしやすい *easy to talk to*; 引きやすい・ひきやすい *easy to pull*; やりやすい *easy to do*; 読みやすい・よみやすい *easy to read, well-written, legible*; 分かりやすい・わかりやすい *easy to understand*; 割れやすい・われやすい *breaks easily*

In fact, there are several hundred possible compound verbs, used with varying degrees of productivity. As a rule, students of Japanese do not use verbal compounds enough. The lists here include a large percentage of the more common compounds.

Sometimes, a single verb combines with many different second verbs for a variety of specific interpretations.

うち・打ち～ *hit, strike,* *knock, slap*	打ち上げる・うちあげる *send up, launch*; 打ち返す・うちかえす *strike back, return a blow*; 打ち勝つ・うちかつ *triumph over, conquer*; 打ち切る・うちきる *end, close, bring to a close*; 打ち消す・うちけす *deny*; 打ち込む・うちこむ *drive into, hammer*; 打ち出す・うちだす *strike, work out*; 打ち立てる・うちたてる *push up, stand*; 打ち解ける・うちとける *be friendly, be at ease with*; 打ち抜く・うちぬく *perforate, punch a hole*; 打ちのめす・うちのめす *knock down*; 打ち寄せる・うちよせる *beat against, dash against*
うり・売り～ *sell*	売り歩く・うりあるく *vend, peddle, hawk*; 売り切る・うりきる *sell out*; 売り切れる・うりきれる *be sold out*; 売り込む・うりこむ *sell, push, promote*; 売りさばく・うりさばく *sell off, dispose of*; 売り付ける・うりつける *palm off on, force on*; 売り飛ばす・うりとばす *sell quickly, dispose of*; 売り払う・うりはらう *dispose of, sell off*; 売り渡す・うりわたす *sell and hand over*
おい・追い～ *chase,* *pursue*	追いかける・おいかける *chase after*; 追い越す・おいこす *overtake, pass*; 追い込む・おいこむ *drive, force into*; 追い付く・おいつく *catch up with overtake*; 追い詰める・おいつめる *drive into a corner, corner*; 追い払う・おいはらう *drive away*; 追い回す・おいまわす *chase around* (closely); 追いやる・おいやる *drive out*

おし・押し〜 *push*	押し入る・おしいる *force one's way in*; 押し返す・おしかえす *push back, beat back*; 押し掛ける・おしかける *invite oneself*; 押し切る・おしきる *force one's way*; 押し込む・おしこむ *be forced in*; 押し込める・おしこめる *force in*; 押し殺す・おしころす *suppress* (a yawn); 推し進める・おしすすめる *push along*; 押し立てる・おしたてる *raise, set up, stand*; 押し付ける・おしつける *push against, pin against*; 押し詰める・おしつめる *pack to, drive back against*; 押し通す・おしとおす *push through, persist*; 押しのける・おしのける *shove aside*; 押しやる・おしやる *push away, push aside*; 押し寄せる・おしよせる *to crowd, flock, swarm*
おもい・思い〜 *think, believe*	思い上がる・おもいあがる *be arrogant, conceited*; 思い浮かべる・おもいうかべる *remember, recall*; 思い起こす・おもいおこす *remember, recollect*; 思い返す・おもいかえす *look back on*; 思い込む・おもいこむ *be convinced that, take for granted that*; 思い知る・おもいしる *realize fully, learn one's lesson*; 思い立つ・おもいたつ *plan, project, decide to do*; 思い出す・おもいだす *recall*; 思い付く・おもいつく *hit, strike on*; 思い詰める・おもいつめる *brood, worry*; 思い直す・おもいなおす *change one's mind*
かい・買い〜 *buy*	買いあさる・かいあさる *hunt high and low for*; 買い換える・かいかえる *buy to replace*; 買いかぶる・かいかぶる *overestimate, overrate*; 買い切る・かいきる *buy all*; 買い込む・かいこむ *buy and hoard*; 買い占める・かいしめる *buy all of, buy out*; 買い取る・かいとる *buy and take away*; 買い戻す・かいもどす *buy back*
かき・書き〜 *write*	書き上げる・かきあげる *finish writing*; 書き起こす・かきおこす *begin writing again*; 書き下ろす・かきおろす *write a new* (novel, play, etc.); 書き込む・かきこむ *write in*; 書き出す・かきだす *begin to write*; 書き散らす・かきちらす *write here and there*; 書き連ねる・かきつらねる *write one after the other, in a line*; 書き飛ばす・かきとばす *write quickly*; 書き取る・かきとる *write down, take down*; 書き直す・かきなおす *rewrite*; 書きなぐる・かきなぐる *write in big letters, boldly*; 書き抜く・かきぬく *write editing out*; 書きまくる・かきまくる *write a lot quickly*; 書き漏らす・かきもらす *forget to write something crucial*
きき・聞き〜 *hear, listen*	聞き入る・ききいる *listen attentively to*; 聞き入れる・ききいれる *comply with, grant*; 聞き落とす・ききおとす *fail to hear, miss*; 聞き返す・ききかえす *ask back, throw back a question*; 聞きかじる・ききかじる *get superficial knowledge of*; 聞き込む・ききこむ *obtain information, get wind of*; 聞き取る・ききとる *hear and understand, comprehend*; 聞き直す・ききなおす *ask again*; 聞き流す・ききながす *take no notice of*; 聞きほれる・ききほれる *be enraptured by, be lost in*; 聞き分ける・ききわける *hear reason, be reasonable*

きり・切り〜   切り上げる・きりあげる *knock off, cut short, stop*; 切り替える・きりかえ
cut   る *change, exchange, switch over*; 切り込む・きりこむ *gash, cut deeply*;
              切り下げる・きりさげる *reduce, devalue*; 切り捨てる・きりすてる *cut
              away, leave out, omit*; 切り出す・きりだす *cut down, start to talk about*;
              切り詰める・きりつめる *cut back, shorten*; 切り抜く・きりぬく *cut out,
              clip*; 切り抜ける・きりぬける *get through, manage*; 切り離す・きりはな
              す *cut off, sever*; 切り開く・きりひらく *cut open, cut through*

さし・差し〜   差し置く・さしおく *ignore, disregard*; 差し押さえる・さしおさえる *seize*;
point ut,   差し替える・さしかえる *replace, exchange*; 差し込む・さしこむ *insert,
indicate   put in*; 差し障る・さしさわる *obstruct, hinder*; 差し迫る・さしせまる *be
              imminent, impending*; 差し出す・さしだす *hold out, reach out*; 差し出る・
              さしでる *thrust oneself forward*; 差し止める・さしとめる *stop, suspend*;
              差し伸べる・さしのべる *extend*; 差し控える・さしひかえる *refrain from*;
              差し引く・さしひく *deduct from*; 差し向ける・さしむける *send, dispatch*;
              差し戻す・さしもどす *send back, remand*

たち・立ち〜   立ち会う・たちあう *to witness*; 立ち遅れる・たちおくれる *begin later,
stand   after*; 立ち込める・たちこめる *hang over, fill*; 立ち直る・たちなおる *get
              over, recover*; 立ち退く・たちのく *leave, clear out*; 立ちはだかる・たちは
              だかる *confront, face*; 立ち回る・たちまわる *conduct oneself, act*; 立ち向
              かう・たちむかう *confront*; 立ち寄る・たちよる *drop in on*

とび・飛び〜   飛び上がる・とびあがる *fly up*; 飛び起きる・とびおきる *jump out of bed*;
fly, jump   飛び降りる・とびおりる *jump down off of*; 飛び交う・とびかう *fly about,
              flitter about*; 飛び掛かる・とびかかる *jump on, pounce*; 飛び越える・とび
              こえる *fly over*; 飛び込む・とびこむ *fly in to*; 飛び出す・とびだす *fly out
              of*; 飛び立つ・とびたつ *fly away from*; 飛び散る・とびちる *fly off in dif-
              ferent directions*; 飛び付く・とびつく *pounce on*; 飛び乗る・とびのる
              jump on to (a means of transportation); 飛び離れる・とびはなれる *jump
              away from*; 飛び回る・とびまわる *fly around* (the sky)

とり・取り〜   取り上げる・とりあげる *pick up*; 取り扱う・とりあつかう *treat, handle*
take   取り入る・とりいる *gain favor with*; 取り返す・とりかえす *regain*; 取り
              かかる・とりかかる *set about, begin*; 取り決める・とりきめる *arrange,
              agree on*; 取り組む・とりくむ *grapple with*; 取り消す・とりけす *cancel,
              revoke*; 取り込む・とりこむ *take in*; 取り仕切る・とりしきる *manage, be
              in charge*; 取り締まる・とりしまる *regulate, manage*; 取り付く・とりつ
              く *cling to*; 取り次ぐ・とりつぐ *tell, convey*; 取り直す・とりなおす *retake*;
              取り払う・とりはらう *clear away, demolish*; 取り巻く・とりまく *cluster
              around*; 取り乱す・とりみだす *be upset about*; 取り持つ・とりもつ *act as
              go-between*; 取り寄せる・とりよせる *order* (products)

ひき・引き～
pull

引き上げる・ひきあげる *pull, draw up*; 引き合わせる・ひきあわせる *introduce, compare*; 引き入れる・ひきいれる *drag, pull in*; 引き受ける・ひきうける *take on, undertake*; 引き起こす・ひきおこす *cause, bring about*; 引き返す・ひきかえす *turn back*; 引き替える・ひきかえる *to exchange*; 引き込む・ひきこむ *draw into*; 引き下がる・ひきさがる *withdraw, back into*; 引き下げる・ひきさげる *bring down, lower*; 引き締まる・ひきしまる *be firm, compact*; 引き締める・ひきしめる *tighten up, shape up*; 引きずる・ひきずる *drag, trail*; 引き出す・ひきだす *pull out*; 引き立つ・ひきたつ *look better, stand out*; 引き立てる・ひきたてる *set off, contrast, cheer up*; 引き継ぐ・ひきつぐ *take over*; 引き付ける・ひきつける *attract, charm*; 引きつる・ひきつる *get a cramp*; 引き止める・ひきとめる *stop, keep, detain*; 引き取る・ひきとる *take back, leave, adopt* (a child を); 引き抜く・ひきぬく *pull out, uproot*; 引き伸ばす・ひきのばす *enlarge, stretch*; 引き離す・ひきはなす *pull apart, separate*; 引き払う・ひきはらう *leave, vacate*; 引き渡す・ひきわたす *pull across, hand out*

ふり・振り～
swing, shake, wave

振り当てる・ふりあてる *assign a role to*; 振り返る・ふりかえる *turn around, look back*; 振り切る・ふりきる *tear oneself away from*; 振り込む・ふりこむ *pay into a bank account*; 振り絞る・ふりしぼる *put forth all one's strength*; 振り捨てる・ふりすてる *abandon*; 振りまく・ふりまく *spread, turn on* (the charm, a smile); 振り乱す・ふりみだす *be disheveled, hanging loose*; 振り向く・ふりむく *look around at*; 振り分ける・ふりわける *divide amongst*

み・見～
see, watch

見合う・みあう *be proportionate to, suit, look at each other*; 見合わせる・みあわせる *compare, look at each other*; 見いだす・みいだす *find*; 見入る・みいる *gaze at*; 見失う・みうしなう *lose sight of*; 見送る・みおくる *see off*; 見落とす・みおとす *overlook, miss*; 見返す・みかえす *go over, re-read*; 見かける・みかける *catch sight of*; 見かねる・みかねる *cannot stand by and watch*; 見極める・みきわめる *make sure of, get to the bottom of*; 見下す・みくだす *despise, look down on*; 見越す・みこす *expect*; 見込む・みこむ *expect, anticipate*; 見損なう・みそこなう *miss seeing, misjudge*; 見そめる・みそめる *fall in love at first sight*; 見違える・みちがえる *change so much that can hardly be recognized*; 見つめる・みつめる *gaze at, stare intently at*; 見積もる・みつもる *to estimate*; 見届ける・みとどける *see through to the end*; 見とれる・みとれる *look in fascination, gaze at*; 見抜く・みぬく *find out, perceive*; 見逃す・みのがす *miss, overlook*; 見計らう・みはからう *make a suitable choice*; 見張る・みはる *guard, keep watch*; 見渡す・みわたす *look out over*

よび・呼び〜   呼び上げる・よびあげる *call the roll*; 呼び起こす・よびおこす *wake up*;
call out   呼びかける・よびかける *call out to*; 呼び込む・よびこむ *call in*; 呼び出す
                ・よびだす *summon*; 呼び立てる・よびたてる *call in a loud voice*; 呼び止め
                る・よびとめる *hail, stop*; 呼び戻す・よびもどす *call back*; 呼び寄せる・
                よびよせる *call near*

Other verbs are very common as the second half of compounds. They have standard
meanings, and the lists give an idea of how frequent particular compounds actually are.

〜合う・あう   落ち合う・おちあう *meet, get together*; 掛かり合う・かかりあう *be
fit, suit,   involved with, be entangled with*; 混み合う・こみあう *be crowded, be
go well with,   jammed in*; 知り合う・しりあう *get to know, become acquainted with*; 抱
reciprocate   き合う・だきあう *embrace each other*; 出し合う・だしあう *chip in, pool*
                (one's money); 釣り合う・つりあう *balance with, be in proportion to,
                match*; 取り合う・とりあう *join* (hands), *take each other's* (something);
                話し合う・はなしあう *talk over, discuss with*; 見合う・みあう *be propor-
                tionate to, suit, look at each other*; 巡り合う・めぐりあう *come across,
                meet by chance*; 向かい合う・むかいあう *face each other*; 向き合う・むき
                あう *face each other*; 譲り合う・ゆずりあう *make way for, make mutual
                concessions, meet half-way*

〜上がる・   浮かび上がる・うかびあがる *rise to the surface, emerge*; 浮き上がる・う
あがる   きあがる *surface, come to the surface*; 起き上がる・おきあがる *get up, sit
rise, be   up, rise*; 駆け上がる・かけあがる *rush up, run up* (stairs); 仕上がる・し
completed   あがる *be finished, completed*; 立ち上がる・たちあがる *stand up, rise to
                one's feet*; 出来上がる・できあがる *be finished, completed*; 飛び上がる・
                とびあがる *jump up, spring to one's feet*; 跳ね上がる・はねあがる *spring
                up, jump up, shoot up*; 晴れ上がる・はれあがる *clear up*; 舞い上がる・ま
                いあがる *soar up, fly up, be blown around*; 燃え上がる・もえあがる *burst
                into flames, burn up*

〜上げる・   書き上げる・かきあげる *finish writing*; 切り上げる・きりあげる *stop,
あげる   knock off, cut short*; 差し上げる・さしあげる *hold high, give* (humbly, to
lift, raise,   a superior); 仕上げる・しあげる *finish off, complete*; 締め上げる・しめ
finish   あげる *tighten up, fasten up*; 吸い上げる・すいあげる *pump up* (water),
                absorb (water); 作り上げる・つくりあげる *construct, make*; 積み上げる・
                つみあげる *pile up*; 釣り上げる・つりあげる *land, catch* (a fish); 引き上げ
                る・ひきあげる *pull up, pull in, withdraw*; 拾い上げる・ひろいあげる
                pick up, pick out, gather; 見上げる・みあげる *up at, raise one's eyes to*;
                持ち上げる・もちあげる *lift up, heave*; 盛り上げる・もりあげる *heap up,
                pile up*; 読み上げる・よみあげる *read out loud, call out*

～合わせる・ あわせる *put together,* *combine,* *get together* *(often by* *chance)*	居合わせる・いあわせる *happen to be present at, be at by chance*; 行き合わせる・いきあわせる *meet by chance*; 埋め合わせる・うめあわせる *make up, make amends, compensate for*; 噛み合わせる・かみあわせる *engage, clench* (one's teeth), *mesh* (two plans); 組み合わせる・くみあわせる *put together, match, combine*; 継ぎ合わせる・つぎあわせる *join together, piece together*; つなぎ合わせる *connect, tie together*; 問い合わせる・といあわせる *ask about, inquire of*; 乗り合わせる・のりあわせる *happen to ride* (on the same train); 縫い合わせる・ぬいあわせる *sew, stitch together*; 混ぜ合わせる・まぜあわせる *mix up, mix with*; 待ち合わせる・まちあわせる *make an appointment with, arrange* (a meeting)
～入る・いる *come in,* *go in*	押し入る・おしいる *force one's way into*; 落ち入る・おちいる *fall into, get caught in*; 聞き入る・ききいる *listen attentively to*; 込み入る・こみいる *be complicated, intricate*; 取り入る・とりいる *gain favor with, curry favor with*
～入れる・ いれる *put in*	受け入れる・うけいれる *accept, grant, comply with*; 聞き入れる・ききいれる *agree to* (a request), *grant, accept*; 取り入れる・とりいれる *take in, gather, harvest*; 運び入れる・はこびいれる *carry in, move in*; 呼び入れる・よびいれる *call* (a person) *in, hail* (someone) *into*
～返す・ かえす *return* *(a thing)*	言い返す・いいかえす *retort, answer back*; 追い返す・おいかえす *send back, turn away*; 送り返す・おくりかえす *send something back* (by post); 聞き返す・ききかえす *ask back, throw back a question*; 繰り返す・くりかえす *repeat oneself, do again and again*; 突き返す・つきかえす *refuse to receive, refuse to accept, return*; 取り返す・とりかえす *get back again, regain, recover*; 殴り返す・なぐりかえす *hit back, return a blow*; 引き返す・ひきかえす *turn back, return, go back*; 見返す・みかえす *go over* (an exam), *stare back*; 読み返す・よみかえす *reread*
～かえる *go back*	生き返る・いきかえる *revive, come back to life*; 入れ替える・いれかえる *replace one thing with another, replace A with B*; 置き換える・おきかえる *rearrange, move around*; 着替える・きがえる *change one's clothes*; すり替える・すりかえる *exchange* (secretly), *change the subject* (cleverly); 立て替える・たてかえる *lend*; 取り換える・とりかえる *exchange, replace, renew*; 乗り換える・のりかえる *change* (buses, trains), *transfer*; 跳ね返る・はねかえる *bounce back, rebound*; 振り返る・ふりかえる *turn around, look back, look around*;

～かかる *be hung,* *be about* *to*	おぼれかかる *be about to drown;* 倒れ掛かる・たおれかかる*fall against;* 飛び掛かる・とびかかる *jump on, spring on, pounce;* 通り掛かる・とおりかかる *pass by, go by;* 取りかかる・とりかかる *set about, start, begin to;* 開きかかる・ひらきかかる *be aboutto open;* もたれ掛かる・もたれかかる *lean on;* 寄り掛かる・よりかかる *lean on, lean over*
～かける *hang,* *begin to*	追い掛ける・おいかける *chase after, pursue;* 押し掛ける・おしかける *crowd in, invite oneself* (to a party); 出掛ける・でかける *go out;* 問い掛ける・といかける *ask a question, put a question to;* 投げ掛ける・なげかける *throw* (light on), *cast* (doubt on); 話しかける・はなしかける *speak to, talk to;* 振り掛ける・ふりかける *sprinkle* (salt on meat); 見掛ける・みかける *catchsight of, find;* 呼び掛ける・よびかける *call to, shout out to*
～切る・きる *cut, to the* *utmost*	言い切る・いいきる *assert;* 押し切る・おしきる *force one's way, in spite of;* 思い切る・おもいきる *give up, make up one's mind;* 嚙み切る・かみきる *bite off;* 締め切る・しめきる *shut, close up;* 断ち切る・たちきる *cut off* (relations), *break off;* 使い切る・つかいきる *make full use of, exhaust;* 張り切る・はりきる *work hard, try hard, be enthusiastic;* 踏み切る・ふみきる *take off, take the plunge* (and marry, begin a new venture); 割り切る・わりきる *take a rational, unsentimental point of view*
～込む・こむ *crowded,* *enter* *(intensifier)*	上がり込む・あがりこむ *come in, walk in, go in;* 売り込む・うりこむ *sell, push, market;* 打ち込む・うちこむ *hammer, drive into, hit* (a ball); 追い込む・おいこむ *drive* (into a corner, into a pen); 落ち込む・おちこむ *sink, fall in, collapse, get depressed;* 思い込む・おもいこむ *be convinced that, take for granted that;* 書き込む・かきこむ *write in, fill in, fill out;* 駆け込む・かけこむ *rush into, run into;* 刈り込む・かりこむ *cut, shear, trim;* 考え込む・かんがえこむ *brood, be in deep thought;* 着込む・きこむ *wear layers of clothing;* 転がり込む・ころがりこむ *roll off of, roll under;* 染み込む・しみこむ *soak through, permeate;* 吸い込む・すいこむ *breathe in, inhale* (smoke); 滑り込む・すべりこむ *slide* (safely into base), *arrive* (just in time); 住み込む・すみこむ *live in someone else's home;* 座り込む・すわりこむ *sit, crouch down;* 頼み込む・たのみこむ *ask earnestly, plead;* 黙り込む・だまりこむ *suddenly become silent;* つけ込む・つけこむ *take advantage of, play on* (his good nature); 詰め込む・つめこむ *cram, stuff, fill;* 連れ込む・つれこむ *take* (into a room), *bring* (into a room); 飛び込む・とびこむ *dive;* 取り込む・とりこむ *take in* (washing), *be in confusion;* 流し込む・ながしこむ *pour* (something) *into;* 流れ込む・ながれこむ *pour in, crowd, stream in;* 逃げ込む・にげこむ *run in to, seek refuge in;* 寝込む・ねこむ *fall asleep;* 覗き込む・のぞきこむ *peep into, pry;* 飲み込む・のみこむ *swallow, gulp;* 乗り込む・のりこむ *get into, get on board;* 入り

込む・はいりこむ *get in, sneak in*; 話し込む・はなしこむ *have a long talk, be absorbed in conversation*; はめ込む・はめこむ *fit, set* (a pane of glass, a diamond); 張り込む・はりこむ *keep close watch on, stake out*; 冷え込む・ひえこむ *freeze, be- come colder*; 引き込む・ひきこむ *draw in, attract, fascinate*; 吹き込む・ふきこむ *blow up, blow into*; 踏み込む・ふみこむ *step into, break into*; 放り込む・ほうりこむ *throw in, throw into*; 巻き込む・まきこむ *catch, catch on, be involved in*; 紛れ込む・まぎれこむ *mingle* (with a crowd), *disappear* (into a crowd); 迷い込む・まよいこむ *stray off* (into some- thing); 丸め込む・まるめこむ *wheedle, sweet-talk*; 申し込む・もうしこむ *propose, request, ask for*; 持ち込む・もちこむ *bring in* (something), *smuggle in*; 呼び込む・よびこむ *call in*; 割り込む・わりこむ *interrupt, cut off*

〜出す・だす
put out, begin

暴れ出す・あばれだす *begin to act violently, go on a rampage*; 歩き出す・あるきだす *set out walking*; 言い出す・いいだす *begin to speak, suggest*; 動き出す・うごきだす *begin to move*; 打ち出す・うちだす *emboss, work out a plan*; 売り出す・うりだす *put up for sale*; 追い出す・おいだす *put out, drive out*; 送り出す・おくりだす *send off, see out*; 押し出す・おしだす *push out*; 思い出す・おもいだす *remember, recall*; 駆け出す・かけだす *run out, break into a run*; 貸し出す・かしだす *loan*; 借り出す・かりだす *borrow, check out*; 考え出す・かんがえだす *think up, devise, invent*; 探しだす・さがしだす *find out, discover, detect*; 差し出す・さしだす *stretch out* (one's hand), *reach out*; 誘い出す・さそいだす *invite out*; 助け出す・たすけだす *rescue from a place, save*; 食べ出す・たべだす *begin to eat*; 突き出す・つきだす *stick out*; 連れ出す・つれだす *take* (someone) *out* (to lunch); 飛び出す・とびだす *jump out, spring out, leap out*; 取り出す・とりだす *take out* (from), *extract from*; 泣き出す・なきだす *cry, burst out crying*; 投げ出す・なげだす *throw out, abandon*; 逃げ出す・にげだす *break into a run, run away*; 抜き出す・ぬきだす *pick out, take* (a card); 抜け出す・ぬけだす *slip, sneak* (out of a room); 乗り出す・のりだす *start, begin, set about*; 吐き出す・はきだす *vomit, throw up*; 話し出す・はなしだす *begin to speak*; 引き出す・ひきだす *pull out, draw out*; 吹き出す・ふきだす *spout out, spurt out*; 踏み出す・ふみだす *step forward, take a step*; 降り出す・ふりだす *begin to rain*; 放り出す・ほうりだす *throw out*; 掘り出す・ほりだす *dig up*; 持ち出す・もちだす *take out, carry out, smuggle out*; 呼び出す・よびだす *call, page*

〜立つ・たつ
be built

浮き立つ・うきたつ *stand out*; 思い立つ・おもいたつ *plan, project, re- solve to do*; 飛び立つ・とびたつ *fly away, take wing*; 成り立つ・なりたつ *be made up of, consist of*; 引き立つ・ひきたつ *look better, look nicer, stand out*

〜立てる・ たてる *build* (intensifier)	言い立てる・いいたてる *state, maintain, allege*; 追い立てる・おいたてる *hurry off, pack off, evict*; 書き立てる・かきたてる *write up, splash* (across the front page); 掻き立てる・かきたてる *stir up, arouse*; 駆り立てる・かりたてる *drive* (to do), *urge on*; 組み立てる・くみたてる *put together, build, construct*; 責め立てる・せめたてる *persecute, torture*; 取り立てる・とりたてる *exact, collect*; 引き立てる・ひきたてる *support, patronize*
〜つく *attach oneself*	追い付く・おいつく *catch up with, overtake*; 落ち着く・おちつく *calm down, settle*; 思い付く・おもいつく *hit on, strike on, think up*; かじり付く・かじりつく *bite into*; 噛み付く・かみつく *bite, snap at*; 絡み付く・からみつく *twist oneself around, get tangled up*; 考え付く・かんがえつく *hit on* (a good idea); 食い付く・くいつく *bite at* (in fishing); 焦げ付く・こげつく *burn, scorch, char*; 住み着く・すみつく *settle down*; 抱き付く・だきつく *cling to, throw your arms around*; たどり着く・たどりつく *finally reach, arrive at*; 飛び付く・とびつく *jump at, pounce on*; 泣き付く・なきつく *beg, entreat, implore*
〜つける *attach* (intensifier)	言い付ける・いいつける *order, tell report*; 植え付ける・うえつける *plant, implant*; 受け付ける・うけつける *accept*; 売りつける・うりつける *palm off, force a sale*; 押さえ付ける・おさえつける *press against, suppress*; かぎ付ける・かぎつける *get wind of, get wise to*; 駆け付ける・かけつける *rush to, run to*; 決め付ける・きめつける *conclude, jump to a conclusion*; 締め付ける・しめつける *tighten* (a screw); 叩きつける・たたきつける *throw, fling* (against something); 突き付ける・つきつける *point, thrust*; 取り付ける・とりつける *fix, fit, install*; 投げ付ける・なげつける *throw, fling, hurl at*; にらみつける *glare at, scowl at*; 跳ねつける・はねつける *reject, turn down*; 張り付ける・はりつける *stick, paste*; 引き付ける・ひきつける *attract, charm*; 吹き付ける・ふきつける *blow, spray against*; 踏み付ける・ふみつける *stamp on, trample down*; 見せつける・みせつける *make a demonstration of, show off, parade*; 見つける・みつける *find, spot, discover*; 結び付ける・むすびつける *tie up, fasten*; 焼き付ける・やきつける *to glaze*
〜出る・でる *stick out, come out*	浮き出る・うきでる *bring to the surface*; 進み出る・すすみでる *take a step forward*; 突き出る・つきでる *stick out, jut out*; 届け出る・とどけでる *report, submit a report*; 飛び出る・とびでる *jump out, spring out*; 流れ出る・ながれでる *flow out, run out*; 名乗り出る・なのりでる *claim to be*; 抜け出る・ぬけでる *slip out of, sneak out of*; 願い出る・ねがいでる *ask for, request, apply for*; 申し出る・もうしでる *offer, propose, report to*

～とる *obtain*	受け取る・うけとる *receive, get*; 買い取る・かいとる *buy, buy out*; 書き取る・かきとる *write down*; 刈り取る・かりとる *cut, mow down*; 聞き取る・ききとる *catch, follow, hear and understand*; 切り取る・きりとる *cut off, cut out*; 汲み取る・くみとる *draw up, pump up, ladle out*; 吸い取る・すいとる *suck up, soak up*; だまし取る・だましとる *cheat out of, trick out of*; 抜き取る・ぬきとる *pull out, extract*; 乗っ取る・のっとる *take over (a company), hijack*; 引き取る・ひきとる *take back, take in*; 読み取る・よみとる *read, read and understand*
～慣れる・なれる *get used to*	歩き慣れる・あるきなれる *get used to walking* (a route); 通い慣れる・かよいなれる *get used to going through, commuting*; 聞き慣れる・ききなれる *get used to hearing* (a dialect); 着慣れる・きなれる *get used to wearing*; 住み慣れる・すみなれる *get used to living* (in a place); 使い慣れる・つかいなれる *get used to using*; 履き慣れる・はきなれる *get used to wearing* (shoes); 見慣れる・みなれる *get used to seeing*; 読み慣れる・よみなれる *get used to reading*
～残す・のこす *leave behind*	思い残す・おもいのこす *regret, remain in memory*; し残す・しのこす *leave things to do*; 食べ残す・たべのこす *leave behind* (after eating); 取り残す・とりのこす *leave behind*
～残る・のこる *be left behind*	生き残る・いきのこる *survive, be left living*; 居残る・いのこる *stay behind, remain*; 売れ残る・うれのこる *not to sell, be unsold*; 勝ち残る・かちのこる *continue winning, stay in the competition*
～回す・まわす *turn around*	追い回す・おいまわす *chase after, chase around*; かき回す・かきまわす *disturb, put out of order, stir*; 乗り回す・のりまわす *ride around, ride about*; 引き回す・ひきまわす *pull around, draw around*; 見回す・みまわす *look around*
～回る・まわる *go around*	歩き回る・あるきまわる *walk around*; 動き回る・うごきまわる *move around*; 駆け回る・かけまわる *run around, run back and forth*; 転げ回る・ころげまわる *roll about, roll around*; 探し回る・さがしまわる *search around*; 飛び回る・とびまわる *fly around, flutter about*; 逃げ回る・にげまわる *run about trying to escape*; 走り回る・はしりまわる *run around*
～寄せる・よせる *move to, approach*	押し寄せる・おしよせる *to crowd, throng, flock*; 取り寄せる・とりよせる *to order*; 引き寄せる・ひきよせる *draw near to, pull up to*; 呼び寄せる・よびよせる *call to, have* (someone) *come*

〜寄る・よる　歩み寄る・あゆみよる *walk up to, step up to*; 言い寄る・いいよる *make*
move to the　*advances to, proposition*; 立ち寄る・たちよる *drop in on, drop by*; 持ち
side　寄る・もちよる *gather and bring*

〜分ける・　かき分ける・かきわける *plow, make your way through a crowd*; かぎ分け
わける　る・かぎわける *smell out*; 聞き分ける・ききわける *recognize* (by listen-
separate　ing), *tell one voice from another*; 使い分ける・つかいわける *use properly,*
use appropriately to one's needs; 振り分ける・ふりわける *divide among,*
divide into (parts); 見分ける・みわける *distinguish, tell* (one thing from
another); より分ける・よりわける *sort out, classify*

2.2.4 Affixing

Typical affixes in English are elements such as *un-* (meaning *not*: *unimportant, unloved,*
etc.) or *-er* (meaning *doer*: *runner, swimmer, jogger, thinker,* etc.). Due to the fact that
many affixes in Japanese are actually Chinese characters with their own meaning, the line
between affixing (as it is understood in English) and compounding is not completely
clear. The words listed here generally have the quality that if the affix is removed, a base
word with the relevant meaning remains. (Removing a character from a compound, on the
other hand, does not generally leave an independent word with the right meaning.) A
great number of example words are given to make the affix meaning as clear as possible.

Affixes here are divided into two broad categories: (i) those which seem to change the
meaning of the base word, and (ii) those which simply change its grammatical category.
The latter type are all regularly productive and many of them may be thought of as in-
flectional endings. Most of them are regularly written in ひらがな. Affixes which occur
only with the names of people (or groups of people) as well as those related to honorifics
have also been grouped separately.

2.2.4.1 Honorification and beautification: 御〜（お・おん・ご）

This prefix makes a word more polite or more formal. The お〜 and おん〜 readings are
for Japanese words as well as for words of foreign origin, while the ご〜 reading is generally limited to noun compounds of Chinese origin. Of the two, the お〜 reading is
probably the more productive. Words prefixed with お〜 or ご〜 show respect to the person being addressed or to a third person. They can never refer back to the person speaking
or to any member of the speaker's in-group. Strictly speaking, honorifics are limited to
people (お忙しいですか。*Are you busy?*) while "beautification" is for non-people (お手紙,
御飯). The lists here are divided into several subcategories depending on the base word.

Nouns related to people

お・おん〜　　お医者さん・おいしゃさん *doctor*; お家・おうち *your house*; お生まれ・おうまれ *your birth town, hometown*; お母さん・おかあさん *your mother*; お上さん・おかみさん *female chief in business*; お体・おからだ *your body, health*; お考え・おかんがえ *your thought*; お気遣い・おきづかい *your concern*; お国・おくに *your home town, country*; お声・おこえ *your voice*; お子様・おこさま *your child*; お先・おさき *going prior to you*; おじいさん *your grandfather, old man*; お仕事・おしごと *your occupation*; お嬢さん・おじょうさん *your daughter, young lady*; お住まい・おすまい *your address, residence*; お宅・おたく *your house*; お勤め・おつとめ *your employment, duty*; お父さん・おとうさん *your father*; お年より・おとしより *senior citizen, old-age pensioner*; お年よりの方・おとしよりのかた *senior citizen, old-age pensioner*; お名前・おなまえ *your name*; お兄さん・おにいさん *your older brother*; お姉さん・おねえさん *your older sister*; おばあさん *grandmother, old woman*; お返事・おへんじ *reply from you*; お巡りさん・おまわりさん *police officer*; お姫さま・おひめさま *princess*; 御中・おんちゅう suffix on a letter address (see page 303)

ご〜　　　　御意見・ごいけん *your opinion*; 御一筆・ごいっぴつ *your brief writing*; 御宴会・ごえんかい *your dinner party*; 御恩・ごおん *your kindness*; 御家族・ごかぞく *your family*; 御兄弟・ごきょうだい *your brothers, siblings*; 御子息・ごしそく *your son*; 御自分・ごじぶん *yourself*; 御姉妹・ごしまい *your sisters*; 御住所・ごじゅうしょ *your address*; 御出身・ごしゅっしん *your home town, country*; 御商売・ごしょうばい *your sales, business*; 御職業・ごしょくぎょう *your occupation*; 御親戚・ごしんせき *your relatives*; 御主人・ごしゅじん *your husband, male chief in business*; 御長男・ごちょうなん *your eldest son*; 御年配・ごねんぱい *old-age pensioner, senior citizen*; 御返事・ごへんじ *your reply*; 御用・ごよう *your errands*; 御両親・ごりょうしん *your parents*; 御令嬢・ごれいじょう *your daughter*

Words referring to activities which people do

The nouns listed here are all formed from the stem of a verb. The verb stems in the first two sets occur regularly with 〜になる, なさる, or くださる to form honorific verbs. In addition, many occur regularly with some form of だ in polite sentences such as お帰り(か)ですか or even お帰り(か)でございますか. Again, these are really honorific verbs so that longer sentences such as 何時にお帰り(か)ですか or どちらの方へお帰り(か)ですか are fine. The most common examples here include お帰り(か)です, お越(こ)しです, お使(つか)いです, お出(で)かけです, お待(ま)ちです, ご案内(あんない)です, ご帰国(きこく)です, ご出発(しゅっぱつ)です, ご卒業(そつぎょう)です, ご入学(にゅうがく)です, ご利用(りよう)です all of which are used naturally as honorific verbs. At the same time, there is a general feeling that many combinations with だ are rather strange, and お届けですか, for example, is not typically understood as the honorific equivalent of 届けます. Nevertheless, even the less typical combinations are often fine when understood as habits or with "What, again?" kinds of interpretations. 毎朝お花をお届けですか "You deliver flowers **every** morning?" and またアメリカ人とご結婚ですか "You're going to marry an American **again**?" are both fine.

お〜	お会い・おあい・お会いになる *meeting, to meet*; お出で・おいで・お出でになる *coming, to come*; お帰り・おかえり・お帰りになる *returning home, to return home*; お聞き・おきき・お聞きになる *hearing from, to hear from*; お越し・おこし・お越しになる *moving, coming, to come*; お知らせ・おしらせ・お知らせくださる *announcement, to inform*; お尋ね・おたずね・お尋ねになる *asking, to ask*; お発ち・おたち・お発ちになる *departing, to depart*; お使い・おつかい・お使いになる *using, to use*; お伝え・おつたえ・お伝えなさる *telling, to tell*; お出かけ・おでかけ・お出かけになる *going out, to go out*; お届け・おとどけ・お届けなさる *delivery, to deliver*; お取り・おとり・お取りくださる *taking, to take for me*; お入り・おはいり・お入りになる *entering, to enter*; お話し・おはなし・お話しになる *speaking, to speak*; お待ち・おまち・お待ちになる *waiting, to wait*; お招き・おまねき・お招きなさる *inviting, to invite*; お寄り・および・お寄りになる *dropping by, to drop by*
ご〜	ご案内・ごあんない・ご案内なさる *guide, to guide*; ご帰国・ごきこく・ご帰国なさる *returning to your home country*; ご協力・ごきょうりょく・ご協力なさる *cooperation, to cooperate*; ご結婚・ごけっこん・ご結婚なさる *marriage, to marry*; ご指導・ごしどう・ご指導なさる *instruction, to instruct*; ご出産・ごしゅっさん・ご出産なさる *having a baby, to give birth to*; ご出席・ごしゅっせき・ご出席なさる *attendance, to attend*; ご出発・ごしゅっぱつ・ご出発なさる *departure, to depart*; ご紹介・ごしょうかい・ご紹介なさる *introduction, to introduce*; ご招待・ごしょうたい・ご招待なさる *invitation, to invite*; ご説明・ごせつめい・ご説明なさる *explanation, to explain*; ご卒業・ごそつぎょう・ご卒業なさる *graduation, to graduate*; ご入学・ごにゅうがく・ご入学なさる *entering school, entering university, to enter university*; ご利用・ごりよう・ご利用なさる *use, to use*; ご連絡・ごれんらく・ご連絡なさる *announcement, to inform*; 御覧・ごらん・ごらんになる *to see*; 御免・ごめん・ごめんなさい *I am sorry*・ごめん下さい *Excuse me*

The verb stem nouns in the second set here occur with する or いたす to form humble verbs. For example, ご案内する or ご案内いたす mean that *I* (humbly) *guide you* (honorifically). In general, the speaker is doing something for the benefit of the listener. Further discussion of this kind of humble verb as well as the contrast between expressions such as お書きしましょう and 書いて差し上げましょう is found on page 150.

お〜　　　　　お会い・おあい・お会いする *meeting, to meet you*; お聞き・おきき・お聞きする *hearing from, to hear from you*; お知らせ・おしらせ・お知らせする *announcement, to inform you*; お尋ね・おたずね・お尋ねする *asking, to ask you*; お伝え・おつたえ・お伝えする *telling, to tell you*; お手伝い・おてつだい・お手伝いする *help, to give hand to you*; お届け・おとどけ・お届けする *delivery, to deliver to you*; お取り・おとり・お取りする *taking, to take for you*; お話・おはなし・お話する *speaking, to speak with you*; お待ち・おまち・お待ちする *waiting, to wait for you*; お招き・おまねき・お招きする *inviting, to invite you*; お寄り・および・お寄りする *dropping by, dropping by at yours*

ご〜　　　　　ご案内・ごあんない・ご案内する *guide, to guide you*; ご一緒・ごいっしょ・ご一緒する *together, to accompany you*; ご紹介・ごしょうかい・ご紹介する *introduction, to introduce you*; ご招待・ごしょうたい・ご招待する *invitation, to invite you*; ご説明・ごせつめい・ご説明する *explanation, to explain to you*; ご連絡・ごれんらく・ご連絡する *announcement, to inform you*

Of course, many of these verbs stems are also real nouns in their own right: 先生の長い話し, 今日のお知らせ, 日本へのご帰国, etc.

Words which describe people (nominal adjectives and adjectives)

お〜　　　　　おかわいそうな *pitiful*; お気の毒な・おきのどく *miserable, pitiful*; おきれいな *beautiful*; お元気な・おげんき *healthy*; お疲れな・おつかれ *tired*; お幸せな・おしあわせ *happy*; お上手な・おじょうず *talented*

お〜　　　　　お忙しい・おいそがしい *busy*; お偉い・おえらい *great*; お寂しい・おさびしい *sad*; お早い・おはやい *early*; お優しい・おやさしい *kind*; お若い・おわかい *young*

ご〜　　　　　ご機嫌な・ごきげん *mood, cheerful*; ご健康な・ごけんこう *health, healthy*; ご幸運な・ごこううん *good luck, fortunate*; ご親切な・ごしんせつ *kindness, kind*; ご心配な・ごしんぱい *concern, worrisome*; ご多忙な・ごたぼう *being busy, busy*; ご不幸な・ごふこう *unhappiness, unhappy*; ご満足な・ごまんぞく *contentfulness, content*; ご無理な・ごむり *unreasonableness, unreasonable*; ご面倒な・ごめんどう *trouble, troublesome*; ごゆっくり *taking time, leisurely*; ご立派な・ごりっぱ *fineness, fine, decent*

Beautification

The prefixed words are all considered more elegant or more beautiful than their nonprefixed counterparts. Many are congratulatory, and in practice, the prefixed form of many of these words is actually much more common than the non-prefixed form.

ご～   御挨拶・ごあいさつ *greetings*; 御縁・ごえん *relation, ties, fate*; 御祝儀・ごしゅうぎ *congratulatory gift*; 御所・ごしょ *Kyoto Imperial Palace*; 御馳走・ごちそう *a feast*; 御殿・ごてん *palace of a noble person*; 御飯・ごはん *rice, food*; 御無沙汰・ごぶさた *a long silence*

お～   お祈り・おいのり *prayer*; お祝い・おいわい *celebration*; お返し・おかえし *return, change*; お陰様で・おかげさまで *thanks to you*; お菓子・おかし *cake, candy*; おかず *food, a side dish*; お金・おかね *money*; お勘定・おかんじょう *accounts, payment, the check, bill*; お代り・おかわり *seconds* (of food); お悔やみ・おくやみ *condolences*; お下がり・おさがり *hand-me-downs*; お酒・おさけ *sake, alcohol*; お札・おさつ *paper money*; お産・おさん *childbirth*; 御辞儀・おじぎ *a bow, bowing*; お塩・おしお *salt*; お絞り・おしぼり *rolled hand towel* (hot or cold); おしゃべり *talk, gossip, chatter*; おしゃれな *fashionable*; お食事・おしょくじ *meal*; お城・おしろ *castle*; お赤飯・おせきはん *red rice, rice cooked with red beans* (congratulatory); お世辞・おせじ *flattery, a compliment*; お節介な・おせっかい *meddlesome, officious*; お世話・おせわ *care, looking after*; お膳立て・おぜんだて *preparations* (for a party or meal); お蕎麦・おそば *buckwheat noodles*; お揃い・おそろい *go together, suit, a set*; お互い・おたがい *each other, one another*; お茶・おちゃ *tea*; お月様・おつきさま *the moon*; おつり *change* (from a purchase); お手洗い・おてあらい *toilet, bathroom*; お電話・おでんわ *telephone*; お握り・おにぎり *rice ball*; おニューの *new*; お願い・おねがい *wish, request*; お値段・おねだん *price*; お化け・おばけ *a ghost*; お開き・おひらき *bringing a meeting to a close*; お盆・おぼん *the Bon Festival* (13-16 August, honoring the spirits of ancestors); お参り・おまいり *a visit, pilgrimage*; お祭り・おまつり *festival*; お守り・おまもり *good luck charm*; 御神籤・おみくじ *fortune slip*; お土産・おみやげ *souvenir*; おめでたい *congratulatory*; おやつ *a snack, tea, a light meal*; お休み・おやすみ *vacation, rest*; お礼・おれい *gratitude, thanks*; お詫び・おわび *an apology*; お笑い・おわらい *funny story, joke*

Other effects

The honorific prefix can also be used to show cynicism, ridicule, deprecation, etc. For obvious reasons, these words should be used with care.

お～   お偉方・おえらがた *a "VIP"* (said cynically); お高い・おたかい *snobbish* (lit. *high*); お調子者・おちょうしもの *a person easily flattered*; お荷物・おにもつ *troublesome matter* (lit. *luggage*); お上りさん・おのぼりさん *country hick* (in the big city); お人好し・おひとよし *a dupe* (lit. *good-natured*); お安くない・おやすくない *in a hot relationship* (lit. *not cheap*)

Note that for some compounds the particular reading can determine the effect. Compare 御前・おまえ *you* (familiar, mild contempt) and 御前・ごぜん *the presence* (of someone important, usually the Emperor).

2.2.4.2 *Prefixes (which change meaning regularly)*

The prefixes listed in this section tend to change the meaning of their base word in regular and predictable ways. Note, however, that a Chinese character occurring as a prefix may also have more than one sound. These different sounds often correspond to different meanings. The various readings are cross-referenced.

おお・大～   大赤字・おおあかじ *large deficit*; 大汗・おおあせ *hard sweat*; 大当たり・
big, extreme,   おおあたり *exactly right*; 大雨・おおあめ *heavy rain shower*; 大慌て・お
important   おあわて *big mix-up, confusion*; 大威張り・おおいばり *big fuss*; 大入り・
                      おおいり *a full house, large audience*; 大男・おおおとこ *big man, giant*;
                      大火事・おおかじ *big fire*; 大風・おおかぜ *strong wind*; 大型・大形・お
                      おがた *large-scale, large size*; 大食い・おおぐい *gluttony, big-eater*; 大声・
                      おおごえ *loud, big voice*; 大騒ぎ・おおさわぎ *big uproar, fuss*; 大仕事・
                      おおしごと *big job*; 大詰め・おおづめ *a* (catastrophic) *end, finale*; 大粒・
                      おおつぶ *large grain, coarse grain*; 大通り・おおどおり *main street, high
                      street*; 大降り・おおぶり *heavy rain or snow fall*; 大馬鹿・おおばか *extremely stupid*; 大真面目・おおまじめ *extremely serious*; 大晦日・おおみ
                      そか *the last day of the year*; 大文字・おおもじ *capital letters, big letters*;
                      大笑い・おおわらい *big laugh*

                      (See だい・大～ below.)

かく・各～   各駅停車・かくえきていしゃ *a local train, a train which makes all stops*;
each   各家庭・かくかてい *each family*; 各角・かくかど *each corner*; 各科目・か
                      くかもく *each subject*; 各議員・かくぎいん *each assemblyman*; 各教授・か
                      くきょうじゅ *each lecturer, professor*; 各区・かくく *each ward, zone*; 各
                      クラス *each class*; 各項目・かくこうもく *each list, each subject heading*;

各個人・かくこじん *each individual*; 各自・かくじ *each person, every person*; 各社員・かくしゃいん *each employee*; 各車両・かくしゃりょう *each* (train) *car, carriage*; 各種・かくしゅ *all kinds*; 各州・かくしゅう *each state*; 各席・かくせき *each seat*; 各段落・かくだんらく *each paragraph*; 各地方・かくちほう *each area, region*; 各方面・かくほうめん *each direction*; 各部・かくぶ *each department, section*; 各部屋・かくへや *each room*; 各プレイヤー *each player*; 各路線・かくろせん *each route, line*

かた・片〜
one

片足・かたあし *one leg*; 片一方・かたいっぽう *one* (of two); 片思い・かたおもい *unrequited love*; 片親・かたおや *single parent*; 片側・かたがわ *one side*; 片隅・かたすみ *one corner* (of a room); 片手・かたて *one hand*; 片方・かたほう *one* (of two); 片道・かたみち *one way* (ticket); 片寄る・かたよる *be partial to, be biased*

から・空〜
empty

空威張り・からいばり *empty bluster*; カラオケ *karaoke* (lit. *empty orchestra*); 空くじ・からくじ *blank ticket*; 空元気・からげんき *false courage*; 空騒ぎ・からさわぎ *a fuss about nothing*; 空箱・からばこ *empty box*; 空振り・からぶり *missing a ball, a strike*; 空返事・からへんじ *an empty reply*; 空回り・からまわり *run idle*; 空約束・からやくそく *empty promise*

ぎゃく・逆〜
counter,
reverse

逆回転・ぎゃくかいてん *reverse spin*; 逆効果・ぎゃくこうか *contrary, opposite, adverse effect*; 逆光線・ぎゃくこうせん *backlighting* (in photography); 逆コース *backwards path*; 逆説・ぎゃくせつ *paradoxical*; 逆転・ぎゃくてん *reversal, come-from-behind* (victory); 逆比例・ぎゃくひれい *inverse proportion*; 逆方向・ぎゃくほうこう *opposite direction*; 逆方面・ぎゃくほうめん *opposite direction, side*; 逆回り・ぎゃくまわり *reverse rotation*; 逆輸入・ぎゃくゆにゅう *re-import*

きゅう・旧〜
old, former

旧仮名遣い・きゅうかなづかい *old way of using kana*; 旧共産党・きゅうきょうさんとう *old Communist Party*; 旧式・きゅうしき *old-style, old way*; 旧住所・きゅうじゅうしょ *old address*; 旧正月・きゅうしょうがつ *lunar New Year's Day*; 旧姓・きゅうせい *maiden name*; 旧制度・きゅうせいど *old system*; 旧石器時代・きゅうせっきじだい *the Old Stone Age*; 旧ソ連・きゅうそれん *the former Soviet Union*; 旧体制・きゅうたいせい *old system, old establishment*

げん・現〜
present,
current

現憲法・げんけんぽう *the current constitution*; 現住所・げんじゅうしょ *one's present incumbent address*; 現首相・げんしゅしょう *the current prime minister*; 現政権・げんせいけん *the current administration*; 現政府・げんせいふ *the current government*; 現総理大臣・げんそうりだいじん *the current prime minister*

こ・小〜
small, little,
light

小粋な・こいき *stylish, smart, chic*; 小売り・こうり *retail sale*; 小枝・こえだ *a twig*; 小柄な・こがら *short, small build*; 小切り・こぎり *pieces of cloth, rags*; 小ぎれいな・こぎれい *neat, trim, tidy*; 小口・こぐち *small mouth*; 小魚・こざかな *small fish, fingerling*; こざっぱり *neat, clean, tidy*; 小皿・こざら *small dish*; 小猿・こざる *small monkey, baby monkey*; 小雨・こさめ *drizzle, light rain*; 小じわ・こじわ *fine lines, fine wrinkles*; 小銭・こぜに *small change, coins*; 小競り合い・こぜりあい *skirmish, brief argument*; 小高い・こだかい *slightly elevated*; 小出し・こだし *taking out a small quantity, frugal use*; 小憎らしい・こにくらしい *mildly provoking*; 小粒・こつぶ *small grain*; 小走り・こばしり *trot*; 小降り・こぶり light rain, drizzle*; 小坊主・こぼうず *acolyte, novice*; 小道・こみち *path, lane*; 小難しい・こむずかしい *troublesome, bothersome*; 小娘・こむすめ young, immature girl*; 小文字・こもじ *small letters* (not capitals); 小物・こもの *small things*

さい・再〜
re-, again

再開発・さいかいはつ *redevelopment*; 再確認・さいかくにん *reconfirmation*; 再検討・さいけんとう*reexamination*; 再婚・さいこん *remarriage*; 再生産・さいせいさん *reproduction*; 再選挙・さいせんきょ *re-election*; 再試験・さいしけん *make-up examination*; 再出発・さいしゅっぱつ *restart, redeparture*; 再出版・さいしゅっぱん *republication*; 再提出・さいていしゅつ *representation*; 再登録・さいとうろく *reregistration*; 再認識・さいにんしき *realize again, come to light again*; 再発行・さいはっこう *reissue, republish*; 再評価・さいひょうか *reevaluation*; 再編成・さいへんせい *reorganization, reshuffle*; 再放送・さいほうそう *rebroadcast*

さい・最〜
most, -est

最愛の・さいあい *most dear, beloved*; 最悪の・さいあく *the worst*; 最下位・さいかい *last place, bottom position*; 最強の・さいきょう *the strongest, most powerful*; 最高級・さいこうきゅう *top class, best class*; 最敬礼・さいけいれい *profound obeisance*; 最上級・さいじょうきゅう *highest rank*; 最善・さいぜん *one's best, the best*; 最前線・さいぜんせん *the front* (of a movement); 最先端・さいせんたん *the very point* (of a sword); 最年少・さいねんしょう *youngest*; 最年長・さいねんちょう *oldest, most senior*; 最優遇・さいゆうぐう *best treatment, most preferred*; 最優先・さいゆうせん *top priority, most preferred*

じゅん・準〜
semi-,
quasi-

準一級・じゅんいっきゅう*junior first rank* (i.e. *second rank*); 準会員・じゅんかいいん *associate member*; 準急行・じゅんきゅうこう *a local express train*; 準教員・じゅうきょういん *assistant teacher*; 準決勝・じゅんけっしょう *semi-finals*; 準社員・じゅんしゃいん *associate employee*; 準々決勝・じゅんじゅんけっしょう *quarter-finals*; 準ミスアメリカ *the Miss America first runner up*; 準優勝・じゅんゆうしょう *first runner up* (i.e. *second*)

しょ・諸〜 *many, several*	諸悪・しょあく *all evil*; 諸縁・しょえん *many ties, binds, relations*; 諸経費・しょけいひ *many kinds of expenses*; 諸説・しょせつ *many theories*; 諸設備・しょせつび *many facilities*; 諸島・しょとう *group of islands, archipelago*; 諸都市・しょとし *many cities*; 諸費用・しょひよう *many expenses*; 諸役・しょやく *a variety of responsibilities*; 諸例・しょれい *many examples*; 諸礼・しょれい *varieties of etiquette*
しょ・初〜 *first*	初演・しょえん *first performance*; 初夏・しょか *early summer*; 初期・しょき *the beginning*; 初旬・しょじゅん *beginning of the month*; 初心・しょしん *beginner's enthusiasm*; 初診・しょしん *first medical examination*; 初段・しょだん *first grade, first step*; 初体験・しょたいけん *first experience*; 初対面・しょたいめん *meeting for the first time*; 初日・しょにち *opening day*; 初任給・しょにんきゅう *starting salary*; 初版・しょはん *first edition*; 初歩・しょほ *the rudiments, the first step*; 初夜・しょや *one's wedding night*
	(See はつ・初〜 below.)
しん・新〜 *new*	新入り・しんいり *newcomer, rookie*; 新会員・しんかいいん *new member*; 新会長・しんかいちょう *new chair, new president*; 新開発・しんかいはつ *new development*; 新学期・しんがっき *new term, new semester*; 新型・しんがた *new type, new model*; 新記録・しんきろく *new record*; 新憲法・しんけんぽう *new constitution*; 新札・しんさつ *new bills, new currency*; 新シリーズ *new series*; 新社員・しんしゃいん *new employee*; 新住所・しんじゅうしょ *new address*; 新人類・しんじんるい *new human race*; 新生児・しんせいじ *a newborn*; 新世紀・しんせいき *new century*; 新世界・しんせかい *a new world, the New World*; 新制度・しんせいど *new system*; 新製品・しんせいひん *new goods, product*; 新政府・しんせいふ *new government*; 新石器時代・しんせっきじだい *New Stone Age*; 新体制・しんたいせい *new system, new establishment*; 新大統領・しんだいとうりょう *new president*; 新茶・しんちゃ *the first tea of the season*; 新内閣・しんないかく *new cabinet*; 新発売・しんはつばい *new release*; 新番組・しんばんぐみ *new program*; 新兵器・しんへいき *new weapon*
す・っす・ 素〜 *bare*	素足・すあし *barefoot* (cf. 裸足); 素顔・すがお *face without make-up*; 素性・すじょう *background, origin, birth*; 素っ裸・すっぱだか *bare naked* (cf. 裸); 素っ破抜く・すっぱぬく *expose, lay bare*; 素手・すで *bare hand*; 素通り・すどおり *passing through without dropping by*; 素肌・すはだ *bare skin*; 素早い・すばやい *quick, swift*; 素振り・すぶり *behavior, manner, attitude*; 素彫り・すぼり *a rough carve*; 素焼き・すやき *unglazed pottery*

ぜん・前～ *previous,* *former, ex-*	前回・ぜんかい *the previous time, the last time*; 前会員・ぜんかいいん *previous assemblyman*; 前会長・ぜんかいちょう *previous chairperson*; 前期・ぜんき *previous term, first term*; 前景・ぜんけい *foreground*; 前号・ぜんごう *the preceding issue or number, the issue or number before*; 前日・ぜんじつ *the previous day, the day before*; 前社長・ぜんしゃちょう *previous company president*; 前首相・ぜんしゅしょう *previous prime minister*; 前世紀・ぜんせいき *a previous century, the preceding century*; 前大統領・ぜんだいとうりょう *the previous president*; 前年度・ぜんねんど *the previous fiscal year*; 前文・ぜんぶん *preamble*; 前ページ *the previous page*; 前編・ぜんぺん *part one, the first volume*; 前方・ぜんぽう *forward, movement forward*; 前夜・ぜんや *the night before, a previous night*; 前例・ぜんれい *a precedent*, 先例; 前列・ぜんれつ *the front row*
ぜん・全～ *all, entire,* *total*	全員・ぜんいん *all the members*; 全快・ぜんかい *complete recovery*; 全開・ぜんかい *full power, fully opened*; 全額・ぜんがく *full amount*; 全科目 ぜんかもく *all school subjects*; 全曲・ぜんきょく *all of a piece of music*; 全校・ぜんこう *the whole school, all the students*; 全国・ぜんこく *the whole country*; 全国民・ぜんこくみん *the entire citizenry*; 全車両・ぜんしゃりょう *all of the cars* (in a train), *all of the carriages*; 全種類・ぜんしゅるい *all kinds, all types*; 全焼・ぜんしょう *total destruction by fire*; 全勝・ぜんしょう *total victory*; 全人口・ぜんじんこう *the entire population*; 全人類・ぜんじんるい *all of humanity*; 全世界・ぜんせかい *the entire world*; 全席・ぜんせき *all seats*; 全責任・ぜんせきにん *full responsibility*; 全速力・ぜんそくりょく *full speed*; 全チーム *the whole team*; 全敗・ぜんぱい *total failure*; 全部・ぜんぶ *all, whole, every*; 全文・ぜんぶん *the whole text*; 全米・ぜんべい *all of the US, the all-American*; 全ページ *all pages*; 全滅・ぜんめつ *total destruction*; 全面・ぜんめん *the whole surface*; 全寮制の学校・ぜんりょうせいのがっこう *a boarding school*; 全力・ぜんりょく *all one's might*
そう・総～ *general,* *entire*	総当たり・そうあたり (playing a match) *against all players*; 総入れ歯・そういれば *full set of false teeth*; 総会・そうかい *general assembly*; 総掛かり・そうがかり *together, as one*; 総額・そうがく *sum total*, 総計; 総崩れ・そうくずれ *a rout*; 総合計・そうごうけい *grand total*; 総攻撃・そうこうげき *full scale attack*; 総支出・そうししゅつ *total expenditure*; 総収入・そうしゅうにゅう *total income*; 総司令部・そうしれいぶ *General Headquarters, GHQ*; 総人口・そうじんこう *entire population*; 総数・そうすう *total number*; 総世帯・そうせたい *general household*; 総選挙・そうせんきょ *general election*; 総立ち・そうだち *a group rising to their feet*; 総返済・そうへんさい *total repayment*; 総目録・そうもくろく *general catalog*; 総領事・そうりょうじ *a consul general*

たい・対～ *vis-a-vis,* *with respect* *to*	対案・たいあん *counterproposal*, (cf. 提案・ていあん *proposal*); 対外・たいがい *with respect to foreign countries*; 対外政策・たいがいせいさく *foreign policy*; 対角・たいかく *opposite corner*; 対策・たいさく *countermeasure, measure against*; 対人・たいじん *vis-a-vis people*; 対人関係・たいじんかんけい *relations with people*; 対日・たいにち *with respect to Japan*; 対日貿易・たいにちぼうえき *trade with Japan*
だい・大～ *big, extreme,* *important*	大移動・だいいどう *mass movement*; 大家族・だいかぞく *big family*; 大企業・だいきぎょう *large trading company*; 大規模・だいきぼ *large-scale*; 大混乱・だいこんらん *total chaos, complete disorder*; 大サービス *very special service, big freebie*; 大事業・だいじぎょう *large business, undertaking*; 大事件・だいじけん *big incident*; 大自然・だいしぜん *the great outdoors*; 大震災・だいしんさい *a great earthquake, a great disaster*; 大都市・だいとし *a big city, a great metropolis*; 大豊作・だいほうさく *a bumper crop*
	(See おお・大～ above.)
だい・第～ ordinal prefix	第一・だいいち *number one*; 第二次・だいにじ *second, secondary*; 第三課・だいさんか *lesson three*; 第四章・だいよんしょう *chapter four*; etc.
ちょう・超～ *super-,* *extremely*	超音速・ちょうおんそく *supersonic speed*; 超音波・ちょうおんぱ *supersonic waves*; 超現実主義・ちょうげんじつしゅぎ *extreme realism*; 超高級ホテル・ちょうこうきゅうホテル *extremely high-class hotel*; 超合金・ちょうごうきん *super alloy*; 超高層ビル・ちょうこうそうビル *extremely high, multi-story building*; 超高速・ちょうこうそく *extremely high speed*; 超国家主義・ちょうこっかしゅぎ *extreme nationalism*; 超短波・ちょうたんぱ *very high frequency*; 超電導・ちょうでんどう *superconductivity*; 超特急・ちょうとっきゅう *a super express* (train); 超能力・ちょうのうりょく *supernatural power*; ちょべリグ *very, very good*; ちょべリバ *very, very bad* (these last two are giggling girl slang)
どう・同～ *same,* *as above*	同学年・どうがくねん *same year in school*; 同学部・どうがくぶ *same academic department*; 同期・どうき *same class, same period of school*; 同級・どうきゅう *same grade, same class*; 同業者・どうぎょうしゃ *person in same trade or profession*; 同系統・どうけいとう *same system*; 同系列・どうけいれつ *two companies with the same affiliation*; 同時の・どうじ *simultaneous*; 同種類・どうしゅるい *same kind, type*; 同時代・どうじだい *same period*; 同質・どうしつ *same quality, homogeneity*; 同姓・どうせい *same surname*; 同性・どうせい *same sex*; 同性愛・どうせいあい *homosexuality*; 同世代・どうせだい *same generation*; 同点・どうてん *a tie*; 同年代・

どうねんだい *same generation*; 同年齢・どうねんれい *same age*; 同列・ど うれつ *same rank or class*

(どう〜・同 as a prefix or on its own often means *the one above* or *as stated above* or something like *ditto*, making specific reference to an earlier occurrence of the particular expression: 同提案 *the previously mentioned proposal, the aforementioned proposal, the above proposal*.)

なま・生〜 *raw, half*	生あくび・なまあくび *a slight yawn*; 生暖かい・なまあたたかい *lukewarm, tepid*; 生意気な・なまいき *conceited, self-absorbed*; 生かじり・なまかじり *superficial knowledge*; 生乾き・なまがわき *half dry*; 生傷・なまきず *a bruise, wound*; 生首・なまくび *freshly severed head*; 生煮え・なまにえ *half-cooked, half-done*; 生ぬるい・なまぬるい *lukewarm, tepid*; 生半可・なまはんか *superficial, shallow*; 生返事・なまへんじ *half-hearted, reluctant reply*; 生焼け・なまやけ *half-cooked*; 生易しい・なまやさしい *simple, easy*
はつ・初〜 *first*	初売り・はつうり *first sale of the New Year*; 初恋・はつこい *first love*; 初公開・はつこうかい *first showing to the public*; 初航海・はつこうかい *maiden voyage*; 初仕事・はつしごと *first job of the year*; 初芝居・はつしばい *Kabuki plays for the New Year*; 初出場・はつしゅつじょう *first participation*; 初登場・はつとうじょう *first appearance on stage*; 初当選・はつとうせん *first time being elected*; 初場所・はつばしょ *January sumo tournament* (first of the year); 初日の出・はつひので *first sunrise of the New Year*; 初舞台・はつぶたい *first appearance on the stage*; 初耳・はつみみ *news to me, something never heard before*; 初詣で・はつもうで *first visit of the year to a shrine*; 初物・はつもの *first* (thing) *of the season*; 初優勝・はつゆうしょう *first victory*; 初雪・はつゆき *first snowfall*; 初夢・はつゆめ *first dream of the New Year*

(See しょ・初〜 above.)

はん・半〜 *half, semi-*	半永久的・はんえいきゅうてき *semi-permanent*; 半円・はんえん *semicircle*; 半音・はんおん *a flat or sharp* (in music); 半回転・はんかいてん *half turn*; 半額・はんがく *half-price*; 半乾き・はんがわき *half dry*; 半強制的・はんきょうせいてき *semi-compulsory*; 半月・はんげつ *half moon*; 半殺し・はんごろし *nearly to death*; 半自動・はんじどう *semi-automatic*; 半熟・はんじゅく *half-boiled*; 半数・はんすう *half* (of a countable amount); 半ズボン *shorts*; 半世紀・はんせいき *half a century*; 半そで・はんそで *half sleeve, short sleeve*; 半月・はんつき *half a month*; 半ドア *half-opened* (car) *door,* (car) *door which is not properly shut*; 半導体・はんどうたい *semiconductor*; 半年・はんとし *half a year*; 半煮え・はんにえ

halfway boiled; 半日・はんにち *half a day*; 半値・はんね *half price*; 半開き・はんびらき *halfway open*; 半面・はんめん *one side* (of two)

は・反〜
anti-,
counter-

反意語・はんいご *antonym*; 反科学的・はんかがくてき *anti-scientific*; 反核運動・はんかくうんどう *anti-nuclear movement*; 反革命・はんかくめい *counter-revolution*; 反感・はんかん *antagonism, antipathy*; 反共産主義・はんきょうさんしゅぎ *anti-communism*; 反差別運動・はんさべつうんどう *anti-discrimination movement*; 反作用・はんさよう *counter reaction*; 反社会的・はんしゃかいてき *anti-social*; 反道徳的・はんどうとくてき *anti-moral*; 反テロ対策・はんテロ たいさく *anti-terrorism measures*; 反比例・はんぴれい *inverse reaction*; 反物質・はんぶっしつ *anti-matter*

ひ・非〜
non-, un-

非アメリカ的・ひアメリカてき *un-American*; 非衛生・ひえいせい *un-sanitariness*; 非化学・ひかがく *chemical-free*; 非科学的・ひかがくてき *unscientific*; 非核保有国・ひかくほゆうこく *nuclear-free country*; 非加盟国・ひかめいこく *non-alliance country*; 非強制的・ひきょうせいてき *non-compulsory*; 非協力的・ひきょうりょくてき *uncooperative*; 非軍事的・ひぐんじてき *non-military*; 非現実的・ひげんじつてき *unrealistic*; 非公開の・ひこうかい *secret, closed-door*; 非公式な・ひこうしき *unofficial*; 非国民・ひこくみん *unpatriotic* (often specifically *un-Japanese*); 非産油国・ひさんゆこく *non oil-producing country*; 非宗教的・ひしゅうきょうてき *unreligious*; 非主要国・ひしゅようこく *a minor power*; 非常識な・ひじょうしき *absurd, unreasonable*; 非人道的・ひじんどうてき *inhumane*; 非生産的・ひせいさんてき *unproductive*; 非対称的・ひたいしょうてき *as-symmetrical*; 非能率的・ひのうりつてき *inefficient*; 非民主的・ひみんしゅてき *undemocratic*

ひ・被〜
recipient,
undergoer

被援助国・ひえんじょこく *aid receiving country*; 被害者・ひがいしゃ *victim*; 被疑者・ひぎしゃ *suspect*; 被験者・ひけんしゃ・ひけんじゃ (experimental) *subject*; 被支配者・ひしはいしゃ *the dominated power, loser*; 被支払い人・ひしはらいにん *payee*; 被選挙権・ひせんきょけん *eligibility*; 被相続人・ひそうぞくにん *one succeeded by his successor*; 被保険者・ひほけんしゃ *the person insured*; 被保険物・ひほけんぶつ *things insured*; 被爆者・ひばくしゃ *bomb victim*

ふ・不〜
un-, not

不安定な・ふあんてい *unsettled, uncertain*; 不衛生な・ふえいせい *un-sanitary*; 不確実な・ふかくじつ *uncertain, unreliable*; 不可能な・ふかのう *impossible*; 不完全な・ひかんぜん *incomplete*; 不規則な・ふきそく *irregular, unsystematic*; 不均衡な・ふきんこう *unbalanced, disproportionate*; 不景気・ふけいき *hard times, bad times*; 不健康な・ふけんこう *unhealthy*; 不幸な・ふこう *unhappy*; 不合格・ふごうかく *failure*; 不合理な・ふごうり *illogical, unreasonable*; 不自然な・ふしぜん *unnatural*; 不始末・

ふしまつ *mismanagement*; 不自由な・ふじゆう *inconvenient, unfree, restricted*; 不十分な・ふじゅうぶん *insufficient*; 不親切・ふしんせつ *unkindness*; 不誠実な・ふせいじつ *insincere, dishonest*; 不正確な・ふせいかく *inaccurate*; 不注意な・ふちゅうい *careless, negligent*; 不調和な・ふちょうわ *disharmonious*; 不釣り合いの・ふつりあい *ill-matched, disproportionate*; 不適当な・ふてきとう *unsuitable*; 不透明な・ふとうめい *opaque*; 不得意な・ふとくい *(skills are) bad, poor, weak*; 不特定の・ふとくてい *indefinite*; 不慣れな・ふなれ *unaccustomed to, unfamiliar with*; 不必要な・ふひつよう *unnecessary*; 不平等な・ふびょうどう *unequal, unfair*; 不真面目な・ふまじめ *not serious*; 不向きな・ふむき *unsuitable, unfit*; 不明瞭・ふめいりょう *lack of clarity, indistinctness*; 不名誉な・ふめいよ *dishonorable, disgraceful*; 不愉快な・ふゆかい *unpleasant*; 不行き届き・ふゆきとどき *negligent*

ぶ・無〜
un-, not,
opposite
of 有〜

無愛想な・ぶあいそう *unsocial*; 不格好な・ぶかっこう *shapeless, ill-shaped*; 不器用な・ぶきよう *awkward, clumsy*; 不器量な・ぶきりょう *not good-looking, not talented*; 不気味な・ぶきみ *weird*; 不作法な・ぶさほう *bad mannered*; 不細工な・ぶさいく *awkward, clumsy*; 無事・ぶじ *safety, peace, without incidence*; 無難な・ぶなん *safe, acceptable*; 無用心な・ぶようじん *not cautious*; 無礼な・ぶれい *impolite, rude*

(See む・無〜 below.)

ふく・副〜
vice-,
deputy-,
secondary

副会長・ふくかいちょう *deputy chief* (of a group); 副作用・ふくさよう *secondary effect*; 副産業・ふくさんぎょう *secondary industry*; 副産物・ふくさんぶつ *by-product*; 副社長・ふくしゃちょう *company vice-president*; 副収入・ふくしゅうにゅう *supplementary income*; 副職・ふくしょく *secondary job*; 副総理・ふくそうり *deputy prime minister*; 副大統領・ふくだいとうりょう *vice-president*; 副知事・ふくちじ *deputy governor*; 副読本・ふくどくほん *supplementary reader*

ほん・本〜
main, actual,
fundamental

本会議・ほんかいぎ *this session* (of the legislature); 本決まり・ほんぎまり *final decision*; 本式・ほんしき *full, formal way*, 正式; 本質・ほんしつ *essence, nature*; 本社・ほんしゃ *head office*; 本州・ほんしゅう *Honshu* (the main island of Japan); 本性・ほんしょう *one's true nature*, 正体; 本職・ほんしょく *one's occupation, profession*; 本筋・ほんすじ *main subject, topic, purpose*; 本籍・ほんせき *legal residence*; 本体・ほんたい *main body, true form*; 本題・ほんだい *main subject*; 本調子・ほんちょうし *the normal condition*; 本店・ほんてん *main store, main office*; 本土・ほんど *mainland*; 本人・ほんにん *the person in question*; 本能・ほんのう *instinct*; 本場所・ほんばしょ *regular sumo tournament*; 本部・ほんぶ *head office*; 本降り・ほんぶり *heavy rain*; 本文・ほんぶん *main body of a* text; 本名・ほんみょう *one's real name*; 本物・ほんもの *the real thing*; 本流・ほんりゅう *main stream or current*; 本塁・ほんるい *home base, home plate*

ま・まっ・まん・真〜 *right, true, pure*	真新しい・まあたらしい *brand new*; 真上・まうえ *directly above*; 真後ろ・まうしろ *directly behind*; 真四角・ましかく *perfectly square*; 真下・ました *directly beneath*; 真っ白・まっしろ *pure white*; 真っ正面・まっしょうめん *directly opposite*; 真っ赤な・まっか *bright red*; 真っ暗・まっくら *complete darkness*; 真っ最中・まっさいちゅう *in the middle of, at the height of*; 真っ青・まっさお *deep blue, pure blue*; 真っ盛り・まっさかり *at the height of* (summer); 真っ先に・まっさきに *first of all, first and foremost*; 真っ只中・まっただなか *in the midst of*; 真っ裸・まっぱだか *being stark naked*; 真っ二つ・まっぷたつ *exactly into two*; 真水・まみず *fresh water*; 真向かい・まむかい *just opposite, just across from*; 真横・まよこ *just beside*; 真夜中・まよなか *the middle of the night, midnight*; 真ん中・まんなか *the middle, the center*; 真ん前・まんまえ *right in front of*; 真ん丸い・まんまるい *perfectly round*
まい・毎〜 *every*	毎朝・まいあさ *every morning*; 毎回・まいかい *every time*; *every turn*; 毎月・まいげつ・まいつき *every month*; 毎時間・まいじかん *every hour*; 毎週・まいしゅう *every week*; 毎食・まいしょく *every meal*; 毎度・まいど *every time*; 毎年・まいとし *every year*; 毎日・まいにち *every day*; 毎晩・まいばん *every night*; 毎分・まいふん *every minute*
み・未〜 *un-*	未開の・みかい *uncivilized, primitive*; 未解決の・みかいけつ *unsolved*; 未開拓の・みかいたく *unexploited*; 未確認飛行物体・みかくにんひこうぶったい *UFO*; 未完成・みかんせい *incompletion*; 未経験の・みけいけん *inexperienced*; 未公開の・みこうかい *unreleased*; 未婚・みこん *unmarried*; 未熟な・みじゅく *immature*; 未成年・みせいねん *minor, underage*; 未知の・みち *unknown, unfamiliar*; 未定・みてい *undecided*; 未納・みのう *in arrears*; 未発達・みはったつ *undeveloped*; 未発表・みはっぴょう *unpublished*; 未亡人・みぼうじん *widow*
む・無〜 *in-, un-, not, opposite of 有〜*	無意識の・むいしき *unconscious, involuntary*; 無意味な・むいみ *without meaning*; 無縁の・むえん *have no relation, irrelevant*; 無害な・むがい *harmless, innocuous*; 無感覚の・むかんかく *insensitive*; 無関係の・むかんけい *lack of a connection, unrelated*; 無関心の・むかんしん *indifference*; 無傷の・むきず *flawless*; 無口な・むくち *quiet, not talking very much*; 無欠席・むけっせき *perfect attendance*; 無限の・むげん *infinity, without limit*; 無言の・むごん *silent*; 無罪・むざい *innocence*, (cf. 有罪); 無差別・むさべつ *no discrimination*; 無惨な・むざん *horrible, cruel*; 無事故・むじこ *no accidents*; 無慈悲・むじひ *without mercy*; 無情な・むじょう *cruel,*

heartless; 無条件・むじょうけん *without conditions*; 無職の・むしょく *without an occupation, unemployed*; 無所属・むしょぞく *unattached, independent*; 無神経な・むしんけい *insensitive, thick-skinned*; 無人島・むじんとう *uninhabited island*; 無数の・むすう *countless*; 無税・むぜい *tax-free, duty-free*; 無責任な・むせきにん *irresponsible*; 無駄な・むだ *a waste, pointless*; 無駄遣い・むだづかい *a waste*, 無駄; 無秩序な・むちつじょ *disorderly, chaotic*; 無能な・むのう *incompetent*; 無表情・むひょうじょう *without an expression, expressionless*; 無謀な・むぼう *thoughtless, reckless*; 無報酬・むほうしゅう *without pay*; 無名の・むめい *unknown, obscure, nameless*; 無免許・むめんきょ *unlicensed*; 無料・むりょう *free of charge*; 無力な・むりょく *powerless, helpless*

(See ぶ・無〜 above.)

もと・元〜 *former*	元首相・もとしゅしょう *former prime minister*; 元大統領・もとだいとうりょう *former president*; 元幹事長・もとかんじちょう *former chief secretary, secretary general*; 元社員・もとしゃいん *former company employee*; 元書記長・もとしょきちょう *former first secretary*; 元公務員・もとこうむいん *former public servant*; 元教授・もときょうじゅ *former professor*; 元同盟国・もとどうめいこく *former allied nations*
ゆう・有〜 *have, possess, opposite of 無〜*	有意義・ゆういぎ *meaningful, significant*; 有益な・ゆうえき *instructive, profitable*, (cf. 無益な); 有害な・ゆうがい *harmful*, (cf. 無害な); 有機物・ゆうきぶつ *organic matter*, (cf. 無有機物); 有限の・ゆうげん *with a time limit*; 有権者・ゆうけんしゃ *voter*; 有効な・ゆうこう *effective, valid*, (cf. 無効な); 有効期限・ゆうこうきげん *term of validity*; 有罪・ゆうざい *guilt*, (cf. 無罪); 有色人種・ゆうしょくじんしゅ *a colored race*; 有税・ゆうぜい *taxed*, (cf. 無税); 有毒な・ゆうどく *poisonous*; 有能な・ゆうのう *with ability, talented*, (cf. 無能); 有名な・ゆうめい *famous*; 有利な・ゆうり *favorable, advantageous*; 有料・ゆうりょう *with a charge, with a cost*, (cf. 無料); 有力な・ゆうりょく *strong, influential*, (cf. 無力)

2.2.4.3 Suffixes (which change meaning regularly)

The suffixes listed in this section tend to change the meaning of their base word in regular and predictable ways. Note, however, that a Chinese character occurring as a suffix may also have more than one sound. These different sounds often correspond to different meanings. The various readings are cross-referenced. Finally, a number of the suffixes here attach not to independent words, per se, but to verbal and adjectival stems (i.e. verbs without 〜ます and adjectives without 〜い.)

〜家・か
*person who
is typically
described as
doing* 〜

演奏家・えんそうか *performer, player*; 音楽家・おんがっか・おんがくか *musician*; 画家・がか *painter*; 切手収集家・きってしゅうしゅうか *stamp collector*; 芸術家・げいじゅつか *artist*; 劇作家・げきさっか *playwright*; 研究家・けんきゅうか *researcher*; 作家・さっか *author*; 作曲家・さっきょくか *composer*; 資本家・しほんか *capitalist*; 小説家・しょうせつか *novelist, writer*; 政治家・せいじか *politician*; 専門家・せんもんか *specialist*; 読書家・どくしょか *a reader*; 勉強家・べんきょうか *hardworking student*; 弁舌家・べんぜつか *a speaker*; 法律家・ほうりつか *a lawyer*, 弁護士・^{べんごし}; 楽天家・らくてんか *optimist*; 浪費家・ろうひか *a waster*

〜化・か
*change,
convert*

アメリカ化 *Americanization*; 安定化・あんていか *stabilization*; 一体化・いったいか *unification*; 一本化・いっぽんか *unification, centralization*; 違法化・いほうか *illegalization*; 映画化・えいがか *dramatization*; 液化・えきか *liquefaction*; 核家族化・かくかぞくか *movement to nuclear families*; 過疎化・かそか *depopulation*; 機械化・きかいか *mechanization*; 擬人化・ぎじんか *personification*; 形式化・けいしきか *formalization*; 軽量化・けいりょうか *lightening* (of a load or amount); 現代化・げんだいか *modernization*; 工業化・こうぎょうか *industrialization*; 合理化・ごうりか *rationalization, streamlining*; 高齢化・こうれいか *aging* (of a society); 国際化・こくさいか *internationalization*; 自由化・じゆうか *liberalization* (of trade); 西洋化・せいようか *Westernization*; 退化・たいか *retrogression, degeneration*; 多角化・たかくか *diversification*; 統一化・とういつか *unification*; 複雑化・ふくざつか *becoming more complicated*; 平等化・びょうどうか *equalization*; 民営化・みんえいか *privatization*; 民主化・みんしゅか *democratization*; 老化・ろうか *aging, senility*

(Many words ending with 〜化・か can be followed by する to create a verb which refers to doing the change.)

〜下・か
under

インフレ下 *subject to inflation*; 〜の影響下・えいきょうか *under the influence of* 〜; 行政下・ぎょうせいか *under an administration*; 支配下・しはいか *under the control of*; クリントン政権下・クリントンせいけんか *under the Clinton administration*; 占領下・せんりょうか *occupied, under occupation*

〜方・かた
*way to,
way of doing*

開ける・開け方・あけかた *way of opening*; 在る・在り方・ありかた *way of living*; 言う・言い方・いいかた *way of saying, way of saying a Chinese character*; 生きる・生き方・いきかた *way of living*; 入れる・入れ方・いれかた *way of putting something in*; 教える・教え方・おしえかた *way of teaching*; 書く・書き方・かきかた *way of writing, stroke order*; 考える・考え方・かんがえかた *way of thinking*; 答える・答え方・こたえかた *way of replying*; 殺される・殺され方・ころされかた *how to be killed*; 探す・探し方・さがしかた *way of searching for*; 死ぬ・死に方・しにかた *how to die*; する・仕方・しかた *way of doing* (something); 頼む・頼み方・たのみかた *way of asking*; 食べる・食べ方 *way of eating, correct way to eat*; 使う・使い方・つかいかた *way of using*; 作る・作り方・つくりかた *way of making, recipe*; つづる・つづり方 *spelling, way of spelling*; 話す・話し方・はなしかた *way of speaking*; 見る・見方・みかた *point of view, stand point*; やる・やり方 *way of doing*; 行く・行き方・ゆきかた・いきかた *way, access*; 読む・読み方・よみかた *way of reading, reading of a Chinese character*

(Compare with 〜様・よう below. An expression such as 話し方 refers to a way or manner of speaking, as opposed to the procedure for making it happen. 話し方が好きだ *I like the way she talks*; 話し方がうまい *She speaks well*; 話し方が変だ *She has a strange way of speaking.* The most common expression overall here is しかたがない *There is nothing to be done.*)

〜方・かた *person, role, group, side*	裏方・うらかた *stagehand*; 親方・おやかた *chief, master, boss*; 父方・ちちかた *paternal side*; 敵方・てきかた *enemy, enemy's group or side*; 母方・ははかた *maternal side*; 味方・みかた *friend, partner*
〜方・がた	For usage as an honorific plural, see page 107 below.
〜型・がた *type, model*	朝型・あさがた *a morning person*; AB型・エービーがた *AB blood type*; 遺伝子型・いでんしがた *genotype*; 依存型・いぞんがた *dependency model*; 薄型・うすがた *thin figure*; 混合型・こんごうがた *blended type*; 従来型・じゅうらいがた *traditional model, type*; 1998年型・ねんがた *1998 model*; 冬型・ふゆがた *winter model, type*; 標準型・ひょうじゅんがた *standard type*; 発作型・ほっさがた *the type of person likely to have a heart attacks*; 痩せ型・やせがた *a slim figure*
〜形・がた *shaped*	扇形・おうぎがた *fan-shaped*; 小判形・こばんがた *koban-shaped* (a coin formerly used in Japan); 卵形・たまごがた *egg-shaped*; ハート形 *heart-shaped*; 箱形・はこがた *box-shaped*; 花形・はながた *flower-shaped*; 半円型・はんえんがた *semicircular*; ひし形・ひしがた *lozenge*; ひょうたん形・ひょうたんがた *gourd-shaped*; 星形・ほしがた *star-shaped*; V字形・ブイじがた *V-shaped*; 船形・ふながた *boat-shaped*; 三日月形・みかつきがた *crescent-shaped*

(See 〜形・けい below.)

〜勝ち・がち *tend to*	ありがちの *common, frequent*; 遠慮がち・えんりょうがち *tend to self-restraint*; 遅れがち・おくれがち *tend to be late*; 曇りがち・くもりがち *tend to be cloudy*; 進みがち・すすみがち *tend to move forward, progressive*; 止まりがち・とまりがち *tend to stop*; 怠けがち・なまけがち *tend to be idle, lazy*; 病気がち・びょうきがち *tend to be ill*; 不足しがち・ふそくしがち *tend to be in short supply*; 休みがち・やすみがち *tend to rest, take time off*; 忘れがち・わすれがち *tend to forget*

(Examples: 忘れがちの人 *a person who tends to forget*; 彼は忘れがちだ。 *He tends to forget. He tends to be forgetful.*)

〜間・かん *between*	会社間・かいしゃかん *between companies*; 家族間・かぞくかん *between families*; 学校間・がっこうかん *between schools*; 教師間・きょうしかん *between teachers*; 業者間・ぎょうしゃかん *between dealers*; 生徒間・せいとかん *between pupils*; 東京大阪間・とうきょうおおさかかん *between Tokyo and Osaka*; 三日間・みっかかん *for three days*
〜気味・ぎみ *tending to;* *verging on*	上がりぎみ・あがりぎみ *tending to increase, about to increase* (of prices); 怒りぎみ・おこりぎみ *tend to get angry, have a short fuse*; 風邪気味・かぜぎみ *catching a cold, about to catch a cold*; 下がりぎみ・さがりぎみ *tend to fall* (of prices); 上昇ぎみ・じょうしょうぎみ *tend to rise* (of prices, temperature, etc.); 疲れ気味・つかれぎみ *tending to tire easily, about to tire*; 太り気味・ふとりぎみ *tending to gain weight*; 弱りぎみ・よわりぎみ *tend to be weak, feeble*
〜位・ぐらい ・くらい *about*	一時間位・ぐらい *for about one hour*; 50人ぐらい *about fifty people*; 5分位かかる *take about ten minutes*; 卵ぐらいの大きさ *about the size of an egg*; 20代前半ぐらい *in her early twenties*; どのぐらい・どのくらい *for about how long*

(ぐらい refers to an approximate quantity, size, amount, or length of time. The sizes or numbers are relatively large, and expressions such as 二人ぐらい are somewhat strange in many contexts; 二、三人 or 二、三人ぐらい are preferred. ぐらい should be contrasted with ごろ below which refers only to an approximate time.)

〜気 ・け・げ *state, flavor,* *indication*	嫌気・いやけ *dislike, disgust*; 色気・いろけ *sexiness*; 大人げ・おとなげ *adult, mature*; 悲しげ・かなしげ *sad, sorrowful*; 可愛げ・かわいげ *innocence, charm of youth*; 寒気・さむけ *a chill, shivers*; 商売っ気・しょうばいっけ *commercial spirit*; 退屈げ・たいくつげ *boredom*; 懐かしげ・なつかしげ *nostalgia*; 吐き気・はきけ *nausea*; 満足げ・まんぞくげ *satisfaction*

〜形・けい *shape*	円形・えんけい *a circle, circular*; 矩形・くけい *a rectangle, rectangular*; 五角形・ごかくけい・ごかっけい *pentagon*; 七角形・しちかっけい *heptagon*; 正方形・せいほうけい *a regular square*; 台形・だいけい *a trapezoid*; 多角形・たかっけい *a polygon*; 長方形・ちょうほうけい *a rectangle, oblong*; 二等辺三角形・にとうへんさんかっけい *an isosceles triangle*; 半円型・はんえんけい *semicircular*

(See 〜形・がた above.)

〜子・こ *woman who does a job, person born in*	いじめっ子 *a bully, a tease*; 売り子・うりこ *salesgirl, sales clerk*; 売れっ子・うれっこ *popular person, sought-after person*; 江戸っ子・えどっこ *native of Tokyo*; 踊り子・おどりこ *dancer, dancing girl*; お針子・おはりこ *embroiderer, needle worker*; 駄々っ子・だだっこ *spoiled, willful child*; 一人っ子・ひとりっこ・ひとりご *an only child*
〜毎・ごと *every*	季節毎・きせつごと *every season*; 国毎・くにごと *every country*; 五分毎・ごふんごと *every five minutes*; 人種毎・じんしゅごと *every race*; 月毎・つきごと *every month*; 一雨毎・ひとあめごと *every rain shower*; 二日毎・ふつかごと *every two days, every other day*; 日曜日毎・にちようびごと *every Sunday*
〜頃・ごろ *approximate time*	三時ごろ *approximately 3 o'clock*; 何時ごろ来たの？ *at about what time did he come?*; 水曜日頃 *around Wednesday*; 終わり頃・ごろ *at around the end*; 食べごろ *time to eat, season*
〜士・し *one who is officially qualified as*	栄養士・えいようし *dietician*; 会計士・かいけいし *accountant, CPA*; 学士・がくし *college graduate, Bachelor's degree*; 技術士・ぎじゅつし *technician*; 建築士・けんちくし *architect*; 歯科技工士・しかぎこうし *dental technician*; 税理士・ぜいりし *licensed tax accountant*; 設計士・せっけいし *planner, designer*; 戦士・せんし *soldier*; 操縦士・そうじゅうし *pilot*; 代議士・だいぎし *a Diet member*; 闘牛士・とうぎゅうし *bullfighter*; 武士・ぶし *samurai*; 兵士・へいし *soldier*; 弁護士・べんごし *lawyer*; 力士・りきし *sumo wrestler*
〜師・し *teacher, someone educated to do something*	医師・いし *doctor*; 恩師・おんし *one's (former) teacher*; 教師・きょうし *teacher, instructor*; 講師・こうし *speaker, lecturer*; 詐欺師・さぎし *swindler*; 宣教師・せんきょうし *missionary*; 調理師・ちょうりし *a cook*; 調律師・ちょうりつし *piano tuner*; 庭師・にわし *gardener*; 美容師・びようし *beautician*; 牧師・ぼくし *minister, vicar*; 薬剤師・やくざいし *pharmacist, chemist*; 漁師・りょうし *fisherman*; 猟師・りょうし *hunter*

〜時・じ
time of

開館時・かいかんじ *opening time*; 革命時・かくめいじ *time of the revolution*; 恐慌時・きょうこうじ *time of* (financial) *panic*; 空腹時・くうふくじ *time of hunger*; 第二次世界大戦時・だいにじせかいたいせんじ *the time of World War II*; 非常時・ひじょうじ *an emergency time*; 幼少時・ようしょうじ *childhood*

〜式・しき
style, type

アメリカ式 *American-style*; 折り畳み式・おりたたみしき *folding-style* (like an umbrella or fan); 回転式・かいてんしき *revolving type*; 時差式・じさしき *staggered* (working hours); スパルタ式 *Spartan*; 電動式・でんどうしき *electric-powered*; 日本式・にほんしき *Japanese-style*; ヘボン式 *Hepburn-style of romanization*; ○×式・まるばつしき *true or false type* (test); 洋式・ようしき *Western-style*; ルネッサンス式 *Renaissance-style*; 和式・わしき *Japanese-style*

〜者・しゃ
person who does

暗殺者・あんさつしゃ *assassin*; 医者・いしゃ *doctor*; 演奏者・えんそうしゃ *player, performer*; 応募者・おうぼしゃ *applicant*; 加害者・かがいしゃ *person who has harmed someone*; 関係者・かんけいしゃ *related person*; 患者・かんじゃ *patient*; 記者・きしゃ *reporter*; 犠牲者・ぎせいしゃ *victim*; 希望者・きぼうしゃ *applicant, hopeful one*; 業者・ぎょうしゃ *dealer*; 芸者・げいしゃ *geisha*; 後継者・こうけいしゃ *successor*; 雇用者・こようしゃ *employer*; 作者・さくしゃ *author, writer*; 参加者・さんかしゃ *participant*; 死者・ししゃ *dead person*; 視聴者・しちょうしゃ *viewer*; 失業者・しつぎょうしゃ *unemployed person*; 支配者・しはいしゃ *ruler*; 勝者・しょうしゃ *winner*; 初心者・しょしんしゃ *beginner*; 身体障害者・しんたいしょうがいしゃ *physically handicapped person*; 製作者・せいさくしゃ *product maker*; 走者・そうしゃ *runner*; 奏者・そうしゃ *player* (of an instrument); 第三者・だいさんしゃ *third party*; 打者・だしゃ *batter, hitter*; 著者・ちょしゃ *author*; 当事者・とうじしゃ *the person involved*; 同乗者・どうじょうしゃ *fellow rider*; 当選者・とうせんしゃ *successful candidate*; 読者・どくしゃ *reader*; 配偶者・はいぐうしゃ *one's spouse*; 反対者・はんたいしゃ *opponent*; 筆者・ひっしゃ *writer, author*; 文学者・ぶんがくしゃ *literary person, writer*; 編者・へんしゃ *editor, compiler*; 申込者・もうしこみしゃ *applicant*; 労働者・ろうどうしゃ *laborer*

〜手・しゅ
person with a skill or role

運転手・うんてんしゅ *driver*; 歌手・かしゅ *singer*; 騎手・きしゅ *rider, jockey*; 交換手・こうかんしゅ (telephone) *operator*; 助手・じょしゅ *assistant*; 選手・せんしゅ *athlete, player*; 狙撃手・そげきしゅ *sniper, sharpshooter*; 投手・とうしゅ *pitcher*; 捕手・ほしゅ *catcher*

(See 〜手・て below.)

~中・じゅう throughout	家中・いえじゅう throughout the house; 一日中・いちにちじゅう all day 一年中・いちねんじゅう throughout the year; 学校中・がっこうじゅう throughout school; 島中・しまじゅう throughout an island; 親戚中・しんせきじゅう in all relatives; 世界中・せかいじゅう throughout the world; 夏中・なつじゅう all summer; 年内中・ねんないじゅう within the year; 日本中・にほんじゅう throughout Japan; 庭中・にわじゅう throughout the garden; 一晩中・ひとばんじゅう all night long; 町中・まちじゅう throughout the town

(See ~中・ちゅう below.)

~主義・しゅぎ -ism	印象主義・いんしょうしゅぎ impressionism; 営利主義・えいりしゅぎ commercialism; 快楽主義・かいらくしゅぎ epicureanism; 共産主義・きょうさんしゅぎ Communism; 現実主義・げんじつしゅぎ realism; 合理主義・ごうりしゅぎ rationalism; 個人主義・こじんしゅぎ individualism; 菜食主義・さいしょくしゅぎ vegetarianism; 自然主義・しぜんしゅぎ naturalism; 資本主義・しほんしゅぎ capitalism; 写実主義・しゃじつしゅぎ realism; マルクス主義 Marxism; 民主主義・みんしゅしゅぎ democracy; 利己主義・りこしゅぎ selfishness, egoism; 理想主義・りそうしゅぎ idealism; ロマン主義 romanticism

~所・しょ・じょ institution, place	居場所・いばしょ one's whereabouts; 休憩所・きゅうけいじょ rest area; 教習所・きょうしゅうじょ school; 近所・きんじょ neighborhood; 刑務所・けいむしょ prison; 研究所・けんきゅうじょ research laboratory; 高所・こうしょ a high place; ゴミ収集所・ゴミしゅうしゅうじょ trash collection place; 裁判所・さいばんしょ Supreme Court; 事務所・じむしょ office; 市役所・しやくしょ city hall; 収容所・しゅうようじょ concentration camp; 出張所・しゅっちょうじょ branch office; 洗面所・せんめんじょ bathroom, washroom; 測候所・そっこうじょ weather station; 託児所・たくじしょ nursery, day care center; 停留所・ていりゅうじょ bus stop; 鉄工所・てっこうじょ iron works; 派出所・はしゅつじょ police box; 発電所・はつでんしょ power station

(See ~所・ところ below.)

~上・じょう from the viewpoint of, viewed in light of	医学上の・いがくじょう medical; 一身上の・いっしんじょう personal; 行きがかり上・いきがかりじょう by force of circumstance; 仕事の関係上・かんけいじょう in relationship to work; 教育上・きょういくじょう from the educational point of view; 行政上・ぎょうせいじょう from an administrative point of view, administratively; 健康上・けんこうじょう from the view of health; 宗教上・しゅうきょうじょう religiously; 通行上・つうこうじょう from the point of view of transportation; 商売の都合上・つご

うじょう *from the view of convenience for work*; 道義上・どうぎじょう *in light of the motion* (e.g. to adjourn); 理論上・りろんじょう *from a theoretical point of view*; 法律上・ほうりつじょう *legally*

〜状・じょう -shaped, -like 渦巻き状の・うずまきじょう *spiral shaped*; 液状の・えきじょう *liquid, fluid*; 円筒状の・えんとうじょう *cylindrical*; 帯状の・おびじょう *long, narrow* (strip of anything); 粉状の・こなじょう *granular*; ゼリー状の *jelly-like, gelatinous*; 箱状の・はこじょう *box-like*; 半円状の・はんえんじょう *semi-circular*; 袋状の・ふくろじょう *bag-like, pouch-shaped*; 粉末状の・ふんまつじょう *powdered*; 棒状の・ぼうじょう *stick-shaped*

〜場・じょう place for an event to take place 運動場・うんどうじょう *playground, sports field*; 宴会場・えんかいじょう *banquet hall*; 会場・かいじょう *meeting place*; 球場・きゅうじょう *baseball field*; 競技場・きょうぎじょう *stadium, athletic field*; 漁場・ぎょじょう *fishery*; 工場・こうじょう・こうばい *factory*; ゴルフ場 *golf course*; 式場・しきじょう *ceremonial hall*; 戦場・せんじょう *battlefield*; 駐車場・ちゅうしゃじょう *parking lot*; 道場・どうじょう *dojo*; 飛行場・ひこうじょう *airport*; 牧場・ぼくじょう *ranch, farm*; 野球場・やきゅうじょう *baseball field*; 浴場・よくじょう *public bath*; 練習場・れんしゅうじょう *practice field*

(See 〜場・ば below.)

〜人・じん person of a race, residence, nationality, speciality アジア人 *Asian*; アメリカ人 *American*; オーストラリア人 *Australian*; 異邦人・いほうじん *foreigner, stranger*; 宇宙人・うちゅうじん *alien*; 欧米人・おうべいじん *Westerners*; 外国人・がいこくじん *foreigner*; 外人・がいじん *foreigner*; 火星人・かせいじん *Martian*; 韓国人・かんこくじん (South) *Korean*; 軍人・ぐんじん *member of the armed forces*; 芸能人・げいのうじん *entertainer*; 原始人・げんしじん *primitive man*; 現代人・げんだいじん *modern man*; 詩人・しじん *poet*; 社会人・しゃかいじん *a member of society*; 西洋人・せいようじん *Westerner*; 台湾人・たいわんじん *Taiwanese*; 知識人・ちしきじん *an intellectual*; 中国人・ちゅうごくじん *Chinese*; 東京人・とうきょうじん *Tokyo resident*; 民間人・みんかんじん *civilian*; ユダヤ人 *a Jew*

(See 〜人・にん below.)

〜製・せい made in, made from イギリス製 *Made in England*; イタリア製 *Made in Italy*; 米国製・べいこくせい *Made in the USA*; 革製・かわせい *made of leather*; 絹製・きぬせい *made of silk*; 銀製・ぎんせい *made of silver*; 純金製・じゅんきんせい *made of pure gold*; 手製・てせい *made by hand*; 銅製・どうせい *made of copper, bronze*; ドイツ製 *Made in Germany*; 日本製・にほんせい *Made in Japan*; ナイロン製 *made of nylon*; 木製・もくせい *made of wood*

～代・だい *era, age*	４０代・よんじゅうだい *the 40s* (period of a century, period of one's life); ７０代・ななじゅうだい *the 70s*; １０代・じゅうだい *teens*; etc.
～代・だい *successive*	三代・さんだい *third generation, number three*; 三代目・さんだいめ *third generation*; 第三十代天皇・だいさんじゅうだいてんのう *the emper-or of the thirtieth generation, thirtieth successive emperor*; 第五十代横綱・ だいごじゅうだいよこづな *the fiftieth successive grand champion sumo wrestler*
～代・だい *charge, rate, price*	印刷代・いんさつだい *printing costs*; 飲食代・いんしょくだい *food and drink costs*; ガス代 *cost of gas* (for heating, etc.); 切手代・きってだい *price of stamps*; 薬代・くすりだい *price of medicine*; コピー代 *copy price*; 車代・くるまだい *car expenses, rental car cost*; 診察代・しんさつだい *cost of a medical examination*; 洗濯代・せんたくだい *cleaning cost*; タクシー代 *taxi fare*; 電気代・でんきだい *electricity costs*; 電話代・でんわだい *telephone rates*; 箱代・はこだい *charge per box*; 場所代・ばしょだい *location costs*; 部屋代・へやだい *room rent*; ホテル代 *hotel rates*; 本代・ほんだい *payment for books*; 洋服代・ようふくだい *cost of clothing*
～だらけ *full of, covered with*	くずだらけ *full of trash*; 毛だらけ・けだらけ *covered with hair*; 欠点だらけ・けってんだらけ *full of faults, defects*; 粉だらけ・こなだらけ *covered with dust, powder*; ゴミだらけ *full of trash, covered in trash*; 借金だらけ・しゃっきんだらけ *deep in debt*; 血だらけ・ちだらけ *covered in blood*; 泥だらけ・どろだらけ *covered in mud*; 灰だらけ・はいだらけ *covered in ash*; 誇りだらけ・ほこりだらけ (overly) *full of pride* (sarcastic); 間違いだらけ・まちがいだらけ *full of errors*
～中・ちゅう *in the middle of*	海水中・かいすいちゅう *in saltwater, in the ocean*; 空気中・くうきちゅう *in the air*; 血液中・けつえきちゅう *in the blood*; 大気中・たいきちゅう *atmospheric, in the air*; 唾液中・だえきちゅう *in saliva*; 地中・ちちゅう *in earth, in soil*
	(See ～中・ちゅう immediately below and ～中・じゅう above.)
～中・ちゅう *during*	会議中・かいぎちゅう *in a meeting*; 開拓中・かいたくちゅう *during cultivation*; 検査中・けんさちゅう *under examination*; 検討中・けんとうちゅう *under investigation*; 工事中・こうじちゅう *under construction*; 午前中・ごぜんちゅう *during the morning*; 今週中・こんしゅうちゅう *during this week*; 仕事中・しごとちゅう *during work, at work*; 授業中・じゅぎょうちゅう *in class, during a lecture*; 準備中・じゅんびちゅう *in preparation*; 食事中・しょくじちゅう *while eating, during a meal*; 先月中・せんげつちゅう *during last month*; 戦時中・せんじちゅう *in wartime*; 戦争中・せんそうちゅう *during war*; 掃除中・そうじちゅう *during cleaning*; 滞在中・た

いざいちゅう *while staying, visiting*; テスト中 *during an exam*; 電話中・でんわちゅう *on the phone*; 取り込み中・とりこみちゅう *being very busy*; 夏休み中・なつやすみちゅう *during summer vacation*; 話し中・はなしちゅう *talking, busy* (on the phone); 勉強中・べんきょうちゅう *during studying*; 旅行中・りょこうちゅう *while traveling*

(See 〜中・ちゅう immediately above and 〜中・じゅう further above.)

〜手・て *person with role as* 〜	歌い手・うたいて *singer*; 売り手・うりて *seller*; 追っ手・おって *pursuer*; 買い手・かいて *buyer*; 書き手・かきて *writer, author*; 貸し手・かして *lender*; 語り手・かたりて *narrator, story-teller*; 借り手・かりて *borrower, tenant*; 聞き手 *hearer, listener*; 使い手・つかいて *user*; 話し手・はなして *speaker*; やり手 *a person of ability*; もらい手 *recipient*

(See 〜手・しゅ above.)

〜所・ところ *place, time*	行き所・いきどころ *destination*; 居所・いどころ *one's whereabouts*; 米所・こめどころ *rice-producing area*; 台所・だいどころ *kitchen*; つかみ所のない・つかみどころのない *pointless, vague, elusive*; 出所・でところ *a source* (of information); 泣き所・なきどころ *weak point*; 見所・みどころ *highlight, good point*

(See 〜所・しょ・じょ above.)

〜人・にん *person who does*	案内人・あんないにん *a guide*; 受取人・うけとりにん *recipient, receiver*; 見物人・けんぶつにん *sightseer, tourist*; 差出し人・さしだしにん *sender*; 死人・しにん *dead person*; 支配人・しはいにん *manager*; 住人・じゅうにん *resident*; 商人・しょうにん *merchant*; 商売人・しょうばいにん *retailer, trades person*; 相続人・そうぞくにん *heir*; 代理人・だいりにん *agent, representative*; 仲買人・なかがいにん *a broker*; 被選挙人・ひせんきょにん *a person eligible for election*; 保証人・ほしょうにん *guarantor*; 見張り人・みはりにん *a guard, lookout*

(See 〜人・じん above.)

〜場・ば *place for, place to do*	足場・あしば *footing, scaffolding*; 市場・いちば *market* (for goods food); 売り場・売場・うりば *sales counter, shop*; 置き場・おきば *a place for*; 踊り場・おどりば *staircase landing*; 酒場・さかば *bar, pub*; 修羅場・しゅらば *battle scene*; 職場・しょくば *one's workplace*; 溜まり場・たまりば *rendezvous, artist hangout*; 乗り場・のりば *station, terminal*; 波止場・はとば *wharf, pier*; 船着場・船着き場・ふなつきば *harbor, port*; 持ち場・もちば *one's post, one's round, one's beat*

(See 〜場・じょう above.)

〜費・ひ
expense, cost

維持費・いじひ *maintenance costs*; 医療費・いりょうひ *medical expenses*; 教育費・きょういくひ *educational expenses, tuition*; 交際費・こうさいひ *social expenses, entertainment costs*; 工事費・こうじひ *construction costs*; 交通費・こうつうひ *transportation costs*; 光熱費・こうねつひ *lighting and heating expenses*; 娯楽費・ごらくひ *recreation expenses*; 食料費・しょくりょうひ *food costs*; 修理費・しゅうりひ *repair costs*; 人件費・じんけんひ *personal expenses*; 生活費・せいかつひ *cost of living*; 設備費・せつびひ *equipment costs*; 暖房費・だんぼうひ *heating costs*; 入院費・にゅういんひ *hospitalization costs*; 燃料費・ねんりょうひ *fuel costs, the cost of fuel*; 冷房費・れいぼうひ *cooling costs*

〜風・ふう
style,
looking like

英国風・えいこくふう *English style*; エスニック風 *ethnic style*; 欧米風・おうべいふう *Western style*; 学者風・がくしゃふう *scholarly, like a scholar*; 学生風・がくせいふう *looking like a student*; 現代風・げんだいふう *modern style*; 職人風・しょくにんふう *craftsman style*; 西洋風・せいようふう *Western style*; 中華風・ちゅうかふう *Chinese food style*; 中世風・ちゅうせいふう *medieval style*; 勤め人風・つとめにんふう *employed person's style, worker style*; 東洋風・とうようふう *Oriental, Eastern*; 日本風・にほんふう *Japanese style*; 昔風・むかしふう *old-style*

〜分・ぶん
worth,
amount

一ヶ月分・いっかげつぶん *one month's worth*; 一年分・いちねんぶん *one year's worth*; 五人分・ごにんぶん *five people's worth*; 今月分・こんげつぶん *this month's amount*; 十ドル分・じゅうどるぶん *ten dollar's worth*; 増加分・ぞうかぶん *increased amount*; 不足分・ふそくぶん *shortage amount*; 来年度分・らいねんどぶん *next fiscal year's amount*

〜味・み
-ness
hint of

青味・あおみ *blueness, greenness*; 暖かみ・あたたかみ *warmth*; 厚み・あつみ *thickness*; ありがたみ *thankfulness*; 重み・おもみ *weight, heft*; 面白み・おもしろみ *interest, degree to which something is amusing*; 悲しみ・かなしみ *sadness*; 親切味・しんせつみ *kindness*; 真剣味・しんけんみ *seriousness, earnestness*; 新鮮味・しんせんみ *freshness*; 楽しみ・たのしみ *pleasure, enjoyment*; 深み・ふかみ *depth*; 弱み・よわみ *weakness*

(A word such as 深み *depth, deepness* should be contrasted with 深さ *depth* (page 108). 〜み is basically unproductive (occurring with a fixed number of words) while the 〜さ suffix is productive with adjectives and nominal adjectives. In terms of their meanings, words with 〜み refer to a hint of, point of, or place of, something that is not objectively measureable, so 深み refers to depth in the sense of vast space or depth of character. Words with 〜さ refer to an objective whole or entity, so that 深さ, for example, refers to the depth of the ocean or the depth of a pool.)

～目・め
-th (one)

一番目・いちばんめ *number one, first*; 二つ目・ふたつめ *second one*; 三人目・さんにんめ *third person*; 四回目・よんかいめ *fourth time*; 五列目・ごれつめ *fifth row*; 六行目・ろくぎょうめ *sixth column*; 七年目・ななねんめ *seventh year*; 十日目・とおかめ *tenth day*; etc.

～目・め
state of,
point of

落ち目・おちめ *decline of fortune*; 変わり目・かわりめ *change, turning point*; つなぎ目 *a joint, a join*; 縫い目・ぬいめ *seam, suture*; 控え目の・ひかえめ *moderate, temperate*; 結び目・むすびめ *knot, tie, bend*; 弱り目・よわりめ *point of weakness*, 弱り目にたたり目 *misfortunes never come singly*

(This suffix combines with verbal stems and can be contrasted with ～目・め immediately below which combines with adjectival stems.)

～目・め
quality

厚め・あつめ *on the thick side, thicker rather than thinner*; 薄め・うすめ *on the thin side*; 多め・おおめ *many* (not fewer); 大きめ・おおきめ *on the large side*; 少なめ・すくなめ *on the few side, at the least*; 高め・たかめ *on the expensive side, higher rather than lower*; 小さめ・ちいさめ *smaller rather than larger*; 長め・ながめ *on the long side*; 早め・はやめ *earlier* (not later); 細め・ほそめ *on the thin, slender side*; 短め・みじかめ *on the short side*; 低め・ひくめ *on the low, short side*

(Many of the words here also occur regularly as adverbs with に, e.g. 少(すく)なめに *at the least*, 早(はや)めに (come) *earlier*, etc. This suffix combines with adjectival stems and can be contrasted with ～目・め immediately above which combines with verbal stems.)

～面・めん
aspect of

運営面・うんえいめん *management-side, point of view*; 技術面・ぎじゅつめん *technological aspect*; 財政面・ざいせいめん *financial aspect*; 資金面・しきんめん *funding aspect*; 税金面・ぜいきんめん *taxing point of view*

(All of these alternate with expressions like 運営(うんえい)の面(めん).)

～物・もの
thing, object

揚げ物・あげもの *deep-fried food*; 洗い物・あらいもの *washing*; 売り物・うりもの *things for sale*; 贈り物・おくりもの *a gift*; 落とし物・おとしもの *something lost* (or found); 織物・おりもの *fabric, something woven*; 買い物・かいもの *shopping, things bought*; 着物・きもの *clothing*; 建物・たてもの *a building*; 食べ物・たべもの *food*; 忘れ物・わすれもの *something forgotten*

(See page 109 for a comparison with こと and の.)

～屋・や *person with* *a quality*	お天気屋・おてんきや *moody, fickle person*; 頑張り屋・がんばりや *an eager beaver*; 気取り屋・きどりや *affected person, snob*; 寂しがり屋・さびしがりや *desolate, lonely person, person who easily feels loneliness*; 締まり屋・しまりや *thrifty, frugal person*; 恥ずかしがり屋・はずかしがりや *shy, bashful person*; やかましや *fastidious, particular person*; 分からず屋・わからずや *obstinate person, a blockhead*
～屋・や *store*	米屋・こめや *rice store*; 魚屋・さかなや *fish store*; 葬儀屋・そうぎや *funeral parlor*; 畳屋・たたみや *tatami store*; 田中屋・たなかや *the Tanaka family store*; たばこ屋 *tobacconist*; 電気屋・でんきや *electronics store*; 肉屋・にくや *butcher*; 飲み屋・のみや *bar, pub*; パン屋 *bread store, bakery*; 本屋・ほんや *book store*; 米屋・こめや *rice store*

(Some expressions with the meaning *store* are sarcastically extended to the meaning *professional*: 技術屋・ぎじゅつや *technician*; 政治屋・せいじや *politician* (very negative); ダフ屋・や *ticket scalper*)

～様・よう *method*	言う・言いよう・いいよう *way of saying*; 書く・書きよう・かきよう *way of writing*; 助ける・助けよう・たすけよう *way of saving*; 止める・止めよう・とめよう *way of stop- ping*; 直す・直しよう・なおしよう *method for fixing*; 始める・始めよう・はじめよう *way of beginning*; 見る・見よう・みよう *way of seeing*; やる・やりよう *way of doing*; 呼ぶ・呼びよう・よびよう *way of calling*

(Compare with ～方・かた above. An expression such as 直しよう・なお refers to a procedure for fixing something, as opposed to the manner in which it is done, i.e. carefully or quickly or badly. Most commonly one says that there is or is not such a procedure, i.e. 言いようがない *there is no way to say this* or 止めようがあるかどうかわからない *I don't know if there is a way to stop this or not*. The most common expression overall here is しようがない *There is no other way for it to be, nothing to be done* which also occurs in しようがないやつ meaning *a useless guy*.)

～用・よう *for the* *use of*	学生用・がくせいよう *for student use*; 家庭用・かていよう *for household use*; 子供用・こどもよう *for children to use*; ゴルフ用 *for use in golf*; 教師用・きょうしよう *for teacher use*; 自家用・じかよう *for private use, family use*; 実験用・じっけんよう *for experimental use*; 事務用・じむよう *for office use*; 社内用・しゃないよう *for company internal use*; 商売用・しょうばいよう *for business use*; 初心者用・しょしんしゃよう *for use by a beginner*; 非常用・ひじょうよう *for emergency use*; 婦人用・ふじんよう *for women*; 冬用・ふゆよう *for winter use*; 来客用・らいきゃくよう *for guests to use*; 練習用・れんしゅうよう *for practice*

〜料・りょう   運送料・うんそうりょう *shipping charge*; 購読料・こうどくりょう *sub-*
fee, charge   *scription fee*; サービス料 *service charge*; 参加料・さんかりょう *partici-*
                pation charge, entry fee; 宿泊料・しゅくはくりょう *hotel charges*; 授業料・
                じゅぎょうりょう *school fees, tuition*; 受験料・じゅけんりょう *examina-*
                tion fee; 使用料・しようりょう *usage fee*; 診察料・しんさつりょう
                doctor's fee; 水道料・すいどうりょう *water charges, rates*; 席料・せきりょ
                う *seating charge, cover charge*; 通行料・つうこうりょう *a toll*; 通信料・
                つうしんりょう *communication charges*; 手数料・てすうりょう *service*
                charge, commission; テレビ放映料・テレビほうえいりょう *TV broadcast*
                fee; 電気料・でんきりょう *electricity charge*; 電話料・でんわりょう
                telephone charge; 入場料・にゅうじょうりょう *admission fee*

2.2.4.4 Suffixes for names

These suffixes are attached to pronouns, proper names, and to words which refer to people
or groups of people.

   As the correct term of address is always crucial (see page 233 of Chapter 3), the correct
suffix on the name is also important. When in doubt use 〜さん. Use familiar suffixes in
particular only when you are sure, and never use a familiar suffix with someone who is
your social superior, regardless of how such a person addresses you.

〜さん   A polite suffix which can mean *Mr., Mrs., Miss, Ms.* when attached to
            proper names, but which can also make certain titles or professional names
            polite, e.g. お医者さん *doctor*, お父さん *father*, お母さん *mother*, 事務員
            さん *clerk, office worker*, お巡りさん *policeman*, お客さん *guest*, etc. 〜さ
            ん is never attached to the speaker's own name or to the name of anyone in
            the speaker's relevant group (unless you are addressing that person).

            Further examples: 社長さん・しゃちょうさん *Mr. Company President*; 魚
            屋さん・さかなやさん *Mr. Fishmonger*; 歯医者さん・はいしゃさん *Mr.*
            Dentist; etc.

〜様・さま   A suffix for people which is significantly more polite that 〜さん. Its use
            in speech is limited to formal and ritualistic interactions, although certain
            words such as お客様 and 皆様 are quite common even in spoken Japa-
            nese. 〜様 more so than 〜さん is never used with the name of anyone in
            the speaker's in-group (again unless you are addressing that person; then
            one might hear something like a young woman addressing her father お父
            様). In writing, this suffix is seen most commonly after the name of the
            addressee on the front of an envelope (see page 303).

Further examples: 神様・かみさま *God*; 仏様・ほとけさま *Buddha*; 殿様・とのさま *feudal lord*; 御馳走様・ごちそうさま *Thank you for the meal*; お粗末様・おそまつさま *You're welcome* (after being thanked for dinner); ご苦労様・ごくろうさま *Good job, Thank you for your effort*

〜殿・どの   Used after the name of the addressee on business and professional corre-spondence which is addressed to an individual (山本昭子殿) or to a partic-ular title (係長殿) and not to an institution or company name. See page 303 for addressing letters to an institution or company.

〜君・くん   A suffix typically for boys and young men used by their equals or their superiors. Its usage brings with it a certain sense of intimacy or responsi-bility (particularly when used by someone older to address someone younger). It is not generally used to address girls, although this may be accepted between some friends. Recently, the trend has been to reduce the distinctions made in addressing men and women. On the one hand, more and more women and girls use 〜君 instead of the diminutive 〜ちゃん when talking to or about other women (friends, classmates, co-workers). In more established circles (particularly in government), there is a movement to use 〜さん all of the time in response to the pervasive presence of the elite "old-boy" network (whose members have been using 〜君 since their student days at Japan's best universities).

〜ちゃん   A diminutive suffix for close friends and relatives (instead of 〜さん). In elementary schools, boys are typically addressed with 〜君 while girls are addressed with 〜ちゃん or 〜さん. The nicknames of childhood, includ-ing 〜君 or 〜ちゃん, are often used throughout the lives of everyone within a family or a circle of friends (in much the same way that my aunts and uncles call me *Billy* to this very day; recall also the passage on page 13). In a romantic relationship, either individual may address the other with 〜ちゃん, although the male partner is more likely to use the term to address the female partner. In more neutral situations outside of the fam-ily, in a circle of college friends or in an office amongst younger workers, for example, 〜ちゃん may be used by women when addressing each oth-er. It may also be used when a man addresses a women although it can be offensive and should be used with care. Nicknames with 〜ちゃん are of-ten shortened to two moras. 恵子ちゃん becomes けいちゃん. 道子ちゃん would probably become みいちゃん. ケンちゃん in the conversation on page 23 might be a nickname for 健二, 健一, 健一郎, etc.

〜氏・し   A more formal (generally written) version of 〜さん. Unlike 〜様, 〜氏 is not really an honorific and is simply more professional sounding. It is often heard in companies when speaking of customers or business partners. It is probably more common with the names of men than with women, and it is used consistently in newspapers.

〜達・たち   A plural marker which is limited to animate (generally human) individuals. It can be attached to pronouns (私たち), proper names (渡辺さん達),
plural   words which refer to humans (女の人たち, 学生たち), and sometimes to words which refer to pets (犬たち). It is neither honorific nor familiar. Unlike the English plural, 〜たち (as well as all of the other plural markers discussed here) means *group of* rather than simply *more than one*. In this sense it might be considered a *collective* marker rather than a simple plural marker. For example:

私たち・私達

us, we, the group of people with me

僕たち・僕達

us, we (male), *the group of people with me* (male)

山田さん達

the Yamada family, the set of people in the room who are named Yamada, the group of people on Yamada's team, the group of people who came in with Yamada

学生達

a group of students, the students (under discussion), *the students standing over there*

うちの犬達

our dogs

Compare:

学生たちが入ってきた。*A group of students came in.*

学生が入ってきた。*A student came in. Some students came in. Students* (and not teachers) *came in.*

どの学生たちが入ってきたの？ *Which set* (team) *of students came in?*

This last example may strike some as odd because it only makes sense in a situation where the students are already divided up into groups or teams. The point, of course, is that the sentence does not mean just: *Which students came in?*

～等・ら plural	An informal plural marker used with pronouns and proper names: 僕ら, 山田ら, 社長ら, 我ら, これら, etc. It is very common in newspapers. Again, it refers to some group rather than meaning just more than one, and it may express humility, familiarity, or mild contempt. A combination like 私等 makes no sense because of the mismatch of polite (わたくし) and informal (～ら) styles (and both 私ら and 我ら are more usual).
～共・ども humble plural	An informal plural marker used with first person pronouns and nouns: 私ども. When used with first person pronouns it is perceived a humble. When used with nouns it conveys a relatively strong sense of contempt (stronger than that associated with ～ら). Examples: 犬ども・いぬども *dogs*; 男ども・おとこども *men*; 女ども・おんなども *women*; 家来共・けらいども *retainers, vassals*; 手前共・てまえども *you, us*; 者共・ものども *people*; 私共・わたくしども *us*
～方・がた honorific plural	As an honorific plural, this suffix occurs basically with second person: あなた方, and with some nouns, 先生方 or お母さん方. Like the word あなた, あなた方 should be avoided whenever possible in polite speech. Again, a combination like 君方 does not make a great deal of sense because 君 is very familiar and ～方 is very polite. 方 alone is a polite word for 人 *person*, while 方々 as in その方々 is a polite version of 人々 *people*. Examples: あなた方・あなたがた *you* (plural); お偉方・おえらがた *you, VIP* (sarcastic); お兄様方・おにいさまがた *older brothers*; お姉様方・おねえさまがた *older sisters*; 奥様方・おくさまがた *wives*; あそこにいらっしゃる方々・あそこにいらっしゃるかたがた *those people over there*; 御夫人方・ごふじんがた *wives*; 先生方・せんせいがた *teachers*; 皆様方・みなさまがた *everyone*
～家・け clan, family name	徳川家 *the Tokugawa family, the Tokugawa line, the Tokugawa clan*, etc. This suffix is found most commonly in books. It appears also on family tombstones and with the names of families with royal lineage.
～屋・や store, shop	三河屋 *the Mikawa family store*, etc. ～屋 is used in words like 本屋 or 米屋 to indicate a store which sells a product like books or rice. After a family name, it indicates a family business of some kind (or serves to give that impression, cf. 明治屋 which is the name of a large corporation that never was a family business).

2.2.4.5 *Grammatical suffixes*

The suffixes discussed in this section affect the grammar of a class of words rather than affecting the meaning of the word, per se. For example, they change any adjective into a noun or any verb into a noun. Most of these affixes are written in ひらがな, and it might be more correct to treat some of them as grammatical endings. Note that a number of the suffixes here attach not to independent words, per se, but to verbal and adjectival stems (i.e. verbs without ～ます and adjectives without ～い.)

～さ nominal adjective ⇄ noun	きれい・きれいさ *prettiness*; 静か・静かさ・しずかさ *quietness*; 誠実・誠実さ・せいじつ *honesty, sincerity*; 単純・単純さ・たんじゅん *simplicity, simpleness*; 真面目・真面目さ・まじめ *seriousness*; 複雑・複雑さ・ふくくざつさ *complexity*; 不愉快・不愉快さ・ふゆかいさ *unpleasantness*; 利口・利口さ・りこうさ *cleverness*; 立派・りっぱさ *degree of excellence*
～さ adjective ⇄ noun	明るい・明るさ・あかるさ *brightness*; 暖かい・暖かさ・あたたかさ *warmth*; 暑い・暑さ・あつさ *heat*; 美しい・美しさ・うつくしさ *beauty*; うれしい・うれしさ *happiness*; 大きい・大きさ・おおきさ *bigness, size*; 恐ろしい・恐ろしさ・おそろしさ *fright, dread, awfulness*; 重い・重さ・おもさ *heaviness, weight*; 面白い・面白さ・おもしろさ *interest, degree of interest*; 堅い・堅さ・かたさ *hardness, stiffness*; 悲しい・悲しさ・かなしさ *sadness*; 苦しい・苦しさ・くるしさ *suffering; frustration*; 寂しい・寂しさ・さびしさ *loneliness, sadness*; 親しい・親しさ・したしさ *intimacy*; すごい・すごさ *wonderful-ness, awfulness, (extremely stimulating)*; 高い・高さ・たかさ *height*; 強い・強さ・つよさ *strength*; 長い・長さ・ながさ *length*; 早い・早さ・はやさ *earliness*; 速い・速さ・はやさ *speed*; 広い・広さ・ひろさ *width, breadth*; 太い・太さ・ふとさ *thickness, girth*; 優しい・優しさ・やさしさ *niceness, kindness*; 若い・若さ・わかさ *youth, youngness*; 悪い・悪さ・わるさ *badness*

Derivations which are themselves adjectival (and subject to ～さ)
伸びる・伸びやすい・伸びやすさ・のびやすさ *easiness to stretch*
力がない・力のない・力のなさ・ちからのなさ *powerlessness*
会う・会いたい・会いたさ・あいたさ *desire to meet*
頭がよい・頭のよい・頭のよさ・あたまのよさ *good-headedness, brains*
理屈・理屈っぽい・理屈っぽさ *reasonableness*
かわいらしい・かわいらしさ *prettiness*

(Where there is more than one Chinese character for a particular adjective, ～さ applies equally to all of them. For example: 暑い・暑さ・厚い become 厚さ・熱い・熱さ. See page 101 for a comparison of ～さ and ～み.)

～∅ adjective ⇄ noun	青い・青・あお *the color blue*; 赤い・赤・あか *the color red*; 黄色い・黄色・きいろ *the color yellow*; 黒い・黒・くろ *the color black*; 白い・白・しろ *the color white*; 茶色い・茶色・ちゃいろ *the color brown*

(The noun forms here all refer to the color itself, as in *What is your favorite color?* This alternation is basically limited to those colors listed here.)

～的・てき noun ⇄ nominal adjective	アメリカ的 *American*; 一般的・いっぱん *general, ordinary*; 印象的・いんしょう *impressionistic*; 科学的・かがく *scientific*; 基本的・きほん *fundamental, basic*; 教育的・きょういく *educational*; 金銭的・きんせん *cash (sale)*; 具体的・ぐたい *concrete* (not *abstract*); 軍事的・ぐんじ *military*; 経済的・けいざい *economic*; 形式的・けいしき *formal*; 芸術的・げいじゅつ *artistic*; 決定的・けってい *conclusive, final, decisive*; 健康的・けんこう *healthy*; 現代的・げんだい *modern, up-to-date*; 個人的・こじん *individual, private*; 社会的・しゃかい *social*; 消極的・しょうきょく *negative* (not *positive*), *passive* (not *active*); 心理的・しんり *psychological*; 政治的・せいじ *political*; 精神的・せいしん *spiritual, mental*; 積極的・せっきょく *positive, up-beat* (not *negative*), *active* (not *passive*); 定期的・ていき *regular, periodical*; 抽象的・ちゅうしょう *abstract* (not *concrete*); 日本的・にほん *Japanese*; 本格的・ほんかく *real, full-scale, complete*; 理想的・りそう *ideal*; 論理的・ろんり *logical*

(All ～的 words are nominal adjectives. Like most nominal adjectives, adding a に turns them into adverbs: 科学的に *scientifically*, 具体的に *concretely*; 決定的に *decisively*, etc.)

～∅ verb ⇄ noun	遊びます・遊び・あそび *playing, relaxation*; 受け付けます・受付・うけつけ *registration*; 生まれます・生まれ・うまれ *birth*; 代わります・代わり・かわり *a change, seconds*; 帰ります・帰り・かえり *returning home*; 調べます・調べ・しらべ *investigation*; 育ちます・育ち・そだち *bringing up, raising* (a child); 話します・話し・話・はなし *speaking, talk*; 晴れます・晴れ・はれ *clear* (weather); 申し込みます・申し込み・もうしこみ *application*; 休みます・休み・やすみ *rest, vacation*; 行きます・行き・行・ゆき *going to, bound for*; 笑います・笑い・わらい *laughter*

(This is a very common alternation and the list of words given here is far from complete. Note that the ひらがな on the noun form is sometimes optional.)

こと・の verb ⇄ noun	Both of these forms change verbs into nouns (and it is not really clear that these two elements are real suffixes). The only difficulty is in distinguishing between the meaning of the こと form and the の form. Briefly, こと seems to refer to information or factual matters, while の seems to refer to

events or things which happen. Compare the implications of the following
pairs of examples.

ピアノを弾いていることを聞いた。（こと）
I heard that he had been playing the piano. (a fact)
ピアノを弾いているのを聞いた。（の）
I heard him playing the piano. (I heard actual piano playing)
明日雨が降ることをイーメールで伝えた。（こと）
I let them know by e-mail that it would rain tomorrow. (a fact)
明日雨が降るのをイーメールで伝えた。（の）
I let them know by e-mail about the raining tomorrow.
(This is as strange in Japanese as it is in English because one cannot convey an event of raining by any means, let alone by e-mail)
アメリカ生活が長くて、お茶を入れることを忘れた。（こと）
*I have lived in America for a long time, and I have forgotten the custom
of making tea.* (the custom is what is forgotten)
お茶を入れるのを忘れて、お客さんに失礼だった。（の）
I forgot to serve tea which was rude to my guests. (a specific instance)

There are a number of verbs where one nominalizer or the other is preferred. The effect is strongest for the verbs of perception (where の is strongly
preferred). Those preferring の include: 見る, 見える, 聞く, 聞こえる, 感じ
る, 止める, and 待つ. Those preferring こと include: 考える, 命じる, and
教える. There are also specific grammatical constructions where only one
or the other can be used.

〜ことがある *have experience of* 〜
〜ことにする *decide to* 〜
〜ことになる *it turns out that* 〜
〜ことができる *possible to* 〜
来たのはジョンだ。*The one who came was John.*
ジョンが来たのは東京からだ。*The place John came from is Tokyo.*
(These last two with の are called *cleft-constructions* in linguistics.)

Finally, both こと and の contrast with 物 *thing* which refers specifically
to concrete objects: 揚げ物 *deep-fried food*, 贈り物 *a gift*, 買い物 *shopping, things bought*, 着物 *clothing*, 建物 *a building*, 食べ物 *food*, 忘れ物
something forgotten, etc. Compare 食べるの and 食べること both of
which refer to the act of eating with 食べ物 which refers only to food. The
only grammatical use of もの is as a sentence final particle where the effect
is to make the sentence more concrete. See page 223.

～い to ～む adjective ⇄ verb	怪しい・怪しむ・あやしむ *be doubtful, doubt*; 悲しい・悲しむ・かなしむ *be sad, mourn*; 苦しい・苦しむ・くるしむ *suffer, endure*; 親しい・親しむ・したしむ *enjoy, take pleasure in, be near to*; 楽しい・楽しむ・たのしむ *enjoy, take pleasure in*; 懐かしい・懐かしむ・なつかしむ *be sentimental about the past, be nostalgic*
	(This particular alternation is limited to a small set of words.)
する noun ⇄ verb	The only regular way to change a noun into a verb is to add some form of する. The grammar of these constructions as well examples are discussed in section 3.8.2 of Chapter 3 (beginning on page 228). Note also that some borrowed words become verbs because of fortunate morphology, e.g. サボる meaning *to skip class* (from *sabotage*). Further examples are found on page 123 in the next section on borrowed words.

2.3 Borrowed words

Japanese borrows extensively from other languages (although historically the most from Chinese and now from English). In the modern language, the term 外来語 refers to words borrowed generally from European languages. In contrast, Chinese words in Japanese are called 漢語. They are often referred to as Sino-Japanese words. Dictionaries of borrowed words (外来語辞典) may list as many as 20,000 words found in print, and yearly publications such as *Imidas* list hundreds of newly borrowed words each year.

Early borrowings into Japanese from European languages include words such as パン *bread*, カステラ *sponge cake*, タバコ *tobacco*, and ジュバン *undershirt*. Many of the earliest borrowings are now usually written in ひらがな or even Chinese characters, たばこ, 長襦袢, or 天ぷら, and many Japanese view them as native Japanese words. Other early words include: ゴム *rubber*, ガラス・硝子 *glass*, ギンガム *gingham*, ギヤマン *diamond*, ハム *ham*, ビール *beer*, コーヒー *coffee*, カピタン *captain*, ホック *hook*, マスト *mast*, カルテ *medical record*, コンペートー・金平糖 *a kind of sugar candy*, カッパ・合羽 *rain jacket*.

As the earlier words come principally from Portuguese (regular contact from 1542 to 1639) and later Dutch (regular contact began in 1609 and continued to influence Japanese development up to the modern era), earlier borrowings often look quite strange from an English perspective. English itself was actually introduced to Japan with the help of the Dutch (who were the only Europeans officially allowed into Japan during the period of self-imposed isolation from 1639 to 1854), and the first textbook of colloquial English was produced (for very limited circulation) in 1811. In the modern era, English borrowings are far and away the most frequent, making up just over seven percent of the Japanese lexicon. Second on the list is French with less than one percent. These are frequently cited figures from the last thorough survey of the Japanese lexicon done in 1964 by the Japanese National Language Research Institute. While more recent surveys are less systematic, the general impression is that English is more and more prevalent in the Japanese language particularly in fields such as advertising, entertainment, sports, business management, and engineering. Many early words have also been "modified" with English help, so that ギヤマン, for example, has ended up meaning *glassware* while ダイヤモンド means *diamond*. Finally, more and more Japanese words are actually being *replaced* by their borrowed equivalents.

百貨店・ひゃっかてん	→	デパート	*department store*
写真機・しゃしんき	→	カメラ	*camera*
装置端末・そうちたんまつ	→	ターミナル	*computer terminal*
査証・さしょう	→	ビザ	*visa*
葡萄酒・ぶどうしゅ	→	ワイン	*wine*

When a word is borrowed into Japanese, the sound as well as the meaning of the word may change quite dramatically. In addition, as more and more have been borrowed, foreign sounding words which are actually completely Japanese have been created. While it is not possible to list all borrowed words here, the various kinds of changes as well as strategies for understanding and using borrowed words are discussed.

2.3.1 Sound changes

With a basic sound inventory of seventeen consonants and five vowels, Japanese has significantly fewer sounds than English, which has a basic sound inventory of twenty-four consonants and twelve vowels. While there are well known consonant convergencies (for example, English *l* and *r* or English *s* and *th* end up sounding the same in Japanese), the relationship between English vowels and Japanese vowels is more subtle. It is further complicated by the fact that different speakers of English will often pronounce the same word in a variety of different ways.

A number of general points to notice. English consonant clusters are broken up with vowels in Japanese (トラベル *travel*; クラス *class*). Likewise, final consonants must be followed by a vowel (チーム *team*; コーチ *coach*). Vowel + *r* sequences usually end up as lengthened vowels in Japanese (バー *bar*; バード *bird*). An English unstressed vowel (known as a *schwa* and usually represented [ə]) is replaced by a full vowel; there are no unstressed vowels in Japanese (サーカス *circus*; チキン *chicken, etc.*). A small ッ is typically inserted after a short vowel before stops such as *k* and *t* (トラック *track*; ペット *pet*). Since Japanese has a more restricted set of possible sounds than English, it is also the case that words which are different in English may end up with the same representation in Japanese, e.g. *staff* and *stuff* (スタッフ) or *low, row, law,* and *raw* (ロー).

Lists of English words which converge to the same sound in Japanese are given below. To the degree possible, all of the English sounds which converge to that sound in

Japanese are represented, and within each list words are grouped more or less according to a common English sound. When an English word contains more than one vowel, the relevant sounds are underlined.

English vowel convergencies (representative)

Converge to ア・アー	アート *art*; アーミー *army*; アクター *actor*; アナウンサー *announcer*; アパレル *apparel*; アラーム *alarm*; アンクル *ankle, uncle*; ユタ *Utah*; カー *car*; カード *card*; カール *curl*; カラー *color, collar*; カレッジ *college*; カヌー *canoe*; サーカス *circus*; サラダ *salad*; シルバー *silver*; シャワー *shower*; スター *star*; スタジアム *stadium*; スタッフ *staff, stuff*; セーター *sweater*; セーラー *sailor*; センター *center*; ターミナル *terminal*; ドライバー *driver*; トラック *track, truck*; パー *par, per*; バースデー *birthday*; パーティ *party*; ハート *heart*; パート *part, part-timer*; バード *bird*; バーナー *burner*; ハーフ *half*; パール *pearl*; バグ *bug* (in a computer); バザー *bazaar*; バス *bath, bus*; バッグ *bag*; パット *pat*, バトン *button; putt*; ハム *ham*; バルブ *valve*; ファーザー *father*; ファーストクラス *first class*; パレード *parade*; ハロー *hello*; ハンガー *hanger*; マザー *mother*; マッサージ *massage*
Converge to イ・イー	キー *key*; チキン *chicken*; チケット *ticket*; ビル *building*; ピン *pin*; ユニコーン *unicorn*
Converge to ウ・ウー	ウルフ *wolf*; グッド *good*; ブック *book*; ビューティフル *beautiful*; フード *food, hood* (clothing); フルサービス *full-service*; ルーキー *rookie*; ルーツ *roots*; ルート *route*; ワンダフル *wonderful*;
Converge to エ・エー	アイスホッケー *ice hockey*; エコノミー *economy*; カーテン *curtain*; カクテル *cocktail*; クラスメート *classmate*; ケース *case*; ケーブル *cable*; サイレン *siren*; スケート *skate*; ステーキ *steak*; ステッキ (walking) *stick*; ステンドグラス *stained glass*; ステンレス *stainless*; スネーク *snake*; セント *cent, saint*; テーブル *table*; デトロイト *Detroit*; ネット *net*; ヘッド *head*; ベッド *bed*; ペット *pet*; ヘルシー *healthy*; ヘルメット *helmet*; ペン *pen*; メーター *meter* (distance and musical); メートル *meter* (distance); メジャー *measure*; メッセージ *message*; レザー *leather*; レバー *liver*; レベル *level*
Converge to オ・オー	コースト *coast*; コーチ *coach*; コース *course*; コート *coat, court*; コード *code, cord*; コーン *cone*; コーンフレーク *corn flakes*; コック *cook, person who cooks* (cf. クックブック *cookbook*; クッキング *cooking*; キャプテンクック *Captain Cook*); コロニー *colony*; コンサート *concert*; チョーク *choke, chalk*; トロリーバス *trolleybus*; トローリング *trolling, trawling*; トロフィー *trophy*; フォーク *folk, fork*; フロア *floor*; ホース *hose, horse*; ; ポーチ *poach, porch, pouch*; ホーム *home,* (train station) *platform*; ; ホール *hole, hall*; ボール *bowl, ball*; ポスター *poster*; ボックス *box*; ポテト *potato*; ボ

トル b*ottle*; ポンド *pound*; メロディー *mel*o*dy*; メロン *mel*o*n*; ロー *law, raw, low, row*; ローン *lawn*; ロサンジェルス *L*o*s Angeles*; ユースホステ ル *youth h*o*stel*; ヨット *yacht*

English consonant convergences (representative)

Converge to サ・ザ, etc.	ガレージ *garage*; サード *third*; サーブ *serve*; サーモスタット *thermostat*; サウス *south*; サンクス *thanks*; サンダー *thunder*; サンデー *Sunday/ sundae*; シーサイド *seaside*; シート *seat, sheet*; シールド *shield*; シーン *scene*; シアター *theater*; シガー *cigar*; シックス *six*; シック *chic*; ジッパー *zipper*; シフト *shift*; ジュース *juice, deuce* (the latter has recently become デュース); シリング *shilling*; シンガーソングライター *singer song writer*; シンクタンク *think tank*; スリー *three*; ゼウス *Zeus*; ニュース *news*; バザー・ バザール *bazaar*; ブラジャー *brassiere*; ブラジル *Brazil*; ブラザー *brother*; ブリッジ *bridge*; ブレザー *blazer* (jacket); ホース *hose*; マザー *mother*; マジック *magic* メジャー *measure, major*; レジスター *resistor, register*; レジャー *leisure*; レザー *leather, razor*
Converge to タ・ダ, etc.	キャッツ *Cats* (the musical); イム *time*; チーク *teak, cheek*; チップ・ティップ *tip*; チキン *chicken*; ツー *two*; ツール *tool*; ツアー *tour*; ツリー *tree*; テープ *tape*; テーマ *theme*; ベンツ *Benz*; ポテトチップス *potato chips*; ルーツ *roots* ロマンチック・ロマンティック *romantic*
Converge to ハ・バ, etc.	コーヒー *coffee*; テレホン・テレフォン *telephone*; バース *birth*; ハーフ *half*; ハイヒール *high heels*; バット *vat, bat*; バルブ *valve, bulb*; バンク *bank*; バンクーバー *Vancouver*; ヒューストン *Houston, TX*; フード *food, hood*; ベース *vase, base*; ベスト *vest, best*; ヘルプ *help*; ホーク・フォーク *fork*; ホーク *hawk*; ホーム・プラットホーム *platform, home*; ホイッスル *whistle*; ホイップ *whip*; ボルト *volt*; ホワイト *white*; ホンコン *Hong Kong*; ラバー *lover, rubber*
	(Recently, the various *v* sounds have been represented ヴァ, ヴィ, ヴ, ヴェ, and ヴォ instead of バ, ビ, ブ, ベ, and ボ.)
Converge to ラ, etc.	クラウン *crown, clown*; スロー *throw, slow*; ハーレム *harem, Harlem*; ブレード *braid, blade*; フライ *fry, fly*; ミール *Mir, meal*; ライター *writer, lighter*; ライト *right, light*; ライン *Rhine, line*; ラック *rack, luck*
Converge to a Japanese vowel	イースト *yeast*; イエス *yes*; イエス・イエズス *Jesus* (this is based on Latin and has recently become ジーザス); イエロー *yellow*; イヤー *year*; エール・イェール *Yale*; イアリング・イヤリング *earring*; イヤー *ear*; エアライン *airline*; ウール *wool*; ウェーター *waiter*; ウォーク *walk*; ウルフ *wolf*; ツアー *tour*; ドア *door*; ピアス *pierced earring*; フォーク *folk, fork*; ベア *bear*

Many words look unfamiliar in カタカナ not because the sounds have changed so dramatically, but because they are not actually borrowed from English: パン *bread* (Portuguese), バッハ *Bach* (German), ゴッホ *van Gogh* (Dutch), モナミ *mon amie* (French), リセ *lycée* (French), イタリア *Italy* (Italian). There are often very specific relationships between the words of one language and particular fields. Italian words, for example, dominate in music, e.g. コンチェルト *concerto*. Common Chinese place names are written in Chinese characters but pronounced more or less as they are pronounced in Chinese (and not as the same characters would be pronounced in Japanese): 北京・ペキン, 上海・シャンハイ, 香港・ホンコン. The original Chinese pronunciations preserved in Japanese may themselves be out of date, or they may reflect regional variation.

Acronyms are usually pronounced as letters but sometimes pronounced as words: アイ・ビー・エム *IBM* versus ナトー *NATO*. This is true in English as well, but which acronyms are pronounced which way does not always correspond. Some acronyms may also be uniquely Japanese: オーエル *OL* (*office lady*) or エルディーケイ *LDK* (*living, dining, kitchen*).

Usually, words which sound alike in the original language end up sounding alike in Japanese, but sometimes such homonyms end up as different words in Japanese.

antique	アンチーク (furniture, also realized アンティーク; アンチック (a type face)
chalk	チョーク (chalk for blackboards); チャコ (chalk for marking clothing)
cook	コック *cook* (of food); キャプテンクック *Captain Cook*
cork	コルク *cork*; コークスクリュー *corkscrew*
cup	コップ (cup for coffee and other hot drinks); カップ (cup, glass (actually derived from the Dutch *kop*))
glass	グラス (cup); ガラス (substance)
hood	フード (clothing); フッド *Robin Hood*
horn	ホルン・ホーン (musical instrument); ホーン (car horn)
iron	アイロン (for ironing); アイアン (golf iron)
me	ミー *me*; ミ (*mi*, the name of the musical note)
salt	ソルト (for food), サルト or ソルト (Strategic Arms Limitation Treaty)
sheet	シーツ (for a bed); シート (paper)
singles	シングルス (in tennis); シングルズ (unmarried people)
strike	ストライキ (labor action); ストライク (in baseball or bowling)

Some words sound different from what one might expect for more obscure (and often idiosyncratic) reasons. For example:

コーポ   *co-op* (based on spelling rather than pronunciation)
セーター   *sweater* (an older word)
マーガリン   *margarine* (an older word)
マツダ   *Mazda* (reflects the actual Japanese pronunciation of 松田)
ツンパ   *pants* (*underwear*, *underpants*, *pants* spelled backwards)
バイク   *motorcycle* (from *motor-bicycle*)

With respect to ツンパ, about twenty years ago, it was quite common for younger people to invert various taboo words (Japanese and borrowed). Some have entered the language more or less permanently. A recent creation along a similar line is ワイハ used instead of the standard ハワイ *Hawaii*.

Many borrowed words also have more than one Japanese spelling because of novel sound representations. For example, the sounds *va, vi, vu, ve,* and *vo* are now commonly represented as ヴァ, ヴィ, ヴ, ヴェ, and ヴォ instead of バ, ビ, ブ, ベ, and ボ. Similarly more specific *s* and *t* sounds include スィ for *see* (as opposed to シ), ズィ for *zee* (as opposed to ジ), ティ for *tee* (as opposed to チ), and ディ for *dee* (as opposed to ヂ). There is an overall tendency to shorten longer sounds (eliminating long vowels and double consonants). In addition, (i) for many English vowel sounds, (ii) for words with *y* and *w*, and (iii) for some consonant combinations (particularly those with *r*), there is still a degree of disagreement as to the best representation.

r	ヘヤ・ヘア *hair*; バリヤー・バリア *barrier*; ホーン・ホルン *horn*; メートル・メーター *meter*; イアリング・イヤリング *earring*
s, z, j	ジョガー・ジョッガー *jogger*; ジェリー・ゼリー *jelly*; セパード・シェパード *shepherd* (dog breed); リシウム・リチウム *lithium*
v	ヴィールス・ウイルス・ビールス*virus*; バイオリン・ヴァイオリン *violin*; ベニス・ヴェニス *Venice*
ga	ギャロン・ガロン*gallon*; ギャラリー・ガラリー *gallery*; ギャレージ・ガレージ *garage*
f, h	テレフォン・テレホン *telephone*; ファイヤ・ファイア *fire*; フイルム・フィルム *film*, マリハナ・マリファナ・マリワナ *marijuana*; ヒューズ・フューズ *fuse*
t, d, ch	スチール・スティール *steel*; ステータス・ステイタス*status*; セロ・チェロ *cello*; ティーク・チーク *teak*; ティケット・チケット *ticket*; メジアン・メディアン *median*; ティップ・チップ *tip*

w, y	セーター・スェーター sweater; スインガー・スウィンガー swinger; スウェット・スエット sweat; ターコイズ・ターコワーズ turquoise
Single/double consonant	ジョッガー・ジョガー jogger
Shortened forms	ジーンズ・ジーパン jeans; トイレ・トイレット toilet; バミューダ・バーミューダ Bermuda; メイク・メイクアップ・メーキャップ makeup; コンピューター・コンピュータ computer
Vowel quality	ジューリー・ジュエリー jewelry; フィナンス・ファイナンス finance, ベビー・ベイビー baby; ポンチ・パンチ punch (US vs. UK pronunciation); リポート・レポート report

2.3.2 Clipping

As we have seen, the sounds of a borrowed word may be quite different from the original. In addition, a borrowed word may be shortened (or clipped) in Japanese. The vast majority of Japanese nouns contain no more than four moras (words like 経済 or 音楽 or names like 山本 and 中島 which are written with four ひらがな). Clipping is very common especially for recently borrowed vocabulary to bring longer words into this range of normal length. These patterns of abbreviation are found within the Japanese vocabulary as well.

Front clipping (using only the beginning of the original word)

携帯・けいたい	cell phone	携帯電話・けいたいでんわ
昼・ひる	lunch	昼飯・ひるめし
アド	advertisement	アドバータイズメント
アニメ	animation	アニメーション
インテリ	intellectual	インテレクチュアル
インフレ	inflation	インフレーション
コンビニ	convenience store	コンビニエント・ストア
スト	(labor) strike	ストライキ
デパート	department store	デパートメント・ストア
デモ	demonstration	デモンストレーション
テレビ	television	テレビジョン
テロ	terrorism	テロリズム
バスケ	basketball (club, game)	バスケットボール
ハンカチ	handkerchief	ハンカチーフ
ヘリ	helicopter	ヘリコプター
マスコミ	mass communication	マスコミュニケーション
ロケ	(movie) location	ロケーション

Back clipping (using only the end of the original word)

察・さつ	*police*	警察・けいさつ
洋式・ようしき	*Western-style*	西洋式・せいようしき
オーレ	*café au lait*	カフェオーレ
ケット	*blanket*	ブランケット
ネル	*flannel*	フランネル
バイト	*arbeit, part-time job*	アルバイト
ペット	*trumpet*	トランペット
ホーム	(train station) *platform*	プラットホーム
マイト	*dynamite*	ダイナマイト
メット	*helmet*	ヘルメット

Using the first element of each word (very common with Chinese compounds as well)

東大・とうだい	*Tokyo University*	東京大学・とうきょうだいがく
特急・とっきゅう	*special express train*	特別急行・とくべつきゅうこう
エアコン	*air conditioner*	エア・コンディショナー
エロシーン	*erotic scene*	エロティック・エロチック・シーン
エンスト	*engine strike* (engine trouble)	エンジン・ストライキ
スケボー	*skate board*	スケート・ボード
セクハラ	*sexual harassment*	セクシュアル・ハラスメント
バッシュ	*basketball shoes*	バスケットボール・シューズ
パソコン	*personal computer*	パーソナル・コンピュータ
ハンスト	*hunger strike*	ハンガー・ストライキ
パンスト	*panty stockings*	パンティー・ストッキング
プラマイ	*plus/minus*	プラス・マイナス
ポケベル	*pocket bell* (beeper)	ポケット・ベル
ミニパト	*compact patrol car*	ミニチュア・パトロールカー
リモコン	*remote control*	リモート・コントロール
ワープロ	*word processor*	ワード・プロセッサー

2.3.3 Meaning changes

When a word is borrowed into Japanese, the meaning of the word in Japanese is usually more restricted than the meaning in the original language because only one sense is borrowed. Likewise, the meaning may shift unpredictably in ways which seem strange to someone familiar with the word in the original language. In addition, and as we have seen, most borrowed words are shortened or modified in ways which may appear quite arbitrary. While knowledge of English is a relatively safe place to begin when translating a word borrowed into Japanese, it is often not quite enough, and some care should always be taken. In addition, Japanese combines borrowed elements with each other and with existing Japanese words to create new words with new meanings. This is best described as an endlessly surprising process, one which many people would say has been accelerating in recent years.

Borrowed words with significant meaning shifts or restrictions

スター	*movie star, TV performer*, etc.
スナック	*bar, place where you drink and eat snack food*
ツナ	*canned tuna*
トースト	*toast* (bread only)
ドライ	*unsentimental*
ビジター	*visitor at a golf club*
フロント	*hotel reception desk*
マザー	*nun*
マンション	(a nicer) *apartment building*
モーニング	*morning* (-service, a Western style breakfast)

Novel borrowed words where all of the various processes apply (i.e. sound changes, clipping, meaning shifts, and novel compounding)

インスタント	*instant food, ready-made food*
コンパ	*company* (a party mainly among college students)
コンペ	(golf) *competition*
コンポ	(stereo) *component*
スキンシップ	*skinship* (touching, e.g. between mother and child, between close friends)
ネガ	(film) *negative*, etc.
ラブホテル	*love hotel*
リヤカー	*rear car* (two-wheeled cart pulled by a bicycle or motorcycle)

Novel words where all the process apply and the base words are a mix of borrowed and Japanese words

板チョコ	いたチョコ	*chocolate bar*
大サービス	だいサービス	*big service* (i.e. *big discount*)
カラオケ	空オケ	*karaoke* (lit. *empty orchestra*)
タオル地	タオルじ	*cloth texture*
子ギャル	こギャル	*younger girls* (in high school)
玉子サンド	たまごサンド	*egg sandwich*
超ベリ・グ	ちょベリ・グ	*very, very good*
超ベリ・バ	ちょベリ・バ	*very, very bad*
天パ・天然パーマ	てんねんパーマ	*naturally permed hair*
生コン	なまコン	*raw concrete*

バタくさい		*butter* (i.e. Western) *-smelling* (not good)
光ファイバー	ひかりファイバー	*optical fiber*
ポリ袋	ポリぶくろ	*plastic bag*
ガラス窓	ガラスまど	*glass window*
輸出ドライブ	ゆしゅつドライブ	*export drive*
和製ポップス	わせいポップス	*Japanese style pop music*

A very recent creation which shows just how far these processes have gone is パンピー which is an abbreviated form of 一般ピープル that might be translated into English as *the little people* or *everyday people* (i.e. people who are not famous). パンピー is derived from a novel combination of a Japanese and a borrowed word where the beginning of the Japanese word and the end of the borrowed word have been clipped. The extent of these adaptations (and the degree to which unknown borrowed words are being used instead of familiar Chinese compounds) is becoming a source of some concern as people encounter more and more words which are both unfamiliar and uninterpretable. (See the front page of the US edition of the 朝日新聞 (29 April 1999, issue no. 40641) for a recent discussion this problem.)

2.3.4 Japanese "borrowed" words and compounds

While most foreign words are borrowed as unanalyzed units, some borrowed elements are so common that they have taken on the status of Japanese word parts. These are now used to create new words within Japanese. Three examples are given here. It is interesting to see how the original English expression has taken on a meaning of its own in Japanese. Presumably this process parallels the way Chinese characters were borrowed into Japanese as well. While the basic meaning of a particular character is the same in Chinese and Japanese, a particular usage of a particular character or compound might well be language specific, and some compounds are quite foreign. From the perspective of the Chinese, of course, the Japanese are the ones who use Chinese characters in unexpected and novel ways. In the lists below, the starred (☆) expressions are thought to be novel Japanese "borrowed" words. The lists here are complete (from one dictionary) to give a sense of the range of use.

アフター from *after*, means 〜の後 in Japanese	アフター・アワーズ *pub, club opening after hours*; アフターエフェクト *secondary effect, consequence*; アフターケア *care after surgery or medical treatment*; アフターケア・コロニー *group of people in aftercare*; ☆アフター・サービス *product care after a purchase; after-sale service*; ☆アフター・サン・ケア *care after a sunburn*; アフターシェーブ・ローション *after shave lotion*; ☆アフターシューズ *loose comfortable shoes for after skiing or skating*; ☆アフター・ショッピング *a rest, short break, bite to eat after*

shopping and before going home; アフタースキー *relaxation after skiing; après-ski;* アフター・ダーク *gatherings after dark,* アフターテイスト *after taste;* アフターバーナー *(jet engine) after burner;* ☆アフター５５ *after retirement;* アフター・ファイブ *after five; after dark;* ☆アフター・フォロー *a product guarantee;* ☆アフターマーケット *a market for product guarantees and repair;* アフターライフ *after life;* ☆アフター・レコーディング *recording to fix, modify the main recording; post re-cording;* アフタヌーン *afternoon;* 午後

ノー
means なし
or 不〜 in
Japanese

ノー *no;* ノー・アイロン *iron is not contained or necessary;* ノー・アウト *no outs (in baseball);* ノー・エラー *no mistakes, no errors (in baseball);* ☆ノー・カー *not using a car;* ノー・カー・デー *a day for using public transportation;* ノー・ガード *no defense, without a guard;* ☆ノー・カーボン *carbonless carbon paper;* ☆ノー・カウント *items or people not counted (abbreviated* ノーカン*);* ☆ノー・カット *uncut (movie);* ノー・カラー *collarless, no collar;* ノー・グー *not good, bad;* ☆ノー・クラッチ車 *automatic car (abbreviated* ノー・クラ*);* ☆ノー・ゲーム *when a sports e-vent is canceled;* ノー・ゴール *no goal (soccer, ice hockey, etc.);* ノー・コメント *no comment (to a reporter);* ☆ノー・コン *no condom;* ノー・コン *no control (of a pitch in baseball);* ノー・サンキュー *no thank you (also* ノー・サンクス*)* ☆ノー・シード *unseeded (athlete);* ノー・ショー *a no show (at a game, at a hotel, at a reservation, etc.);* ノー・ストッキング *without socks;* ノー・ストリング *no strings, freely;* ノー・スモーキング *no smoking;* ノー・スリーブ *sleeveless;* ☆ノー・ズロ *chip shot (in golf);* ☆ノー・タイム *beginning a game again (after a time out), free time at a skate rink; limitless;* ☆ノー・ダウン *no outs (in baseball);* ノー・タックス *no tax, tax-free;* ノー・タッチ *not to touch, to keep your hands off (a problem), to remain uninvolved;* ノー・チップ *no tip;* ノー・ネーム *no brand, generic;* ノー・ネクタイ *without a necktie;* ノー・パーキング *no parking;* ☆ノー・バウンド *without bounds (in baseball, sports);* ☆ノー・パン *not wearing underwear or panties;* ノー・パンク・タイヤ *no puncture tire, solid tire;* ノー・ヒット *no hit (game);* ☆ノー・ブラ *no bra, braless;* ノー・ブランド *no brand, generic brand;* ☆ノー・ブレ *no breakfast;* ☆ノー・ブレ *no breath (swimming while holding your breath);* ☆ノー・プレー *a baseball play with no effect on the game;* ☆ノー・プロ *no problem; cf.* オーケー*;* ノー・フロスト *frost-free (refrigerator);* ノーペーパー・ソサイエティ *no paper society, paperless society (office);* ☆ノー・ポイ・デー *no garbage day (*ぽい *=* *throwing away, tossing);* ノー・ボール *no ball (baseball game);* ノーホン地帯 *no honking zone;* ノー・マネー *not having any money;* ☆ノー・ミス *no mistakes;* ☆ノー・メイク *without* *makeup*; ノー・モア *no more, never again*, cf. ノー・モア・ヒロシマ; ノー・モーション *not moving, not warming up* (before a game); ノー・ラン *no runs* (in baseball); ノー・ワーク・ノー・ペイ *no work, no pay*; ノー・ワインドアップ *pitching without a big wind-up*; ☆ノンティ *no panties*

マイ means 自分の (じぶん) *private* in Japanese	マイ *my*; ☆マイカー *a private car, one's own car*; ☆マイカー・リース *long term leasing of a private car*; ☆マイコン *personal computer*; マイ・ペース *at your own speed*; ☆マイ・ホーム *your own home* (owned not rented); ☆マイ・ボール *"I've got it," "Mine!"* (in baseball)

Note that マイ does not actually mean 私の (わたし) because it is possible to say things like 田中さんのマイ・ペースで (たなか) which means *at a speed Tanaka is comfortable with* or マイ・ホームはいつ買いましたか (か) which means, "When did you buy your own home?"

2.3.5 *Native versus borrowed versus Chinese vocabulary*

The extensive borrowed vocabulary of Japanese contributes to its richness. Many what might be called synonyms actually differentiate aspects of traditional Japanese culture and borrowed elements. Words of Chinese origin add a further level of possibilities. At any given point in time a particular word may sound old-fashioned or trendy or erudite. For example:

Japanese	Borrowed	Chinese
飯・めし	ライス	御飯・ごはん
恋・こい	ラブ	愛・あい
十・とお	テン	十・じゅう・じゅ
間・ま	ルーム・スペース	室・しつ
札・ふだ	チケット	券・けん

Japanese	Borrowed
戸・と, 扉・とびら	ドア
いちご	ストロベリー
灰色・はいいろ	グレー
こころ	ハート
贈り物・おくりもの	プレゼント

Borrowed	Chinese
ウェディング	結婚式・けっこんしき
デモクラシー	民主主義・みんしゅしゅぎ
インターナショナリズム	国際主義・こくさいしゅぎ
ジョーク	冗談・じょうだん
アメリカ	米国・べいこく

Japanese	Chinese
学ぶ・まなぶ	勉強する・べんきょう
選ぶ・えらぶ	選択する・せんたく
昨日・きのう	昨日・さくじつ
難しい・むずかしい	困難な・こんなん

2.3.6 The grammar of borrowed words

Most borrowed words are nouns. And as nouns, they can become verbs by adding する. This is of course the common pattern for Chinese compounds as well (see section 3.8.2 on page 228). For example:

> ゴールインする *score a goal, reach a goal, (marry well)*; アメリカナイズ する *Americanize*; ドライブする *go for a drive*; パレードする *have a parade*; パンクする *puncture, get a flat*; ダウンロードする *download*; ブートアップする *boot up*; マージする *merge* (data); マスターする *master, learn*; エンジョイする *enjoy*, リクエストする *request*, オーダーする *order*

Words which are adjectives in the original language tend to become nominal adjectives. For example:

> セクシーな *sexy*; ダンディーな *dandy*; パブリックな *public*; ボーイッシュ な *boyish*; ハンサムな *handsome*; ホットな *hot (new)*; メインな *main, the main*; ユーモラスな *humorous*; ルーズな *loose*; タフな *tough*; エキゾチックな *exotic*; ヘルシーな *healthy*; オイリーな *oily*; メローな *mellow*; etc.

Once upon a time there were a very small number of borrowed words which become verbs, usually due to lucky sound patterns (where a る-sound occurred near the end of the word). Recently, the production of new verbs seems to have reached a threshold of possibility, and it is now both common and trendy (at least among young people). It remains to be seen, however, how many of these words will enter the language permanently.

> サボる *sabotage, skip class*; サドる *be sadistic*; マゾる *be masochistic*; ダ フる *duff* (in golf to hit the ground not the ball); ダブる *double*; デコる *decorate*; デモる *march, demonstrate*; トラブる *have trouble*; バイブる *use a vibrator*; パニクる *panic*; ミスる *make a mistake*; レズる *be a lesbian* (can be discriminatory); ホモる *be gay* (can be discriminatory); メ モる *write a memo*; ハモる *harmonize*

I know of only one borrowed adjective: ナウい, meaning *trendy* or *cool*.

3 Grammar and verbal strategies

In a very broad sense, all Japanese sentences consist of nouns which are related to their verbs by particles. Nouns, verbs, and whole sentences can be modified by adjectives, adverbs, and relative clauses (which are themselves sentences). This chapter will touch on each of these elements to some degree, although the emphasis will be on topics which are often problematic or not well understood or not extensively discussed in traditional textbooks. More importantly, many of the discussions are focused not on points of grammar, but on the relationship between grammar and correct usage. When making a request in English, we can contrast "Get out!," "Please leave," and "Won't you please leave me alone for a while." In Japanese as in English, there are a number of different ways to say the same thing. What are the different implications of each form, and why might one be preferred over another?

3.1 Being vague and indirect

Japanese is well-known for vague speech, and the language is full of grammatical expressions which allow explicit (and often difficult or awkward) details to be left unspoken. Of course, the accommodating listener plays a crucial role in such exchanges because he or she *expects* the difficult details to be left unspoken. In general, a less direct expression is considered more polite, even more sophisticated. It is more humble to sound ineffective, and the most powerful people often sound the least in control of events.

3.1.1 なる versus する

なる means *become*; する means *do*. These two words occur in parallel expressions where なる indicates an accidental or unforeseen development while する indicates a purposeful choice. なる expressions leave open the question of who is responsible for the change. When talking about a decision, for example, this same effect can be achieved in English with a pronoun such as *they* in "This is the way they said it is going to be" or "They decided that you will go to Paris and I will go to Edinburgh." Nevertheless, speakers of English are often not happy not knowing who made a particular decision, and these kinds of explanations might be seen as purposely evasive. Within Japanese society, it is often considered irrelevant or unnecessary to identify the source of an idea or decision. Further, while it is possible to turn many なる expressions into equivalent expressions with する, it is often very presumptuous to do so, and in many contexts (where decisions are supposed to be reached only after a period of consensus building) it may actually be impossible to identify the particular source of an idea or change.

In the examples below, the expressions on the left with なる all refer to inevitable or uncontrolled changes. The speaker did not decide to become an adult. The piano player did not decide to become good. She may have hoped to improve; she may have practiced a great deal, but none of this guaranteed that she would actually develop the right skills. Note that these two sentences are completely beyond the control of any individual and do not have sensible する equivalents. Likewise, the speaker in the third sentence did not choose to have sushi for dinner, although here it is clear that someone did in fact make the decision. In contrast, the する expressions on the right all involve questions of will. When did you decide to have the party? What are you having for dinner? What did you do?

知らないうちに大人になりました。

I became an adult without realizing.

ピアノが上手になりました。

She has become very good at the piano.

晩ご飯はすしになったらしい。

It seems we are having sushi for dinner.

どうなりましたか。

What happened?

宴会は木曜日にしました。

We decided to have the party on Thursday.

きのうテニスをしましたか。

Did you play tennis yesterday?

晩ご飯は天ぷらにしました。

I decided on tempura for dinner.

どうしましたか。

What did you do?

なる indicates either (i) that the speaker had no control over the change, or (ii) that the speaker does not know why something occurred. It may also be used to give this impression, regardless of the truth. なる may be used to avoid taking responsibility for an unpleasant decision, or to avoid taking credit for a good (or self-serving) decision.

高くなってしまった。

It has become expensive.

もう少し安くなりませんか。

Won't it become a little less expensive?

高くした。

I raised the price.

もう少し安くしていただけますか。

Can't you make it a bit cheaper?

The speaker may or may not be responsible for pricing, but with なる the increase can be blamed on a group decision or a head office. With する the speaker is taking more direct responsibility. Note that it is strange to say something like 高くなってしまってください since the command form implies control while なってしまう implies its lack.

〜ことになる and 〜ことにする both refer to decisions. (The parallel expressions for adjectives are 高くなる and 高くする, and for nouns あしたになる and あしたにする.)

私が海外に行くことになりました。

It has been decided that I will go abroad.

天ぷらを食べることになりました。

It happens that we are having tempura.

中国に残ることになりました。

It has turned out that I will stay in China.

私が海外に行くことにしました。

I decided to go abroad.

天ぷらを食べることにしました。

I decided to have tempura.

中国に残ることにしました。

I have decided to stay in China.

Looking at the final pair of examples above, if it has just turned out that the speaker will stay in China, the 〜ことになる expression is most appropriate. If the speaker consciously made the decision to stay, the 〜ことにする expression is appropriate. If, however, the speaker has consciously decided to stay in China to avoid marriage but is afraid to admit this to his bride-to-be waiting at home, he may use なる to imply that circumstances have conspired against him. One can also convey what might be construed as bad news the same way. If everyone loves the job in China, and even if you secretly lobbied hardest to keep it, なる conveys an implicit denial of personal involvement in the decision.

　〜ようになる implies that some change in behavior or plan occurs, although how the change comes about is not clear. Conversely, 〜ようにする implies a conscious effort to bring about the change. Note that expressions with 〜ように do not actually imply success of the main verb.

3月に行くようになっている。

It has turned out that I will go in March.

理解するようになった。

I have gotten to where I understand.

来週までにできるようになるだろう。

It should turn out that we can do it
*　by next week.*

3月に行くようにしている。

I am making an effort to go in March.

理解するようにした。

I made an effort to understand.

来週までにできるようにする。

I will make an effort to do it by next week.

　The contrast between なる and する may also be reflected in related honorific expressions. While it is overstating the case, superiors may be said to behave in mysterious unknowable ways: なる. Inferiors (including oneself) behave in mundane, totally knowable ways: する.

お帰りになりますか。

Are you going home?

おかけになってくださいませんか。

Won't you please have a seat?

お書きしましょうか。

Shall I write it for you?

お聞きしてもよろしいでしょうか。

Is it okay if I ask you a question?

See pages 11 and 12 in Chapter 1 (and pages cited there) for a more extensive discussion of these two kinds of honorific expressions.

3.1.2 Transitive and intransitive pairs

The terms *transitive* and *intransitive* refer to kinds of verbs. A sentence like *John ate a sandwich* is transitive because it involves two nouns: the person eating and the thing being eaten. The action of John has an affect on the sandwich. In contrast, *John swam* is intransitive because it involves only one noun: the person swimming. A list of transitive verbs in English would include: *eat, drink, watch, study, hit,* etc. Intransitive verbs would include: *swim, run, crawl, sit, wait,* etc.

Many verbs in English are *both* transitive and intransitive, which means they can occur with both a subject and an object or with just a subject:

Takako opened the door.   (subject and object = transitive)
The door opened.   (subject only = intransitive)

Both sentences can be used in a situation where a door opens. In the first sentence, however, we also learn who caused the door to open. The second sentence tells us only that the door is no longer closed. The implication is that it somehow opened itself. Characteristically, the object of the transitive verb is the subject of the intransitive verb. Other verbs which alternate the same way in English are *close, break, get up,* or *burn* (i.e. *I burned the toast* and *The toast burned*).

These verbs are a problem when learning Japanese because, as a rule, a single English verb like *open* always has two Japanese translations: transitive 開ける (with particle を) and intransitive 開く (without).

隆子がドアを開けた。   (subject and object = transitive)
Takako opened the door.
ドアが開いた。   (subject only = intransitive)
The door opened.

Again, in the first sentence, Takako is given credit for opening the door, while in the second sentence the door has apparently opened itself. The Chinese character is the same, although the sounds are not always related in a straightforward manner. Unfortunately, there is no easy way to predict what the two verbs will sound like, and they have to be learned more or less one at a time. The verbs 入れる and 入る in the second pair of sentences below are possibly the most common example of a verb pair where the sounds of the two verbs appear unrelated. (Historically, however, there is a relation, and 入る is derived from 這い入る *enter crawling*.)

The basic difference in meaning between the two verbs in transitive and intransitive pairs is reflected in a variety of ways. Most of these differences are a reflex of the fact that transitive verbs have subjects who control the action of the verb while intransitive verbs do not.

隆子が窓ガラスを壊した。*Takako broke the window.*
窓ガラスが壊れた。*The window broke.*

荷物をここに入れてください。*Please put your luggage in here.*
私たちはこの小さい車には入らない。*We aren't going to fit into this small car.*

First, as with なる and する, the intransitive version makes it possible to avoid the question of who opened the door or who broke the window (although, as an excuse, this may not work in Japanese any better than it does in English; when looking at a shattered vase, "I don't know, it just broke" is not a very effective defense).

Second, a simple verb form like ジョギングをする can be used to mean that I jog every day or that I will jog this afternoon at 3 o'clock. This first usage is habitual (i.e. a daily habit) while the second usage is a future.

毎日ジョギングをします。

I jog everyday.
三時にジョギングをします。

I will jog at three o'clock.

With the intransitive verbs in transitive and intransitive pairs, there is a further interpretation. While the transitive verbs are just like *jog*, the intransitive versions have what is called a potential interpretation as well. *I can come at 3 o'clock* is a statement about what is possible. It is potential, and it contrasts with both *I come every day at 3 o'clock* (habitual) and *I will come at 3 o'clock* (future). Intransitive verbs like 開く, 壊れる, or 入る can be used to talk about what is possible: 開く can be used to mean *can open*, 壊れる to mean *can break, is breakable*, and 入る to can mean *fits, can go in*. Compare the following sets of sentences.

毎日お風呂に入る。

I take a bath every day.
三時にお風呂に入る。

I will take a bath at three o'clock.
私の象は大きくてお風呂に入らない。

My elephant is big, and it doesn't fit in the bath.

窓のどれかが毎日壊れる。

Some window breaks everyday.
三時に窓が壊れる。

A window will break at three o'clock. (a bit mysterious in Japanese as well as English)
この窓は壊れない。

This window does not break.

Verb forms which refer to what is possible are usually said to have a *potential* interpretation. Intransitive verbs like 開く, 壊れる, or 入る which have an inherent potential meaning typically do not occur in a derived potential form. While both 行く and 行ける occur regularly, there is no grammatically derived potential for 開く. (This is not actually true for 入る; see the discussion on page 137.)

Third, compare intransitive ～ている with ～てある and the passive. ～てある is discussed on page 137, the passive beginning on page 139. As with なる, none of these sentences makes explicit reference to the person who brought the change about.

ドアが開いている。 *The door is open.*
ドアが開けてある。 *The door has been opened.*
ドアが開けられた。 *The door was opened.*

火が消えている。 *The fire is out.*
火が消してある。 *The fire has been put out.*
火が消された。 *The fire was put out.*

In all three sentences of the first set, the door is open. In the second set, the fire is out. Nevertheless, the underlying assertions of each sentence are different, and a speaker can choose how to talk about a situation based on the implications which he or she wishes to convey. ドアが開いている is the most neutral: the door is open. The speaker makes no commitment as to how it got that way. Perhaps someone opened it. Perhaps the wind opened it. Perhaps it was never closed. The emphasis is on the existing condition of the door. In contrast, ドアが開けてある makes implicit reference to the fact that an event has taken place: someone opened the door. While the door is now open, it did not start this way, and it did not get this way on its own. Such a sentence can be used if the speaker does not know who did the action or has chosen not to say. In contrast to this, the passive makes implicit reference to the individual who brought the condition about: someone is responsible for the fact that the door is now open. In addition, the passive is frequently used when the action of the unnamed individual is perceived as unpleasant or negative. Neither ～ている nor ～てある is particularly negative.

3.1.2.1 Examples

Here is a list of just over sixty common transitive and intransitive pairs. The verbs are generally written with the same Chinese character with related sounds (although as we have seen, there are exceptions). The transitive verb describes an action taken by a person which affects something else. The intransitive verb talks just about the affected object. Note that the English translations are not always the same (unlike *open* and *open* above).

Transitive	Intransitive

開ける・あける *open*
その窓を開けてください。

Please open that window.

開く・あく *open*
二階の窓が開かない。

The second floor windows do not open.

開ける and 開く refer to concrete openings (windows, doors, books, etc.). 開ける is transitive while 開く is intransitive except for one usage: 赤ちゃんが目を広く開いた *The baby opened its eyes wide* which requires a volitional subject who is not in control of the action (like a baby or an animal). If the subject decides to open its eyes, 開ける is the correct verb. 開ける and 開く contrast with ひらく and ひらける which are more abstract (and are discussed below).

上げる・あげる *raise*
話す前に手を上げてください。

Please raise your hand before speaking.

上がる・あがる *rise*
気温が３０度に上がった。

The temperature rose to thirty degrees.

集める・あつめる *gather, collect*
情報を集める

gather information

集まる・あつまる *gather*
人が大勢駅の前に集まった。

A crowd gathered in front of the station.

表す・あらわす *show, reveal, express*
気持ちを外に表さない。

He keeps his feelings to himself.

表れる・あらわれる *appear*
努力が結果に表れた。

The effort was apparent in the result.

These words are also written 現す and 現れる which refer to the appearance of concrete objects. Compare, for example, 霧の中から船が現れた "The boat appeared out of the mist."

入れる・いれる *put in*
お金を駐車メーターに入れてください。

Please put money into the parking meter.

入る・はいる *go in, enter*
入ってはいけないよ。

You may not go into there.

動かす・うごかす *move*
車を動かしてください。

Please move the car.

動く・うごく *move*
時計の針が動いている。

The clock hand is moving.

移す・うつす *move, shift, transfer*
机を窓ぎわに移す

move the desk near the window

移る・うつる *move, remove*
京都から東京に移る

move from Kyoto to Tokyo

動かす and 動く emphasize the movement itself while 移す and 移る emphasize the outcome of the move. In the example with 動かす, it is important only that the car not stay where it is (perhaps it is in the way), while in the example with 移す, it is important that the desk end up near the window (perhaps because the light is better).

生む・うむ *give birth to*   生まれる・うまれる *be born*
子供を生む   娘が生まれた。
give birth to a child   *My daughter has been born.*

These words are also written 産む and 産まれる.

起こす・おこす *wake up*   起きる・おきる *get up*
赤ちゃんを起こしてしまった。   今日五時に起きた。
I ended up waking the baby.   *I got up at five today.*

起こす・おこす *cause, create*   起こる・おこる *happen, occur*
革命を起こす   革命が起こった。
cause a revolution   *A revolution happened.*

落とす・おとす *drop*   落ちる・おちる *fall*
本を床に落とした。   テーブルから落ちる
I dropped the book on the floor. *fall from the table*

かえす *return*   かえる *return*
本を図書館に返す   答えが返って来た。
return a book to the library   *His reply came back.*

かえる *change*   かわる *change*
ヘアスタイルを変えた。   住所が変わった。
I changed my hair style.   *Their address has changed.*

かける *hang*   かかる *hang*
服をハンガーに掛ける   ジャケットがいすに掛かっている。
hang the clothes on a hanger   *A jacket is hanging on the chair.*

消す・けす *extinguish, put out*   消える・きえる *go out*
テレビを消して下さい。   街灯が消えた。
Please turn the television off.   *The streetlights went out.*

聞く・きく *hear, listen, ask*   聞こえる・きこえる *be audible*
そういううわさを聞いた。   鳥の声が聞こえる。
A heard that rumor.   *I can hear a bird singing.*

決める・きめる *decide*   決まる・きまる *be decided*
進路を決めた。   専攻が決まった。
I decided my future course of action. *My major has been decided.*

切る・きる *cut*   切れる・きれる *become cut*
はさみで紙を切る   このはさみは紙がよく切れる。
cut paper with scissors   *These scissors cut paper well.*

加える・くわえる *add*
もう一人グループに加える
add one more person to the group

加わる・くわわる *join*
新入生が生徒会に加わった。
New students joined the student council.

壊す・こわす *break*
時計を壊してしまった。
I broke my watch.

壊れる・こわれる *break*
テレビが壊れている。
This television is broken.

下げる・さげる *lower*
ブラインドを少し下げてください。
Please lower the blinds a bit.

下がる・さがる *become lower*
物価が下がった。
Prices fell.

閉める・しめる *close*
窓を閉めて下さい。
Please close the windows.

閉まる・しまる *close*
店が閉まっている。
The store is closed.

閉める may be contrasted with 閉じる which means *close* with the meaning of tying or binding. See 締める on page 46.

過ごす・すごす *exceed, spend*
つい酒を過ごす *drink too much*
楽しく時を過ごす *spend time enjoyably*

過ぎる・すぎる *go past*
あらしが過ぎる *the storm will pass*
それから3年が過ぎた。 *Three years passed.*

育てる・そだてる *raise*
子供を育てるのに苦労した。
I struggled with raising three children.

育つ・そだつ *grow up*
赤ちゃんは育つのが早い。
Children grow up quickly.

倒す・たおす *knock down*
大木を倒すのは大変だ。
Knocking over a big tree is difficult.

倒れる・たおれる *fall down*
古くなって木が倒れた。
The tree became old and fell down.

出す・だす *take out, put out*
封筒から手紙を出す
take a letter out of an envelope

出る・でる *come out*
月が出ている。
The moon is out.

助ける・たすける *help, aid*
川に落ちた子を助けた。
I saved the child who fell into the river.

助かる・たすかる *be helped*
手術のおかげで命が助かった。
Thanks to the operation, his life is saved.

立てる・たてる *stand*
ろうそくを床の上に立てる
stand the candle on the floor

立つ・たつ *stand*
ゲレンデにポールが立っている。
My poles are standing on the ski slope.

付ける・つける *attach*
服にしみを付ける
get a stain on your clothes

付く・つく *adhere to*
服にしみが付く
clothes get stained

伝える・つたえる *transmit*
上司に伝言を伝える

convey a message to your superior

続ける・つづける *continue*
ピアノの練習を続けた。

I continued practicing the piano.

通す・とおす *let by, let through*
客を奥の部屋に通す

Let the guest through to the back room

止める・とめる *stop*
急に車を止めた。

I stopped the car suddenly.

直す・なおす *fix*
明日まで車を直してください。

Please fix my car by tomorrow.

無くす・なくす *lose*
ハンカチを無くした。

I lost my handkerchief.

並べる・ならべる *line up*
ここにいすを並べてください。

Please line the chairs up here.

悩ます・なやます *trouble*
その問題が彼を悩ませた。

That problem troubled him.

残す・のこす *leave*
ご飯を半分残した。

I left half of my dinner.

延ばす・のばす *extend*
仕事が入ったので出発を延ばした。

Work came in, so we put off our

departure.

伝わる・つたわる *passed down, transmitted*
メッセージがみんなに伝わった。

The message was passed to everyone.

続く・つづく *continue*
会議が三日も続いた。

The meeting continued for three days.

通る・とおる *go by, go through*
この道は人がよく通る。

People often go down this road.

止まる・とまる *stop*
急に前の車が止まった。

The car in front stopped suddenly.

直る・なおる *get better*
車はもう直りましたか。

Is your car repaired yet?

無くなる・なくなる *become lost*
知らないうちにピアスが無くなった。

My earring fell out without me realizing.

並ぶ・ならぶ *line up, queue*
木が一列に並んで立っている。

The trees are standing in a single line.

悩む・なやむ *be troubled*
私は家庭内の問題で悩んでいる。

I am troubled by problems at home.
その会社は赤字に悩んでいる。

That company is troubled by debt.

残る・のこる *remain*
きのうは遅くまで会社に残った。

I remained at work until late yesterday.

延びる・のびる *extend*
平均寿命が延びた。

Our average lifespan has increased.

乗せる・のせる *give a ride to, put on*
彼を新車に乗せた。
I gave him a ride in my new car.
子供をジェットコースターに乗せた。
I put the child on the roller coaster.

乗る・のる *get on*
バスに乗って、隣の町に行った。
I got on the bus and went to the next town.

始める・はじめる *begin*
先生が講義を始めた。
The teacher began the lecture.

始まる・はじまる *begin*
新学期が始まった。
The new school term began.

外す・はずす *take off*
腕時計を外して泳いだ。
I took my watch off and swam.

外れる・はずれる *come off*
知らないうちにねじが外れていた。
Before I realized, the screw had come out.

離す・はなす *separate*
机をいすから離した。
I separated the chair and desk.

離れる・はなれる *move away from*
夫と離れて住む。
I live away from my husband.

冷やす・ひやす *cool*
ワインを冷やして飲む
cool the wine and drink it

冷える・ひえる *become cool*
ビールがよく冷えている。
The beer is well-cooled.

開く・ひらく *open, clear*
包みを開く
open a package
店を開く
open, establish a store
道を開く
clear a road

開ける・ひらける *open, develop*
眺めが開けた。
A view opened up.
開けた国
a developed nation
運が開けてきた。
Luck is turning my way.

ひらく and ひらける have a broader and more metaphorical range of meanings than あける and あく. This is particularly true of ひらける. Note (somewhat incredibly) that transitive あける and intransitive ひらける are both written as 開ける, while intransitive あく and transitive ひらく are both written as 開く.

広げる・ひろげる *spread out, enlarge*
ふろしきを床に広げる
spread the furoshiki on the floor

広がる・ひろがる *become spread out*
視野が広がった。
My field of vision widened.

増やす・ふやす *increase, add to*
新しいメンバーを増やした。
We added new members.

増える・ふえる *increase*
東京の人口が増えている。
Tokyo's population has increased.

曲げる・まげる bend
事実を曲げる
distort the truth

曲がる・まがる bend, turn
道の曲がった所
a bend in the road

混ぜる・まぜる mix
卵と牛乳を混ぜる
mix eggs and milk

混ざる・まざる become mixed with
油と水が混ざらない。
Oil and water do not mix.

まとめる put into order
荷物をまとめる
organize the luggage

まとまる take shape
論文がよくまとまっている。
His thesis is well organized.

回す・まわす turn
車のハンドルを回す
turn the steering wheel

回る・まわる turn
地球が回る
the earth spins

見る・みる see
何を見ていますか。
What do you see?

見える・みえる be visible
富士山が見えない。
Mt. Fuji is not visible.

見付ける・みつける find
仕事を見付ける
find a job

見付かる・みつかる be found
財布がまだ見付からない。
My wallet is still missing.

向ける・むける meet, welcome
研究に心を向ける
put all your heart into your research

向かう・むかう face
目標に向かう
face the goal

燃やす・もやす burn
紙を燃やす
burn paper.

燃える・もえる burn
紙が燃える
paper burns

戻す・もどす return
本を本棚に戻す
return a book to the bookshelf

戻る・もどる return
席に戻る
return to one's seat

焼く・やく burn, cook
野菜を焼く
roast vegetables

焼ける・やける burn, cook
火事で原稿が焼けた。
The manuscript burned in the fire.

破る・やぶる tear
服を破る
tear your clothes

破れる・やぶれる tear
破れた服
torn clothes

止める・やめる *stop*   止む・やむ *stop*
ストライキを止める   雨が止む
stop the strike   *the rain stops*

寄せる・よせる *allow to approach*   寄る・よる *approach*
いすをテーブルに寄せる   近くに寄って下さい。
pull the chair close to the table   *Come close.*

沸かす・わかす *boil*   沸く・わく *boil*
風呂を沸かす   湯が沸いている。
warm the bath water   *The water is boiling.*

湯 means *hot water*. Note that 水が沸いている makes no sense since 水 means *cold water*.

わける *divide*   わかれる *be divided*
ケーキを三つにわける   川が二つにわかれる
divide the cake into three pieces   *the river divides into two*

渡す・わたす *hand over*   渡る・わたる *reach*
手紙を友達に渡す   手紙が友達に渡った。
hand the letter to a friend   *The letter reached my friend.*

An intransitive verb like 渡る does in fact occur regularly with what might be taken to be a direct object: 橋を渡る *cross a bridge*. This kind of direct object which indicates a route of motion is discussed on page 197.

割る・わる *break*   割れる・われる *break*
窓ガラスを割る   窓ガラスが割れる
smash a window pane   *the window pane breaks*

3.1.2.2 Controllable versus non-controllable

All of the *transitive verbs* in the above list take people as subjects. These people are in control of the action of the verb. As such, it makes sense to give commands like 口を開けてください *Open your mouth* or 落としてください *Drop it!* Verbs which are controlled by people are compatible with 〜ておく: 開けておいた *I opened it now* (since we will want it opened later) or 決めておきましょう *Let's decide now* (so we won't have to later). Finally, verbs which are controllable occur in the 〜ましょう form as well: 辞めましょう *Let's stop* or 始めよう *Let's begin*.

The *intransitive verbs* in the above list can be divided into two types: those which are controllable and those which are not. Compare: *Get in line!* (said to a group of students) and *Open!* (said to a door). Both verbs are intransitive, but a command to a door is nonsense. Again, only the intransitive verbs which allow human subjects can be done on purpose or with intent. With most such verbs, commands, 〜ておく, and 〜ましょう are fine as well. Further, intransitive verbs which can be done on purpose can also occur in the grammatical potential. やっとあのバーに入れた, for example, means that, having turned twenty-one, I was finally able to get into that bar.

Intransitives which a person can do	どうぞお上がり下さい・あがる *Please come in*; あそこに集まってください・あつまる *Please gather over there*; お風呂に入ってもいいですよ・はいる *It is okay to take a bath*; 動かないで下さい・うごく *Please don't move*; 他校へ移ろう・うつる *Let's transfer to another school*; 遅れるから早く起きなさい・おきる *Get up now or we will be late*; 帰ってください・かえる *Go home*; 仕事にかかってください・かかる *Apply yourself to your job*; お変りありませんか・かわる *I hope nothing has changed with you*; 仲間に加わる・くわわる *join the group*; 一歩後ろに下がってください・さがる *Take one step back*; 倒れるな・たおれる *Don't fall over*; 立ってください・たつ *Please stand up*; あの人に付こう・つく *Let's follow that person*; 田中さんのあとに続きましょう・つづく *Let's follow Tanaka*; 出よう・でる *Let's leave*; この道を通ろう・とおる *Let's take this street*; あそこに止まってください・とまる *Please stop over there*; 並ぼう・ならぶ *Let's make a line*; バスに乗ってください・のる *Please get on the bus*; グループから離れよう・はなれる *Let's separate from the group*; 校庭に広がって下さい・ひろがる *Spread out in the school yard*; 左に曲がって下さい・まがる *Please turn left*; 回らないで下さい・まわる *Please don't spin around*; こちらに向かって下さい・むかう *Please look this way*; 上を向こう・むく *Let's look up*; ついに戻ってきた・もどる *Eventually, he came back*; わかれましょうか *Shall we separate?*; どの橋を渡ろうか・わたる *Which bridge shall we cross?*

3.1.3 ～てある

The ～てある construction is possible with almost any verb with a direct object を (not just those which occur in transitive and intransitive pairs). It makes implicit reference to an event which has taken place. The を-marked object is usually but not necessarily marked with が. The identity of the agent can only be implied. This implication can be made stronger by the use of the particle を on the object.

お茶のためにお湯が沸かしてある。
The water has been boiled for tea.
(emphasizes the fact that the water has been boiled)
お茶のためにお湯を沸かしてある。
The water has been boiled for tea. I have boiled water for tea.
(emphasizes the unnamed person who is responsible for boiling the water)

ドアが開けてあるからいつでも入って来て下さい。

The door is opened, so please come in at any time.

(emphasizes the fact that the door is not closed)

ドアを開けてあるからいつでも入って来て下さい。

The door is opened, so please come in at any time. The door has been opened, so please come in at any time. (emphasizes the unnamed person who is responsible for the door)

The 〜てある construction is also compatible with the causative of any verb and with the passive of transitive verbs.

何度も生徒に日本語のテープを聞かせてある。

I have made my students listen to Japanese tapes many times (so they remember).

犬にその匂いを一度嗅がせてある。

I have made my dog sniff the smell once (so he now remembers it).

洗濯物が外に干されてあった。

My clothes have been hung outside.

開拓のために木が何本も倒すされてあった。

Many trees had been cut down for reclamation.

The 〜てある construction is essentially incompatible with intransitive verbs (a few exceptions: 沸いてある *has been boiled*, 届いてある *has been delivered*, 落ちてある *has fallen*, わたってある *has been passed to*). 〜てある is also difficult with the transitive verbs listed here. Note that the great majority of them describe psychological states.

object, but no 〜てある

愛する・あい *love* (a person を); 諦める・あきらめる *give up* (a cause を); 飽きる・あきる *lose interest in* (a cause を); 呆れる・あきれる *be astonished at* (a fact に); 痛む・いたむ *feel pain* (at a death を); 疑う・うたがう *doubt* (a person を); 影響する・えいきょう *influence* (a person に); 追う・おう *chase after* (a person を); 恐れる・おそれる *fear* (a person を); 思い出す・おもいだす *recall* (a fact を); 思う・おもう *believe* (a fact を); 悲しむ・かなしむ *grieve* (a loss を); 構う・かまう *mind, care about* (a problem を); 感謝する・かんしゃ *be grateful for* (something を・に); 感じる・かんじる *feel* (an emotion を); 嫌う・きらう *hate* (a person を); 後悔する・こうかい *regret* (an action を); 誤解する・ごかい *misunderstand* (a meaning を); 従う・したがう *follow, obey* (a person に); 親しむ・したしむ *be in close contact* (with a person に); 知る・しる *know* (something を); 信じる・しんじる *believe* (the news を); 信用する・しんよう *put trust in* (a doctor を); 尊敬する・そんけい *respect* (a person を); 代表する・だいひょう *represent* (a group を); 近寄る・ちかよる *approach* (a place に); 同情する・どうじょう *pity* (a person に); 憎む・にくむ *hate* (a person を); 待つ・まつ *wait for* (a person を); 持つ・もつ *have, carry* (something を); 喜ぶ・よろこぶ *be happy about* (something を・に); 理解する・りかい *comprehend* (the question を・について)

3.1.4 Active and passive

The passive is just another way of looking at an event: *I ate the cake* versus *The cake was eaten by me*. Someone did something (active) versus something happened to something (passive). In both situations, a cake was eaten. Of course, the same distinction is found in Japanese: 田中さんがケーキを食べた versus ケーキが田中さんに食べられた, although both of the Japanese sentences are probably more natural if the subject is actually left unspoken (and derived from the context): ケーキを食べた versus ケーキが食べられた.

Now, it is sometimes observed in English that students *get* good grades, but *are given* bad ones: *John got 100%* (because he is such a smart boy) while *Jack was given a failing score* (by his teacher). Likewise, *I talked to my best friend on the phone*, but *I was talked to by my mother* or *I was given a talking to by my mother*. In both of these cases, turning the sentence around and presenting it from the viewpoint of the person affected seems to imply an underlying unpleasantness or tension.

This is not to say that a passive sentence in English is necessarily negative. "I was left behind so that I could study" might very well be exactly what was wanted, and it is very easy to find sentences like "I think *Star Wars* has been seen by everyone I know" which are not at all negative. This book (this page) includes many passive sentences which are nothing more than simple declarations.

In a typical passive sentence in Japanese, the を-marked direct object becomes the subject and the が-marked subject is marked with a に or によって (where によって gives a more neutral reading). As with English, the subject is often omitted altogether.

Active
兄がドアを開けた。
My brother opened the door.

Passive
ドアが兄によって開けられた。
ドアが兄に開けられた。
The door was opened by my brother.

学生が日記を読んだ。
The students read my diary.

日記が学生によって読まれた。
日記が学生に読まれた。
My diary was read by the students.

ワープロを使いましたか。
Did you use a word processor?

私のワープロがみんなに使われている。
My word processor is used by everyone.

The passive sentences here are not necessarily pleasant or unpleasant; they simply present the event from the point of view of the object which was affected. At the same time, however, it is very easy in Japanese to make it explicit when a person has benefited from an event. And as is discussed beginning on page 147, the overt acknowledgement of benefit is probably more common in Japanese than in English.

Active	Beneficial
兄がドアを開けた。	兄がドアを開けてくれた。
My brother opened the door.	*My brother opened the door for me.*
学生が日記を読んだ。	学生が日記を読んでくれた。
My students read my diary.	*My students read my diary as I asked.*
ワープロを使いましたか。	皆がワープロを使ってくれた。
Did you use a word processor?	*Everyone used a word processor as I asked.*

The possible contrast with an explicitly beneficial form makes it easier to give the passive in Japanese a negative interpretation, and use of the passive is one way of hinting that things might be better than they are. Such a tendency is probably strongest in very informal speech where the passive is the most unusual. The tendency is greatly reduced as speech becomes more formal and in all written language particularly with verbs such as 行われる *is carried out, performed*, 表現される *is expressed*, 言われる *is said*, or 思われる *is thought* (which occur very frequently in the passive).

There are other devices for increasing the likelihood that a particular passive sentence reflects someone's unhappiness. Note that によって for に is odd here since the sentences are no longer simple (neutral) passives.

Active	Passive (unpleasant most likely)
兄がドアを開けた。	兄にドアを開けられた。
My brother opened the door.	*The door was opened by my brother.*
学生が日記を読んだ。	日記を学生に読まれた。
My students read my diary.	*My diary was read by my students.*
ワープロを使いましたか。	みんなにワープロを使われた。
Did you use my computer?	*My word processor was used by everyone.*

The passive sentences in this second group still have the object marker を which is very odd from an English perspective since a passive construction normally lacks a direct object. While it is not unambiguous, this is a clearer sign that the speaker is unhappy about something. My brother opened the door and now the room is full of flies. My students read my diary which I had accidentally left open on my desk. Someone has been using my word processor and changing the settings. When you encounter a passive sentence with an を-marked noun, it is frequently a sign that something is wrong. Likewise, によって is unlikely to occur when the sentence has a more negative feeling.

A final type of passive sentence in Japanese is very strange from an English perspective because the active verb does not include a direct object at all. The English translations are usually somewhat odd as a result. More often than the other constructions discussed here, this kind of passive indicates that something is in fact viewed negatively.

Active	Passive (unpleasant)
雨が降った。	雨に降られた。
It rained.	*I was rained on.*
友達の田中さんが去った。	友達の田中さんに去られた。
My friend Tanaka left.	*I was left behind by my friend Tanaka.*
お母さんが来た。	お母さんに来られた。
My mother came.	*My mother barged into my room.*

In general, the active sentence is the preferred, neutral way to describe any situation in Japanese. The use of the passive can be viewed as a special signal, and as such it can convey the speaker's unhappiness with a situation in a relatively subtle manner. Nevertheless, the listener must often figure out what exactly is wrong, even if something actually is wrong. Compare the first pair of sentences with the second.

雨が降ってそれで風邪をひいてしまった。

It rained, and I ended up catching a cold.

雨に降られてしまった。

I was rained on (and ended up catching a cold).

三日後にようやく雨が降って、おかげで畑が潤った。

Three days later, it rained, and thanks to that, the fields became wet.

三日後にようやく雨に降られ、おかげで畑が潤った。

Three days later, we were rained on at last, and thanks to that, the fields became wet.

The passive alone raises a signal, but it is not necessarily enough to mean that something bad has happened. The second pair of sentences above clearly refers to a good event. As is often the case in Japanese, accommodation plays a role in the correct interpretation. Does the speaker seem unhappy with the situation or not? Are there any other signs of stress? Does it make sense to cast the entire sentence in a negative light? If there is no supporting evidence, be careful before assuming that something has gone wrong.

Recall, finally, that a passive verb may in fact be honorific as well. This usage is discussed on page 12 of Chapter 1.

3.1.5 Evidence

There are a number of different expressions which allow one to be quite explicit about the source of information as well as one's commitment to its truth. These are usually called *evidentials*. Using them correctly can soften the impact of statement as well as allowing a speaker to distance him or herself from the truth of a statement.

〜みたい is probably the most neutral translation of conversational English *seem*. It is used when the sentence reflects the speaker's judgment (as opposed to a third party's judgment) and the confidence level is reasonably high. The judgment is often based on observed evidence. 〜みたい is quite common in informal speech. In contrast to expressions softened with something like だろう, an expression with 〜みたい is always more than a simple guess. (See page 145 for discussion of expressions like だろう.)

田中君はもう元気みたいですよ。

Tanaka seems to be better.

明日は雨が降るみたいだ。

It seems it is going to rain.

誰も来ないみたいですよ。

It seems no one is going to come.

安くなってきたみたい。

It seems that it has come down in price.

〜よう is the neutral translation of English *seem* in written Japanese. Like 〜みたい it is used when the sentence reflects the speaker's judgment, again usually based on observed evidence. In speech, it is taken to indicate a greater degree of confidence than 〜みたい, although this may simply be a reflection of the increased sense of formality. 〜よう can be written with the Chinese character 〜様.

田中君はもう元気なようですよ。

Tanaka seems to be better.

明日は雨が降るようだ。

It seems it is going to rain.

誰も来ないようですよ。

It seems no one is going to come.

安くなってきたようだ。

It seems that it has gotten cheaper.

In contrast to 〜みたい and 〜よう, 〜らしい is used when the statement does not directly involve the speaker's judgment. This is the clear line between 〜らしい on the one hand and 〜みたい and 〜よう on the other. Use of 〜らしい indicates that the statement is second-hand information (learned by being told, by reading, by hearing it on television, etc.). The speaker is not really in a position to evaluate the truth or falseness of the claim, although they should know the source of the information. 〜らしい usually means something like *I was told* 〜 or *I heard that* 〜.

田中君はもう元気らしいですよ。

Tanaka seems to be better. I hear that Tanaka is better.

明日は雨が降るらしい。

It seems it is going to rain. I hear that it is going to rain.

誰も来ないらしいですよ。

It seems no one is going to come. I heard that no one is going to come.

安くなってきたらしい。

It seems that it has become cheaper. They say that it has become cheaper.

〜らしい can also be used consciously to create a distance between the speaker and the information. Perhaps the speaker disagrees with the statement, feels there is no basis for the judgment, or does not want to be associated with bad or unpopular news. 〜らしい indicates that this is someone else's idea, allowing the speaker to remain relatively uncommitted.

Generally speaking, 〜らしい is less common in speech than 〜みたい or 〜よう, and it is more or less equivalent to the hearsay expression そうだ. In contrast to 〜らしい, however, そうだ implies that the source of the information is not necessarily clear or reliable. It may, for example, be no more than a rumor. そうだ is often translated into English as *They say that*〜 where the *they* refers to no one in particular.

田中君はもう元気だそうですよ。

Tanaka seems to be better. They say that Tanaka is better.

誰も来ないそうですよ。

It seems no one is going to come. I heard that no one is going to come.

安くなってきたそうだ。

It seems that it has gotten cheap. They say that it has gotten less expensive.

Remember also the fixed two-part expression: 〜によると 〜そうだ or 〜によると 〜らしい *According to* 〜 〜 *is true.*

〜みたい, 〜よう, and 〜らしい also occur in the following patterns where similar differences in degrees of confidence are reflected.

イギリス人みたいな日本人

a Japanese person who seems English

イギリス人のような日本人

a very English Japanese person, a Japanese person who seems very English

イギリス人らしいイギリス人

a real English man, an Englishman's Englishman

あの人は日本人みたいに日本語を話す。

That person speaks Japanese as if he were a Japanese person.

日本人のように日本語を話す。

That person speaks Japanese as if he really were a Japanese person.

日本人らしく日本語を話す。

That person speaks Japanese like a typical Japanese person.

With 〜みたい and 〜よう, the two nouns being compared are not the same thing. Basically, a Japanese person is not an English person, but in the opinion of the speaker, the Japanese person under discussion has many English qualities. Again, 〜みたい and 〜よう assert the opinion of the speaker with 〜よう being stronger and more confident. In contrast, with 〜らしい the two nouns being compared really are examples of the same thing. The Englishman under discussion is a real, stereotypical Englishman. The claim is that the person under discussion is (in some absolute sense) an ideal example of the given attribute. Likewise with the second set of expressions, 〜みたい and 〜よう say that the person speaking is not Japanese but nevertheless speaks Japanese like a Japanese person. 〜らしく says that the person speaks Japanese like the true Japanese person he or she is. Note that 〜らしい can in fact be used when the person speaking is not actually Japanese. 日本人らしく日本語を話す said of a non-Japanese person is an authentic compliment (which the foreigner who sounds Japanese will immediately deny). As before, expressions with 〜みたい and 〜よう are relatively common while expressions with 〜らしい are less frequent.

There is a second kind of expression with a different 〜そう which is based not on hearsay but on immediate sensory experience (what you see, hear, feel, etc.). There are a number of situations where it (and only it) is expected and appropriate, in particular, situations where you are commenting on the food in front of you or where you are commenting on the way the weather looks outside.

とてもおいしそうな天ぷらだね。
It is really delicious looking tempura, isn't it.
雨が降りそうだ。
It looks like rain.
田中君はとても元気そうだった。
Tanaka looked really healthy.
すぐに来られそうじゃなかった。
He didn't look like he would be able to come anytime soon.

Compare the implications of the following three expressions when a plate of tempura has been placed in front of you. If you are actually looking at a plate of tempura, the second two expressions are strange, as is discussed below.

ここの天ぷらはおいしそうだ。
The tempura here looks delicious.
ここの天ぷらはおいしいみたいだ。
The tempura here seems delicious.
ここの天ぷらはおいしいらしい。
I have been told that the tempura here is delicious.

おいしそう (not おいしいそうだ which means *I hear that it is delicious*) says that the tempura in front of you looks delicious. This is an immediate visual evaluation. In contrast, おいしいみたい says that in your judgment, the tempura in front of you is delicious. The implication is that you have reasons for reaching this conclusion (i.e. past experience with the cook, a good review of the restaurant, etc.). Crucially, however, visual appearance on its own is not enough, or you would have said おいしそう. The underlying implication is that the tempura does not actually look good but you are confident for other reasons that it will taste delicious. The overall effect is not necessarily complimentary. ～らしい is even worse. The speaker can assert only that he or she has been told that the tempura is good (even though this may contradict the direct experience).

The implications change if you are discussing the tempura at a particular restaurant but you are not actually staring at a plate of food or reading the menu. In such a situation, おいしそう is simply inappropriate. おいしいみたい means that based on what you have heard, read, saw, or smelled (but not actually eaten), you have concluded that the tempura is good. おいしいらしい says that you have been told or you have read (in a guide, for example) that the food is good, but you are not in a position (or are unwilling) to commit yourself to that claim.

Note finally that these expressions can be combined to achieve a subtle effect.

やさしくなさそうだったらしい。
I hear that he did not look like a kind person (when you meet him face to face).
やさしくないらしいそうだ。
I have heard that someone was told that he is not a kind person.
日本人らしいようだ。
It appears that he really seems to be a Japanese person.
アメリカ人のようであるらしい。
I have been told that he seems like an American.

3.2. Softening

Remember that polite speech in Japanese is almost always indirect. As we have seen, various verbal expressions as well as assumptions about accommodation allow one to be indirect. Japanese also has a large number of grammatical devices which let you soften the impact of your own opinion. All of these expressions can be used with the most honorable of intentions (expressing actual ignorance or at least humility about one's knowledge), but they can also be used simply to avoid unpleasant encounters, even if you are quite sure of what you are saying, and quite sure, for example, that your boss is wrong on some point. In Japanese as well as in English, it is presumably better and more polite to avoid making others look foolish. These expressions can be added to the end of almost any Japanese sentence to soften its overall impact, and, like all speech in Japanese, they must be modulated to the person you are talking to.

そうだろう。（だろう）
そうでしょう。
そうであろう。
そうでございましょう。
Maybe it is so. Possibly it is so.

そう？
そうかなあ。（〜かなあ）
そうかしら。（〜かしら）
そうですか。（か）
Hmm. I wonder if it is so.

そうかもね。
そうかも知れない。（かも知れない・かもしれない）
そうかも知れません。
For all I know, it is so. Probably.

ホンコンに行くと思う。（〜と思う・〜とおもう）
ホンコンに行こうと思う。
ホンコンに行くと思います。
ホンコンに行こうと思います。
ホンコンに行くと思っている。
ホンコンに行こうと思っている。
ホンコンに行くと思っています。
ホンコンに行こうと思っています。
ホンコンに行くと思っております。
ホンコンに行こうと思っております。
ホンコンに行くだろうと思います。
She thinks that she will go to Hong Kong.
She thinks that she will probably go to Hong Kong.

ホンコンに行かないだろう。
ホンコンに行かないでしょう。
ホンコンに行くまい。（〜まい）
I probably will not go to Hong Kong

〜まい is a formal written ending meaning ないだろう *probably not*. It is formed:

行くまい	行かないだろう	*probably not go*
するまい	しないだろう	*probably not do* (sometimes すまい)
高くはあるまい	高くないだろう	*is probably not expensive*
先生ではあるまい	先生ではないだろう	*is probably not a teacher*

Rhetorical expressions such as *Don't you think that* ～ or *Isn't* ～ are as common in Japanese as in English.

会議は明日じゃないですか。　（～じゃないですか）
会議は明日ではないですか。
会議は明日じゃありませんか。
会議は明日じゃないでしょうか。
会議は明日ではないでしょうか。
Isn't it the case that the meeting is tomorrow?

ちょっと高いと思わない？　（～と思わない・～とおもわない）
ちょっと高いとは思わない？
ちょっと高いと思いませんか。
ちょっと高いとは思いませんか。
ちょっと高いと思わないでしょうか。
ちょっと高いとは思わないでしょうか。
Don't you think that it is a bit expensive?

There are also any number of expressions which can be used to lead up to a statement of doubt in order to soften its effect (and possibly forewarn its coming).

本当かどうかわかりませんが～
I don't know if it true or not, but ～
いいかどうかわかりませんが～
I don't know if it is good, but ～
聞いたかどうかわかりませんが～
I don't know if you have heard this but ～
ご存じかもしれませんが～
You may know this but ～
ちょっと話したいことがあるんですが、よろしいでしょうか。
I have a little something to talk about. Is now a good time?

3.3 Giving and receiving

In Japanese it is important to acknowledge the source of your information and your degree of confidence. Likewise, it is important to indicate that you have benefited from someone else's actions (intentionally or not). This is related to the fact that when you have a relationship with someone you often greet them with an expression like どうも or いつもお世話になっております or この間、どうもありがとう. Cynics might say that relationships between Japanese people are like contests to see who can be nicer to the other person. Certainly many actions are motivated by little more than a sense of obligation, but, for better or for worse, an awareness of who is doing what for whom is crucial to all relationships in Japan.

To this end, overt expressions of giving and receiving are significantly more common in Japanese than in English. While speakers of English may feel all of the appropriate emotions and obligations, in Japanese it is necessary to recognize indebtedness in speech. People who do not use these expressions sufficiently seem insensitive, even selfish. As usual, a non-native speaker will be forgiven, but using these expressions correctly signals a sensitivity to Japanese inter-personal relations which is well-appreciated. Compare the Japanese examples with their English translations where overt expressions of benefit are much less frequent.

くれる・くださる（くれる・下さる）

買い物に行ってくれた。

He went shopping (so I wouldn't have to).

私が考えていることを言ってくれた。

He said what I was thinking (so I didn't have to).

赤ちゃんが元気に産まれてきてくれた。

The baby was born healthy.

先生が私の言いたいことをわかってくださった。

The teacher understood what I was trying to say.

秀明君は私と遊んでくれた。

Hideaki played with me.

息子がよく食べてくれた。

My son ate everything.

ドアを開けてくださいました。

He opened the door for me.

もらう・いただく（貰う・頂く）

英会話を教えてもらおう。

Let's have someone teach us English.

うちの下の子が隣の子によく遊んでもらった。

My youngest child often had the child next door over to play.

荷物を持ってもらった。

They brought my luggage. I had them bring my luggage.

答えを教えてもらった。

I had her tell me the answer.

やる・あげる・さしあげる（やる・上げる・差し上げる）

うちの下の子が隣の子と遊んであげた。

My youngest child played with the child next door.

電話をかけてあげた。

I called them (to tell them the good news).

書いて差し上げましょうか。

Shall I write it for you?

While あげる and くれる both mean *give*, くれる means specifically *give to me* (or *to a member of my in-group*). An expression such as 私にくれた therefore sounds redundant although it is not ungrammatical. In contrast, 私がくれた is basically ungrammatical since it can only mean that I gave something to myself. Similarly, the unspoken subject of もらう is the speaker (or a member of the speaker's in-group) so that 私にもらった is also ungrammatical since it means that I received something from myself. If it is the case that you have in fact given something to someone, 私が彼にあげた *I gave it to him* is preferred to 彼が私にもらった *He received it from me*, although the latter expression is not impossible. Given a choice between くれる and もらう, the former is generally more polite because the speaker's role as recipient seems passive. It is also possible with くれる (and only with くれる) to put yourself into the position of the person you are speaking to, allowing either 誰がくれたの？ meaning *Who gave that to you?* or 誰にもらったの？ meaning *Who did you get that from?*

When speaking of acts of giving and receiving between two third parties, the verbs あげる and もらう are used freely. With もらう, the source of what is received may be marked with に or から, although から is more likely when the source is not an actual human being (田中君にもらう versus 国からもらう).

As noted on page 10, やる is really just a colloquial version of 上げる. While typical examples with やる involve giving water to plants and food to babies (i.e. giving to inferiors), it is in fact possible to use やる when speaking of giving to a relatively wide range of people.

It should be obvious that when used correctly verbs of giving and receiving make explicit use of pronouns redundant (particularly any reference to oneself). Verbs of giving and receiving can also disambiguate sentences by making it explicit exactly who has benefited in a particular situation. Compare the following:

田中さんが手伝いました。

Tanaka helped. (someone quite unlikely the speaker)

田中さんが手伝ってくれました。

Tanaka helped me. (must be the speaker, the speaker's in-group)

田中さんが山本君に手伝った。

Tanaka helped Yamamoto. (Yamamoto is most likely unrelated to the speaker)

田中さんが山本君に手伝ってあげた。

Tanaka helped Yamamoto. (Yamamoto is explicitly unrelated the speaker)

田中さんが山本君に手伝ってくれた。

Tanaka helped Yamamoto. (Yamamoto is in the speaker's in-group)

行こうか。

Shall I go? Shall we go?

行ってあげようか。

Shall I go? (for you, in your place)

中島さんは山本さんが自分の車を洗ったと言いました。

Nakajima said that Yamamoto washed his car. (Nakajima's car or Yamamoto's car?)

中島さんは山本さんが自分の車を洗ってくれたと言いました。

Nakajima said that Yamamoto washed his car. (must be Nakajima's car)

　Finally, there is a point of contrast between expressions like お書きしましょうか and 書いて差し上げましょうか. While both expressions are offers, お書きしましょうか is given even when the other person is clearly capable of doing the activity, in this case writing. A helpful clerk offers to fill in a form simply as a courtesy. In contrast, 書いてあげましょうか and 書いて差し上げましょうか carry the implication that the person being addressed is in some way incapable of doing the activity. The helpful clerk makes such an offer to someone who has left their reading glasses at home, or to a foreign student who is unsure of how to fill in the form. As a result the latter can in some circumstances be insulting. On a bus, for example, it is polite to offer your seat with a polite お譲りしましょうか. It may be dangerous to offer your seat with an equally polite 譲って差し上げましょうか unless the person you are addressing obviously needs to sit down. Said to someone with no clear need to sit may imply that you believe them to be old, feeble, and in need of assistance. For people who do not feel themselves to be particularly old, this may come as something of a shock (cf. おじさん and おばさん on page 233).

3.4. Modals

Modals in English are words such as *may*, *must*, *can*, *could*, or *should*. None of these expressions has a direct translation into Japanese. Rather the meaning associated with these words is represented by particular expressions in Japanese.

3.4.1 Commands and requests

When you give a command or make a request you are in effect asking another person to do something for you (obey your command or respond to your request). With permission, you are asking the other person to let you do something. It should not come as a great surprise that commands, requests, and permission often involve expressions of giving and receiving. Even the most basic word meaning *please*, 下さい (as well as 下さいませ), is a frozen form of the humble verb 下さる.

　Here we compare over twenty different ways to express a command or make a request. Some of these expressions are real commands which require compliance. Even if the command is very polite, it is expected that the listener will respond. The three sets which follow are increasingly indirect command forms disguised as other kinds of sentences. In general, the easier it is to refuse or ignore a command (overt or implied), the more polite it is felt to be, because the overall goal is to avoid the potential difficulty of having to refuse. When making a request (which is to say when trying to have done what you want done), it is natural to use one of the more polite expressions. And as with English, the more complicated or difficult your request, the more polite and circumspect you should probably be.

止まれ。 *Stop!*

The most direct kind of command; military, official, angry. 止まれ is what is written on stop signs in Japan. The negative version of this is 止まるな *Don't stop!*

止まってくれ。 *Stop!*

くれ is the direct command form of くれる. The overall effect is still quite strong.

止まりなさい。 *Please stop.*

Intimate sounding, generally adults speaking to children.

止まって。 *Stop!*

A somewhat less direct command form. Some form of くれる has been omitted.

止まってください。 *Please stop.*

The most neutral command form. The negative here is 止まらないでください *Please don't stop.*

止まってちょうだい。 *Please stop.*

Very intimate sounding, for use within a family. ちょうだい on its own is an intimate way to say *please* when you want something.

お止まりください。
お止まりになってください
Please stop.

These are softer, female, characteristic of people working in hotels, restaurants and other service industries.

Three more general types of commands are discussed below. In the first set, the command is disguised as an invitation. As an invitation it is up to the person being invited to accept or decline. This command is considered more indirect because the person being invited is given an implicit (if very weak) choice. More direct forms like 止まれ or 止まって or even 止まってください lack this sense of choice.

止まってくれない？
止まってくれないか。
止まってくれませんか。

止まって下さらない？
止まって下さいませんか。
Won't you please stop?

In the second set, the command is disguised as a question about what is possible (もらえ
る is the potential form of もらう). This kind of command is less direct than the invitation because it is even less personal. An invitation must be accepted or declined by a
person. In contrast, something may not be possible for any number of reasons, many of
which have nothing to do with the people at hand. Again, taking individual responsibility out of the equation results in an more polite interaction.

止まってもらえない？
止まってもらえないか。
止まってもらえませんか。
止まっていただけない？
止まっていただけないか。
止まっていただけませんか。
Can you stop? Could you stop? Could I have you stop?

In the final set of examples, the requests are made with expressions containing 〜たい or
ほしい. These are really no more than just hints. One person announces that such and
such would be really helpful. The obvious implication is, can you help me? The person
listening can choose to act on the obvious implication (いいですよ or 何かいたしましょ
うか) or they can choose to ignore it (そうですか、それは大変ですねえ or どうしてです
か). This is the least direct command because it does not require any explanation whatsoever. It is not a literal command, and should the listener decline to act on the obvious
implication, everyone can act as if nothing ever happened.

止まってほしい。
止まってほしいんですが。
止まってもらいたいんだけど。
止まってもらいたいんですが。
止まっていただきたいんですか。
I would really like you to stop. I would like to have you stop.

While there are a great number of different expressions discussed above, a student should
be comfortable with about four, in essence one of each kind. For example:

待って。待ってよ。	for friends
待って下さい。	for strangers
待って下さいませんか。	polite
待っていただけますか。	most polite, for more difficult requests
or 待っていただけませんか。	

3.4.2 Permission

Commands and requests are really just attempts by one person to get another person to do something. Asking for permission is the same thing, but the person being asked must make the decision. They may grant permission or not. Requests for permission in English begin with the words *May I ~* or *Please let me ~* or *Do you think it would be possible for me to ~*. There is a parallel variety in Japanese, and the degree of politeness increases in the expected ways and for the expected reasons (i.e. social distance between speaker and listener, difficulty of what is about to follow: *Could I borrow this pen?* versus *I know you are very busy, but do you think you could take a look at this essay and check my English?* etc.).

英語で話していい？（～て）
英語で話してもいい？（～ても）
英語で話してもいいですか。
英語で話してもよろしいですか。
英語で話してもよろしいでしょうか。
英語でお話ししてもよろしいでしょうか。
May I speak English?

The forms below (with 話させる which is the causative form of 話す) literally mean something like: *Please make me speak* or *Please let me speak*. They are a very polite way of making a request which can be made more polite by adding the appropriate command or request ending as discussed above (i.e. くれ versus いただけませんか).

話させて。
話させてくれ。
話させてください。
話させてくれませんか。
話させてくださいませんか。
話させていただけないですか。
話させていただけませんか。
話させていただけないでしょうか。
Please let me speak. May I speak?

In general, using causative expressions is the most polite way to ask for permission or to announce your compliance with someone else's wish. For example, before beginning a self-introduction, it is very common to say "I will now introduce myself."

これから自己紹介します。
これから自己紹介いたします。
これから自己紹介させていただきます。
I will now introduce myself.

The third expression here literally means something like: *I will now have you make me introduce myself.* While exceedingly polite, this style of statement which combines causative forms with some form of もらう is quite common in a number of ritualized situations. For example:

before almost any kind of public speech
先生のお話では、聞かせていただきます。
We will now hear the professor's words.

before beginning your own speech
〜について少しの間お話しさせていただきます。
〜について少しお話しさせていただきたいと思います。
I will now make a short speech about 〜
I would like to make a short speech about 〜

when beginning an introduction
お客様を紹介させていただきます。
I will now introduce our guest.

when accepting a duty or heavy responsibility
行かせていただき、頑張らせていただきます。
I will be the one to go (as the company representative), *and I will try my hardest.*

3.4.3 Should

Expressions of advice in English are often expressed with *should*. While there is no word which translates *should* in Japanese, there are a number of different ways to make suggestions in Japanese. Many involve conditionals (discussed beginning on page 172).

早く出かけた方がいい。（方がいい・ほうがいい）
早く出かけた方がいいです。
早く出かけた方がいいだろう。
早く出かけた方がいいでしょう。
早く出かけた方がいいんじゃないですか。
早く出かけた方がいいんじゃないでしょうか。
早く出かけた方がいいと思わない？
早く出かけた方がいいと思いませんか。
早く出かけた方がいいかも知れない。
早く出かけた方がいいかも知れません。
It would be better if you left early. You should leave early.

早<ruby>早<rt>はや</rt></ruby>く<ruby>出<rt>で</rt></ruby>かけたらどう？ （〜たら）
早く出かけたらどうですか。
早く出かけたらどうでしょうか。
早く出かけたらいがですか。
早く出かけたらいかがでしょうか。
How would it be if you left early? If you left early, how would that be?

早く出かけたらいい。
早く出かければいい。 （〜れば）
You should leave early.

<ruby>早<rt>はや</rt></ruby>く<ruby>出<rt>で</rt></ruby>かけたほうがよかった。 （方・ほう）
早く出かけたらよかった。
早く出かければよかった。
I should have left early. You should have left early.

<ruby>早<rt>はや</rt></ruby>く<ruby>出<rt>で</rt></ruby>かけたほうがいいのに。 （〜のに）
早く出かけたらいいのに。
早く出かければいいのに。
It would be better if you leave early (but I doubt you will).

<ruby>早<rt>はや</rt></ruby>く<ruby>出<rt>で</rt></ruby>かけたほうがよかったのに。
早く出かけたらよかったのに。
早く出かければよかったのに。
I should have left early (but I didn't). *You should have left early* (but you didn't).

ビッグベンを<ruby>見<rt>み</rt></ruby>るべきですよ。 （〜べき）
You really should see Big Ben.
<ruby>早<rt>はや</rt></ruby>く<ruby>帰<rt>かえ</rt></ruby>るべきだ。
You should really go home early.

Advice phrases with 〜べき indicate something which should be done because it is the general expectation. Everyone who visits London sees Big Ben. You should go and see it as well. In order to be on time for your son's birthday party, you should really go home early. It is only natural.

Should in English actually has a second usage as well, unrelated to advice. "He should be here at two o'clock" refers to an expectation about future events. This may be translated as something like <ruby>二時<rt>にじ</rt></ruby>までに<ruby>来<rt>く</rt></ruby>るだろう or as an expression with はず: <ruby>二時<rt>にじ</rt></ruby>までに<ruby>来<rt>く</rt></ruby>るはずだ.

3.4.4 Must

〜ては on its own has a conditional *if* interpretation (discussed on page 179). As such 行
かなくてはいけない might be literally translated as "If you do not go, it will be bad."
The effect of this in Japanese is, "You must go." Again, there is no word which actually
means *must* in Japanese. In conversation, the combination 〜ては contracts to 〜ちゃ.

行かなくちゃ。（〜ては）
行かなくちゃいけない。（〜てはいけない）
行かなくてはいけない。
行かなくてはいけません。
行かなくちゃならない。（〜てはならない）
行かなくてはならない。
行かなくてはなりません。
行かなくちゃだめだ（〜てはだめだ）
行かなくてはだめだ。
行かなくてはだめです。
We must go.

Expressions with 〜てはいけない are in general very blunt and somewhat legalistic
sounding. As such, an honorific expression such as いらっしゃらなくてはなりません is
possible but unusual; it is rare to be both very polite and very direct at the same time. If
someone important must be encouraged, repeated advice statements are better: いらっしゃ
らなくてはならないと思いませんか or いらっしゃらなくてはならないのではないでしょ
うか or even a more general いらっしゃらなくてはならないことになりました "It has
turned out that everyone must go."

   Prohibition with 〜れば is generally considered somewhat less harsh than the more
direct 〜ては form.

行かなければならない。（〜ればならない）
行かなければなりません。
行かなければならないでしょう。
行かなければいけない。（〜ればいけない）
行かなければいけません。
行かなければいけないでしょう。
We must go.

   A general necessity can also be expressed with 必要: 行くことが必要です. This may
be for legal or for more personal reasons where it can sound like strong advice. 〜べき is
ambiguous in the same way and may be quite strong. The effect in Japanese is similar to
the distinction in English between "You should go and see Big Ben" (advice) and "You
really must go and see Big Ben" (very strong advice).

3.4.5 Can

Can, as in "I can eat more pancakes than you can," is known as the *potential*. Like all of the other modal expressions discussed in this section, there is no word for *can* in Japanese. Rather, the potential of a verb like 行く is the separate verb form 行ける *can go*. The potential of a verb like 食べる is 食べられる *can eat*. The potential of する is できる.Due to the fact that 食べられる is identical to the *passive* form of 食べる, *can eat* is often abbreviated to 食べれる in conversation. However, this abbreviation is strongly frowned on by the powers that be in Japan (i.e. the Ministry of Education), and non-native speakers may sometimes be corrected. In addition, a phrase such as *can eat sushi* may be realized in Japanese as either すしが食べられる or すしを食べられる. Both particles が and を are acceptable on the direct object. For more on this continue on to the next section for a discussion of the relationship between predicate types and particles.

A second potential construction is 〜ことができる as in のどが痛いから大きい声で話すことができない "My throat hurts so I am unable to speak in a loud voice." Students of Japanese can sometimes be accused of over-using this latter expression and avoiding the grammatical potential (話せる in this case) because forms like 話せる or 食べられる are sometimes felt to be harder to pronounce or more difficult to remember.

Finally, recall from the discussion of transitive and intransitive pairs (page 127) that intransitive verbs like 開く, 壊れる, 冷える, 燃える, are in some sense inherently potential. As such, they do not usually occur in the grammatical potential as well. This inherent potential meaning is also present in verbs like 聞こえる, 見える, and わかる. Note that an expression like できることができる is in fact possible, although it means something like "I can do what I can do" or "I can do some (but probably not all)."

3.5 Tense and aspect

Verbs in Japanese might be divided into two overall categories: verbs which refer to facts or situations and verbs which refer to things which happen (or things which a person does). Verbs which refer to facts or situations are generally called *statives*. In addition to real verbs, adjectives, nominal adjectives, and all potential verbs should be thought of as stative predicates.

Stative verbs	ある *have, exist*; 要る・いる *to need*; 居る・いる *exist*; 聞こえる・きこえる *be audible*; テニスができる *be able to play tennis*; 見える・みえる *be visible*; 日本語がわかる *understand Japanese*
Potentials	漢字が書ける *be able to write Chinese characters*; etc.
〜たい	すしが食べたい・たべたい *want to eat sushi*; etc.
Adjectives	ありがたい *be grateful for*; いとしい *think tenderly of*; うまい *be good at, tasty*; うらやましい *be envious of*; 恐ろしい・おそろしい *be fearful, fear,*

be afraid of; 面白い・おもしろい *interesting, be interested in*; 可愛い・かわいい *cute, hold dear*; 楽しい・たのしい *enjoyable*; つまらない *boring*; なつかしい *to miss, feel yearning for*; にくらしい *be hateful of*; ねたましい *be jealous of*; はずかしい *be bashful, ashamed*; ほしい *to want*; まずい *taste bad, be bad*; etc.

Nominal adjectives	可能な・かのう *be possible*; きらいな *dislike*; 困難な・こんなん *be difficult*; 好きな・すき *like*; 得意な・とくい *be good at*; 苦手な・にがて *be bad at*; 必要な・ひつよう *needed, necessary*; 下手な・へた *be bad at*; etc. (See the list on page 227 for many more examples.)

Stative predicates are simply true or not, or possibly true to some degree. They are not normally thought of as things which a person "does," and they may be true even if a person is not doing anything particular at the moment. *John likes sushi* is a fact about John which, if true, is true even when he is sleeping or playing tennis. As there is no control, it is not usual to use statives as commands. お金をあってください makes no sense, and non-verbal predicates such as nominal adjectives and adjectives do not even have a command form. For the same reason, statives do not combine with predicates like 〜ておく which imply doing something on purpose for some later use. The same is true of volitional forms like あろう which are quite strange. In addition, the direct object of a stative predicate is marked with が rather than を, sometimes obligatorily, sometimes optionally: only お金がいる, but both すしが食べたい and すしを食べたい are grammatical. All verbs in the potential as well as verbs in the 〜たい form are statives derived from regular verbs. The case marker on their direct objects shifts optionally from を to が. See page 196 for more discussion of が-marked direct objects.

が-object obligatory	ある, 居る・いる, 要る・いる, 聞こえる・きこえる, 見える・みえる, 分かる・わかる, any adjective or nominal adjective which might be thought of as taking a direct object (e.g. ほしい)
optional	好き・すき, 嫌い・きらい, 〜たい forms, potentials

A possible counter-example to these generalizations about statives is a sentence like 私の気持ちをわかってください although this sentence really means "Please try to understand how I feel." Quite likely わかる is not actually stative here, and means instead something like *come to understand*. A second apparent exception is the verb いる which may be a true stative *exist* but might also be something which a person does: *remain* or *stay*. Under this interpretation, いる is not stative; ここにいてください *Stay here*.

In contrast to statives, happenings are all dynamic. They involve changes, and to a great degree they reflect the choices of their participants. All transitive and intransitive verbs (page 127) as well as Noun＋する combinations (page 228) are examples of things which happen.

3.5.1 Simple tenses in English and Japanese

In general, one needs to be able to talk about things which will be true in the *future*, things which were true in the *past*, and things which are true *now*. How do stative and non-stative verb types interact with normal tenses (*future, past, present*) in Japanese?

3.5.1.1 Will do, do *(future)*

三時_{さんじ}まで泳_{およ}ぐからそのあと会_あいましょうか。

I will swim until three, so shall we meet after that?

彼_{かれ}が二時_{にじ}に着_つくそうです。

He said he will arrive at two o'clock.

三時_{さんじ}まで会議_{かいぎ}がある。

I have a meeting until three.

Note that some stative predicates are difficult to interpret in the future. 明日_{あした}までにすしが 好_すきだ is pretty strange because a predicate like 好_すき is not clearly related to free will: unlike meeting times, one rarely schedules changes in one's preferences. Compare the above sentence with 明日_{あした}までにすしが好きになる which is no longer stative.

The simple future form (identical to the dictionary form) can also be used to talk about a habit. Habits are anything which one does on a regular basis. It can be true that one takes a bath every night after dinner even if one is not taking a bath at the moment. In English, the simple present of a verb is used to represent habits.

健康_{けんこう}のために毎日_{まいにち}プールで泳_{およ}ぐ。

I swim in the pool every day for my health.

そのおじさんが毎日_{まいにち}二時_{にじ}に入_{はい}ってくる。

That man comes in everyday at two.

It is odd to think of statives themselves as habits, again since statives are not usually thought of as things which a person does, let alone does on a regular basis. Think about "I have an envelope every day at three o'clock" which is a rather odd claim to make.

3.5.1.2 Have done, did *(past)*

きのうプールで泳_{およ}いだ。

Yesterday, I swam in the pool.

お客_{きゃく}さんが時間通_{じかんどお}りに着_ついた。

The guest arrived right on time.

何_{なに}もなかった。

She didn't have anything.

All three verb types occur in the simple past.

3.5.1.3 ～ている

For many verbs, the ～ている form is best described as a perfect form which means *has verb-ed*. These verbs are often called *change of state* verbs since they refer to events which have definite final states. For these verbs, the ～ている form means that the final state obtains. 着いている means *has arrived, is in the station*. 着く, on the other hand, means that the final state will come to pass in the future (perhaps in the very near future). Crucially for a verb like 着く, there is no exact Japanese equivalent to the English progressive *is arriving*. None of the verbs in this list has a progressive interpretation (at least when referring to a single event). Note the English translations. All of the lists in the section are representative.

Change of state only	諦めている・あきらめる *has given up*; 飽きている・あきる *is tired of*; 開いている・あく (the door) *is open*; 浮いている・うく *has floated* (to the surface); 遅れている・おくれる *is late*; 思い出している・おもいだす *has recalled, remembers*; 外出している・がいしゅつ *has gone out, is out*; 買っている・かう *has bought*; 帰っている・かえる *is at home, has returned*; 隠れている・かくれる *is hidden, concealed*; 欠けている・かける *is chipped, has chipped*; 貸している・かす *has lent*; 傾いている・かたむく *has leaned over, is tilting*; 借りている・かりる *has borrowed*; 固まっている・かたまる *is hard, has hardened*; 勝っている・かつ *is best, has won*; 変わっている・かわる *is different, has changed*; 決まっている・きまる *is decided*; 許可している・きょか *has permitted*; 禁止している・きんし *is prohibited*; 腐っている・くさる *is rotten, has gone bad*; 夫している・くふう *has found a way, invented*; 曇っている・くもる *is cloudy*; 来ている・くる *is here, has come*; 結婚している・けっこん *is married*; 凍っている・こおる *is frozen*; 故障している・こしょう *is broken, out of order*; 断わっている・ことわる *has refused*; 込んでいる・こむ *is crowded*; 壊れている・こわれる *is broken*; 下がっている・さがる *is down, has gone down*; 咲いている・さく *is in bloom*; 冷めている・さめる *is cooled down*; 沈んでいる・しずむ *is sunk*; 死んでいる・しぬ *is dead, has died*; 閉まっている・しまる *is closed*; 出発している・しゅっぱつ *is departed, is gone*; 知らせている・しらせる *has let someone know, is informed*; 捨てている・すてる *is thrown away*; 揃っている・そろう *is gathered together*; 倒れている・たおれる *has fallen down, is down*; 助けている・たすける *is saved*; 建っている・たつ *is built*; 足りている・たりる *is sufficient*; 縮んでいる・ちぢむ *is shrunk*; 貯金している・ちょきん *is saved up*; 疲れている・つかれる *is tired*; 着いている・つく *is here, has arrived*; 潰れている・つぶれる *is crushed*; 積もっている・つもる *is piled up*; 到着している・とうちゃく *is here, has arrived*; 独立している・どくりつ *is independent, has become independent*; 止まっている・とまる *stops, is stopped*; 直っている・なお

る *is better, is recovered*; 無くなっている・なくなる *is gone, disappeared*; なっている・なる *is made of*; 慣れている・なれる *is used to, has gotten used to*; 抜けている・ぬける *is out, has come out*; 濡れている・ぬれる *is damp, wet*; 願っている・ねがう *wishes for*; 寝ている・ねる *has lied down, has gone to sleep*; 残している・のこす *is left behind, remains, has left behind*; 残っている・のこる *remains, has stayed*; 生えている・はえる *has spring up*; 始まっている・はじまる *is begun*; 外れている・はずれる *is off, has slipped off*; 発行している・はっこう *has issued, published*; 発達している・はったつ *is developed, has progressed*; 離れる・はなれる *is separate from, has separated from*; 晴れている・はれる *is cleared up*; 広がっている・ひろがる *is extended, is spread out*; 不足している・ふそく *lacks, is short of*; 返事している・へんじ *has replied*; 募集している・ぼしゅう *is recruited*; 保存している・ほぞん *is preserved*; 太っている・ふとる *is fat, has gotten fat*; 報告している・ほうこく *has reported, reports*; 混じっている・まじる *is mixed, has mixed*; 間違っている・まちがう *is mistaken, has made a mistake*; 迷っている・まよう *is lost, has gotten lost*; 間に合っている・まにあう *is on time, has been on time*; 認めている・みとめる *recognizes, has recognized*; 向いている・むく *is turned toward, faces, has turned*; 痩せている・やせる *is thin, has lost weight*; 止んでいる・やむ *is stopped*; 輸出している・ゆしゅつ *is exported*; 輸入している・ゆにゅう *is imported*; 汚れている・よごれる *is dirty*; 汚している・よごす *has dirtied* (something); 予定している・よてい *has scheduled*; 割れている・われる *is broken*; 弱っている・よわる *is weak, has weakened*; 沸いている・わく *has reached boiling*; 分かれている・わかれる *is separated, has split off*

Imagine you are waiting for a bus and reporting to a friend who can hear you but cannot see you or the street. The following sequence of sentences is normal in Japanese. Note in particular that 来ている is not possible *until the bus has stopped*. As such, it must mean something like "The bus is here" or "The bus has arrived." Contrary to what might be expected, Japanese 来ている and English *is coming* do not correspond.

Before the bus comes into sight (in English, *Where is the bus?!*):
バスは来ないね。
バスはまだだよ。

When it first comes into sight (in English, *The bus is here* or *The bus is coming*):
あっ、バスが来た。
あっ、バスが来るよ。

As it approaches (in English, *It's here!* or *The bus is coming. Hurry up!*):
あっ、バスが来る。
あっ、バスが来た、来た。早くしろよ。

When it has stopped (in English, *It's here!* or *The bus is here. Hurry!*):
バスが来てるよ。早く早く。

There are in effect two different contexts in the above situation. First, the bus is in sight or it is not. Second, the bus is coming to a stop or it has stopped. In English it is actually possible to shout "The bus is here" at least twice, once when the bus first comes into sight and once again after it has stopped. Crucially, 来てる (or more properly 来ている) is possible only after the bus has come to a complete stop. This discussion of 来る applies equally to all verbs found in the change of state list above. And while many of the verbs are naturally thought of as changes, others are more surprising. Note in particular that if you meet a friend who is looking at an item while shopping, in English it is natural to ask "Are you buying that?" In Japanese this must be それを買うの？ since それを買っている usually means *has bought that*. This is not a completely clear case, however. At the cash register, as a person is going through what might be called the "buying process," 買っている may also be understood to mean *is buying*.

Turning now from change of state verbs, we find that for other verbs, the 〜ている construction is a progressive. 泳いでいる, for example, is best translated into English as *is swimming*. *Is swimming* is something which can be understood as going on "now." Verbs which are usually interpreted as progressive with 〜ている are usually thought of as *processes*. Swimming (along with running, walking, talking, watching television, studying) are all processes or activities which people do. Note that very few verbs are progressive under 〜ている *all* of the time. Like 買う above, most of these verbs are to some degree ambiguous in one way or another (given the right circumstances), and as such there may be some disagreement from one native speaker of Japanese to the next.

Progressive primarily
遊んでいる・あそぶ *is playing*; 扱っている・あつかう *is dealing with*; 洗っている・あらう *is washing*; 争っている・あらそう *is competing*; 急いでいる・いそぐ *is hurrying*; 歌っている・うたう *is singing*; 運転している・うんてん *is driving*; 運動している・うんどう *is exercising*; 追っている・おう *is chasing after*; 行っている・おこなう *is carrying out*; 押している・おす *is pushing*; 踊っている・おどる *is dancing*; 溺れている・おぼれる *is drowning*; 泳いでいる・およぐ *is swimming*; 飼っている・かう *is taking care of* (a pet); 数えている・かぞえる *is counting*; 活動している・かつどう *is playing a role in*; 頑張っている・がんばる *is trying one's best*; 競争している・きょうそう *is competing with*; 協力している・きょうりょく *is cooperating with*; 暮らしている・くらす *is making a living*; 比べている・くらべる *is comparing*; 繰り返している・くりかえす *is repeating, doing*

again; 苦しんでいる・くるしむ *is suffering*; 苦労している・くろう *is having trouble with*; 削っている・けずる *is shaving*; 喧嘩している・けんか *is arguing*; 研究している・けんきゅう *is researching*; 建設している・けんせつ *is building*; 見物している・けんぶつ *is sightseeing*; 交際している・こうさい *is hanging about*; 行動している・こうどう *is acting, behaving*; 裂いている・さく *is cutting up* (a fish); 探している・さがす *is looking for*; 叫んでいる・さけぶ *is crying out*; 騒いでいる・さわぐ *is making a lot of noise*; 叱っている・しかる *is scolding*; 実験している・じっけん *is conducting an experiment*; 質問している・しつもん *is asking a question*; 指導している・しどう *is guiding*; しゃべっている・しゃべる *is speaking*; 修理している・しゅうり *is repairing*; 使用している・しよう *is making use of*; 吸っている・すう *is breathing, inhaling*; 過ごしている・すごす *is spending* (time); 住んでいる・すむ *is residing*; 生活している・せいかつ *is making a living*; 製造している・せいぞう *is manufacturing*; 洗濯している・せんたく *is washing*; 掃除している・そうじ *is cleaning*; 想像している・そうぞう *is imagining*; 闘っている・たたかう *is fighting against*; 叩いている・たたく *is striking, hitting* (an object); 注意している・ちゅうい *is being careful*; 使っている・つかう *is using*; 続けている・つづける *is continuing* (the conversation); 努めている・つとめる *is working, is employed*; 照っている・てる *is shining*; 電話している・でんわ *is telephoning*; 努力している・どりょく *is making an effort, is trying*; 眺めている・ながめる *is staring*; 泣いている・なく *is crying*; 鳴っている・なる *is ringing, is jingling*; 匂っている・におう *smells* (good); 臭っている・におう *smells* (bad); 塗っている・ぬる *is painting*; 拍手している・はくしゅ *is clapping*; 運んでいる・はこぶ *is carrying* (a load); 働いている・はたらく *is working*; 比較している・ひかく *is comparing*; 光っている・ひかる *glitters, is glittering*; 弾いている・ひく *is performing*; 拭いている・ふく *is wiping away*; 降っている・ふる *is raining*; 勉強している・べんきょう *is studying*; 放送している・ほうそう *is broadcasting*; 掘っている・ほる *is excavating*; 翻訳している・ほんやく *is translating*; 磨いている・みがく *is polishing*; 向かっている・むかう *is heading in a direction*; 燃やしている・もやす *is burning* (leaves); 揺れている・ゆれる *is shaking, quivering*; 読んでいる・よむ *is reading*; 練習している・れんしゅう *is practicing*; 笑っている・わらう *is laughing*

As noted above, almost all verbs which are progressive under 〜ている are actually ambiguous, allowing either interpretation (perfect or progressive) to some degree. Such ambiguity is dependent on the context but is nonetheless very common. For example, 手術している spoken during an actual operation is progressive and means *is operating on*. Said by the doctor *after* the operation, however, it is more naturally interpreted as *have performed an operation* or *have operated on*. Similarly for the following verbs where both interpretations are judged to be more or less equally accessible:

Ambiguous　祝っている・いわう *is celebrating, celebrates* (a birthday); 植えている・うえる *is planting, has planted*; 写している・うつす *is imitating, imitates, is a copy of*; 希望している・きぼう *is hoping for, hopes for* (good luck);切っている・きる *is chopping, has chopped*; 配っている・くばる *is distributing, has distributed*; 計画している・けいかく *is planning, has planned* (an event); 誘っている・さそう *is inviting, has invited* (the neighbors); 冷ましている・さます *is cooling, has cooled* (a pie); 敷いている・しく *is spreading out, has spread out* (a futon); 従っている・したがう *is following, follows* (an order); 縛っている・しばる *is tying up, has tied up* (an intruder); 手術している・しゅじゅつ *is operating on, has operated on* (a person); 主張している・しゅちょう *is asserting, has asserted* (one's rights); 準備している・じゅんび *is preparing, has prepared*; 調べている・しらべる *is investigating, has investigated* (a crime); 推薦している・すいせん *is recommending, recommends* (a person); 勧めている・すすめる *is advising, recommending, advises* (a course of action); 説明している・せつめい *is explaining, explains, has explained* (the answer); 確かめている・たしかめる *is confirming, has confirmed* (times and places); 建てている・たてる *is building, has built* (a skyscraper); 頼んでいる・たのむ *is requesting, has requested* (advice); 食べている・たべる *is eating, has eaten* (dinner); 黙っている・だまる *is falling silent, is silent*; 試している・ためす *is trying out, has tried out* (a new product); 注文している・ちゅうもん *is ordering, has ordered* (dinner); 取り替えている・とりかえる *is exchanging, has exchanged* (one thing for another); 並べている・ならべる *is lining up, has lined up* (the chairs); 発表している・はっぴょう *is announcing, making public, has announced*; 反対している・はんたい *is disagreeing with, disagrees with*; 否定している・ひてい *is denying, has denied* (past statements); 冷やしている・ひやす *is cooling, has cooled* (beer); 防いでいる・ふせぐ *is preventing, prevents*;増やしている・ふやす *is increasing, has increased* (one's savings); 訪問している・ほうもん *is paying a call on, is at*; 干している・ほす *is drying, has dried* (laundry); 誉めている・ほめる *is praising, praises* (someone); 混ぜている・まぜる *is mixing, has mixed* (one thing into another); 守っている・まもる *is protecting, protects*; 命令している・めいれい *is ordering, has ordered*; 用心している・ようじん *is taking care, takes care*; 予防している・よぼう *is preventing, prevents* (fires); 沸かしている・わかす *is boiling, has boiled* (water)

Most of these are extended activities which come to natural conclusions (like building a house or lining something up). Others are are events which are complex when looked at "closely" but are more simple when looked at from "far away." Thus *ordering dinner* may involve lengthy discussion with the waiter and several individual decisions: a process. Alternatively, it may refer to a simple placing of an order: a change of state.

Recall that simple verb forms in Japanese may refer to a specific future event (明日三時に電話する) or to a habit (毎日三時に電話する). Habits themselves may also be talked about in the past, future, or present.

先月まで毎日三時に電話しました。
Until last month, he called everyday at three.
来月から毎日三時に電話します。
From next month, he will call everyday at three.
毎日三時に電話します。
He calls everyday at three.
今は毎日三時に電話しています。
He is now calling everyday at three.

Under a habitual reading, a normally change of state verb like 行く is completely acceptable as a progressive; 今は毎日電車で行っています means "He is now going by train everyday." Each act of going by train is a discrete change of state; it is the habit which is progressing.

Finally, many 〜ている predicates have a weak experiential reading. Usually 家を建てている means "We are building a house" or "We have built this house (in front of us)," but it can also be used to mean "We have built some house (in the past)" or the more literal "We have the experience of building a house." When contrasted with 家を建てたことがある, use of the experiential 〜ている implies a relevance to the present situation (i.e. "We have built houses in the past so you can trust us to do a good job on your house as well").

3.5.2 *Sequences of aspect and tense*

The particular interpretation of a 〜ている form varies with the tense found on the いる.

もう駅に着いている (から早く迎えに行かなくちゃ)。
She has already arrived at the station. (so we had better go and get her).
(私たちが着いたとき、彼女は) もう駅に着いていた。
(When we arrived) *she had already arrived at the station.*

勉強している。

They are studying.

（私たちが電話したとき彼らは）勉強していた。

They were studying (when we called).

ご飯を食べている。

They are eating dinner. They have eaten dinner.

（僕らが着いたとき）ご飯を食べていた。

They were eating dinner (when we arrived). *They had eaten dinner* (when we arrived).

毎日車で行っている。

I am now going by car everyday.

昔は毎日車で行っていた（が、今はバスで行っている）。

I used to go by car everyday (but now I go by bus).

In sentences with more than one verb, the rule of thumb is that any verb inside a sentence is understood relative to the final verb. In most sentences, there are no restrictions on which verb forms may go where, and all interpretations (including habitual ones) are possible. In some constructions, however, particular verbs must be in particular forms.

Sometimes, the internal verb is not tensed (often corresponding to English *and*).

家に帰ってテレビを見ます。（〜て）

She will go home and watch television.

家に帰ってテレビを見ました。

She went home and watched television.

家に帰ってテレビを見ています。

She went home and is watching television.

Other times, the inner and outer verbs may vary freely (aspect as well as negation). The Japanese sentences here and below are probably no more or less obscure than their English translations.

明日行くと思う。

I think that she will go tomorrow.

明日行くと思っている。

I have thought that she will go tomorrow.

明日行くと思った。

I thought she would go tomorrow.

もう行っていると思う。

I think she has already gone.

もう行っていると思っている。

I have thought that she has already gone.

もう行っていると思った。
I thought that she had already gone.
きのう行ったと思う。
I think she went yesterday.
きのう行ったと思っている。
I have thought that she went yesterday.
きのう行ったと思った。
I thought that she went yesterday.
明日行くと思う。
I think she will go tomorrow.
明日行かないと思う。
I think she will not go tomorrow.
明日行くと思わない。
I do not think she will go tomorrow.
明日行かないと思わない。
I do not think she will not go tomorrow.

The same effects occur with verbs in modifying sentences (usually called *relative clauses*) with specific interpretations limited to those possible for the verb in question.

私の友だちは日本語を勉強している人だ。
My friend is the person who is studying Japanese.
私の友だちは日本語を勉強している人じゃない。
My friend is not the person who is studying Japanese.
私の友だちは日本語を勉強していない人だ。
My friend is the person who is not studying Japanese.
私の友だちは日本語を勉強していない人じゃない。
My friend is not the person who is not studying Japanese.
私の友だちは日本語がよくわかっている人だ。
My friend is the person who understands Japanese well.
私の友だちは日本語がよくわかっている人じゃない。
My friend is not the person who understands Japanese well.
私の友だちは日本語がよくわかっていない人だ。
My friend is the person who does not understand Japanese well.
私の友だちは日本語がよくわかっていない人じゃない。
My friend is not the person who does not understand Japanese well.

3.5.3 Where the tense of the verb is determined

In these expressions, the first verb must be past or future with respect to the main verb of the sentence. Some involve temporal order while others refer to possibility and necessity. Likewise, there may be restrictions on whether the first verb must be affirmative or negative. Where relevant, other discussions are referenced.

前に・   でかける前に電話して下さい。
まえに

            Please call before you leave.

            (The calling is always before the leaving. Affirmative only.)

後で・   でかけた後で電話して下さい。
あとで

            Please call after you leave.

            (The calling is always after the leaving. で here is optional. Affirmative only.)

かもしれない 来週フランス料理を作るかもしれない。

            I might make French food next week.

            (The first verb, 作る here, is never in the past, but it may be negative or affirmative.)

ことがある   外国に行ったことがある。

            I have been abroad (once or twice).
            外国に行くことがある。

            I go abroad. I have occasion to go abroad.

            (The first verb, 行く here, is almost always affirmative, although it is possible to say something like 食べないこともあるよ when someone accuses you of always helping yourself to the contents of their refrigerator.)

ことができる ピアノを弾くことができる。

            I can play the piano.
            一週間何も食べないでいることができる。

            I can go a week without eating.

            (The first verb, 弾く in the first sentence 食べない in the second, is never in the past. The affirmative and negative versions of this expressions are different. Compare also with the potential 弾ける. See page 157.)

ことにする   行くことにしていたが、結局、行かなかった。

            I had decided to go, but in the end I didn't.

            (The going always follows the decision making. Affirmative or negative. See page 126.)

ことになる   行くことになっていたが、結局、誰も行かなかった。

It had turned out I would go, but in the end no one went.

(The going always follows the decision making. Affirmative or negative. See page 126.)

ように言う   明日来ないように言いました。

I told him not to come tomorrow.

(The action being spoken about, *coming* in this case, will always follow the speaking itself. Affirmative or negative.)

ようにする   8時までに着くように出ました。

I left in order to arrive at eight.

(The effort to leave always precedes the arrival. Affirmative or negative. See page 126.)

ようになる   日本語がうまく話せるようになりました。

He has gotten to the point that he can speak Japanese well.

(The coming about always precedes the actual result, speaking Japanese well in this case. Affirmative or negative. See page 126.)

ため   晩ご飯を作るために買い物に行った。

I went shopping in order to make dinner.

(The first verb, 作る here, is never in the past. For other usages of ため, see pages 202 and 268 as well.)

まで   わかるまで勉強しなくちゃ。

You must study until you understand.

(The first verb, わかる here, is never in the past and it is usually affirmative.)

つもり   明日行くつもりだ。

I plan to go tomorrow.

行くつもりだったけど行かなかった。

I planned to go I didn't.

コロンブスはインドに行ったつもりだったけど、そこはアメリカだった。

Columbus thought he had gone to India, but it was America.

(Note that つもり in the third example does not really mean *plan*, and is used instead to mean something like と思った in a situation where Columbus was wrong but he didn't realize it. This is really a kind of counterfactual. See page 180.)

予定・よてい　明日行く予定だ。

I plan to go tomorrow.

(The first verb, 行く here, is never in the past, but it may be negative or affirmative.)

3.5.4 Temporal adverbs

A number of Japanese equivalents are given for several English temporal adverbs. Japanese equivalents of *if* and *when* are the specific topic of section 3.6 beginning on page 172.

before　　家を出る前に電話して下さい。　（前・まえ）

Please call me before you leave home.

家を出る時に電話して下さい。　（時・とき）

Please call me before you leave home, when you are leaving.

年を取りすぎないうちにもう一度行きたいと思う。　（うちに）

I would like to go again before I get too old.

知らせが来るまで長くはかからなかった。　（まで）

It was not long before the news came.

during　　食事の間何も言わなかった。　（間・あいだ）

He said nothing during dinner.

会議中に電話が入った。　（〜中・ちゅう）

The telephone rang during the meeting

旅行している時多くの有名人と知り合いになった。　（時・とき）

During my travels, I became acquainted with many celebrities.

夏休みには何もしなかった。　（には）

I did nothing during summer vacation.

after,　　テレビを見てから寝た。　（〜てから）
and then

We watched television and then went to bed.

テレビを見て、それから寝た。　（〜て、それから）

We watched television and then went to bed.

駅に着いた時に電話します。　（時・とき）

I will call you after I arrive at the station.

駅に着いたあと電話します。　（あと）

I will call after I have arrived at the station.

これを食べるとお腹が痛くなる。　（と）

When you eat this, your stomach will start to hurt.

(See page 178 for further discussion of this と. Turn to page 244 for adverbial expressions which also mean *and then*.)

when	ご飯を食べている時にちょっとした地震があった。（時・とき）

There was a small earthquake when we were eating dinner.
日が沈むころに停電になりました。（頃・ころ）

The electricity went out when the sun went down.
出ようと思ったところに宅急便がきた。（ところに）

There was a delivery when we were about to go out.

while	よく勉強しながらテレビを見ます。（～ながら）

I often watch television while I am studying.
子供が寝ている間にプレゼントを包んだ。（間・あいだ）

I wrapped presents while the children were asleep.
食べているうちに電話が入った。（うちに）

There was a phone call while we were eating dinner.
話している最中にプツッと電話が切れた。（最中・さいちゅう）

The phone cut off while we were talking.

as soon as	家を出た途端に雨が降り出した。（途端・とたん）

As soon as I went out, it started to rain.
食べてすぐ帰った。食べてからすぐに帰った。（すぐ）

He went home as soon as he ate.
出かけると雨が降り始めた。（と）

As soon as I went out, it started to rain.

(See page 178 for further discussion of this と.)
家に着き次第電話します。（次第・しだい）

I will call as soon as I get home.
家を出るや否や雨が降りだした。（や否や・やいなや）

As soon as I left home, it started to rain.

(This last is rather old-fashioned sounding.)

just	ちょうどその時に～　（時・とき）

just at that time
来たばかりだ。（ばかり）

She has just arrived.
すぐ行きます。（すぐ）

I am just about to go. I will leave soon.
腰をおろしたかと思うとまた赤ん坊が泣き出した。（したか）

I had just sat down when the baby started to cry again.
たった今ここに着いた。（たった今・たったいま）

I arrived just now.
出かけるところだ。（ところ）

I am just leaving. I am just about to leave.

出^でかけようとしているところに電話^{でんわ}があった。（ところ）

Just when as I was leaving, the phone rang.

出^でかけたところだ。（ところ）

He has just left.

(Note the usages of ところ in the last three examples. More discussion of ばかり is found on page 217.)

3.6 *If* and *when*

Japanese has a great number of expressions which might be translated into English as *if* or *when*. Sentences with *if*, about what might happen or might have happened, are called *conditionals*: "If you build it, they will come" and "If you had built it they would have come." Many of the sentences with *when* are related to the temporal expressions introduced in the previous section.

To begin, compare the implications of the following sentences. Each sentence type (as well as a few others) is discussed in greater detail in the following sections.

大統領^{だいとうりょう}が通^{とお}ったら、ハタをふります。

When the President goes by, I will wave my flag.

If the President goes by, I will wave my flag.

The President may or may not be scheduled to go by. I won't wave my flag until he is going by. This sentence emphasizes the order of events. (See page 173.)

大統領^{だいとうりょう}が通^{とお}れば、ハタをふります。

If the President goes by, I will wave my flag.

The President may or may not go by. If he actually does appear, I will wave my flag. This sentence makes clear the conditions under which flag-waving will in fact occur. (See page 174.)

大統領^{だいとうりょう}が通^{とお}る時^{とき}、ハタをふります。

When the President goes by, I will wave my flag.

If the President goes by, I will wave my flag.

The President may or may not be scheduled to pass by. If he is, *when* is an appropriate translation. If he is not, *if* is appropriate. In either case, I will wave my flag as he is going by. This sentence tells you the time that I will wave my flag. The 時^{とき} phrase gives a time, not a condition, and if we know that the President is scheduled to come by at 2:15, an equivalent statement would be 2時^じ１５分^{ふん}に、ハタをふります. (See page 179.)

大統領^{だいとうりょう}が見^みえてくるとハタをふります。

Whenever the President comes into view, they wave their flags.

They are great fans of the President who follow him to all of his public appearances. They wave flags whenever they see him. From the viewer's perspective, the sequence of events is automatic, and seeing the President seems to elicit a flag-waving response. (See page 178.)

大統領がここを通るのなら、ハタをふります。
If the President is going to go by, I will wave my flag.

Given that the President is in fact going to drive by, I will wave my flag, perhaps starting immediately. The sequence of events is not relevant. (See page 177.)

3.6.1 ～たら

The two basic conditionals are ～たら and ～れば. ～たら first.

田中君が帰ってきたら、私に電話してください。
If Tanaka comes home, please phone me.
When Tanaka comes home, please phone me.

できたら、手を上げてください。
If you are done, please raise your hand.
When you are done, please raise your hand.

Problematically for speakers of English, ～たら may be translated into English as *if* or *when* with circumstances determining which interpretation is better. In English, an *if*-clause is used when the event is not necessarily going to happen: *if Tanaka comes home* implies that no one is sure of Tanaka's plans. Use of もし assures this interpretation: もし田中君が帰っきたら *if Tanaka comes home*. In contrast, a *when*-clause is used when it is assumed that the event will necessarily happen: *when Tanaka come home* is appropriate if we know that Tanaka has made specific plans to return (that evening, for example). A ～たら sentence says only that the first event will begin (and often end) before the second event begins. It offers no comment on the probability that the first event will actually happen. In the examples above, Tanaka's arrival will precede your telephoning me. Likewise, your finishing will precede your raising your hand.

Putting such sentences into the past tense affects the range of English translations because the sentences are no longer ambiguous between *if* and *when*.

薬を飲んだら元気になった。
I felt better when I took medicine.
大統領が見えてきたら、皆、ハタをふりはじめた。
When the President came by, everyone began to wave flags.

Given that a sequence of events has already occurred, the use of *if* no longer makes sense. Since everything is in the past, we *know* what happened, and only a *when* interpretation is sensible. (Note that "If she took her medicine, she felt better" is not particularly grammatical in English either. Rather, one might say "If she had taken her medicine, she would have felt better." In Japanese this ends up as 薬を飲んでいたら元気になっていたはずだ which is discussed on page 180.)

Note that it is not necessarily the case that the first event must completely precede the second; there may be significant overlap especially if the first predicate is stative.

わからないところがあったら、聞きます。
If there is something we don't understand, we will ask about it.
いたら確認できる。
If he is there, we can check with him.
本当に好きだったらはっきり言ったほうがいいと思うよ。
If you really like him, I think you should tell him directly.

Likewise, the first event may be a process which is ongoing (and does not necessarily stop) when the second event occurs.

寝ていたら、起こします。
If you are asleep, I will wake you up.
外に寝ていたら、雨が降ってきた。
It started raining while I was taking a nap outside.
勉強していたら、邪魔はしない。
If she is studying, we will leave her alone.

Finally, the entire sentence may express a habitual relationship. Here the two parts of the sentence are in an on-going relationship where the first generally leads to the second.

おなかがすいていたらいつもそこでうどんを食べる。
Whenever he is hungry, he eats udon there.
ゴミが落ちていたら、必ず拾う。
If there is a piece of trash on the floor, he always picks it up.
わからないところがあったら、たいてい聞きます。
Whenever there is something we don't understand, we usually ask about it.

3.6.2 ～れば

Like ～たら、～れば can also be translated into English as both *if* and *when*.

東京に来れば、私に連絡をよこすだろう。 東京に来れば、私に連絡をよこすはずだ。
If he comes to Tokyo, he should give me a call.
When he comes to Tokyo, he should give me a call.
できれば、手を上げてください。
If you are able to do it, please raise your hand.

A 〜れば sentence says that a first event is a condition for a second event. There is almost a causal relationship between the two events, and the second will not occur unless the first one does. Unlike 〜たら, 〜れば says nothing about the actual occurrence of either event. As such, a sentences with 〜れば cannot be used in the past when it refers to a specific instance. Contrast the following:

パリに行ったらフランス語が上手になる。

If you go to Paris, you will become good at French.

パリに行ったらフランス語が上手になった。

When I went to Paris, I became good at French.

パリに行けばフランス語が上手になる。

As long as you go to Paris, you will become good at French.

パリに行けばフランス語が上手になった is as strange in Japanese as "Provided you went to Paris you became good at French" is in English. In contrast, a 〜れば sentence *can* occur in the past or present if it refers to a habit. In such a sentence it is the habit (and not the condition per se) which was true in the past: ゴミが落ちていれば、必ずひろった "Whenever there was litter on the floor, he would pick it up" or more literally "It was always the case that if there was litter on the floor, he would pick it up."

Finally, sentences with 〜れば can be used in commands only when the first part of the sentence is a stative of some kind:

暑ければ、窓を開けてください

If you are hot, please open the windows

聞こえなければ、手を上げてください。

Raise your hand if you cannot hear.

駅に来ていれば知らせてください。

If he is at the station, please let me know.

The examples here are not particularly different from their 〜たら counterparts. This is probably because of the stative verb in the conditional part of the sentence. Recall that, in general, conditional statives do not occur "before" the second part of the sentence. The notion of temporal order is therefore made irrelevant, and the differences between 〜たら and 〜れば are neutralized.

Their slightly different grammatical distributions aside, the problem with distinguishing 〜たら and 〜れば is that both forms are acceptable in a great number of situations. Note also that conditional sentences (with 〜たら or with 〜れば) are often no more than guesses or expectations. As such it is common to find modification with expressions such as だろう, はずだ, と思う, or にちがいない. Contrast the implications of the following pairs:

できたら手を上げてください。
If you are done, please raise your hand.
できれば手を上げてください。
If you are able to do it, please raise your hand.

If you are done applies only after the task has been completed. Then raise your hand. In contrast, *if you are able to do it* is a question of ability. If you have the ability, please raise your hand now. Having the ability to do a task, and actually doing the task, however, are two different things.

わからないところがあったら、聞きます。
If we have a problem, we will ask.
わからないところがあれば、聞きます。
If there are things we don't understand, we will ask.

The first sentence promises that we will disturb you only after we have encountered a problem. The second sentence sets up a precondition: we will disturb only if we have a problem. The effect may be the same (you get disturbed when we have a problem), but the reasoning is slightly different.

たくさん食べたら元気が出るだろう。
You will probably feel better once you have eaten.
たくさん食べれば元気が出るだろう。
Provided you eat, you should feel better.

The first sentence sets up a time line: if you eat, you will then feel better. The second sentences says that in order to feel better you have to eat. It is a sentence about what kind of behavior should help your condition improve.

兄が帰ってきたらすぐ出かけます。
I will go out as soon as my brother comes home.
兄が帰ってくれば出かけます。
If my brother comes home, I will go out.

The first sentence again sets up a time line: my brother will come home, and then I will go out. The second sentence establishes conditions: I will be able to go out as long as my brother comes home.

部屋を掃除したら、＄１０払う。
I will pay you ten dollars after you have cleaned your room.
部屋を掃除すれば、＄１０払う。
I will pay you ten dollars if you will clean your room.

While both statements are contracts about cleaning your room, the first promises payment only upon completion. The second is ambiguous. Payment requires that you clean your room. If you accept payment now, however, you are in effect promising to clean your room in the near future.

～れば also occurs in a number of idiomatic expressions:

もう少し勉強すればよかったのに。

It would have been better if only I had studied a little more

行儀のいい人といえば、田中さんは必ずそれに入るでしょう。

Speaking of well-mannered people, Tanaka would certainly be included as one.

食べれば食べるほど好きになる。

The more you eat, the more you like it.

(See page 219 for the parallel expression with だけ.)

行かなければならない。

We must go.

(See page 156 for more on *must*.)

3.6.3 ～なら *or* ～ならば

～なら and ～ならば are both conditional forms of だ (which is not as strange as it might seem; the classical form of だ is なり). These two forms are essentially interchangeable, although the form with ～ば is increasingly rare. ～なら means *if it is the case that* ～ or *if we assume this, then* ～. In contrast to ～たら, expressions with ～なら are most often associated with discussions of the hypothetical. Compare the following:

京都へ行ったら、金閣寺を見に行くべきだ。

If they go to Kyoto, they should go and see the Golden Pavilion.

京都へ行くのなら、金閣寺を見に行くべきだ。

If you are planning to go to Kyoto, you should plan on going to see the Golden Pavilion.

読み終わったらこの本を上げます。

I will give you this book after I have finished reading it.

読むのならこの本を上げます。

If you are going to read this book, I will give it to you.

In both sets, the sentence with ～たら indicates the temporal sequence. In contrast, ～なら presents the first sentence as the assumed condition in a hypothetical discussion. The の which intervenes after the verb, adjective, or noun appears because なら is really a form of だ. As 行くだ is ungrammatical, 行くなら should also ungrammatical. Nevertheless, the の is generally optional. 行くのなら and 行くなら are both fine Japanese.

高くないならたくさん買うの？

If it is the case that they are not expensive, do you plan on buying a lot of them?

会議が明日なら、行けないと思います。

If the meeting is tomorrow, I do not think I will be able to go.

仕事が早く終わったのなら、きっと早く寝ていただろう。

If work finished early, then surely he has gone to sleep.

3.6.4 と

暇だと家にいてテレビを見る。

Whenever she is free, she stays at home and watches TV.

御飯を食べないとおなかが空きます。

If you do not eat, you will get hungry.

午後になるとこの道が買い物をする人で混んでくる。

In the afternoon, this street becomes crowded with shoppers.

僕が着くとすぐ田中さんが帰った。

I arrived, and Tanaka left immediately.

家を出ると外は雨が降っていた。

When I left home, it was raining outside.

These are all situations where the event or state of the first sentence leads inevitably (for whatever reason) to the second sentence. Inevitability is the crucial element here. The sequence may reflect habit or custom (having free time does not lead inevitably to the watching of television). It may be causal (not eating does in fact eventually make one hungry). It may also be coincidental, implying only that one thing happened and the second was true (going outside, I was surprised to find that it was raining). Under a causal interpretation, there is not necessarily a great deal of difference with 〜たら. With a と sequence, the first predicate is always in the dictionary form; tense is realized only on the final predicate.

Compare the interpretations of the following, nearly identical sentences.

暇だったら家にいてテレビを見る。

If she is free, she stays at home and watches TV. When she is free, she stays at home and watches TV.

暇なら家にいてテレビを見る。

Given that she is free, she stays at home and watches TV (although she is not free now).

暇だと家にいてテレビを見る。

Whenever she is free, she stays at home and watches TV.

A sentence with と cannot be a command. できると手を上げてください might mean something like "You are done and then please raise your hand" (which is as odd in English as it is in Japanese).

3.6.5 時・とき

時 means *time* or *hour*. When used as a temporal expression, it refers to occasions, and is best translated as *on the occasion that*. More often than not it is translated into English as *when* although *if* is also possible. In the examples below, note the type of word which precedes 時 (noun, adjective, etc.) as well as alternations.

家を出る時コートを着なさい。
Please put on a coat when you leave the house.
Please put on a coat if you leave the house.
ドルが高い時は外国に行く日本人が少なくなる。
Fewer Japanese go abroad when the dollar is strong.
Fewer Japanese go abroad if the dollar is strong.
学生だった時パリに住んでいた。学生のときパリに住んでいた。
I lived in Paris when I was a student.
暇な時に手紙を書いた。暇があった時手紙を書いた。
I meant to write when I had some free time, but I was busy continuously.

In this last set of examples, the tense of the first verb is understood relative to the tense of the final verb. See page 168 for more discussion and examples.

彼が帰って来るとき電話で呼ぶ。（cf. 帰る前に～）
I will call you when he is leaving for home.
彼が帰って来たとき電話で呼ぶ。（cf. 帰った後～）
I will call you when he has left for home.
彼が帰って来るとき電話で呼んだ。（cf. 帰る前に～）
I called you when he was leaving for home.
彼帰って来たとき電話で呼んだ。（cf. 帰った後～）
I called when he had left for home.

The two actions may also be concurrent.

エクササイズをする時はテレビを見る。（cf. エクササイズをしながらテレビを見る。）
When I exercise, I watch television.
If I exercise, I watch television (but I haven't recently, so I haven't seen much TV lately).

3.6.6 ては and ても

While the ては construction plays a central role in expressions the notion of *must* (行ってはいけないよ, discussed on page 156), when ては (or its contracted form ちゃ) is not followed by a predicate like いけない it has a distinctly conditional meaning (setting up states and facts as conditions). Note that ては is not compatible with もし. Compare:

コンピュータがなくちゃ、仕事ができない。

If we don't have a computer, we will not able to do the job.

講義がわからなくては心配です。

It is a concern if we do not understand the lecture.

辞書がなくちゃ、読めない。

If I don't have a dictionary, I can't read it. I can't read it without a dictionary.

〜ても on the other hand is most generally translated as *even if*, so that a request for permission such as 行ってもいい？ really means something like "Even if I go, is that acceptable?" Compare:

来週でも無理だ。

Even if it is next week, it is impossible.

薬を飲んでも治らない。

Even if I take medicine, I don't get better.

どんなに安くても見に行きたくない。

No matter how cheap it is, I don't want to go and see it.

3.6.7 What might have been

In Japanese as in English, it is possible to talk about things which might be or might have been. These are often called *counterfactuals* (i.e. *going against the actual facts*). Again, embedded predicates are understood relative to the final predicates. The mistaken condition is almost always in the 〜ている form for non-stative verbs. The examples here become increasingly complex (as do their English translations), and they do no more than give a sense of what is possible. In the first set of examples, 思った and 思っている are both possible, but the latter is more natural because the mistaken thought was presumably still relevant when the mistake was realized.

あると思っていたけど、なかった。

I thought I had it, but I didn't.

もう帰っていると思っていたけどいなかった。

I thought they were home, but they weren't.

勉強していると思ったけど、テレビを見ていた。

I thought she was studying, but she was watching television.

勉強していたと思ったけど、まだしていなかった。

I thought she had studied, but she hadn't yet.

Putting conditionals into counterfactual constructions (to create phrases like *if I were a rich man* 〜) is confusing because few of these sentences are necessarily counterfactual. In the examples below, the mistaken condition is again almost always in the 〜ている form, if it is not stative. Alternative interpretations are given in parentheses.

お金_{かね}があったらいい。

It would be good if I had some money. I wish I had some money.

(In a context where I have a rich uncle who is about to die, this can also mean *It will be good when I have some money.*)

お金_{かね}があったらよかった。

It would have been good if I had had some money.

(Past tense on a main stative verb strongly indicates a counterfactual meaning.)

お金_{かね}があったらいいのに。

It would be good if I had some money. I wish I had some money.

(のに strongly indicates a counterfactual situation.)

お金_{かね}があったらあげるよ。

If I had some cash, I would give it to you.

(This can also mean *I will give you some money when I get some* or habitual *I give you money when I have it.*)

もちろん、お金_{かね}があったらあげたよ。

Of course, if I had had some money, I would have given it to her.

(This can also refer to a habitual *Of course, I used to give her money when I had some.*)

早_{はや}く着_ついていたら電話_{でんわ}します。

If they have arrived early, they will call.

(This can also refer to a habitual *If they arrive home early, they call* or *When they arrive home early, they call.*)

早_{はや}く着_ついていたら電話_{でんわ}しました。

If they had arrived early, they would have called.

(This can also refer to a habitual *When they arrived home early, they used to call.*)

早_{はや}く着_ついていたらもう帰_{かえ}っているだろう。

If they have arrived early, they are probably at home already.

If they had arrived early, they would probably be at home already.

(As the two translations indicate, this sentence can be used when the speaker does not know the truth. *If they have arrived early, they are probably at home already* is just an opinion and not a counterfactual. If the speaker does in fact know that they arrived late, the same sentence is naturally taken to be counterfactual as in the second translation.)

早_{はや}く着_ついていたら帰_{かえ}っていただろう。

If they arrived early, they were probably at home.

If they had arrived early, they would probably have been at home.

(Similar comments apply here. The first translation indicates that the speaker does not know the truth. The second is a counterfactual.)

3.7 Particles

3.7.1 は

If a perfect stranger walks up to you and says, "Jack was wearing a blue shirt today," quite likely you will not know how to respond. The statement (which is very simple) is strange because there is no reason that you and a perfect stranger should share an acquaintance named Jack let alone an interest in what he was wearing today. The crucial assumption behind the statement is that you and the speaker both know someone named Jack, but this assumption makes no sense in the situation, and the statement sounds odd. In contrast, the sentence is completely normal when you and your best friend are discussing a friend in common named Jack. You both have a crush on Jack, and you talk about him all the time. The two of you regularly discuss his appearance and activities, but you were sick at home so you have to get the day's gossip from your best friend. Your friend walks into your bedroom where you lying in bed and announces "Jack was wearing a blue t-shirt today."

If we translate this statement into Japanese (in the same situation although we are talking about a Japanese boy now), we get:

田中君は今日、青いTシャツを着てたよ。

A perfect stranger would be surprised if you announced this. Your best friend (who also likes Tanaka) would understand perfectly. The first phrase in this sentence is marked with a particle は. The function of this particle is to record the underlying assumption that both you and the person you are talking to know something about Tanaka, and in doing so it actually splits the sentence into two parts.

田中君は～

I've got news about Tanaka ～   I'm going to tell you something about Tanaka ～

～今日、青いTシャツを着てたよ。

　～ he was wearing a blue t-shirt today.

The part of the sentence before は says, this is what I am going to talk about. It sets the stage for the second part of the sentence, which contains the interesting information. In English, we do not have a particle は, but we divide a sentence into two parts with stress and intonation. Imagine that Jack had never once worn a blue t-shirt. In fact, he is a very formal person who always wears a white shirt and a striped tie so everyone was very surprised that he was wearing just a blue t-shirt. Your friend announces to you very excitedly:

*Jack was wearing a **blue t-shirt** today.*

If you imagine this situation and you say this sentence out loud, you will find that you almost skip over the name *Jack* as well as the phrase *was wearing a*. Your stress and emphasis will be on the two words *blue* and *t-shirt*. In English, the part of the sentence that is interesting receives extra stress or an exaggerated pronunciation. The part of the sentence which is unimportant because you and your friend know you are talking about Jack (you talk about nothing else) is said very quickly, with no particular emphasis.

In most grammars of Japanese, the part of the sentence which is marked with は is called the *topic*. It is the thing you are talking about, and it is usually at the beginning of the sentence. Japanese has a grammatical device (the particle は) to mark the topic, while English uses stress and intonation (to mark the parts of the sentence which are not part of the topic). In English, the topic is the part of the sentence which does not stand out.

We can now look at a second situation. You are throwing Jack a birthday party. Your friend arrives early to help set up, and upon seeing a fabulous cake exclaims (in amazement because your friend had no idea that you could bake, let alone decorate a cake):

*Did **you** make this cake?*

The underlying question is, who made this cake? Where did this cake come from? In this sentence, the person who made the cake is the focus of surprise or doubt. Did *you* make the cake? Did someone else make the make? The cake which is sitting on the table in full view of everyone is the topic of the discussion. A sensible Japanese translation might be:

このケーキは君が作ったの？

As expected, the word ケーキ is marked with は. Again, the part of the sentence after the は is the real question. Did you make it?

If we compare the two Japanese examples so far, we find the following:

田中君は今日、青いTシャツを着てたよ。
このケーキは君が作ったの？

The topic of the first sentence is *Tanaka*, who was wearing the t-shirt. The topic of the second sentence is the *cake*, who made it? Of course, in a context where 田中君 or このケーキ are not the topic, the particle は can be replaced by a different particle, が for the subject in the first sentence, and を for the direct object in the second sentence. Putting everything back into the more typical subject before object order gives the following:

田中君が今日、青いTシャツを着てたよ。
君がこのケーキを作ったの？

Of these four sentences, the first with は on the subject and を on the direct object is the most neutral. The effect of marking the subject with が is discussed immediately below. The effect of placing the object before subject is discussed beginning on page 191.

3.7.1.1 は versus が or を

Understanding the difference between は on the one hand and が or を on the other is a matter of understanding the underlying assumptions of the statement or question. And such an understanding is dependent on the context in which a sentence is spoken. Compare the following questions and answers. Note how the answer will vary based on the structure of the question (i.e. Is there a は or not? Which part of the question of statement is after the は?). Note also that a word marked with は in the question is rarely repeated in the answer. In a context where both speakers know who or what they are talking about, there is no need to repeat the は-marked phrase again and again.

Someone named Smith has just been introduced to all of us. I am asking my friend about her nationality.
スミスさんはアメリカ人ですか。
Is Smith (は) an American?
いいえ、オーストラリア人です。
No, she is Australian.

I have heard there is an American here. I want to know who that person is.
アメリカ人はスミスさんですか。
Is the person who is American (は) Smith?
いいえ、アメリカ人は田中さんですよ。
No, the person who is American (は) is Tanaka.   No, Tanaka (は) is the American.

I want to know which of these people is American. Is it Smith?
この中でだれがアメリカ人ですか。スミスさんがアメリカ人ですか。
Who (が) of these people is American? Is Smith (が) an American?
いいえ、田中さんですよ。スミスさんはオーストラリア人ですよ。
No, Tanaka (is American). Smith (は) is Australian.

I know that different people are going to different places, and I have a question about where Suzuki is going.
鈴木さんは京都に行きますか。
Is Suzuki (は) going to Kyoto?
いいえ、神戸です。
No, to Kobe.

I know that different people are going to different places, and I want to know specifically who is going to Kyoto.
京都にはだれが行きますか。
Who (が) is going to Kyoto (は)?
山本さんですよ。
Yamamoto.

I know someone is supposed to go to Kyoto. Who is it?
京都_{きょうと}に行_いくのはだれですか。

Who is it that is going to Kyoto (は)? The person going to Kyoto (は) is who?
山本_{やまもと}さんですよ。

Yamamoto.

I know that someone in every group is supposed to go to Kyoto. I want to know if Suzuki is that person.
このグループでは鈴木_{すずき}さんが京都_{きょうと}に行_いきますか。

From the group (は), is it Suzuki (が) who is going to Kyoto?
いいえ、山本_{やまもと}さんですよ。鈴木_{すずき}さんは神戸_{こうべ}に行_いくと思_{おも}います。

No, Yamamoto is. Suzuki (は) is going to Kobe, I think.

I have a question about your Japanese. Why do you speak so well?
日本語_{にほんご}は大学_{だいがく}で勉強_{べんきょう}しましたか。

Did you study Japanese (は) in college? (Why do you speak Japanese so well?)
いいえ、十歳_{じゅっさい}まで日本_{にほん}に住_すんでいたんです。

No, I lived in Japan until I was ten.

I want to know about your college studies. What was your major?
大学_{だいがく}の時_{とき}、何_{なに}を勉強_{べんきょう}しましたか。心理学_{しんりがく}を勉強_{べんきょう}しましたか。

What (を) did you study in college? Did you study psychology (を)?
ええ、児童心理学_{じどうしんりがく}を勉強_{べんきょう}しましたよ。

Yes. I studied child psychology (を).

    Note in each of the above conversations, that the pattern of stress and intonation in the English changes based on the particular meaning of the sentence. At the simplest level, we have the following:

*Is Smith (は) **an American**?*
*Is **Smith** (が) an American?*

The part of the sentence which is not stressed is taken for granted (and is marked は in Japanese). The focus of the question, the part of the sentence which is taken as produced or as the answer to a question, receives extra stress or more careful pronunciation (and is marked が in Japanese). Similar observations can be made about all of the English translations above. Here is one set of examples. Think carefully about how each of the questions must be pronounced in order for the given answers to be natural.

Someone named Smith has just been introduced to all of us. I am asking my friend about her nationality.
*Is Smith (は) **an American**?*
*No, she is **Australian**.*

I have heard there is an American here. I want to know who that person is.
Is the person who is American (は) **Smith**?
No, the person who is American (は) *is* **Tanaka**.

I want to know which of these people is American. Is it Smith?
Who (が) *of these people is American? Is* **Smith** (が) *an American?*
No, **Tanaka** (is American). *Smith* (は) *is* **Australian**.

Note in the last exchange how Smith is reintroduced with は in the answer. The speaker is in effect saying, "Your guess about Smith (that she is American) is wrong, but I will tell you that she is in fact Australian."

The difference between は on the one hand and が or を on the other is difficult for speakers of English because the function of the particle は is realized in English usually by stress and intonation and not by anything normally thought of as grammar. In many textbooks, the は -marked phrase is called the *topic* or the *old-information*. It is often stated that は marks phrases which have already been mentioned in the conversation, and a typical example might look like the following:

昔々、山の奥におじいさんが一人住んでいました。おじいさんは～
A long time ago, an old man (が) *lived in the mountains. The old man* (は) ～

The first instance of おじさん is marked が (new), while the second is marked は (old). But if this is the case, why does は occur so often at the very beginning of the very first sentence in a conversation or passage? Even in the above short conversations, は can occur in the first sentence. How can the first person or thing mentioned already be known to the listener?

3.7.1.2 Shared background

The topic of a sentence is not limited to what has already been overtly mentioned. Rather, any fact which is shared by the speaker and the listener is a potential topic. Such a thing may be the cake which is sitting on the table or Jack who is the constant topic of our gossip. In the short conversations above, the speakers share knowledge of people such as Smith and Tanaka. They also have information about languages, nationalities, travel plans. Objects such as the moon, the sun, etc. are often mentioned as the kinds of things which all people share knowledge of. People may also share experiences, although the nature of these experiences will vary quite dramatically. They may range from the impatience of two people waiting in the rain for a bus (バスはおそいですね) to the experiences which you have had in school. The Japanese, for example, all have assumptions and opinions about university entrance examinations. No one is unaware of them, and the common views (the exams are too difficult, they are irrelevant, they destroy creativity; they are a necessary evil, etc.) are probably known to everyone. Just mentioning entrance examinations (入学試験は〜) brings these experiences and opinions into the immediate background of any conversation. All of this information about context (where you are, the date, time, place, the objects in the room, etc.), common experiences, and culture is potentially shared information. Although much of it may change from one context to the next (shared experiences and cultural information in particular), depending on what you want to talk about, any of it can be marked with は at the beginning of a sentence.

3.7.1.3 Changing or announcing the topic

Along the same line, particle は can also be used to announce, "this is what we are going to talk about **now**." は can be used to change the subject. The listener hears an unexpected phrase followed by は. The only sensible conclusion is that this is a new topic of conversation, and the accommodating listener adjusts his or her background assumptions accordingly. For example, I decide that I want to discuss the typical English breakfast, and I begin:

イギリスの朝ご飯は大体おいしいんですよ。
*The English breakfast is generally **really good**.*

Perhaps I know you are interested in breakfast customs; perhaps not. Perhaps we have been talking about the cuisine of various countries, and now I want to give my opinion of English breakfasts. Regardless, the use of は out of the blue, so to speak, comes with an expectation that the listener will change their focus to this new topic of conversation. And in the case here, the speaker is clearly conveying what he or she believes is new information to the listener (reinforced by よ at the end of the sentence).

Note that the notions of shared and new topic can be confused or used incorrectly. What you believe to be shared may not be shared. Likewise, attempts to establish a new topic may fail if the topic you suggest is completely outside the experience of the listener and accommodation is impossible. For example, I could start talking about the movie *Star Wars* thinking that you had seen it and had opinions about it. In fact, you have not seen *Star Wars* and you are not even sure what it is (perhaps because you have been living in a cave for the past thirty years or so).

スターウォーズはよかったよ。もう見た？
Sutaauoozu was great. Have you seen it already?
えっ？スターウォーズって？
Huh? What's a sutaauoozu?

The topic of the first sentence is the movie *Star Wars*. The speaker assumes that the person listening has some knowledge of this movie and has quite possibly seen it already. The listener responds with a question which is about the topic itself, indicating that the speaker's underlying assumptions are wrong. The question, もう見た？, makes no sense because the topic is totally outside the listener's experience. It seems like the very word スターウォーズ makes no sense, and even if the listener tries to accommodate the speaker ("Okay, this is a question about a *sutaauoozu* that I am supposed to have seen..."), the word スターウォーズ may be so odd that the listener has no idea what it might be ("...but I have no idea what a *sutaauoozu* is...."). Changing the subject or introducing a new topic will be successful only if the listener does in fact have some awareness of the new topic.

If I assume you do not actually know very much about *Star Wars*, I might introduce the new topic in a more explicit way. (Here particle は is replaced with a pause.)

スターウォーズっていう映画、もう見た？
Have you seen the movie called Star Wars?

Here, the speaker explains that *Star Wars* is a movie. Even if the listener has never heard of *Star Wars* specifically, chances are greater that the listener knows something about movies. Accommodation to the new topic is possible because of the explanation, and the listener can respond that they have not seen the movie. They might go on to say "Actually, I've never even heard of it" indicating just how much accommodation is necessary ("Well, I know it is a movie because you have said so, so I know I have not seen it since I never go to the movies, but you are really asking me about *Star Wars* specifically, so I will let you know that I actually have no idea what *Star Wars* is.").

3.7.1.4 Contrasting topics

Thinking about what it means to change a topic, clearly any new topic comes with an implicit comparison to the old topic, and the underlying message is "we are not going to talk about **that** any more; we are going to talk about **this**." To some degree, は always establishes a contrast between what we *are* talking about and what we are *not* talking about. When I pull English breakfasts out of the blue, I am implicitly contrasting this new topic with all the other potential topics which exist in our shared background. Related to this, は is used in sentences which indicate explicit contrasts ("this is **big**, but that is **small**" kinds of sentences). Here are some examples. The English translations of these sentences put emphasis on the contrasted words, and here は *corresponds* to stress in English (which was not the case in the so-called topic は).

今日は授業に出ますが、あしたは出られないと思います。
*I'm going to class **today**, but I don't think I'll be able to go **tomorrow**.*
青いのは高いけど赤いのはあまり高くないです。
*The **blue** one is expensive, but the **red** one is not.*
ケーキは買ったが、おにぎりは作った。
*I **bought** the cake, but I **made** the rice balls.*

ニューヨークには行ったことがあるが、ロンドンには行ったことがない。
*I **have** been to New York, but **never** to London.*
よくレストランで食べるとは思わないけど時々外食する。
*I don't think I eat at restaurants **often**, but I **do** go out sometimes.*

3.7.1.5 Negative は

In addition, implicit contrasts are often found in negative sentences, particularly in negative answers to questions. The implication with a negative response is "The answer to your question as stated is no, but there is some other (presumably related) question where the answer would be yes." The implicit contrast is with the positive, presumably preferred answer, and the use of は implies that some kind of accommodation is possible. It is often said that Japanese do not like to say "no" directly. The use of は in a negative answer is an escape valve which may be taken to indicate that a positive answer is near at hand. This overall meaning is reinforced with a が〜 *but* left hanging at the end of the sentence. In English, the contrasted element is again given extra stress, and sentences where the further explanation has been left unsaid often end with a kind of rising intonation. Think about how to say, "Well, it isn't **difficult** but....(it isn't easy either)."

日本語はむずかしいですか。
Is Japanese difficult?
まあ、むずかしくはないですが〜
*Well, it is not **difficult** but (it is not easy either).*

新しい車を買ってきたの？
Did you go and buy a new car?
新しいのは買わなかったが〜
*Well, I didn't buy a **new** one but (I got a used one).*

田中先生はいらっしゃいますか。
Is Prof. Tanaka coming?
田中先生はいらっしゃいませんが〜
***Prof. Tanaka** is not coming but (a different professor is).*

3.7.1.6 Grammar

Students should know already that particles が and を are replaced with は. Other particles (に, で, から, と, etc.) generally occur in combination with は (giving には, では, からは, とは, etc.) although に in particular may be completely replaced as well. Compare: 東京にはアメリカ人がたくさんいる and 東京はアメリカ人がたくさんいる. Typically, the phrase with は is at the beginning of the sentence where it is interpreted as something like "this is what I am going to talk about," the typical "topic" interpretation.

Students should also know that the elements of a Japanese sentence can be moved around quite freely. (This is called *scrambling* by most linguists.) 田中さんがすしを食べた and すしを田中さんが食べた are both grammatical sentences. In spite of this freedom, Japanese does have a typical word order: topic (は), subject (が), indirect object (に), direct object (を). When the phrases of a sentences are moved around, any phrase which is not in its typical position is felt to stand out and therefore be emphasized. Thus, the direct object すし stands out in the sentence すしを田中さんが食べた *Tanaka ate **sushi*** or *It is **sushi** which Tanaka ate* in English. This emphasis induces the contrastive interpretation discussed above: *Tanaka ate **sushi** (**not** fried chicken)* or *It is **sushi** which Tanaka ate, (**not** fried chicken)*.

Sometimes the topic interpretation of は and the contrastive effect of atypical word order are in conflict.

すしは田中さんが食べた。

Here, すし is the topic. If we are talking about some missing sushi, I can tell you that Tanaka ate it. At the same time, the direct object すし is emphasized because it is displaced; the direct object is normally found after the subject. The sentence may therefore be used to contrast the fact that the sushi was eaten by Tanaka, although other food was eaten by other people. Whether the sentence is contrastive or not may depend on context as much as anything. Is the sentence used in a situation where we are looking for some missing sushi or is it used in a situation where many people have eaten many different things? Stress can also be used in Japanese the same way it is used in English. Stressing すしは will emphasize the contrastive interpretation, while stressing 田中さんが will emphasize the what-happened-to-the-sushi interpretation.

Another way to achieve a contrastive effect is to mark the direct object with は but not to move it to the front of the sentence:

田中さんがすしは食べた。

Here, the は-marked phrase is displaced, and the effect is strongly contrastive: *Tanaka ate **sushi***. The contrastive effect is so strong that the example is actually felt to be incomplete because the food contrasted with すし is not clear. A sentence such as 田中さんがすしは食べたが、フライドチキンは食べなかった is felt to be more natural (and a sentence beginning 田中さんは〜 is probably the most natural). The only time that the effect of word order and usual topic position are not in conflict is with subjects (and to a lesser extent with time expressions) because all of these expressions occur at the beginning of a sentence: 田中さんがすしを食べた and 田中さんはすしを食べた. In all other cases, word order and the usual topic position are in conflict resulting in varying degrees of contrastiveness.

The various usage of particle は are listed here with the degree of contrastiveness noted. In general, the strongest contrastive interpretation occurs when は is not found at the beginning of the sentence. Likewise, whenever parallel elements are marked with は in consecutive sentences, the contrastive interpretation is very strong.

instead of が	田中さんが泳いでいる。
	田中さんは泳いでいる。(topic or contrastive)
	田中さんは泳いでいるが山田さんは浜辺でジョギングをしている。
	(highly contrastive)
	(Given a choice between putting は or が on the subject, は is felt to be more normal or unmarked — at least on a sentence used to introduce a new topic of conversation or on a sentence used with no particular context. Note that the opposite is true for a direct object where を is preferred.)
after a time expression	今日田中さんが来る。
	今日は田中さんが来る。(topic or contrastive)
	今日は来るがあしたは来ない。(highly contrastive)
	(Time expressions usually occur even before the subject.)
instead of object を	田中さんがすしを食べた。
	すしは田中さんが食べた。(topic or contrastive)
	田中さんがすしは食べた。(highly contrastive)
	ケーキは食べたがパイは食べなかった。(highly contrastive)
with particle に	田中さんがニューヨークに行ってきた。
	ニューヨークには田中さんが行ってきた。(topic or contrastive)
	ニューヨークは田中さんが行ってきた。(topic or contrastive)
	田中さんがニューヨークには行ってきた。(highly contrastive)
	ニューヨークには行くがロスには行かない。(highly contrastive)
with particle で (also から, まで, etc.)	田中さんが図書館で宿題をしました。
	図書館では田中さんが宿題をしました。(topic or contrastive)
	田中さんが図書館では宿題をしました。(highly contrastive)
	図書館では勉強するが家では勉強できない。(highly contrastive)
with adverbs	速く話さなかった。
	速くは話さなかった。(highly contrastive)
	速くは話したが長くは話さなかった。(highly contrastive)
	(Explicit comparisons of adverbs are, relatively speaking, rare.)
with quotative と	今の大統領はいい人だと思いますか。
	今の大統領はいい政治家だとは思いますが〜　(highly contrastive)
	(Rhetorically, the following pattern is a common way to express your own opinion (and contrast it with others): 大学の学費がとても高いと私たちは思いますが〜 *That the cost of university is high is what **we** think, but ~*.)

with adjective forms	高いですか。高くないけど〜
	高いですか。高くはないけど〜 (highly contrastive)
	安くならない。
	安くはならない。(highly contrastive)
with verb forms	疲れているが、まだやろうとしている。
	疲れてはいるが、まだやろうとしている。(highly contrastive)
	待ってくれないだろう。
	待ってはくれないだろう。(highly contrastive)
	食べません。
	食べはしません。(highly contrastive)
	何度も行ったり来たりできない。
	何度も行ったり来たりはできない。(highly contrastive)
with classifiers	お金があまりなかったから五本買わなかった。
	お金があまりなかったから五本は買わなかった。(highly contrastive)

The following two constructions are consistent with the idea of contrastive は (although they are not generally thought of in these terms).

must	食べてはいけない。
	Eating is bad (although other things might be okay) =
	You must not eat this.
	(See page 156 for more on *must*.)
negative of だ	日本語ではない。
	It is not Japanese. (It is something else.)
	(は is again associated with a negative interpretation implying a contrast with a positive answer. This contrast is even stronger in the negative versions of the である literary form where both でない and ではない are possible. The first sounds like a blunt denial, while the second is taken to be more accommodating.)

If there is more than one は in a sentence, topic interpretations precede contrastive interpretations. The specific meaning depends almost completely on the overall context, and it is not necessary to have both interpretations. Intonation plays a role here as well. (And while sentences with two は are relatively common, those with three or more are really very rare.)

topic before	今日は田中君はケーキは作るよ。
contrast	今日は (topic) 田中君は (contrast) ケーキは (contrast) 作るよ。

*Today, **Tanaka** is going to make a **cake***

(while **Suzuki** is going to make something **else**).

今日は (topic) 田中君は (topic) ケーキは (contrast) 作るよ。

*Today, **Tanaka** is going to make a **cake*** (he is not going to make a **pie**).

今日は田中先生はいらっしゃる。

今日は (topic) 田中先生は (contrast) いらっしゃる。

***Prof. Tanaka** is coming today* (but not **Suzuki**).

今日は (contrast) 田中先生は (contrast) いらっしゃる。

***Prof. Tanaka** is coming today* (while **Suzuki** is coming **tomorrow**).

We can also see that the topic really is an "extra" position in a Japanese sentence, so that a sentence can have *both* a topic and a subject. Many such sentences are "generic," meaning that they are about *types* of animals or general *kinds* of behavior (cf. habits), and not about specific animals or specific incidents. Compare: *My dog barked at the mailman* which is specific and *Dogs bark at mailmen* which is general. If you want to make a broad statement about a class of animals or people, the group is usually marked with は. Several of these sentences are very famous in the linguistic literature.

象は鼻が長い。

Elephants have long noses.
アメリカ人は行儀が悪い。

Americans behave badly.
僕はうなぎだ。

I will have the eel.
この建物は部屋の窓が開かない。

The windows in this building do not open.

3.7.1.7 Other topic indicators

The expressions here might all be used instead of は to indicate the topic of a sentence.

Ø	その男、うわさ通りのプレイボーイなんだ。

That man, like the rumors say, he is a playboy.

(An empty topic markers is most common in informal speech, although there are highly ritualized situations like introductions where no particle is best: こちら、東京大学の田中さんです.)

だって	僕だっていつかヨーロッパに行く。

Me, someday I will go to Europe.

って	男って案外感情的なものね。
	Speaking of men, they are unexpectedly emotional.
	(also というのは〜)
ですが	あしたの会議ですが、何時ごろ出ましょうか。
	It's tomorrow's meeting, but when should we show up?
といえば	猫といえば、うちのはあまり性格がよくないよ。
	If we are talking about cats, ours is not very friendly.
なんか	ゴルフなんかつまらないよ。
	Speaking of golf, it is very boring.
について	この件について少しお話しさせていただきます。
	With respect to this matter, I'd like to say a few words.

3.7.2 も

Particle も is in many respects similar to particle は. It replaces が and を, and it occurs in combination with other particles to produce にも, からも, とも, etc. も, however, does not have a separate meaning like "topic," and it does not have a typical position in a sentence (in the way that は is usually the first element of a sentence). Rather, も is usually translated as *also, as well, too.* It can occur anywhere in a sentence, and it indicates that something else is consistent with the discussion so far. も is heavily dependent on the proceeding discussion, and it rarely if ever occurs "out of the blue."

田中君がケーキを作ったよ。そうか。僕も作ったよ。
Tanaka baked a cake. Really? I baked one too.
きのう東京に行ってきたよ。そうか。横浜にも行ってきたの？
We went to Tokyo yesterday. Oh, did you go to Yokohama as well?
今日は暇ですか。ええ、今日も明日も暇ですよ。
Are you free today? Yes, I am free both today and tomorrow.
食べもしなかった。
I didn't eat it either.

も occurs anytime there is an overt comparison in a single sentence.

東京にも横浜にも行って来ました。*We went to Tokyo as well as to Yokohama.*
ケーキもパイも作った。*I made both a cake and a pie.*
私も兄も外国語が弱いです。*My brother and I are both bad at foreign language.*

も occurs in a construction which parallels 行ってはいけない. Permission expressions such as 行ってもいいですか might be literally translated as "Is going okay as well?" Finally, も occurs in combination with words such as だれ, 何, or どれ to produce だれも,

何も and どれも. These and related expressions are discussed beginning on page 248.

These last three expressions might occur instead of も. さえ and すら have the emphatic meaning of でも *even*.

といい	このコンピュータは便利さといい値段といい一番だ。
	This computer, when it comes to convenience and price, is best.
	(This expression establishes a list as a topic.)
さえ	この魚はうちの猫さえ食べないよ。
	Even our cat wouldn't eat this fish.
	(さえ places extreme emphasis on the noun in question, and is often followed by a negative.)
すら	この魚はうちの猫すら食べないよ。
	Even our cat wouldn't eat this fish.
	(すら is even more emphatic than さえ.)

3.7.3 が

Particle が has one main function: it indicates the subject of a sentence. It occurs with all verbs, all adjectives, and all nominal adjectives in Japanese.

田中さんが着きました。
このクラスでは田中さんがとてもおもしろい人です。
今は田中さんが大好きです。

As discussed in the previous section, が is frequently replaced by particle は, but this is related to the overall context in which a sentence is used. 田中さんが着きました and 田中さんは着きました are both grammatical, and both can be translated into English as *Tanaka arrived* (with differing stress patterns). The choice of particle is determined by conversational context. If you are telling me who arrived, 田中さんが着きました makes sense. If you are telling me what has happened with regards to Tanaka, 田中さんは着きました is appropriate.

Particle が is often said to mark the direct object of stative verbs and adjectives, resulting in sentences such as 象は鼻が長い *Elephants have long noses* with more than one が. These are discussed below and on page 157.

3.7.4 を

3.7.4.1 Direct objects

A direct object in English is the noun which follows the verb: *eat cake, watch television, study Japanese,* or *hit the ball*. In Japanese, the direct object is usually marked with the particle を, although there are certain kinds of exceptions. Sometimes the Japanese direct object (を) is marked with a preposition in English (cf. *listen to, look after, look for, wait for, wish for* etc.). There are also cases where the English direct object is marked with が or に or について rather than with を in Japanese (cf. 何かについて議論する *discuss something* or 人に伝える *inform a person that* 〜).

direct
object を
(examples
only)

人を愛する・あい *love a person*; 新しい車を買うのを諦める・あきらめる *give up buying a new car*; ドアを開ける・あける *open a door*; 荷物を預かる・あずかる *look after luggage*; タバコを遠慮する・えんりょ *refrain from smoking*; 犬の後を追う・おう *chase after a dog*; 音楽を聞く・きく *listen to music*; 何かを希望する・きぼう *wish for something*; 予定を決める・きめる *decide the schedule*; シャツを着る・きる *put on a shirt*; 電気を消す・けす *turn out the lights*; 物を探す・さがす *look for a thing*; 身体の一部を手術する・しゅじゅつ *operate on a part of the body*; ケーキを食べる・たべる *eat cake*; 知らせを人に伝える・つたえる *inform a person of something*; 人を手伝う・つたう *help a person*; 仕事を手伝う・てつだう *help with work*; いい点数を願う・ねがう *hope for a good mark*; ご飯を残す・のこす *leave food*; 風邪をひく *catch a cold*; 部屋を間違う・まちがう *mistake the room*; 友達を待つ・まつ *wait for a friend*; 結婚することを認める・みとめる *approve of the marriage*; 鳥を見る・みる *watch a bird, see a bird*; 政治家に解決を求める・もとめる *seek a resolution from the politicians*; 手を休める・やすめる *rest your hands*; 約束を忘れる・わすれる *forget an appointment*; etc.

Japanese also has what might be called が-marked direct objects (at least based on their English translations). These are all stative predicates which means that they describe mental states, feelings, abilities, etc. They do not refer to things which people do (and most of them do not occur in any command form). Some of these words are real verbs. Others are adjectives or nominal adjectives. Almost all of these predicates allow subjects as well (marked with は or が) resulting in sentences like ジョンさんは金がいる *John needs money* or ジョンさんが金がいる *John needs money*. As expected, the choice of は or が is determined by the overall purpose and direction of the conversation. Sentences with as many as three が are possible but extremely rare. (See page 157 for further discussion of stative and other kinds of predicates.)

direct
object が

金がある *have money*; 犬がいる *have a dog*; 金がいる *need money*; 日本語がおもしろい *Japanese is interesting, have an interest in Japanese*; 声が聞こえる・きこえる *his voice is audible, can hear his voice*; ジョンさんが嫌いだ・きらい *dislike John*; ジョンさんが好きだ・すき *like John*; テニスができない *cannot play tennis*; 山が見える・みえる *mountains are visible, can see mountains*; 日本語がわかる *understand Japanese*; etc.

英語が読める *can read English*; すしが食べたい *want to eat sushi*; etc.

All potential forms and all 〜たい forms are considered stative (since both forms describe a state of mind or ability). Along with 好き and きらい, potential and 〜たい forms can in fact occur with particle を as well.

3.7.4.2 *Other usages*

In addition to indicating the direct object, を has several other typical usages. These include marking two kinds of locations as well as quantities, professions, and emotions.

point of departure を	バスを降りる・おりる *get off the bus*; 成田を出発する・しゅっぱつ *depart from Narita*; 大学を卒業する・そつぎょう *graduate from university*; 家を出る・でる *leave the house*; 成田を発つ・たつ *depart from Narita*; いやな仕事を逃げる・にげる *avoid, run away from unpleasant work*; チームを抜ける・ぬける *leave the team*; いつものコースを外れる・はずれる *deviate from the normal course*; イギリスを離れる・はなれる *leave England*; アパートを引っ越す・ひっこす *move from an apartment*; 練習を休む・やすむ *take a break from practice*

To a great degree, から can be substituted for this use of を, although departure from an を-marked location means only that a place has been left, while departure from a から-marked location implies a corresponding goal or future location as well. Compare:

家を出る *leave the house* (inside then outside)
家から出る *leave from the house* (and set off)

イギリスを離れる *leave England*
イギリスから離れる *leave from England* (on a journey to somewhere)

バスを降りる *get off the bus*
バスから降りる *get off from the bus* (and walk away)

route of motion を	道を歩く・あるく *walk along a road*; 川を泳ぐ・およぐ *swim the river*; 道を急ぐ・いそぐ *hurry along a road*; 夜道を帰る・かえる *return home along a late night street*; 大通りを駆ける・かける *gallop down a big road*; 道を通う・かよう *commute along a road*; 山道を下る・くだる *go down the mountain road*; 峠を超える・こえる *cross the mountain pass*; テーブルの上を転がる・ころがる *roll across the top of a table*; 公園を散歩する・さんぽ *walk in the park*; 前を失礼する・しつれい *pass in front of someone*; 学校の前を過ぎる・すぎる *pass in front of a school*; 道を進む・すすむ *progress along a street*; 雪の上を滑る・すべる *slide on top of snow*; 駅を通過する・つうか *pass a station*; 公園を通る・とおる *walk*

through the park; 山の上を飛ぶ・とぶ *fly over a mountain*; 小川が谷間を流れる・ながれる *a small river flows through a valley*; 山を登る・のぼる *climb a mountain*; 道の右側を走る・はしる *drive along the right side of the road*; 先生のお宅を訪問する・ほうもん *visit a teacher's house*; 角を左へ曲がる・まがる *turn left at the corner*; 太陽のまわりを回る・まわる *orbit around the sun*; この道を戻る・もどる *return along a road*; アメリカを旅行する・りょこう *travel* (all over) *America*; 橋を渡る・わたる *cross a bridge*

The route of motion を defines the range of motion. It answers the question along what route did the movement occur? It contrasts with particle で which indicates location of motion without indicating its route or its extent: 砂浜で歩く *walk on a beach* (possibly in circles); 山の上で飛ぶ *fly* (perhaps in circles) *over the mountain*

quantity を 百キロの距離を行く・いく *go a distance of 100 kilometers*; ３０歳を超す・こす *pass the age of thirty*; 五年間を過ごす・すごす *spend five years*; 夏休みをゴルフで楽しむ・たのしむ *spend the summer enjoying golf*; 時計が５時を回るところだ・まわる *It is just about five o'clock*

occupation を 医者をしている *be a doctor* (lit. *do a doctor*); 看護婦をしている *be a nurse* (lit. *do a nurse*); 歯医者をしている *be a dentist* (lit. *do a dentist*); 英語の教師をしている *be an English teacher* (lit. *do an English teacher*); 案内役を努める・つとめる *work as a guide*; 強盗を働く・はたらく *work as a burglar*

を with verbs of emotion いぬを恐れる・おそれる *fear dogs*; 友達の死を悲しむ・かなしむ *grieve a friend's death*; 日本の生活を懐かしむ・なつかしむ *long for my life in Japan*; 将来のことを悩む・なやむ *worry about the future*; 死を悼む・いたむ *feel pain at a death*; 田中さんを嫌う・きらう *hate Tanaka*; 離婚を後悔する・こうかい *regret my divorce*; 親を憎む・にくむ *hate one's parents*; 成功を喜ぶ・よろこぶ *be happy at a success*

Many of these verbs have adjective forms where the direct object of the verb becomes the subject of the adjective. The verbs of emotion sound much more active than their adjective counterparts. 恐れている sounds like you are quaking, and 悲しんでいる sounds like you are in active mourning, while the adjectives are more passive, describing an internal state, not an ongoing activity or change: いぬが恐ろしい *I am afraid of dogs* or 日本の生活が懐かしい *I am sentimental about my life in Japan*. The same verb/non-verb distinction exists for pairs like 好いている and 好き *like* or 嫌っている and 嫌い *hate*.

3.7.4.3 Grammar

There are two principle constructions where the direct object can end up as the が-marked subject: the 〜てある construction and the (neutral) passive. However, only the "real" direct objects in the first group (i.e. predicates like 開ける) occur freely in either construction. In contrast, objects which indicate a route, point of departure, or quantity are often felt to be more awkward in these constructions. Discussions with lists of relevant predicates are found beginning on pages 137 (〜てある) and 139 (passive).

3.7.5 に

に seems in general to mean "location in space or time," although the location might be a place where you are going, a place you are coming from, or a place where you simply exist. Many of these locations are metaphorical as well as actual. に also has grammatical usages where it does not seem to "mean" anything in particular.

3.7.5.1 With verbs of motion

A verb of motion is characterized by the fact that it cannot occur without the subject changing location. に can indicate the beginning or end of a motion. Here it often alternates with へ, まで, or から. Examples of each type are listed here. The lists are only representative.

goal に   先生に挨拶する・あいさつ *greet a teacher*; 姉に上げる・あげる *give to my sister*; 学生に宿題を与える・あたえる *assign homework to students*; ボールが窓に当たる・あたる *the ball strikes a window*; 本屋の前に集まる・あつまる *gather in front of a bookstore*; 妻に謝る・あやまる *apologize to my wife*; 人に言う *speak to a person*; 何かを箱に入れる・いれる *put something in a box*; 兄に何かを売る・うる *sell something to my brother*; テーブルの上に置く・おく *put on top of the table*; 生徒に何かを教える・おしえる *teach something to students*; 紙に印鑑を押す *press your seal onto the paper*; 友達に貸す・かす *lend to a friend*; 外側に傾く・かたむく *lean to the outside*; 内側に傾ける・かたむける *tilt to the inside*; 人に責任を被せる・かぶせる *put the blame on someone*; 先生に聞く・きく *ask a teacher*; 千円を小さいお金に崩す・くずす *break ¥1000 into small change*; 生徒に配る・くばる *hand out to students*; 私にくれる *give to me*; 仲間に加える・くわえる *include in the group*; くぎが足に刺さる・ささる *a nail stabs my foot*; 人をパーティーに誘う・さそう *invite a person to a party*; 自然に親しむ・したしむ *be close to nature*; 人に紹介する・しょうかい *introduce to a person*; 家に招待する・しょうたい *invite to your home*; 大人に成長する・せいちょう *grow into an adult*; 人に説明する・せつめい *explain to a person*; 書類に署名を添える・そえる *attach a signature to a* document; 床(ゆか)に倒(たお)れる・たおれる *fall to the floor*; ふろに水(みず)を足(た)す・たす *add water to the bath*; 人(ひと)に近付(ちかづ)く・ちかづく *approach a person*; 銀行(ぎんこう)に貯金(ちょきん)する・ちょきん *deposit in the bank*; 駅(えき)に着(つ)く・つく *arrive at the station*; 人(ひと)に名前(なまえ)を付(つ)ける・つける *name, give a name to a person*; 人(ひと)の後(あと)に続(つづ)く・つづく *continue after someone*; 船(ふね)を岸(きし)に繋(つな)ぐ・つなぐ *tie the boat to the shore*; ロシア語(ご)を日本語(にほんご)に直(なお)す・なおす *translate Russian into Japanese*; 新(あたら)しい生活(せいかつ)に慣(な)れる・なれる *get used to a new life*; 人(ひと)に述(の)べる・のべる *express to a person, say*; 飛行機(ひこうき)に乗(の)る・のる *get on an airplane*; みんなに発表(はっぴょう)する・はっぴょう *announce to everyone*; 黒板(こくばん)に貼(は)る・はる *stick to the blackboard*; こちらに引(ひ)っ張(ぱ)る・ひっぱる *pull this way*; 壁(かべ)にぶつける *throw against a wall*; 手(て)で物(もの)に触(ふ)れる・ふれる *touch something with your hand*; 人(ひと)に返事(へんじ)する *reply to somebody*; 先生(せんせい)に報告(ほうこく)する・ほうこく *make a report to a teacher*; ロシア語(ご)に翻訳(ほんやく)する・ほんやく *translate into Russian*; 頭(あたま)に巻(ま)く・まく *wrap around your head*; 「く」の字(じ)に曲(ま)げる・まげる *bend into a "ku"*; 右(みぎ)の方向(ほうこう)に回(まわ)す・まわす *turn to the right*; 先生(せんせい)に見(み)せる *show to the teacher*; 元(もと)に戻(もど)す・もどす *return to its original position*; 席(せき)に戻(もど)る・もどる *return to your seat*; 人(ひと)に何(なに)かを用意(ようい)する・ようい *prepare something for someone*; ここに呼(よ)ぶ・よぶ *call here*; 母(はは)に到着時間(とうちゃくじかん)を連絡(れんらく)する・れんらく *contact mother with my arrival time*

While many of the usages of に above are metaphorical, the alternation between に and へ is generally limited to movement of something physical from one location to another. The movement tends to be caused by a human, and there are instances when both に and へ are possible with a human subject while only に is possible with a non-human subject. In addition, with verbs of motion with a human subject, へ is generally considered softer and more polite.

goal に・へ alternation	テーブルの上(うえ)へ上(あ)げる・あげる *put on a table*; 東京(とうきょう)へ行(い)く・いく *go to Tokyo*; 田中(たなか)さんのお家(うち)へ伺(うかが)う・うかがう *call on, visit Tanaka*; 右(みぎ)の方(ほう)へ動(うご)かす・うごかす *move to the right side*; ある場所(ばしょ)へ移(うつ)す・うつす *shift to*; 東京(とうきょう)へ送(おく)る・おくる *send to Tokyo*; ある場所(ばしょ)へ落(お)とす・おとす *drop to*; ある場所(ばしょ)へ降(お)ろす・おろす *put down to*; 家(いえ)へ帰(かえ)る・かえる *return home*; 学校(がっこう)へ来(く)る・くる *come to school*; ある場所(ばしょ)へ下(さ)げる・さげる *lower to*; ここへしまう *put away here*; パリへ出発(しゅっぱつ)する・しゅっぱつ *depart for Paris*; そこへ進(すす)む・すすむ *proceed to there*; そこへ捨(す)てる・すてる *throw out to there*; 下(した)へ倒(たお)す・たおす *knock down*; 外(そと)へ出(だ)す・だす *put out*; そこへ近寄(ちかよ)る・ちかよる *come near there*; そこへ出掛(でか)ける・でかける *go out to*; 東京(とうきょう)へ出(で)る・でる *leave for Tokyo*; ある場所(ばしょ)へ通(とお)す・とおす *let by*; 会社(かいしゃ)へ届(とど)ける・とどける *deliver to the company*; 木(き)の上(うえ)へ飛(と)ぶ・とぶ *fly to the top of a tree*; 海(うみ)へ流(なが)れる・ながれる *flow to the sea*; そこへ投(な)げる・

なげる *throw to*; その方向へ逃げる・にげる *flee in that direction*; そこへ入る・はいる *come in, go in*; ある場所へ干す・ほす *hang to dry in*; そちらへ参る・まいる *go there*; 右へ曲がる・まがる *turn to the right, bend to the right*; 社長室へ回す・まわす *pass to the office of the company president*; 北の方向へ向かう・むかう *face north*; 外国へ送る *send to a foreign country*; アメリカへ輸出する・ゆしゅつ *export to the US*; そばへ寄る・よる *come near*; 海外へ留学する・りゅうがく *study abroad*; 向こう側へ渡る・わたる *cross to the other side*

In general, all occurrences of に here can be replaced with まで. The difference between に and まで might be translated into English as *to* and *as far as*. まで refers to extent, so that 東京まで行く literally means *go as far as Tokyo*, leaving open whether you actually crossed the city limits or not. In addition, まで implies that Tokyo is not the final destination: 今日は東京まで行って、明日は〜 Note that some verbs of motion, especially those which emphasize the manner of motion rather than the direction (e.g. 走る, 泳ぐ, 急ぐ, etc.) do not actually occur very naturally with a simple に, and compounds such as 走って行く are much better (since 行く and に are fine together). Examples of such compound verbs include:

〜て行く compounds	歩いて行く・あるいていく *go walking*; 急いで行く・いそいでいく *go hurrying*; 運転して行く・うんてんしていく *go driving*; 泳いで行く・およいでいく *go swimming*; 駆けて行く・かけていく *go galloping*; 散歩して行く・さんぽしていく *go walking*

Somewhat surprisingly perhaps, に can also be used to indicate the source of a motion. Some verbs allow only に while the majority alternate with から.

from に	神に運を願う・ねがう *wish for luck from a god*; 人に見返りを望む・のぞむ *hope for a reward from person*
from に・から	先生からいただく *receive from a teacher*; 先生からうわさを伺う・うかがう *hear a rumor from a teacher*; 学生から教わる・おそわる *learn from your students*; 兄から借りる・かりる *borrow from my brother*; 先生から聞く・きく *hear from a teacher*; 人から助言を頼む・たのむ *ask a person for advice*; 先生から習う・ならう *learn from a teacher*; ある事から始まる・はじまる *begin from*; 兄からもらう *receive from my brother*; 友達から助言を求める・もとめる *ask a friend for advice*

Here are three regular and general constructions for expressing purpose, all of which involve the particle に.

〜に行く   勉強しに行く *go to study* (in order to study)
　　　　　　食べに帰る *go home to eat* (in order to eat)
　　　　　　友達に会いに来る *come to meet a friend* (in order to meet a friend)
　　　　　　取りに来る *come to get* (in order to get something)
　　　　　　呼びに行く *go and call* (in order to get a person)

The purpose expressed here is generally not very significant. The main verb must be a verb of motion like 行く, 帰る, or 来る; the し (する) in expressions like 勉強しに行く may be omitted: 勉強に行く. In contrast to 〜のに and 〜ために which relate two different events (the first of which is done to accomplish the second), an expression like 食べに行く refers to a single event of going which includes a reason: *go in order to eat.*

〜のに   日本語の宿題をするのに辞書を使う。
I use a dictionary to do my Japanese homework.
成田へ行くのには電車に乗るのが一番速い。
In order to go to Narita, taking the train is fastest.

In general, the two predicates both *occur* (as opposed to simply being true), and they occur at the same time. The overall effect emphasizes the relationship between two concrete processes.

〜ために   勉強するために図書館に行った。*She went to the library to study.*
子どものために苦しんでいます。*I suffer for the sake of my children.*
上手になるために毎日練習する。*I practice every day in order to improve.*
生きるために食べなくちゃ。*One must eat to live.*

ために is the most formal of the three expressions here, and the purpose expressed is felt to be significant (at least by the speaker). It may be used with nouns as well as verbs, and the particle に is often deleted. In contrast to expressions with 〜のに, the two predicates may be more abstract, and they do not have to co-occur. Thus 生きるのに食べなくちゃ is strange because the whole claim is rather abstract and eating does not really co-occur with living (it is if anything a "sub" activity). ために also occurs in constructions where it means *because*: お金がないために買えない. Turn to page 268 for further ways to express *because.*

3.7.5.2 Location

に is used to indicate a point of existence. Here it contrasts with particle で which indicates the location within which an event occurs (see page 209 below for discussion of で). To understand the difference, it is useful to look at verbs which are actually compatible with both particles. The choice of particle usually affects the specific interpretation of the verb. Usage with 寝る seems to be most idiomatic (and contrasts with that of 眠る).

東京に地震があった。
There was an earthquake in Tokyo (destroying Tokyo).
東京で地震があった。
There was an earthquake (somewhere) *in Tokyo.*

黒板に書く
write on the blackboard
隣の部屋で書く
write in the next room

大宮に土地を買う
buy land in Omiya (land found in Omiya, but purchased at an office in Tokyo)
大宮で車を買う
buy a car in Omiya (presumably at a car dealership in Omiya)

床に転ぶ
roll, fall on the floor, fall to the floor
外で転ぶ
roll, fall somewhere outside (not inside)

水に溶く
dissolve in water
水で溶く
dissolve with water

上野公園に走る
run to Ueno Park
上野公園で走る
run in Ueno Park

事業に成功する
succeed at business, succeed at an enterprise
事業で成功する
succeed in business

家<ruby>いえ</ruby>で寝<ruby>ね</ruby>る

sleep, go to bed in one's home (at a location)

ベッドで寝<ruby>ね</ruby>る

use a bed to sleep (at a location), *go to bed in a bed*

ベッドに寝<ruby>ね</ruby>る

go to bed, get into bed (= ベッドに横<ruby>よこ</ruby>たわる *lie down on a bed*)

ふとんに寝<ruby>ね</ruby>る

go to bed, get into a futon

(寝る can mean either *get into bed* or *lie down, sleep*. The first interpretation assumes a goal with に while the second assumes a location with で. 寝る also contrasts with 眠<ruby>ねむ</ruby>る which is actually closer to English *to sleep, rest*. Compare すやすや眠<ruby>ねむ</ruby>る *sleep soundly* and よく眠<ruby>ねむ</ruby>れましたか "Did you sleep well?" Both expressions are strange with 寝<ruby>ね</ruby>る.)

Here is a (very partial) list of verbs which indicate location with particle に. These locations are thought of as points of location (not as areas within which something occurs). For many specific verbs the actual difference between a goal and a location is actually very subtle. Think about 画面<ruby>がめん</ruby>に写<ruby>うつ</ruby>る *show, appear on a screen*. Is the screen a goal (where an image ends up projected) or a location (where an image is viewed)? Likewise, 椅子<ruby>いす</ruby>に座<ruby>すわ</ruby>る *sit in a chair*. Is the chair where you end up or where you are? As such, the lists offered here should not be taken as definitive. It is meant only to illustrate the range of behavior associated with the particle. Note also that you may sometimes encounter the particle combination において as in 次<ruby>つぎ</ruby>の全国大会<ruby>ぜんこくたいかい</ruby>は東京<ruby>とうきょう</ruby>において行<ruby>おこな</ruby>われます "The next national sports meet will take place in Tokyo." This is a formal alternative to に which indicates location.

location に (real and abstract)	勉強<ruby>べんきょう</ruby>に飽きる・あきる *tire of study*; まずさに呆れる・あきれる *be amazed at the bad taste*; 胃に穴<ruby>あな</ruby>があく *get a hole in one's stomach*; 顔<ruby>かお</ruby>に現す・あらわす *express on your face*; あそこにある *it is over there*; 仕事<ruby>しごと</ruby>に自分<ruby>じぶん</ruby>の才能<ruby>さいのう</ruby>を生かす・いかす *bring one's talents to life in one's work*; 息子<ruby>むすこ</ruby>が二<ruby>に</ruby>階<ruby>かい</ruby>にいる *my son is upstairs*; 人間<ruby>にんげん</ruby>の生活<ruby>せいかつ</ruby>に水<ruby>みず</ruby>が要る *Water is necessary for human life*; 庭<ruby>にわ</ruby>に植える・うえる *plant in a garden*; 空中<ruby>くうちゅう</ruby>に浮かぶ・うかぶ *float in the air*; 画面<ruby>がめん</ruby>に写す・うつす *show on a screen*; 画面に写る・うつる *appear on a screen*; ある国<ruby>くに</ruby>に革命<ruby>かくめい</ruby>が起きた・おきる *a revolution occurred in some country*; 火鉢<ruby>ひばち</ruby>に火<ruby>ひ</ruby>を起こす *build a fire in the hibachi*; 人気<ruby>にんき</ruby>に溺れる・おぼれる *drown in popularity*; 東京<ruby>とうきょう</ruby>にアパートを買う・かう *buy a flat in Tokyo*; 火の光が海面<ruby>かいめん</ruby>に輝く・かがやく *sunlight shines on the ocean surface*; 壁<ruby>かべ</ruby>にかかる *hang on a wall*; 黒板<ruby>こくばん</ruby>に書く *write on the blackboard*; 机<ruby>つくえ</ruby>の中<ruby>なか</ruby>に隠れる・かくれる *be hidden in a desk*; 彼<ruby>かれ</ruby>に知性<ruby>ちせい</ruby>が欠ける・かける *lack intelligence*; 机<ruby>つくえ</ruby>の上<ruby>うえ</ruby>に重ねる・かさねる *pile up on a desk*; テニスの試合<ruby>しあい</ruby>に勝つ・かつ *win a tennis match*; 背中<ruby>せなか</ruby>に痛<ruby>いた</ruby>みを感じる・かんじる *feel pain in one's back*; 彼の努力<ruby>どりょく</ruby>に感心する・かんしん *admire*

his effort; 町に建設する・けんせつ *construct in the town*; 物に腰掛ける・こしかける *sit down on a thing*; 庭に花が咲く・さく *flowers bloom in the garden*; クラブ活動に参加する・さんか *participate in club activities*; 提案に賛成する・さんせい *agree with the proposal*; 庭に草が繁る・しげる *weeds grow thickly in the garden*; 日記に記す・しるす *write down in one's diary*; その町に住む・すむ *live in that town*; 小指に指輪をする *wear a ring on your pinky*; 椅子に座る・すわる *sit in a chair*; 道が川に沿う・そう *the road goes along the river*; スタートラインに揃う・そろう *gather at the start line*; 地球に存在する・そんざい *exist on earth*; 人が店の前に立つ・たつ *people stand in front of a store*; 空き地に建つ・たつ *build on open land*; 庭に建てる・たてる *build in the garden*; 一ヵ所に溜まる・たまる *accumulate in one place*; 市役所に勤めている・つとめる *be employed at city hall*; 勉学に努める・つとめる *make an effort at studying*; 机の上に詰む・つむ *pile up on the desk*; リンゴを箱に詰める・つめる *pack apples in a box*; 足元に照らす・てらす *shine light at one's feet*; ホテルに泊まる・とまる *stay in a hotel*; けがに泣く・なく *cry at an injury*; 駅の前に並ぶ・ならぶ *queue in front of the station*; 栗の木に実が生る・なる *chestnut trees produce nuts*; ふとんに寝る・ねる *lie down in a futon, sleep*; 東京に残る・のこる *remain in Tokyo*; 川に臨む・のぞむ *overlook a river*; 植物が庭に生える・はえる *plants grow in the garden*; 花を本に挟む・はさむ *press a flower in a book*; 川に魚を放す・はなす *release fish in a river*; 頭に髪を生やす・はやす *grow hair on your head*; その知らせにびっくりする *be surprised at an announcement*; 町に店を開く・ひらく *open a store in a town*; テーブルの上に広げる・ひろげる *spread out on a table*; ファイルに保存する・ほぞん *keep in a file*; 顔に疲れが見える・みえる *exhaustion is visible in his face*; エンジンに異状を認める・みとめる *recognize something unusual in the engine*; 私には日本語がわかる *I understand Japanese*; 電車の中に傘を忘れる・わすれる *forget an umbrella in the train*

3.7.5.3 Quantities, limits, and times

に quantity or limit
深夜に及ぶ・およぶ *extend into the late night*; 二つに折れる・おれる *break into two*; 一に二を加える・くわえる *add two to one*; 体重が７０キロに下がる・さがる *body weight goes down to seventy kilograms*; 体重を７０キロに下げる・さげる *reduce your weight to seventy kilograms*; 場所をきれいに整理する・せいり *straighten up a place*; ２週間の休暇が１週間に縮む・ちぢむ *a two week vacation is shortened to one week*; ２週間の休暇を１週間に縮める・ちぢめる *shorten a two week vacation to one week*; 死者が１００人に上る・のぼる *the number of deaths goes up to*

100; 貯金を百万円に増やす・ふやす *increase one's savings to one million yen*; こづかいを千円に減らす・へらす *reduce someone's allowance to ¥1000*; 一万円に負ける・まける *reduce to ¥10,000*; 二つに分かれる・わかれる *be divided into two*; 二つに分ける・わける *divide into two*; 二つに割る・わる *break into two*; 二つに割れる・われる *be broken into two*

Temporal expressions in Japanese are marked with particle に or with no particle. Note in contrast that English uses *at, in, on*, or no preposition (actually making English more idiomatic than Japanese).

に time   9時に会いましょう。

Let's meet at nine.
6月に東京に行く。

I will go to Tokyo in June.
8月13日に結婚しましょう。

Let's get married on the 13th of August.
1962年に生まれた。

She was born in 1962.
この電車は何時に着きますか。

What time will this train arrive?

The following kinds of time expressions do not take particle に when used as adverbs: 今日, 明日, 昨日, 去年, 今, 夕べ, anything with 来〜, anything with 先〜, anything with 今〜, anything with 毎〜, anything with 作〜, anything with 明〜, anything with 再来〜, and いつ. Note that their English translations also require no preposition (*today, tomorrow, yesterday, next week*, etc.). The difference between a time expression like 明日 *tomorrow* and one like 午後3時 *3pm* is that 明日 does not make sense unless you know when it was said; 明日 is different each day. Such expressions are defined relative to when they are spoken. In contrast, 午後3時 is always a specific time independent of when it is spoken. Time expressions made vague by ごろ・ころ・頃 take に optionally as do days of the week and reference to months. Compare 6月 *June* (absolute) and 今年の6月 *June of this year* (relative).

今日は何をするつもりですか。

What do you plan to do today?
明日も明後日も雨だろう。

It will probably rain tomorrow and the day after.
新しい先生が来週来ると思います。

I think the new teacher will come next week.

去年の夏は暑かったよ。

Last summer was hot.

いつ映画を見に行きますか。

When will you go and see the movie?

What day will you go and see the movie?

何時頃に行くつもりですか。

About what time are you planning to go?

Here is a list of time expressions which are relative to the speech time. They do not co-occur with particle に. Note that 前, 先, and 後, all of which indicate location in space as well as time, normally do occur with specific particles (on their own or in combination with other expressions, e.g. 二日前に, 一ヶ月前に, etc.). While いつ does not require a particle, all question words with 何 do (i.e. 何時に, 何日に, 何年に, etc.). In the lists below, when two readings are given, the second is Chinese and more formal, e.g. 昨日の朝・きのうのあさ・さくじつのあさ:

order | 前に・まえに *before, in front of*; 先に・さきに *before, in front of*; 今・いま *now*; 後で・あとで *after*; いつ *when*

with 〜朝 | 一昨日の朝・おとといのあさ・いっさくじつのあさ *morning before last*; 昨日の朝・きのうのあさ・さくじつのあさ *yesterday morning*; 今朝・けさ *this morning*; 明日の朝・あしたのあさ・みょうにちのあさ *tomorrow morning*; 明後日の朝・あさってのあさ・みょうごにちのあさ *morning after tomorrow*; 朝晩・あさばん *morning and evening*; 毎朝・まいあさ *every morning*

with 〜晩 | 一昨日の晩・おとといのばん・いっさくじつのばん *night before last*; 昨晩・さくばん *last night*; 今晩・こんばん *tonight, this evening*; 今夜・こんや *this evening*; 明日の晩・あしたのばん・みょうにちのばん *tomorrow night*; 明後日の晩・あさってのばん・みょうごにちのばん *night after next*; 毎晩・まいばん *every evening*

with 〜日 | 一昨日・おととい・いっさくじつ *day before yesterday*; 昨日・きのう・さくじつ *yesterday*; 今日・きょう・こんにち *today*; 明日・あした・みょうにち *tomorrow*; 明後日・あさって・みょうごにち *day after tomorrow*; 明明後日・しあさって・みょうみょうごにち *two days after tomorrow*; 毎日・まいにち *every day*

with 〜週 | 先々週・せんせんしゅう *two weeks ago*; 先週・せんしゅう *last week*; 今週・こんしゅう *this week*; 来週・らいしゅう *next week*; 再来週・さらいしゅう *week after next*; 毎週・まいしゅう *every week* with 〜月   先々月・せんせんげつ *two months ago*; 先月・せんげつ *last month*; 今月・こんげつ *this month*; 来月・らいげつ *next month*; 再来月・さらいげつ *month after next*; 毎月・まいつき・まいげつ *every month*

with 〜年   一昨年・おととし・いっさくねん *year before last*; 去年・きょねん *last year*; 昨年・さくねん *last year*; 今年・ことし *this year*; 来年・らいねん *next year*; 再来年・さらいねん *year after next*; 毎年・まいとし *every year*

Time of completion, specifically, is often compatible with に, で, まで, and even までに.

仕事が金曜日に終わる。
This job will finish on Friday (not before, not after).
仕事が金曜日で終わる。
This job will finish as of Friday (and not a day later).
仕事が金曜日まで終わる。
This job will finish by Friday (at the latest, possibly earlier).
仕事が金曜日までに終わる。
This job will finish by Friday (at the latest, possibly earlier).

3.7.5.4 Grammatical usages of に

The subject of the active sentence (with が) is marked に in the passive sentence. See page 139 for discussion of the passive.

に with the   猫が魚を食べた。   (猫が)
passive   *The cat ate the fish.*
               魚が猫に食べられた。   (猫に)
               The fish was eaten by the cat.
               友達が行った。   (友達が)
               My friend left.
               友達に行かれた。   (友達に)
               I was left by my friend.

The subject of the active sentence (with が) is marked に or を in the causative sentence. Note the contrast in interpretations when the active subject is marked with に (*let go, allow to go*) and when it is marked with を (*make go*).

に with the   兄が行った。   (兄が)
causative   *My brother went.*
               母が兄に行かせた。   (兄に)
               My mother let my brother go.
               母が兄を行かせた。   (兄を)
               My mother made my brother go.

These two effects are combined in the causative passive although the に・を alternation is not possible here. Japanese has a general rule that there can be no more than one を in a single Japanese sentence. See page 229 as well.

に with the	兄がレバーを食べた。	(兄が)
causative	*My brother ate liver.*	
passive	母が兄にレバーを食べさせた。	(母が・兄に)
	My mother made my brother eat liver.	
	兄が母にレバーを食べさせられた。	(兄が・母に)
	My brother was made to eat liver by my mother.	

3.7.6 で

3.7.6.1 Location of an event

で indicates a location where an event occurs. The list here is representative as で is compatible with almost any verb which describes an action (and which is not otherwise compatible with に). You may sometimes encounter にて which is a more formal version of で: 次の全国大会は東京にて開催されます "The next national sports meet will take place in Tokyo."

で location 二つの道がここで合う・あう *the two roads meet here*; 駅の前で会う *meet in front of the station*; 公園で遊ぶ・あそぶ *play in the park*; 川で溺れる・おぼれる *drown in a river*; プールで泳ぐ・およぐ *swim in a pool*; 戦争で敵国に勝つ・かつ *win over an enemy country in a war*; オフィスで考える・かんがえる *think in one's office*; 玄関で失礼する・しつれい *take one's leave in the entrance hall*; バリ島で休みを過ごす・すごす *spend your vacation on Bali*; アパートで生活する・せいかつ *live in an apartment*; 公園で時間を潰す・つぶす *kill time at the park*; ベッドで眠る・ねむる *sleep on a bed*; 家で寝る・ねる *sleep in one's home*; 工場で働く・はたらく *work in a factory*; アメリカで流行る・はやる *be popular in America*; 図書館で勉強する・べんきょう *study in the library*; 交差点でぶつかる *crash in the intersection*; 駅の前で待つ・まつ *wait in front of the station*; 山の中で迷う・まよう *get lost in the mountains*; 二階で休む・やすむ *rest upstairs*; 新聞で読む・よむ *read in a newspaper*; etc.

While an event is usually indicated by the verb, で is compatible with ある if the subject of the sentence is an event: 公園でコンサートがあった *There was a concert in the park*. Typical "event nouns" include: パーティー *party*; 講演 *speech, lecture*; 授業 *class, lecture*; スポーツ大会 *sports meet, tournament*; 映画 *movie, film*; ピクニック *picnic*; etc.

Particle に is typically used to indicate a location where something exists (or where it ends up). Nevertheless, many verbs mark location with both particles に and で, where the choice of particle affects the specific interpretation. に treats the location as a point of existence, while で treats the location as an area, within which the action occurs. Turn to page 203 for a series of specific examples.

3.7.6.2 Means or materials

Particle で indicates the device used to accomplish a task or the material out of which a product is made. While the list here is very long, it is still incomplete. で is appropriate whenever an object can be thought of as a tool or a material.

で means or materials	火で暖める・あたためる *warm with a flame*; 言葉で表す・あらわす *express with words* (に is also good here meaning *express in words*); 飛行機で行く *go by plane*; バットで玉を打つ・うつ *hit a ball with a bat*; カメラで写す・うつす *photograph with a camera*; 目で追う・おう *follow after with your eyes*; 手で押さえる・おさえる *hold down with your hands*; 手で押す・おす *push with your hand*; ボールペンで書く・かく *write with a pen*; 新聞で顔を隠す・かくす *hide your face with a newspaper*; フェンスで囲む・かこむ *surround with a fence*; 雪を手で固める・かためる *make the snow into a ball in your hand*; 風で傾く・かたむく *lean over because of the wind*; ストーブの火で乾かす・かわかす *dry with the heat of the stove*; ビデオで記録する・きろく *record on video* (に is also good here); ナイフで切る・きる *cut with a knife*; 台風で電線が切れる・きれる *power lines are cut by a typhoon*; 地震で崩れる・くずれる *collapse because of an earthquake*; 水で火を消す・けす *put the fire out with water*; えらで呼吸する・こきゅう *breathe with gills*; 手で目を擦る・こする *rub your eyes with your hands*; 大きい声で叫ぶ・さけぶ *shout in a loud voice*; 雷で木が二つに裂ける・さける *the tree is split by lightning*; ナイフで刺す・さす *stab with a knife*; 音で目を覚ます・さめす *wake up because of a sound*; 手で触る・さわる *feel with your hand*; ロープで縛る・しばる *tie with rope*; グラフで示す・しめす *show with a graph* (に is also good here); 示談で済む・すむ *finish with an out of court settlement*; 薬で命が助かる・たすかる *his life is saved by medicine*; 手で叩く・たたく *hit with your hand*; バスで通学する・つうがく *commute to school by bus*; 手で掴む・つかむ *catch with your hand*; ナイフで突く・つく *stab with a knife*; マッチで火を点ける・つける *light with a match*; 手で潰す・つぶす *squash with your hand*; 光で照らす・てらす *illuminate with light*; その説明で誤解が解ける・とける *the misunderstanding was cleared up with the explanation*; 熱で雪が溶ける・とける *the snow melts from the heat*; 虫をピンで止める・とめる *mount insects on pins*; 薬で痛みを取る・とる *take away*

pain with medicine; ガンで亡くなる・なくなる *die of cancer*; 針^{はり}で縫う・ぬう *sew with a needle*; 液体で濡らす・ぬらす *make wet with a liquid*; 液^{えきたい}体で濡れる・ぬれる *get wet with a liquid*; 水でペンキを伸ばす・のばす^{みず} *extend the paint with water*; クレジットカードで払う *pay with a credit card*; 言葉^{ことば}で表現する・ひょうげん *express with words* (に is also good here meaning *express in words*); ぞうきんで拭く・ふく *wipe with a cloth*; 手^てで物^{もの}に触れる・ふれる *touch something with your hand*; シャベルで掘る・ほる *dig with a shovel*; ノリで巻く・まく *wrap in seaweed*; 紙^{かみ}ひもで結ぶ・むすぶ *tie with paper string cord* (used to tie up packages); 水で戻^{みず}す・もどす *bring back with water*; ドライバーでねじを緩める・ゆるめる *loosen a screw with a screwdriver*

3.7.6.3 Limits and numbers

で is used to mark limits and numbers. Some of these might be thought of as abstract locations. Others might really be thought of as no more than conjunction with the て -form of だ (which is also で). Note the various alternations.

で groups	このクラスで一番^{いちばん}いい学生^{がくせい}
	the best student in this class
	一人^{ひとり}で勉強^{べんきょう}する。
	I study alone
	(cf. *I am alone and I study*)
	数学^{すうがく}で百点満点^{ひゃくてんまんてん}を取^とる
	get full marks in mathematics
	この三人^{さんにん}の中^{なか}でだれが一番背^{いちばんせ}が高^{たか}いですか。
	Who of these three people is the tallest?
	この三人^{さんにん}のうちでだれが一番背^{いちばんせ}が高^{たか}いですか。
	Who of these three people is the tallest?
で numbers	二冊^{にさつ}で三百円^{さんびゃくえん}です *two (of the notebooks) are ¥300*
	200グラムで¥1500のコーヒー *coffee for ¥1500 per 200 grams*
	一万円^{いちまんえん}で売^うる *sell for ¥10,000*
	一万円^{いちまんえん}で売^うれる *be sold for ¥10,000*
	一^{ひと}つで足^たりる *one is enough*
	150キロで飛^とばす *fly along at 150 kph, travel at 150 kph*
	10万円^{まんえん}で間^まに合^あう *¥100,000 is enough*

3.7.6.4 Conditions and reasons

These last two usages of で might simply be conjunction with だ since most of these examples have two-sentence parallels. Again, the more literary にて might sometimes be found in similar constructions.

で
conditions

会長_{かいちょう}で一年_{いちねん}を通_{とお}す *spend one year as chair, be chair for one year*
試合_{しあい}に3対1で負_まける *lose the game three to one*
マージャンで負ける *lose at mahjong*
総合力_{そうごうりょく}で勝_{まさ}る *be superior to in overall strength*

朝_{あさ}ご飯_{はん}を食_たべない。学校_{がっこう}に行_いく。 *I don't eat breakfast. I go to school.*
朝ご飯を食べないで学校に行く。 *I go to school without eating breakfast.*
(cf. 朝ご飯を食べずに学校に行く。)

The 〜ないで pattern is generally taken as a precondition. 〜ずに is still common in place of 〜ないで (食_たべずに学校_{がっこう}に行_いく) although it is somewhat old-fashioned sounding.

Reason or cause interpretations are really the most difficult to identify with any confidence. Many of these might simply be conjunction with です. Others might be interpreted as "means" (for example: 風_{かぜ}で開_あく; is the wind a device for opening the door or the cause of the door opening?). As such, it is difficult to say that there is clear reason で or a clear cause で.

で
cause/reason

風邪_{かぜ}で頭_{あたま}が痛_{いた}い・いたい *my head hurts because of my cold*; 引_ひっ越_こしで腰_{こし}を痛_{いた}める・いためる *injure your back moving*; 火事_{かじ}で家_{いえ}を失_{うしな}う・うしなう *lose your house to fire*; ガンで死_しぬ・しぬ *die of cancer*; 事故_{じこ}でけがをする *be injured in an accident*; 赤字_{あかじ}で倒_{たお}れる・たおれる *collapse due to debt*; 不景気_{ふけいき}で潰_{つぶ}れる・つぶれる *collapse because of a bad economy*

Compare the following sets of examples. Sometimes a condition interpretation seems most natural. Other times, a causative interpretation seems most natural. The ambiguity of a plain で is probably a function of context more than anything else. (This is one reason that it is difficult to say that で here is a real particle.)

病気_{びょうき}です。仕事_{しごと}に行_いけない。 *I am ill. I can't go to work.*
病気で仕事に行けない。 *I am ill so I can't go to work.*
(cf. 病気だから仕事に行けない。 *I am ill so I will not go to work.*)
病気_{びょうき}です。医者_{いしゃ}に行_いきます。 *I am ill. I go to the doctor.*
病気で医者に行きます。 *I go to the doctor ill.*
(cf. 病気なので医者に行きます。 *I am ill so I will go to the doctor.*)

生です。食べます。 *It is raw. I eat it.*
生で食べます。 *I eat it raw.*

ただです。映画を見に行った。 *It is free. I went and saw a movie.*
ただで映画を見に行った。 *I went and saw a movie for free.*

3.7.7 と

Many usages of と are discussed in other places. These are cross-referenced below.

3.7.7.1 With

A number of usages of と correspond conceptually with a notion of *with* (and occasionally *from*). This is further related to conjunction of nouns (page 265) as well as the と conditional (page 178).

田中さんと東京に行ってきた。
I went to Tokyo with Tanaka.
友達と三人でキャンプをしに行くことにした。
Two friends and I decided to go camping together.
人と別れる
split up with a person

と	
with, to, (from)	隣の子と遊ぶ・あそぶ *play with the child next door*; 友達と競争する・きょうそう *compete with a friend*; 人と組む・くむ *work together with a person, cooperate*; 人と結婚する・けっこん *marry a person*; 人と喧嘩する・けんか *argue with a person*; 彼女と交際する・こうさい *hang around with her*; 私のと異なる・ことなる *be different from mine*; 人と試合する・しあい *play a game with a person*; 人とする *do* (something) *with a person*; 闘う・たたかう *fight against* (a person, a disease), *fight with*; 人と違う・ちがう *be different from a person*; 人と並ぶ・ならぶ *get in line with a person*; 並べる・ならべる *line up* (something) *with*; 人と離れる・はなれる *separate from a person*; 彼と比較する・ひかく *compare to him*; 結ぶ・むすぶ *tie together*; 恋愛する・れんあい *to love*

With other verbs, both と and に are possible. と indicates a reciprocal relationship while に indicates a one way exchange. For a small set of verbs including: 会う, 相談する, 協力する, and 話す, the と version is actually an on-going process (だれかと話している *is talking back and forth*) while the に version is more likely to indicate a discrete event or change of state (だれかに話している *has talked to someone*).

と・に	合う・あう *agree with* (my tastes); 会う・あう *meet with* (a person); 合わ
with, to,	せる・あわせる *put together with*; *gather with*; 重なる・かさなる *pile up,*
(from)	*stack together*; 代わる・かわる *substitute with*; 関係する・かんけい *be*

related to, involved with; 協力する・きょうりょく *cooperate with*; 比べる・
くらべる *compare with*; 親しむ・したしむ *be close to*; しゃべる *speak to*;
相談する・そうだん *consult with*; 繋がる・つながる *be connected to*; 繋ぐ・
つなぐ *fasten to, tie to*; 取り替える・とりかえる *exchange with* (this); 似
る・にる *resemble* (a person); 話す・はなす *speak with*; ぶつかる *hit,*
strike against; 混ざる・まざる *mix with*; 混じる・まじる *be mixed with*;
混ぜる・まぜる *mingle with*; 間違う・まちがう *mistake with*; 人と約束す
る・やくそく *promise a person*; 連絡する・れんらく *make contact with*;
分かれる・わかれる *split off from*; 分ける・わける *divide from*

A further set of contrasts is found when particles と and に interact with なる and する. (This discussion is related to that found on page 124). 〜となる indicates that one thing has taken on the role of another. In the first set of examples, the speaker is possibly substituting for the teacher. An empty room is now being used for a specific purpose. In terms of purchases, one does not buy ¥2000. One buys ¥2000 worth of goods or services. 〜になる indicates that one thing actually *is* another. In the second set of examples, the speaker will become an actual teacher. The speaker actually has nothing to do. The price is ¥2000. While both 〜となる and 〜になる are heard in stores, 〜となる is more polite.

先生となります。
I will become a teacher. (= *I will take on the role of teacher.*)
隣の部屋が鈴木のオフィスとなりました。
The room next door has been made into Suzuki's office. (i.e. not its original purpose)
¥2000となります。
It will be ¥2000. (more polite)

先生になります。
I will become a teacher. (= *I am going to be a teacher.*)
隣の部屋が鈴木のオフィスになりました。
The room next door has been made into Suzuki's office. (That is the decision.)
¥2000になります。
It will be ¥2000.

In contrast (and as illustrated in the examples on the next page), 〜にする indicates a decision while the expression 〜にして or 〜にしては means something like *considering* or *given the fact that* 〜, indicating the presumed actuality of the statement in question. This assumption is exactly what is missing with 〜として or 〜としては (from 〜とする) meaning *as* or *as if*.

子供にしてはとても語彙が豊富である。

Considering that he is a child, he has a large vocabulary. (said about an actual child)

2月にしてはあまり寒くないですねえ。

This is not very cold for February, is it. (said about a warm February)

子供としてはとても語彙が豊富である。

He has a large vocabulary for a child.

(said about an actual child or as a roundabout insult about an adult)

2月としてはあまり寒くないですねえ。

It is not very cold for February. (said about a warm February or a very cold April)

3.7.7.2 *Quotative* と

と occurs before verbs such as 思う, 言う, 考える, 感じる to mark quotes or linguistic information (as opposed to the names of objects). It occurs in conversation as って or て. と also occurs with onomatopoeic expressions (see pages 262) which are like quotes in that they are "informational."

Quotative
と
こんにちはと挨拶する・あいさつ *greet with a "Hello"*; 田中と言う・いう *say "Tanaka," be called Tanaka*; 犯人だと訴える・うったえる *charge as a criminal, accuse*; 先生が来ないと教える・おしえる *teach, inform that the teacher is not coming*; いいと思う・おもう *think, believe, feel that it is good*; 否認と解釈する・かいしゃく *interpret as denial*; いいと考える・かんがえる *think that something is good*; いいと感じる・かんじる *feel that something is good*; よくできる人だと感心する・かんしん *admire his ability*; やろうと頑張る・がんばる *stick it out to succeed*; 行ってもいいかと聞く・きく *ask if it is okay to go*; 行かないと決める・きめる *decide that I won't go*; 事故が多かったと記録する・きろく *record that there were many accidents*; 頑張ろうと苦心する・くしん *be at pains to do well, try hard*; やめようと決心する・けっしん *decide, resolve to quit*; 無理だと決定する・けってい *conclude, decide that it is impossible*; すればよかったと後悔する・こうかい *regret not doing something*; 海を渡ろうと試みる・こころみる *try, attempt to cross the ocean*; はいと答える・こたえる *respond, answer "yes"*; 「用事があるから」と招待を断わる・ことわる *refuse an invitation with a "I've got things to do"*; 早くしなさいと催促する・さいそく *urge one to do something quickly*; 万歳と叫ぶ・さけぶ *shout out "Banzai!"*; そんなことしてはだめだと人を叱る・しかる *scold a person for doing that kind of thing*; わかるかと人に質問する・しつもん *ask someone if they understand*; 帰ると主張する・しゅちょう *insist on going home*; 遅くなると人に知らせる・しらせる *let someone know you will be late*; 無理だと信じる・しんじる *believe that it is impossible*; やめ

たらどうかと人に勧める・すすめる *advise someone to stop*; 貸してくれと頼む・たのむ *ask someone to lend you something*; ゆっくり運転しなさいと注意する・ちゅうい *warn someone to drive slowly*; 遅くなると人に伝える・つたえる *convey the message, tell that you will be late*; 行こうと努める・つとめる *try, make an effort to go*; 行かせていただきたいと述べる・のべる *say that you would like to be allowed to go*; 定年すると発表する・はっぴょう *announce that you will retire*;「明日は遅くなる」と話す・はなす *say "I will be late tomorrow"*; 無理だと判断する・はんだん *judge, decide, conclude that something is impossible*; そんなことは知らないと否定する・ひてい *deny knowledge of*;「はい」と返事する・へんじ *reply "yes"*;「試合が終わりました」と報告する・ほうこく *report, "the game is over"*;「試合が終わりました」と放送する・ほうそう *broadcast "the game is over"*; よくできたと誉める・ほめる *praise with "you did a good job"*; 魚がきらいだと見える・みえる *appear not to like fish*; 彼は彼女を２０歳だと見ている・みる *he sees her as being twenty years old*; 入ってはいけないと人に命令する・めいれい *order someone not to come in*; 田中と申します・もうす *my name is Tanaka*; 明日までにすると約束する・やくそく *promise to have it done by tomorrow*; 借りたお金を返してほしいと要求する・ようきゅう *demand repayment of a loan*; 負けるだろうと予想する・よそう *expect that they will lose*; 子犬をポチと呼ぶ・よぶ *call, name the puppy "Pochi"*; 元気だと連絡する・れんらく *contact with the news that you are well*; 無理だと分かる・わかる *understand that something is impossible*

The expression before the と may be a person's exact words (a direct quote) or second person's recasting of those words (an indirect quote). Especially in speech, the distinction is often blurred in Japanese. In writing, quotation marks (which look like this: 「 」) are used regularly.

Direct quote
田中先生が「明日参ります」と言いました。
Prof. Tanaka said, "I will come tomorrow."

Indirect quote
田中先生がいらっしゃると言いました。
Prof. Tanaka said that he will come.
田中先生がいらっしゃるとおっしゃいました。
Prof. Tanaka said that he will come.
田中先生が来ると言った。
Prof. Tanaka said that he will come.

In the "direct" sentence, it is quite likely that Prof. Tanaka actually uttered the word 参^{まい}り ます. In contrast, both "indirect" sentences are potentially ambiguous. It is not possible that Prof. Tanaka said いらっしゃる with respect to himself, although he may have been speaking about a third person. Only knowledge of the context would answer that question clearly. Likewise, Prof. Tanaka may have said 来^くるabout himself or about a third person. Again, only knowledge of a particular context could answer the question definitively.

3.7.7.3 Idioms with quotative と

～という～	スミスというアメリカ人から電話^{でんわ}があった。
	There was a phone call from a person named Smith.
～という ことは	行^いかないということはお金^{かね}がないことですか。
	By saying you won't go, do you mean you don't have the money?
～というと	スミス君^{くん}と言^いうと、どの人^{ひと}ですか。
	Speaking of Smith, which person is he?
～というのは	日本語^{にほんご}がわからないというのはどういうことなの？
	By saying she doesn't understand Japanese, what are you saying?
～といわず	もう無理^{むり}だといわず、頑張^{がんば}ってください。
	Don't say it's impossible; just hang in there.
～とのことだ	遅^{おそ}くなるとのことです。
	He said that he would be late. He left a message that he would be late.
～とはいえば	スミス君^{くん}とは言^いえば、さっき電話^{でんわ}があった。
	Speaking of Smith, he called just a moment ago.

The following structure is very common for explanatory sentences: ～ということは～とい うことだ "Saying ～ is to say ～." The double こと is not considered redundant. It may also be realized as の: ～というのは～というのだ. For example: イギリスに留学^{りゅうがく}したいと いうことは英語^{えいご}を勉強^{べんきょう}したということだ.

3.7.8 Only

Four words commonly translated as *only* are: だけ, しか, のみ, and ばかり. Both ￥１０ ０００だけかかった and ￥１００００しかかからなかった can mean "It only cost ￥10,000." The implication with だけ is that the price was not particularly high. のみ is best considered a more literary version of だけ. The implication with しか is that the price was actually lower than expected. Similarly for the following examples where there is always an expectation of some kind which is not satisfied. しか occurs necessarily with a negative predicate.

三人<ruby>さんにん</ruby>しか来<ruby>こ</ruby>なかった。

Only three people came (although we invited everyone).

一<ruby>ひと</ruby>つしか食<ruby>た</ruby>べられない。

I can only eat one (although they look wonderful).

一本<ruby>いっぽん</ruby>しか飲<ruby>の</ruby>まなかったよ。

I only had one drink (even though I have been out all evening).

　　ばかり means *only* in the following pattern with verbs, nouns, and adjectives. The affirmative implication with ばかり is that there is no alternative. In the first sentence below, for example, we spend all of our time studying so there is no time for other things. Likewise, we drink only coffee; other drinks are not even on the menu. Both sentences might be recast with しか, 勉強<ruby>べんきょう</ruby>しかしない or コーヒーしか飲<ruby>の</ruby>まない, although these may imply greater discontent (because しか implies an expectation which is not satisfied).

勉強<ruby>べんきょう</ruby>ばかりする。

All we ever do is study. We only study.

コーヒーばかり飲<ruby>の</ruby>みます。

All he ever drinks is coffee. He only drinks coffee.

遊<ruby>あそ</ruby>んでばかりいます。

All she is doing is playing. The only thing she is doing is playing.

もう寝<ruby>ね</ruby>るばかりだ。

All that is left is to go to bed.

このレストランは安<ruby>やす</ruby>いばかりが評判<ruby>ひょうばん</ruby>です。

The restaurant is well-known only for being inexpensive.

Turn to page 242 for examples of expressions like 食<ruby>た</ruby>べたばかり meaning *just ate*. A useful idiom with だけ is できるだけ〜 meaning *as 〜 as* (lit. *only as possible*): できるだけ早<ruby>はや</ruby>く *as quickly as possible* or できるだけ小<ruby>ちい</ruby>さい *as small as possible*.

3.7.9 ほど

ほど occurs with negative predicates in patterns where it defines a standard for comparison (which is not reached). With affirmative predicates it defines an extent or upper limit. See page 260 for further discussion of ほど after classifiers and expressions of amount.

今日<ruby>きょう</ruby>は昨日<ruby>きのう</ruby>ほど寒<ruby>さむ</ruby>くない。

Today is not as cold as yesterday.

日本語<ruby>にほんご</ruby>は中国語<ruby>ちゅうごくご</ruby>ほど漢字<ruby>かんじ</ruby>を使<ruby>つか</ruby>わない。

Japanese does not use as many Chinese characters as Chinese.

その車<ruby>くるま</ruby>は買<ruby>か</ruby>いたかったが買<ruby>か</ruby>えるほど安<ruby>やす</ruby>くなかった。

I wanted to buy that car but it is was not cheap enough for me to buy.

三つほど下さい。

Please give me three (as many as three, about three).

山ほどすることがある。

I have a lot to do (as much as a mountain of things to do).

涙が出るほどうれしい。

I am so happy I could cry.

遅れるにも程がある。

I have limits as to tardiness.

年をとればとるほど英語の習得はむずかしくなる。

The older you grow, the harder it is to learn English.

This last kind of example occurs less frequently with だけ: 年をとればとるだけ〜. Likewise, 三つほどください contrasts with 三つだけください where the latter means *only three* or *no more than three*.

3.7.10 より

より defines a minimum standard for comparison or a starting point.

今日は昨日より寒い。

Today is colder than yesterday.

郵便局は駅より手前です。

The post office is closer than the station.

愛より金を大事にする。

He values money more than love.

愛よりも金を大事にする。

He values money even more than love.

直るまで待つよりほかはない。　（cf. 直るまで待つしかない。）

Until it is repaired, there is nothing else to do but wait.

ローマに向けロンドンより出発した。

They left London for Rome.

１０時より開会する。

We will start the meeting at 10 o'clock.

田中より〜

from Tanaka (on a letter or present)

When referring to a starting point, より is more formal or written while から is more conversational.

3.7.11 Sentence final particles

The vast majority of sentence particles are found only in spoken Japanese (with the exception of か). Many of these particles are quite informal as well as being gender specific.

Questions

か   いいですか。そうですか。行きますか。

             Is this okay? Is that so? Are you going?

             (formal, written or spoken, gender neutral)

             いいか。そうか。行くか。

             (informal, spoken, more masculine than not)

かな   いいかな。あしたかな。高すぎるかな。

・かなあ   *I wonder if it is good, if it is tomorrow, if it is too expensive.*

             (informal, spoken, more masculine than not)

Ø   いい？そう？行く？

             Is this okay? Is that so? Are you going?

             (conveyed with intonation, informal, spoken, gender neutral)

かしら   いいかしら。あしたかしら。高すぎるかしら。

             I wonder if it is good, if it is tomorrow, if it is too expensive.

             (informal, spoken, more feminine than not, indicates a nearly rhetorical question)

っけ   会議は明日だっけ？

             The meeting is tomorrow, right?

             (quite colloquial, used when checking the truth of something you are already pretty sure about)

かい   いいかい。あしたかい。高すぎるかい。

             Is it good, tomorrow, too expensive?

             (This is informal, more masculine than not, spoken. 〜かい is actually a combination of question 〜か and emphatic 〜い.)

Emphasize the point of view of the speaker (often exclamatory)

よ   よ is a conversational particle which is most common in informal speech. It emphasizes the knowledge or desires of the speaker rather than the listener, with different kinds of effects. Because of its focus on the speaker, it is rarely used when speaking to superiors.

アメリカに行きたいよ。
I want to go to America (that is what I want).

いいですよね。
This is great, isn't it!
(This is used to make an emphatic statement where you expect agreement. The combination is very common in colloquial speech. See the discussion of ね below.)

これはスペイン語ですか。いいえ、ポルトガル語ですよ。
Is this Spanish? No, it is Portuguese.
(よ is used to make a correction, although its overuse can come across as arrogant; it is more polite to say something like いいえ、そうじゃないと思いますよ。)

行こうよ。
Let's get out of here. Let's go already.
(There is a sense that the speaker is trying to persuade the listener, and an unmodified 行こう is a slightly stronger statement.)

食べてくださいよ。
Eat! Please eat.
(There is a sense that the speaker is trying to persuade the listener. Again an unmodified 食べてください is a slightly stronger request.)

ぞ	いいぞ。あしただぞ。高すぎるぞ。 *It is good, tomorrow, too expensive!* (informal, spoken, very masculine version of よ)
ぜ	いいぜ。あしただぜ。高すぎるぜ。行こうぜ。 *It's good, tomorrow, too expensive. Let's go.* (informal, spoken, very masculine version of よ, related to ぞ)
さ	いいさ。あしたさ。高すぎるさ。〜だってさ。 *It is good, tomorrow, too expensive! I hear 〜* (informal, spoken, associated with Tokyo youth)
わ	きれいだわ。会わなかったわ。明日行くわよ。 *It is pretty. I didn't meet him. I'll go tomorrow.* (overtly feminine, softens a statement or marks a mild exclamation)
い	それ、俺のだい。 *That is mine!* (informal, spoken, masculine, most commonly here and with かい)

Emphasize the point of view of the listener (checking for confirmation)

ね   いいですね？

This is good, right?

(Much like the tag *right?* at the end of an English sentence, ね is a gender neutral way to confirm your understanding of your listener's thoughts. ね may also be used sentence internally at any natural juncture, and in the speech of little children, it may actually occur after almost every particle (something to be avoided by adults). ええ, はい, or even そうですね are all appropriate replies if you do in fact agree. A less committal まあ or a more explicit そうですか indicate hesitation or even disagreement. With falling, assertive intonation, ね may also be interpreted as a softer version of よ: いいですね "You agree, right." This interpretation is strongest when ね and よ occur in combination: いいですよね. The listener here has little choice but to agree.)

ねえ   このセーターはきれいですねえ。

This sweater is pretty, isn't it.

(The implication here is that I think the sweater is pretty and I fully expect you to agree. そうですねえ is the obvious reply which can be said because you agree (if you do feel it is pretty) or because you are being polite (if you actually feel that the sweater is quite ugly). If you feel the sweater is ugly and you want to make this known, you may respond そうですか which while indirect makes it clear that you do not agree.)

Explanatory

のだ・んだ   A combination of の and some form of だ. In informal speech, の is usually contracted to ん. A sentence final だ is realized as な: そうなんですか. Sentence final のだ is often translated into English as *it is the case that* which has the right meaning but is overly cumbersome. もう行って来ましたか is a question about facts: have you gone already or not? In contrast, もう行って来たの？ (here without だ) is checking the truth of the question: is it the case that you have already gone? Am I correct in making this assumption? The formulation with の seems to imply an unspoken reason for asking the question, and the astute respondent might add something like "Why do you ask?" to his or her response. Questions with の invite more than a simple yes/no response. Similarly, the form んだ at the end of a declarative sentence suggests an indirect reason for making the statement and implicitly asks for a response of some kind. 山本さんが好きなんですよ is hinting about reasons and history: it is the case that I like Yamamoto

(and there is a story to tell if you want to hear it). Likewise, 行きたいんで
すが〜 implies that I have a reason for telling you about my desire to go,
i.e. I need to borrow some money or I need time off from work. 行きたい
です is a statement of fact: I am thinking that I want to go. This effect is
very subtle, but it should not be ignored. Avoiding のだ all the time can
sound harsh and overly direct since のだ compels the listener to join into
the conversation. のだ is directly related to ので below.

んで・ので   ので (なので after nouns and nominal adjectives) is usually translated into
English as *because*, *so*, or *since*. While から indicates real cause and effect,
ので is more subtle, usually indicating background conditions. Consider:
お店に行くのでついで何か買ってきましょうか *I am going to the store, so
is there anything you want?* から rather than ので in this sentence is a bit
odd since my going to the store does not actually cause you to want me to
buy you something (but not odd enough to make the sentence with から
actually ungrammatical). This interpretation of ので is replaced quite naturally with が because it is setting up the background to the subsequent
question: お店に行きますがついで何か買ってきましょうか. Overall, ので
is softer and more common in polite conversation (where the harsh specifics of cause and effect facts are more likely to be addressed only in-
directly).

もの・もん   The effect of もの is to nominalize a sentence and in some sense make it a
tangible thing (which is the general meaning of 物). The result is often a
(concrete or emphatic) generalization of some kind. Compare:

その交差点は交通事故が多いです。

There are a lot of accidents at that intersection.

(statement of fact)

その交差点では交通事故が多いんです。

It is a fact that there are a lot of accidents at that intersection

(so don't you think we should do something about it?)

交差点は交通事故が多いものです。

Accidents are frequent at intersections.

(an emphatic generalization)

In conversation, もの conveys greater emotion than の, often verging on
exasperation. もの or もので (often contracted to もんで) can also be used
as a conjunction, almost like から *because*. This greater sense of emotion
is linked to a sense that もの (without だ or か) is a somewhat feminine
exclamation.

まだ子どもだもの！

He is only a child! (so there is no way he could know better)

It is because he is only a child.

A. 奥様、フランス語がお上手ですねえ。

   Madam, you do speak French well, don't you.

B. だって、長くパリにおりましたもの。

   Well, I did live in Paris for a long time (so it is really nothing)

大人だもの。自分でできるよ。

I'm an adult; I can do it by myself.

すごく高かったもんで、びっくりして何も買わずに帰ってきた。

They were really expensive, and I was so shocked, I came home without buying anything.

何だ！そんなものか？

Eh? Is that the way it is!

なんて   そんなことをするなんて、ばかじゃない？

           Doing such a thing, isn't he an idiot!

           ベッドで朝食なんて。いいですねぇ。

           Breakfast in bed! How nice.

           (informal, often sarcastic or critical)

Gender specific differences

The following gender contrasts are found in informal language. Traditionally, expressions with だ and か are associated with men while those with Ø instead of だ as well as わ and の are associated with women. At least amongst younger people, however, both だ and の are becoming more gender neutral, while わ is becoming increasingly rare. Because of this state of flux, there may be some disagreement as to which expression is in fact appropriate for speakers of which gender. Two paradigms are given here, noun and adjective. Verbs parallel adjectives.

Overtly feminine	Gender neutral	Overtly masculine
そうだわ。	そう。（そうだ。）	そうだ。
そうだわよ。そうわよ。	そうよ。（そうだよ。）	そうだよ。
そうだわね。そうわね。	そうね。（そうだね。）	そうだね。
--------	そう？	そうか。
--------	そうなの。	そうなんだ。
そうなのよ。	--------	そうなんだよ。
そうなのね。	--------	そうなんだね。
	そうなの？	そうなのか。

いいわ。	いい。	--------
いいわよ。	いいよ。	--------
いいわね。	いいね。	--------
--------	いい？	いいか。
--------	いいの。	いいんだ。
いいのよ。	--------	いいんだよ。
いいのね。	--------	いいんだね。
--------	いいの？	いいのか

3.8 Nouns

Nouns are conjugated with some form of だ. Some nouns have honorific or more "beautiful" alternatives (see the discussions beginning on page 76), but any noun can be made more polite or more beautiful with the right realization of だ. Forms below are labelled modern or archaic, formal or literary, as well as beautiful. The combination 〜では can always be contracted to a more conversational 〜じゃ. The various forms here are less of a mystery when you realize that だ equals である and ある equals ござる.

Present affirmative

本だ。	(modern familiar)
本です。	(modern polite)
本である。	(formal speech, literary)
本であります。	(archaic)
本でござる。	(super-polite, archaic)
本でございます。	(super-polite, beautiful)
鈴木さんでいらっしゃる。	(honorific)
鈴木さんでいらっしゃいます。	(honorific)

Present negative

本ではない。	(modern familiar)
本ではないです。	(modern polite)
本ではありません。	(modern polite)
本ではございません。	(super-polite, beautiful)
本ではあるまい。	(archaic)

(Negatives without は are possible, but upon reflection are felt to be somewhat uncompromising.)

Past affirmative

本<small>ほん</small>だった。	(modern familiar)
本でした。	(modern polite)
本であった。	(formal speech, literary)
本でありました。	(archaic)
本でございました。	(super-polite, beautiful)

Past negative

本<small>ほん</small>ではなかった。	(modern familiar)
本ではなかったです。	(modern polite)
本ではありませんでした。	(modern polite)
本ではございませんでした。	(super-polite, beautiful)

(Again, negatives without は are possible, but upon reflection are felt to be somewhat uncompromising.)

本<small>ほん</small>だろう。	(modern familiar)
本でしょう。	(modern polite)
本であろう。	(literary)
本でありましょう。	(archaic)
本でございましょう。	(super-polite, beautiful, slightly archaic)

Sentence internal versions of だ are listed below. Recall that the classical form of だ is なり, resulting in the occasional occurrence of な.

本<small>ほん</small>だと思<small>おも</small>う。

本だそうだ。

本<small>ほん</small>で〜	本<small>ほん</small>であって〜	(literary)
本だったら〜	本であったら〜	(literary)
本なら〜	本であるなら〜	(literary)
本ならば〜	本であれば〜	(literary)
本なので〜	本でるので〜	(literary)
本なのだ。	本であるのだ。	(literary)

だ is often referred to as the *copula*. It is best translated as *to be* or *to be equal to*. だ contrasts with いる and ある which really mean *to exist*. Nouns modify other nouns using の: 私<small>わたし</small>の心理学<small>しんりがく</small>の先生<small>せんせい</small>の本<small>ほん</small>. An expression like *mine* is translated as 私<small>わたし</small>の (and not as 私<small>わたし</small>のの). Nouns are linked to verbs with は, が, を, etc. They are modified directly by adjectives and relative clauses: おもしろい本<small>ほん</small> and 兄<small>あに</small>が夕<small>ゆう</small>べ買<small>か</small>った本<small>ほん</small>. Unlike adjectives and verbs, nouns in Japanese do not have special endings, and borrowed words almost all end up as nouns.

There are a small number of common Japanese words which are exceptions to the general conventions of the language. There is one noun 同じだ *is the same* which modifies other nouns like an adjective (i.e. without an intervening の): 同じ人. A few words which look like く-adverbs can be nouns: 近くだ *is nearby*; 遠くだ *is far away*; 多くだ *is many*; 早くだ *is early*; 遅くだ *is late*.

There are also two classes of nouns which are worth a brief discussion: nominal adjectives and nouns which become verbs by combining with する.

3.8.1 Nominal adjectives

In some grammars, these words are called な-adjectives. In others, they are called な-nominals. The Japanese name (形容動詞) actually means something like *adjectival verb*. Nominal adjectives are difficult to classify because they conjugate a great deal like nouns while they have meanings normally associated with adjectives.

First, nominal adjectives conjugate exactly like nouns, and every occurrence of 本 in the table above could be replaced by the word 好き *is pleasing, likes*.

Present affirmative

好きだ。	(modern familiar)
好きです。	(modern polite)
好きである。	(formal speech, literary)
好きであります。	(archaic)
好きでござる。	(super-polite, archaic)
好きでございます。	(super-polite, beautiful)
etc.	

Unlike regular nouns, however, 好き modifies nouns with な (thus the name): 好きな人. The *one I like* is translated 好きなの. Nominal adjectives are also be modified by adverbs like other adjectives and verbs: とても好きだ. Compare this too とても日曜日だ which is nonsense. They also become adverbs in combination with に: きれいに書いてください. Here is a representative list of nominal adjectives. Some words have both a nominal adjective and a regular adjective form (compare 大きい人 and 大きな人). Others allow both な and の (compare 別な人 and 別の部屋). A great number of the words borrowed into Japanese from English are also nominal adjectives (see page 123). Although they are often treated as an extraordinary part of speech, nominal adjectives are probably more common than the standard い-adjective.

Some nominal adjectives	安全な・あんぜん *safe*; 嫌な・いや *nasty, offensive*; 色々な・いろいろ *various, variety of*; 大きな・おおき *big* (大きい); おかしな *strange, funny* (おかしい); 簡単な・かんたん *simple, easy*; 急な・きゅう *sudden*; 嫌いな・きらい *displeasing, hated*; きれいな *pretty*; グロテスクな *grotesque*; 元気な・げんき *healthy, chipper*; 健康な・けんこう *healthy*; 幸運な・こううん

lucky; 強欲な・ごうよく *greedy*; 孤独な・こどく *lonesome, solitary*; 残念な・ざんねん *regrettable*; 静かな・しずか *quiet*; 失礼な・しつれい *rude*; 自由な・じゆう *free, unrestricted*; 十分な・じゅうぶん *sufficient*; 丈夫な・じょうぶ *healthy, strong*; 上手な・じょうず *talented, good*; 親切な・しんせつ *kind*; 好きな・すき *pleasing*; 素敵な・すてき *handsome*; スムーズな *smooth*; センチメンタルな *sentimental*; 大事な・だいじ *important, significant*; 大丈夫な・だいじょうぶ *okay, safe, permitted*; 大切な・たいせつ *important*; 大変な・たいへん *terrible, grave*; 平らな・たいら *flat*; 確かな・たしか *sure, certain*; 駄目な・だめ *bad, prohibited*; 単純な・たんじゅん *simple, naive*; 単調な・たんちょう *monotonous, dull*; 小さな・ちいさ *small* (小さい); 丁寧な・ていねい *polite*; 適当な・てきとう *appropriate*; にぎやかな *noisy, festive*; のどかな *peaceful, mild*; 馬鹿な・ばか *stupid*; 非常な・ひじょう *extreme, great, emergency*; 必要な・ひつよう *necessary*; 暇な・ひま *free, not busy*; フォーマルな *formal*; 複雑な・ふくざつ *involved, complicated*; 平気な・へいき *calm, cool, indifferent*; 下手な・へた *untalented, bad*; 別な・べつ *separate, different*; 変な・へん *strange*; 便利な・べんり *convenient*; 不便な・ふべん *inconvenient*; 真っ赤な・まっか *deep red, crimson*; 真っ暗な・まっくら *pitch-dark, black*; 真っ白な・まっしろ *pure white*; 無理な・むり *impossible*; 迷惑な・めいわく *bothersome, troublesome*; 面倒な・めんどう *troublesome, bothersome*; 柔らかな・やわらか *soft, tender* (柔らかい); 楽な・らく *relaxed, easy*; 有名な・ゆうめい *famous*; 余計な・よけい *extra, needless*; 立派な・りっぱ *great, splendid*; ロマンチックな *romantic*

A number of suffixes regularly create nominal adjectives: ～的な, ～みたいな, ～様な, ～そうな.

A few words which look like い-adjectives are conjugated as nominal adjectives: 嫌いだ *is distasteful, hated*; きれいだ *is pretty*. In slang one actually hears expressions like きれくない *not pretty* or even すきくない *not like*, but these are basically ungrammatical.

3.8.2 Noun + する *combinations*

Words borrowed from Chinese become nouns in Japanese, and the only regular and productive way to use them as verbs is to add する to create a Noun + する combination. Some native-Japanese nouns as well as more and more nouns written in カタカナ occur in this pattern as well. Many Noun + する combinations have native Japanese synonyms. Compare 到着する and 着く, both of which mean *arrive*. As a rule, the native Japanese word is more conversational and more familiar than its Chinese counterpart. A lengthy list of the most useful of these verbs is given at the end of this discussion.

3.8.2.1 Grammar

Noun + する predicates have two specific grammatical properties which should be considered. First, a given Noun + する combination may or may not take a direct object marked with particle を.

日本語を研究している。   (transitive, with a direct object)
I am researching Japanese.
イギリスに帰国する。   (intransitive, without a direct object)
I am returning home to England.

Second, many Noun + する combinations may also be realized as Noun をする where the noun itself is marked as the direct object.

研究している *I am researching.*
研究をしている *I am researching* (lit. *I am doing research*).

The Noun をする option is obligatory whenever the noun is modified in any way.

難しい研究をしている。
I am conducting difficult research.
日本語の研究をしている。
I am conducting Japanese language research.
日本への帰国をする。
I will return to Japan (lit. *I will do a return to Japan*).
久しぶりの帰国をしょうと思っている。
I am thinking of returning home to Japan for the first time in a long while.

These two properties interact in the following way. There is a general rule in Japanese which says there can be only one を-marked noun in a single sentence, which means if you find yourself saying を twice in a single sentence, something is probably wrong. See page 209 as well. For a Noun + する combination which is transitive, either the direct object, or the head noun itself, but not both, may be marked with particle を.

日本語を勉強する   or   日本語の勉強をする

These two properties also mean that 日本語を勉強をする with two direct objects and 日本語の勉強する with a modified head noun and no を are both ungrammatical.

There are also some Noun + する combinations which never occur as Noun をする. For these verbs, direct modification of the head noun is in general not possible.

3.8.2.2 Examples

The lists here are long but still incomplete (there are hundreds of these combinations). The predicates are divided into two broad categories: transitive and intransitive. Within these categories, there are verbs which allow the Nounをする alternation and those which do not. Note the variety of object types (with を, に, or と). Remember also that Chinese compounds often sound more formal than their native Japanese counterparts. Where appropriate, more colloquial synonyms are listed.

Transitive Noun + する

〜をする alternation possible	挨拶する・あいさつ *greet, salute* (a person に); 案内する・あんない *guide lead* (a person を); 運転する・うんてん *drive* (a car を); 延期する・えんき *postpone, put off* (one's departure を); 解釈する・かいしゃく *interpret, translate* (a text, behavior を); 開発する・かいはつ *develop, exploit* (natural resources を); 拡大する・かくだい *enlarge, expand, magnify* (a photo を), 大きくする, 広げる, 延ばす; 我慢する・がまん *be patient, endure, put up with* (bad behavior を), 耐える; 歓迎する・かんげい *welcome* (a person を); 観察する・かんさつ *observe* (the stars を), *watch closely*, 注意して見る; 感謝する・かんしゃ *thank for* (a favor を); 期待する・きたい *expect, hope for* (a letter を), 願う, 希望する, 楽しみにする; 競争する・きょうそう *compete with* (a team と); 許可する・きょか *permit, authorize* (payment を); 記録する・きろく *to record, write down* (daily events を), 書き留める; 議論する・ぎろん *argue, discuss* (a problem について, 良し悪しを *the good and the bad*); 工夫する・くふう *invent* (a device を), *find a way*; 経験する・けいけん *to experience, undergo* (an ordeal を); 計算する・けいさん *calculate* (the cost を); 研究する・けんきゅう *study* (mathematics を), *research* (more academic sounding than 勉強する); 検査する・けんさ *examine* (something を); 建設する・けんせつ *build, construct* (a house を); 見物する・けんぶつ *go sightseeing* (a place を); 交換する・こうかん *to exchange, change* (the car's oil を), 取り換える; 攻撃する・こうげき *to attack* (an enemy を), *charge, criticize*, 攻める; 誤解する・ごかい *misunderstand* (what was said を); 作動する・さどう *operate* (a machine を); 実験する・じっけん *conduct* (an experiment を); 失敗する・しっぱい *fail* (a test に); 指導する・しどう *lead, guide, advise* (a student を); 自慢する・じまん *be proud of* (your children を), *boast, brag*; 修理する・しゅうり *repair, fix* (a car を), *mend*, 直す; 手術する・しゅじゅつ *operate* (on a person を); 準備する・じゅんび *prepare* (dinner を), 用意する; 紹介する・しょうかい *introduce* (one person を to another に); 証明する・しょうめい *prove* (one's identity を), *testify, certify*, 明らかにする; 心配する・しんぱい *worry* (about something を), 気にかける; 生産する・せいさん *produce,*

manufacture (cars を); 製造する・せいぞう *manufacture, produce* (a product を), 生産する; 整理する・せいり *to tidy, straighten up* (a file を) 片付ける; 説明する・せつめい *explain* (the meaning を); 節約する・せつやく *economize* (on expenses を), *skimp, save*; 世話する・せわ *take care of, look after* (a person を); 選択する・せんたく *select* (a topic を), 選ぶ; 掃除する・そうじ *sweep, clean, vacuum* (a room を); 探検する・たんけん *explore* (an island を); 忠告する・ちゅうこく *warn* (a person に・を・と); 注文する・ちゅうもん *to order* (a book を), 頼む; 調査する・ちょうさ *investigate* (an accident を), 調べる, 研究する; 訂正する・ていせい *to correct, put right* (a misprint を), 直す; 配達する・はいたつ *deliver* (a letter を), 届ける; 拍手する・はくしゅ *applaud* (a performance に); 発見する・はっけん *discover* (a new planet を), 見つける; 発行する・はっこう *publish* (a newspaper を), *issue, bring out,* 出版する; 発表する・はっぴょう *announce, make public* (test results を); 発明する・はつめい *invent* (the telephone を), 作り出す; 反省する・はんせい *to reflect* (on what happened を); 批判する・ひはん *criticize* (a politician を); 評価する・ひょうか *evaluate, appraise* (a used car を); 勉強する・べんきょう *to study* (mathematics を), 学ぶ; 返事する・へんじ *to reply to* (a letter に), 答える; 報告する・ほうこく *to report* (facts を), *inform*; 訪問する・ほうもん *call on, visit* (London を), 訪ねる; 募集する・ぼしゅう *recruit* (new club members を), *collect,* 集める, 募集を行う; 保証する・ほしょう *assure, guarantee* (quality を); 保存する・ほぞん *preserve, conserve* (letters, records を); 翻訳する・ほんやく *translate* (an essay を), 訳す; 命令する・めいれい *to order, command* (a person に); 約束する・やくそく *to promise* (payment を); 輸出する・ゆしゅつ *to export* (steel を); 輸入する・ゆにゅう *to import* (steel を); 用意する・ようい *prepare, arrange* (lodging, money を); 要求する・ようきゅう *claim, demand, require* (uniforms を), 求める; 予想する・よそう *expect* (that と), *anticipate* (the future を); 予約する・よやく *reserve* (tickets を), *make a reservation*; 料理する・りょうり *to cook* (fish を); 練習する・れんしゅう *to exercise, practice* (the piano を)

no alternation

愛する・あい *to love* (a person を); 影響する・えいきょう *to influence* (a person に), 影響を与える, 影響を及ぼす; 感心する・かんしん *admire* (a person を), *be impressed by*; 記憶する・きおく *memorize* (a fact を); 希望する・きぼう *hope for* (something good を); 後悔する・こうかい *regret* (what you did を); 賛成する・さんせい *agree with* (an opinion に), 同意する; 刺激する・しげき *stimulate* (production を), *excite*; 実現する・じつげん *realize* (a dream を), *come true*; 招待する・しょうたい *invite* (a person を); 承知する・しょうち *know, be aware of* (a fact を); 所有する・しょゆう *possess* (a car を), 持つ, ある; 推薦する・すいせん *recommend* (a person を); 説得する・せっとく *persuade* (a person を); 増加する・ぞうか *increase* (number, amount を), *grow*, 増える; 組織する・そしき *organize, form* (a club を); 尊敬する・そんけい *look up to, respect* (a person を); 組み立てる; 代表する・だいひょう *represent, act for* (Japan を); 注目する・ちゅうもく *observe, take notice of* (a thing に), よく見る; 同情する・どうじょう *sympathize with, have pity for* (an orphan に); 爆発する・ばくはつ *explode* (a gas tank を); 反対する・はんたい *oppose, be against* (a person, an opinion に); 表現する・ひょうげん *express* (an idea を); 放送する・ほうそう *to broadcast* (on television or radio) (news を・について); 理解する・りかい *understand, appreciate* (classical music を), わかる

The verbs in this section are transitive but they rarely if ever occur in the Nounをする construction. Note here and below that most verbs which do not allow the alternation tend to be verbs of emotion or verbs which describe naturally occurring processes. At the same time, however, realize that almost all Noun+する combinations do allow を insertion in one way or another (as long as the general constraint on more than one を is not violated).

そんなことにいちいち感心をしているわけにはいかない。
I shouldn't be caring about any of those things.
こうしてその許可をするに至った。
It got to the point he where gave his permission.
ご安心をなさってください。
Please don't worry (lit. *please feel relief*).

Insertion of を in these examples adds a flavor of controllability canceling a natural process or emotional interpretation. The agent of control may be a person, an institution, or some machines (e.g. computers).

Intransitive Noun + する

〜をする
alternation

外出する・がいしゅつ *go out, be away*; 活動する・かつどう *be active*; 休憩する・きゅうけい *take a break, rest*, 休む; 競争する・きょうそう *compete*; 協力する・きょうりょく *cooperate with*; 苦心する・くしん *take pains at*; 契約する・けいやく *make a contract with* (a record company と), *contract*; 結婚する・けっこん *marry* (a person と); 化粧する・けしょう *put on make-up*; 決心する・けっしん *decide, make up one's mind*, 心を決める, 決意する; 喧嘩する・けんか *fight with, quarrel*, なぐり合う, 口論する; 見物する・けんぶつ *go sightseeing*; 交際する・こうさい *hang about*; 作業する・さぎょう *operate, work*; 参加する・さんか *participate*; 散歩する・さんぽ *take a walk*; 自殺する・じさつ *commit suicide*; 失敗する・しっ

ぱい *fail* (a test に); 質問する・しつもん *ask* (a teacher に), 尋ねる, 聞く; 失礼する・しつれい *be rude*; 就職する・しゅうしょく *find employment*, 仕事を見付ける, 職に就く; 出席する・しゅっせき *attend* (a meeting に), 出る; 出発する・しゅっぱつ *depart, leave*; 生活する・せいかつ *make a living*, 暮らす; 遅刻する・ちこく *be late, tardy*, 遅くなる; 注意する・ちゅうい *pay attention, be careful of* (what you say に), 気をつける; 到着する・とうちゃく *arrive*, 着く; 独立する・どくりつ *become independent*; 努力する・どりょく *make an effort, endeavor*, 一生懸命働く, 頑張る; 発達する・はったつ *develop, make progress*, 進歩する; 優勝する・ゆうしょう *win*, 勝つ; 留学する・りゅうがく *study abroad*; 旅行する・りょこう *travel*, 旅をする

| no alternation | 安心する・あんしん *feel relieved, feel secure*, ほっとする; 回転する・かいてん *revolve, rotate*; 緊張する・きんちょう *be nervous, be tense*; 苦労する・くろう *have trouble with*; 合格する・ごうかく *pass* (an examination に); 故障する・こしょう *break down*; 混乱する・こんらん *be confused*; 振動する・しんどう *vibrate, tremble*; 進歩する・しんぽ *to progress*, 進む; 成功する・せいこう *succeed* (business が・に), うまく行く; 成長する・せいちょう *grow up, develop*, 育つ; 増加する・ぞうか *increase, grow*, 増える; 卒業する・そつぎょう *to graduate*; 入学する・にゅうがく *enter* (school, college, etc.), 入る; 発展する・はってん *develop into, expand*; 不足する・ふそく *be in short supply, be lacking*, 欠く, 足りない; 変化する・へんか *altar, change, be transformed*, 変わる; 満足する・まんぞく *be satisfied with*; 用心する・ようじん *take care of, be careful of* |

3.9 Personal reference

3.9.1 Terms of address

Japanese typically address each other by last name (with an appropriate suffix), position, or title (also with an appropriate suffix): 田中君, お兄ちゃん, 課長. Turn to page 104 for discussion of these suffixes. Teachers, politicians, doctors, and dentists may all be addressed as 先生. Kinship terms are used with (older) relatives, but they can also be used as a familiar form of address outside of the family. In this case, the appropriate term is determined by the gender of the person being addressed and their (apparent) age relative to the speaker.

familiar boy	お兄さん・おにいさん
familiar girl	お姉さん・おねえさん
familiar man	叔父さん・おじさん
familiar woman	叔母さん・おばさん
familiar old man	おじいさん
familiar old woman	おばあさん

It is also possible to add a name to a kinship term to produce a form like *Bill-*おじさん which may be used with your real Uncle Bill or with a friend of your father's who happens to be named Bill. Because such terms are based on apparent age, there is a progression as you start to look older (and being referred to as おじさん for the first time may be very much like being called *Sir* for the first time; likewise for おばさん). To get the attention of someone, any of the following will do: すみません, ちょっとすみません, ちょっとすみませんが～, 恐れ入りますが～, もしもし, あのう～, おおい. All are polite expect for おおい which sounds very much like "Yo!" or "Hey you!"

3.9.2 Pronouns

The main rule of thumb about pronouns in Japanese is to avoid them completely in very polite conversation, and to avoid them as much as possible everywhere else. This is especially true of any word meaning *you*, and even a polite term such as あなた is insulting when used with a superior. (Address them by name or by title.) If you are speaking and you say something like 夕べ夜中まで勉強しましたよ, it will be assumed that you are the subject of the sentence. There is no need to begin with 私は～. Likewise, if you ask パーティーへ行くの？, it will be assumed that *you* are the subject of the question. If you ask 今夜のパーティーへいらっしゃいますか, there can be no doubt. In either case, there is no need to begin with あなたは. Correct use of honorific speech as well as verbs of giving and receiving (page 147) make most pronouns redundant. Even in informal conversation, there is no need to repeat a phrase like 私は～ in sentence after sentence (and doing so is one of the hallmarks of the non-native speaker of Japanese). A は-phrase is used to establish the topic of conversation. The accommodating listener assumes the topic is the same until there is an indication that topic is changed, and until there is a change, no other は-phrase is necessary. Personal reference, on the phone for example, may also be highly stylized and quite metaphorical. The one place where words for *you* are heard a lot is in the lyrics to popular songs (which is appropriate since words for *you* indicate intimacy).

I, we	こちら	very polite, common on the phone and in introductions of various kinds
	私・わたくし	most polite spoken
	私・わたし	neutral polite
	あたくし	female
	僕・ぼく	informal, young, generally male
	あたし	informal female
	俺・おれ	very informal male, tough

you,	貴〜・き〜	As a prefix means *your* in very formal (usually written) contexts. For example: 貴国 *your country;* 貴家 *your home;* 貴意 *your will,* 貴社 *your company;* etc.
you [plural]		
	貴様・きさま	once very polite, but now used angrily with rising intonation to mean something like *you bastard*
	お宅・おたく	highly stylized, from お宅 meaning *your home*
	そちら・そちら様 ・そちらさま	also stylized; used frequently on the telephone and during introductions; to ask *who* どちら様ですか.
	貴方・貴女・あなた	most neutral to address either gender; あなた is also used by some (generally older) women to address their husbands (where it would be written 貴方)
	君・きみ	informal, used by both genders to equals or inferiors
	僕・ぼく	used by older people to address boys who refer to themselves as 僕
	あんた	informal (usually) female speech
	お前・おまえ	informal male speech

The distinction between male and female third person pronouns is a relatively late development in Japanese (and Chinese) coming after contact with European languages.

he, she	彼・かれ *he*
they	彼女・かのじょ *she*
	彼ら・かれら, 彼女ら・かのじょら *they* (masculine)
	彼たち・かれたち, 彼女たち・かのじょたち *they* (feminine)
	(彼 and 彼女 are also used informally to refer to a boyfriend or girlfriend: 今日彼女と会うんだよ。*I'm gonna see my girl today.*)

guy, one	こいつ *this guy*
	そいつ *that guy*
	あいつ *that guy over there*
	(These are informal and convey a strong sense of contempt.)

Suffixes which mark overt plurals or groups are discussed beginning on page 106.

3.9.3 Self

自分 is usually translated into English *oneself, himself, herself,* etc. 自分 refers to a person. Typically, that person is also the subject of the sentence.

中島君は自分の家を持っている。

Nakajima owns his own home.

学生達はそれぞれ自分の靴がわかる。

The students all know their own shoes.

ジョンは中島に自分の家で殺された。

John was killed by Nakajima in his house.

(in John's house, not in Nakajima's house)

拓也はとてもびっくりしました。大介が自分の車を洗ったからです。

Takuya was very surprised because Daisuke washed his car.

(There are two subjects here; as in English, *his* may refer back to Takuya or to Daisuke. This ambiguity can be eliminated in this example by adding くれる: 拓也はとてもびっくりしました。大介が自分の車を洗ってくれたからです. 自分 must now refer to Takuya.)

When the subject of the sentence is the speaker, 自分 can actually be replaced with a pronoun meaning *I* (particularly in informal speech). When the subject is obvious, of course, the possessive with の can also be eliminated altogether.

自分の辞書を家に置いてきたので図書館のを使った。

私の辞書を家に置いてきたので図書館のを使った。

辞書を家に置いてきたので図書館のを使った。

I left my dictionary at home, so I used the library's.

An expression such as 御自分の makes it possible to avoid あなたの, although 御自分 is a relatively ritualized expression which should not be over used. An emphatic form of 自分 is 自分自身:

自分でしました。

I did it by myself.

それはしてもらいましたが、これは自分自身でしました。

That one I had done, but this one, I did all by myself.

田中さんは自分で作りました。田中さんは一人で作りました。

Tanaka made it by himself.

Although 自分 usually does refer back to the subject of the sentence, this is not always the case. It is possible to say that the interpretation of 自分 may vary with respect to the perspective of the speaker. Where does the speaker's empathy lie? While this is sufficiently vague to allow just about any interpretation of 自分, the student should be aware of the possibility when interpreting complex sentences which contain 自分.

中島君は恵子さんにだれかが自分の車を売ってしまったことを知らせた。

Nakajima told Keiko that someone sold his car. (Nakajima's car)

Nakajima told Keiko that someone sold her car. (Keiko's car)

As the translations indicate, 自分 can refer back to Nakajima (the grammatical subject) or to Keiko, even though Keiko is not the grammatical subject of the sentence. Such an interpretation would be particularly strong if it was known that Nakajima did not own a car.

In addition, there are many Chinese compounds where the element *self-* is an inherent part of the word:

じ・自〜 *self-*	自惚れ・うぬぼれ *self-conceit, vanity*; 自衛・じえい *self-defense*; 自営業・じえいぎょう *self-employed*; 自我・じが *the self, ego*; 自活・じかつ *self-support*; 自家用・じかよう *private use*; 自給・じきゅう *self-sufficiency*; 自国・じこく *one's own country*; 自殺する・じさつ *kill oneself*; 自賛する・じさん *praise oneself*; 自粛・じしゅく *self-control*; 自叙伝・じじょでん *an autobiography*; 自信・じしん *self-confidence*; 自制・じせい *self-control*; 自尊心・じそんしん *self-respect, pride*; 自体・じたい *itself*; 自宅・じたく *one's own home*; 自治・じち *self-government*; 自転する・じてん *revolve around oneself*; 自動・じどう *automatic, self-moving*; 自費・じひ *one's own expense*; 自慢する・じまん *boast about oneself*; 自滅・じめつ *self-destruction*; 自立する・じりつ *establish oneself*

3.10 Adverbs

Adverbs modify the verb of a sentence. They may tell us how something was done or when it was done. Broadly speaking, times expressions (今日, 三時半に, 毎日, etc.) as well as classifiers, onomatopoeic expressions, and locative expressions are all adverbial. Two productive types of adverbs are the く-form of adjectives and nominal adjectives with に.

大きく書いてください。
Please write in large letters.
ご自由にお取りください。
Please take one. Please don't hesitate to take one of these.

3.10.1 Frequency

Many adverbs which refer to frequency occur necessarily with negative or affirmative predicates, or seem to change meaning based on the predicate. Often, the negative predicates may be grammatically negative (with a form of 〜ない) or they may be predicates with "bad" meanings (だめ, きらい, 下手だ, etc.).

あまり *not much*	テニスがあまりできない *can't play tennis very well* あまり上手だとは言えない *can't really say that he is talented* (usually negative, pronounced emphatically あんまり)
あまり *too much,* *excessively*	あまり食べ過ぎる *over eat* 今日はあまりにも暑い。 *Today is really too hot.* (cf. 今日はとても暑い) (less often affirmative, often with に or にも)

いつも *always*	いつも勉強している。 *He is always studying.*
	いつも間に合わない。 *He is always late. He is never one time.*
	(affirmative or negative, although the negative versions can usually be re-cast as a sentence with 全然: 全然間に合わない.)

必ず・ かならず *always,* *necessarily*	必ず〜する *do 〜 without fail*
	食べる前に必ず手を洗おう。 *Always wash your hands before eating.*
	必ず合格する。 *I will definitely pass.*
	(only affirmative, similar to まちがいなく)

必ずしも・ かならずしも *not always*	必ずしもそうとは限らない。 *It is not necessarily so.*
	光るものは必ずしも金ではない。 *All that glitters is not gold.*
	(only negative, not particularly conversational)

かなり *pretty, fairly*	彼はピアノがかなり上手だ。 *He is pretty good at the piano.*
	今年の冬はかなり雪がつもった。 *A fair amount of snow has accumulated this year.*
	(only affirmative)

きっと *surely*	明日はきっと晴れるだろう。 *It will definitely clear up tomorrow.*
	きっと行く。 *I will be sure to go.*
	(only affirmative)

決して・ けっして *never,* *by no means*	決して十分ではない。 *It is far from satisfactory.*
	そうだとは決して言えない *It is not possible for me to say so.*
	(only negative)

さっぱり *not at all*	さっぱりわからない *not know at all*
	さっぱり連絡がない *have no word from*
	(さっぱり with a negative verb is similar to 少しも and occurs most commonly with わからない. It is somewhat less negative than まったく or 全然, and implies only a lack of affirmative instances. In contrast, まったくわからない implies only negative instances ("I tried to understand but failed"), while 全然わからない implies an entire set of negative instances ("I tried to understand many different things but failed each time"). さっぱり also occurs in combination with する in a number of generally positive idioms. For example: さっぱりする *feel refreshed*; さっぱりした味 *a refreshing taste, a simple taste*; さっぱりしている人 *frank, not fussy person*.)

少しも・ すこしも *not at all*	少しも役に立たない *be of no use at all* 英語の知識が少しもない。 *I have no knowledge of English at all.* ６月まで少しも雨が降らなかった。 *We had absolutely no rain until June.* (only negative; similar to but less colloquial than ちっとも)
全然・ ぜんぜん *wholly,* *completely*	彼は全然知らない人だ。 *He is a person I don't know at all.* 全然だめだ。 *It it totally bad.* 全然いい。 *It is completely good, exactly right* (cf. とてもいい, ちょうどいい) (Almost always very negative. Check under さっぱり for comparisons with さっぱり and まったく. Instances with affirmative predicates are very colloquial and have more polite alternatives.)
大して・ たいして *not very*	大して役に立たない。 *This is not particularly useful.* 大して高くない。 *It is not particularly expensive.* 大して興味のあることではない。 *It is not something I'm very interested in.* (Only negative, implying that something is not as useful, good, etc. as it might be. あまりis similarly negative but without the implication that a thing might be better than it is.)
たまに *occasionally*	たまに来る人 *a person who comes occasionally* たまには家で食べよう。 *Let's eat in for a change.* たまに学校に来ない。 *Sometimes, he does not come to school.* (affirmative or negative, less frequent than 時々)
ちっとも *not at all*	ちっともかまわない *not care a bit* ちっともびっくりしなかった。 *I wasn't surprised in the least.* お腹すいている？いや、ちっとも。 *Are you hungry? Not at all.* (only negative, more colloquial than 少しも, not as negative as 全然)
とうてい *impossible*	君の夢はとうてい現実できない。 *There is no way to realize your dream.* それはとうてい私の力ではできない。 *That is beyond my power.* (only negative, less conversational than an expression like どうしても)
どうにも *in no way*	どうにもそれが理解できない。 *I can't understand that at all.* どうにもしかたがない。 *There is nothing that can be done about it.* どうにもこの月給では暮らせない。 *There is no way I can live on this pay.* (only negative, less conversational than an expression like どうしても)
時々・ ときどき *sometimes*	時々外食する。 *Sometimes I eat out.* 曇り時々雨 *cloudy with occasional rain* (only affirmative)

とても   とてもおもしろい人 *a very interesting person*
very,   今日はとても元気だ。*We are full of energy today.*
extremely   とても分かりにくい。*It is very difficult to understand.*

(usually affirmative, pronounced emphatically とっても)

とても   とても助からない *well beyond saving*
not at all,   とても３０代には見えない。*He doesn't look to be in his thirties at all.*
by no means   (cf. 全然３０代には見えない)

(only negative, pronounced emphatically とっても)

なかなか   なかなかりっぱだ *very good, wonderful*
very, quite, なかなかすてきな人 *a pretty good-looking individual*
rather   なかなかの学者だ。*She is a scholar of some significance.*

(only affirmative)

なかなか   なかなかできない *can't do this very well*
not readily, このドアがなかなか閉まらない。*This door does not shut easily.*
not easily   金をなかなか払わない *does not pay money out very readily*

(only negative)

ほとんど   彼にほとんど会わない *almost never meet him*
hardly,   よく来るの？ほとんど来ない。*You come here often? Almost never.*
scarcely   本を読む機会はほとんどない。 *I have almost no opportunity to read.*

まさか   まさか信じられないだろう。 *You don't really believe him, do you?*
by no means   まさかそんなことはあるまいと思った。 *I never thought it possible.*
                まさか！*No! Say it isn't so.* うそだ！*No! That is a lie.*

(only negative, a very emphatic expression)

全く・   まったくわからなかった。 *I didn't understand at all.*
まったく   まったく疲れきっていた。 *He was completely exhausted.*
absolutely   まったく同感です。 *I agree completely.*

(まったく is always emphatic and usually negative. On its own, まったく can be used as an exclamation of mild disgust meaning something like "Good grief!" or "Good heavens!")

まるで   まるで子供のようだ。*He is just a like a child.*
as if,   まるで若いころの母親そっくりだ。*She is just like her mother as a child..*
as though   (まるで is common with both negative and affirmative predicates.)

まるで   そのこととまるで関係がない。
not at all   *I have no relationship to that. I know nothing about that.*
                それはまるでだめだ。*That is no good at all.*

(negative usage is often similar to まったく)

めったに *rarely*	こんな機会はめったにない。 *We rarely have a chance like this.* めったに病気はしない。 *I am almost never ill.* めったにしか行かない *only rarely go* (only negative)
よく *well*	よく焼けた。 *It is well-done.* フランス語がよくわからない。 *I don't speak French very well.* よく知っている人 *a person I know well* よくない *not good* (よく is most naturally interpreted as *well* with verbs of ability. It is usually affirmative, but can occur with negative verbs as well.)
よく *often*	よくロスに行く。 *I go to LA often.* よくあること *a common thing to happen* よくテニスをする *play tennis often* (With events which occur spontaneously or which people do on purpose, よく is naturally interpreted as *often*.)
よく *well* or *often*	よく見てください。 *Look at it carefully.* or テレビをよく見る。 *I often watch television.* (よく is sometimes ambiguous; does it modify ability or frequency?)
ろくに *not well* or *sufficiently*	ろくに眠れない *do not sleep well* 英語もろくに話せない。 *He can't even speak English properly.* ろくに口をきかない *speak very little* (negative only, more literary than あまり)

The adverbs here are ordered relative to their strength of assertion.

Strongest affirmative	*Weakest negative*
かならず	あまり, たいして
かなり	めったに
とても	すこしも, ちっとも
よく	さっぱり
ときどき	ぜんぜん, まったく
たまに	けっして
Weakest affirmative	*Strongest negative*

3.10.2 Temporal

These adverbs answer questions about when, in what order, or how soon. Time expressions such as 五時に or 今年 are also part of this category, but they are discussed on page 206 with discussion of particle に.

already,	もう食べている。（もう）
yet	*They are already eating. Are they eating yet?* 駅に着いたとき電車はすでに出ていた。（すでに） *When I got to the station, the train had already left.*
at once	早速返事を書いた。（早速・さっそく） *I responded at once. I responded immediately.* 今すぐ行きます。（今すぐ・いますぐ）*I will go immediately.* (今すぐ is faster and more automatic than 早速, almost without any forethought. 早速, on the other hand, is fast but still purposeful.)
at that time	その頃は電車がここまで来なかった。（その頃・そのころ） *In those days, the train didn't come this far.* あの時は値段はもっと安かった。（あの時・あのとき） *Prices were lower then.*
just	出かけたところだ。（ところ） *He has just gone out.* 帰ってきたばかりだ。（ばかり） *She has just come home.* (Turn to page 217 for further discussion of ばかり.)
next time	今度来るとき〜（今度・こんど）*Next time you come 〜* この次来るとき〜（この次・このつぎ）*Next time you come 〜* 次回の会議はいつ開かれますか。（次回・じかい） *When will the next meeting be held?*
once (upon a time)	前に台湾に住んだことがある。（前に・まえに） *We once lived in Taiwan.* 昔台湾に住んだことがある。（昔・むかし） *We once lived in Taiwan. We used to live in Taiwan.* 一度台湾に住んだことがある。（一度・いちど） *We once lived in Taiwan. We used to live in Taiwan.* 彼は以前より勉強する。（以前・いぜん） *He studies more than he once did, more than before.* 私たちはかつて台湾に住んだことがある。（かつて） *We once lived in Taiwan. (literary sounding)*

originally	元々彼がきらいだった。（元々・もともと） *I have always disliked him.* (conversational) ここは元来小さい村だった。（元来・がんらい） *This was originally a small village.* (not very conversational) 初めは彼女がきらいだったが今は好きになってきた。（初め・はじめ） *Originally, I disliked her, but I like her now.*
presently, *at the* *moment*	ただいま、会議中でございます。（ただいま） *He is presently in a meeting.* 現在、外出しております。（現在・げんざい） *At the moment, he is away from the office.*
presently, *about to*	やがて雨が雪になった。（やがて） *In time, the rain turned to snow.* 間もなく電車がまいります。（間もなく・まもなく） *The train is about to arrive.*
recently	近ごろの社会問題（近ごろ・ちかごろ） *recent social problems* 最近はあまり食欲がない。（最近・さいきん） *Recently, I don't have much of an appetite.*
still, yet	まだわからない。（まだ） *I still don't understand.* まだ暑いですね。（まだ） *It is still hot, isn't it.* まだ行かない。（まだ） *We aren't going yet.* まだここにいる。（まだ） *They are still here.*
soon, *before long*	そのうち着くだろう。（そのうち） *She should arrive soon.* 近いうちにまた会いましょう。（近いうちに・ちかいうちに） *Let's meet again soon.* もうすぐ梅雨が上がるだろう。（もうすぐ） *The rainy season should end soon.* もう少しで梅雨が上がるだろう。（もう少しで・もうすこしで） *The rainy season should be over before long.*

the other day   この前のちょっとした地震（この前・このまえ）
                   the small earthquake the other day
                   この間の会議（この間・このあいだ）
                   the meeting the other day

then,   部屋を掃除した。それから洗濯もした。（それから）
and then   *I cleaned my room, and then I did laundry.*
                   部屋を掃除し、そうしたら洗濯もする。（そうしたら）
                   I will clean my room, and then I will do laundry.
                   部屋を掃除した。そして洗濯もした。（そして, also そうして）
                   I cleaned my room, and then I did laundry.
                   部屋を掃除した。その後洗濯をした。（その後・そのあと・そのご）
                   I cleaned my room, and then I did laundry.
                   二年生の次に三年生が入ってくる。（次・つぎ）
                   The second years students will come in, and then the third year students.
                   (Turn to page 170 for verbal expressions which can also mean *and then*).

3.10.3 Emphasis (and de-emphasis)

of course,   新鮮な空気はもちろん健康によい。（もちろん）
naturally   *Naturally, fresh air is good for your health.*
                  行くね？もちろん！（もちろん）
                  You're going, right? Of course!
                  当然の結果　（当然・とうぜん）
                  a natural result

definitely,   それは確かに田中君の財布だ。（確かに・たしかに）
certainly   *That is definitely Tanaka's wallet.*
                  それは間違いなく田中君の財布だ。（間違いなく・まちがいなく）
                  That is definitely Tanaka's wallet.
                  必ず返事をします。（必ず・かならず）
                  I will definitely reply.
                  絶対にわからない。絶対わからない。（絶対・ぜったい）
                  I will definitely not understand.

anyway   とにかく始めよう。（とにかく）
                  Anyway, let's begin.
                  雪が降るかも知れないがともかく行く。（ともかく）
                  It may snow, but I will go anyway.
                  (a dialectal version of とにかく)
                  いずれにせよもう一度やって見ます。（いずれにせよ）
                  Anyway, I will try it one more time.

思ったより高いけど、やはり買うことにした。（やはり）

It was more expensive than I thought, but I decided to buy it anyway.
(やっぱり is a spoken version of やはり.)

especially   私は京都が好きだ。特に秋がいい。（特に・とくに）

I like Kyoto. In particular, autumn is nice.
京都は特別好きなわけじゃない。（特別・とくべつ）

I am not especially fond of Kyoto.
私は京都が好きだ。とりわけ秋がいい。（とりわけ）

I like Kyoto. In particular, autumn is nice. (more literary)
格別これといったことはなかった。（格別・かくべつ）

Nothing particular happened. (more literary)

in this way   こうして彼は彼女の心をとらえた。（こうして）

In this way, he won her heart. Thus, he won her heart.
このようにして天ぷらができる。（このようにして）

In this way, you can make tempura.

ever, even   思ったよりも難しかった。（よりも）

(emphasis)   *It is even more difficult than how I thought.*
彼も背が高いが弟はなお高い。（なお）

He is tall, but his younger brother is even taller.
薬を飲んだためになおさら悪くなった。（なおさら）

He got even worse from taking the medicine.
うちの犬でもこんな物を食べないよ。（でも）

Even my dog wouldn't eat this stuff.
うちの犬さえこんな物を食べないよ。（さえ）

Even my dog wouldn't eat this stuff.

Turn to page 145 for discussion of ways to de-emphasize the impact of a statement.

3.10.4 Other rhetorical devices

The expressions here allow one to introduce new ideas, change the subject, contrast ideas, and indicate the order of thoughts in an argument.

introduction   今日は歩いて来た。なぜかと言うと天気がとてもよかったから。（なぜか
to a reason   というと）*Today I walked. To say why, it's because the weather was so*
or further   *nice.* (also なぜかって言うと and なぜかと言えば)
explanation   今日は歩いて来た。なぜなら天気がとてもよかったから。（なぜなら）

Today I walked because the weather was so nice. (also なぜならば which
is more formal)

that is to say, だれも百点がとれなかった。つまりテストは難しかったということだ。

in other   （つまり）*No one got full marks, which is to say, the exam was difficult.*

words,   二人の近代日本の有名な作家すなわち漱石と鴎外（即ち・すなわち）

in short   *two famous modern Japanese writers, namely Soseki and Ogai*

いわゆる知識人が集まった。（いわゆる）

A bunch of so-called intellectuals gathered together.

お金がないと言うのはさびしいことだ。（と言うのは・というのは）*We have no money, which is to say, we are sad and lonely.*

契約は明日までだ。言い換えるとあさってからの仕事は契約以外になる。

（言い換えると・いいかえると）*This contract is for tomorrow. Which means that from the day after tomorrow we will be doing work unrelated to this contract.* (relatively formal also realized as 言い換えれば・いいかえれば)

明日までするという契約だ。要するに明日までにしないと私たちは首になる。（要するに・ようするに）*I have promised to be done by tomorrow. In other words, if we don't do it by tomorrow, we will be fired.*

話せば長いが、結局大学を止めることにした。（結局・けっきょく）*Well, it is a long story, but, in a nutshell, I've decided to quit university.*

contrast   お金が一番大切だと思っている人がいます。それに対して愛が一番だと思っている人もいますよね。（それに対して・それにたいして）*There are people who think money is the most important. But, on the other hand, there are also people who think love is the most important.*

一方では生産量が延びているが、他方では倒産している会社も多い。（一方・いっぽう，他方・たほう）*On the one hand output has increased, but on the other, many companies have gone bankrupt.* (a very formal manner of expression)

田中さんは英語はよくできると思ったが、それと反対に外国語は全然だめだ。（それと反対に・それとはんたいに）*I thought that Tanaka understood English, but in fact he is terrible at foreign languages.*

for example   外国語、例えばフランス語、ドイツ語など〜（例えば・たとえば）

Foreign languages, for example, French, German, etc. 〜

例を挙げると（例を挙げると・れいをあげると）*to give an example 〜*

to change   話は変わりますが〜・はなしはかわりますが〜 *to change the subject 〜*

the subject   (Also ところで, and それはそうと. Many Japanese textbooks translate ところで into English as *by the way*. This is a misleading translation to the degree that ところで usually means that you are coming to the point of the conversation while *by the way* signals what is usually an afterthought or a side matter.)

if	もしできなかったら〜　*If you can't do it 〜*　（もし）
well now,	さて、休憩しましょう。（さて）
so	*Well, let's take a break. So, let's take a break.*
	では、始めようか。（では）
	Well then, shall we begin?
	(Contracted to じゃ; the same contraction is found in ではない and じゃない as well is in 行かなくてはいけない and 行かなくちゃいけない.)
first,	まず場所を決めよう。（まず）
to begin	*To begin, let decide on the place.*
	はじめに東京タワーを見に行った。（はじめに）
	First, I went to see the Tokyo Tower.
	まずはじめに東京タワーを見に行こう。（まずはじめに）
	First, let's go see the Tokyo Tower.
	最初に窓拭きをしましょう。（最初・さいしょ）
	First, let's clean the windows.
finally,	最後に何をしましょうか。（最後に・さいごに）
at last	*What shall we do last?*
	終わりに皆で万歳しましょう。（終わりに・おわりに）
	Let's give a cheer together to end.
	ついに梅雨があがった。（ついに）
	At last the rainy season ended.
	とうとう先生の長い話が終わりました。（とうとう）
	At last the teacher's long lecture came to an end.
	結局台湾に旅行することにした。（結局・けっきょく）
	Finally, they decided to travel to Taiwan.
next, after	次はだれですか。（次・つぎ）*Who is next?*
	その次はだれですか。（その次・つぎ）*Who is next?*
	その後彼らは幸せに暮らした。（その後・そのあと・そのご）
	They lived happily ever after. (literally, After that, they lived happily.)

3.11 Quantities and classifiers

This section is about how to use expressions like *everyone*, *almost no one*, and *three people* in "Everyone arrived on time," "Almost no one knows the answer, " and "Three people sent me a birthday card." Most of these words have properties of both nouns and adverbs.

3.11.1 *Question words with* か, も, *and* でも

Question words like 誰, 何, なぜ, いつ, etc. occur in combination with particles か, も, and でも to create combinations which correspond to words like *someone*, *no one*, *anyone*, and *everyone* in English. The interpretation of a particular expression will vary depending on the predicate which follows (and whether it is affirmative or negative). Like all nouns, these expressions co-occur with particles, although note where they are missing in the examples. It should also be noted that there seems to be a fair amount of individual variation as to what kinds of combinations are possible or not. どうも is treated separately on page 253.

Who, what, where, etc.

who	誰が来たの？ （誰・だれ）	*Who came?*
what	何が聞こえた？ （何・なに）	*What did you hear?*
where	パーティーはどこですか。 （どこ）	*Where is the party?*

when 新学期はいつからですか。 （いつ） *When does the new school term begin?* (A question like パーティーはいつですか is usually answered something like 明日ですよ or 日曜日です. If you want to know the actual starting time of the party, it is more prudent to ask パーティーは何時ですか or パーティーは何時からですか.)

why なぜ行かないの？ （なぜ） *Why won't you go?*
どうして行くの？ （どうして） *Why will you go?*
(なぜ is a bit more formal than どうして.)

how どうですか。 （どう） *How is it?*
どうしましょうか。 （どう） *What should we do? How should we behave?*
肉の焼き加減はどうですか。 （どう） *How do you like your meat?*
(こう, そう, ああ, and どう refer to something like *ways* so that どうですか literally means "Which way is it?" and そうですか literally means "Is that the way it is?")

which   どれが好きなの？（どれ）*Which do you like?*

(どちら, どの＋Noun, and どんな＋Noun have the same distribution as ど
れ with accompanying differences in meaning. どちら refers to a choice of
two as well as to directions. どの＋Noun means *which Noun*, while どんな
＋Noun means *what kind of Noun.*)

how much,   いくらですか。おいくらですか。（いくら）*How much is it?*
how many   どのくらいですか。（どのくらい）
               How much is it? (weight, volume, etc.)
               いくつですか。（いくつ）
               How many things do you have? How old are you?
               (いくら can be used with both exact numbers of items as well as masses,
               quantities, and abstractions. いくつ can be used only with exact numbers
               of countable items (including ages).)

how many   何人来ると思う？（何人・なんにん）
               How many people do you think will come?
               三人来ると思う？（〜人・〜にん）
               Do you think three people will come?

Someone, something, somewhere, etc.

someone   誰かが来た。（誰か・だれか）*Someone came.*
               (more politely, 何方か)
               ある人があそこで待っている。（ある人・あるひと）
               Someone is waiting over there. A certain person is waiting over there.
               七時に人と会う約束がある。（人・ひと）
               I have an appointment with someone at seven.

something,   そこで何か見付けたの？（何か・なにか）*Did you find something there?*
(anything)   そこで何かを見付けたの？ *Did you find something there?*
               何か食べ物がある？ *Do you have some food?*
               食べ物が何かある？ *Do you have some food?*
               何かご用がありますか。*Is there anything I can do for you?*

somewhere   どこかへ行くの？（どこか）*Are you going somewhere?*
               (usually affirmative, but sometimes with negative)

sometime   いつか遊びに来て下さい。（いつか）*Please come over sometime.*

somehow　　　なぜか行かないそうです。（なぜか）

For some reason it seems he is not going.

どうしてか何も言わなかった。（どうしてか）

Somehow he managed to say nothing.

どうやら間に合った。（どうやら）

Somehow I managed to get there on time.

some way　　　どうかしたの？（どうか）*What's the matter? What is wrong?*

行くかどうか分からない。*I don't know if they will go or not.*

（どうか is most common in the embedded question pattern: *whether or not ~*, although it can occur as the main question in a sentence: どうかお願いします *Please do it some how.*)

some thing　　このうちのどれか貸してくれない？（どれか）

Would you lend me some of these?

（どれか must refer to discrete items (usually in the context of some larger well-defined set) while 何か may refer to substances as well.)

some, a little,　貯金はいくらかできましたか。（いくらか）

few　　　　　*Have you been able to save a little?*

いくらか気分がいい。*I feel a bit better today.*

物価がいくらか下がったようだ。*It seems prices have dropped a bit.*

いくつか質問があります。（いくつか）*I have a few questions.*

some number　何人かもう帰っていった。（何人か・なんにんか）

Some number of people have already gone home.

Everyone (anyone), everything (anything), everywhere (anywhere), etc.

everyone,　　誰でもこの仕事が好きになる。（誰でも・だれでも）

anyone　　　*Anyone will end up liking this job.*

誰もが酒を飲んだ。（誰も・だれも）

Everyone drank alcohol.

皆が来ている。（皆・みな・みんな）*Everyone is here.*

(also 皆さん, 皆様, 全ての人, 全員, 誰でもみんな)

誰でもできるわけではない。（だれでも）

It is not the case that anyone can do this.

誰にでもできるわけではない。*It is not the case that anyone can do this.*

誰にでも上げる。*Give some to anyone.*

everything,	彼のことなら何でも知っている。（何でも・なんでも）
anything	*If it is about him, I know everything.*
	万事オーケーだ。(万事・ばんじ) *Everything is ok.*
	全部食べなさいよ。（全部・ぜんぶ）*Eat it all.*
	お金が全てではない。（全て・すべて）*Money isn't everything.*
everywhere,	店はどこも閉まっている。（どこも）*Stores everywhere are closed.*
anywhere	至る所から（至る・いたる）*from all over, from everywhere.*
	方々から（方々・ほうぼう）*from various places*
	どこもかしこも人で混んでいるようだ。（どこもかしこも）
	Everywhere seems to be crowded. Every place seems to be crowded.
	この本はどこでも買える。（どこでも）*You can buy this book anywhere.*
always	いつもテレビを見ている。（いつも）
	He is always watching television.
	先生は常に早くいらっしゃる。（常・つねに）
	The teacher is always early.
	彼は始終テレビを見ている。（始終・しじゅう）
	He is always watching television.
any time,	いつでも家にいる。（いつでも）
every time	*I am home at any time. I am home all the time.*
	いつでも好きなときお電話ください。*Call me at any time.*
	いつも家にいるようだ。（いつも）*It seems they are always home.*
	（いつも means *always, continuously*. It refers to states of being which are true all the time. いつでも is more like *at any time, whenever*. It is compatible with a continuous state but really means that no point of time is more significant than any other. Thus, いつも家にいる and いつでも家にいる are more or less synonymous, although いつも家にいる implies that I never leave home, while いつでも家にいる might imply "whenever something happens, I am at home.")
at any cost	どうしても会いたがっている。（どうしても）
	She really want to meet with him.
every way	どうでもいい。（どうでも）*Anyway is fine.*
every one,	どれでもいい。（どれでも）*Any one is okay.*
any one	どれもいい。（どれも）*Every one is okay.*

as much as	彼はいくらでも本が買える。（いくらでも）
one likes,	*He can buy as many books as he likes.*
any number	リンゴをいくつでも食べて下さい。（いくつでも）
	Eat as many apples as you like.
	まだいくらもある。（いくらも）*There are still a lot left.*
	いくつも持っている。（いくつも）*I have quite a few.*
every number,	何人でもいい。（何人でも・なんにんでも）
any number	*Any number of people is fine.*

No one, nothing, nowhere, etc.

no one,	人は誰も来なかった。（誰も・だれも）*No one came.*
anyone	手紙は誰からももらわなかった。*I didn't get a letter from anyone.*
	（誰も in this interpretation occurs with negative predicates only. が and を are generally prohibited, although combinations such as 誰からも, 誰にも, 誰とも, etc. are fine. A positive interpretation of 誰も is in fact possible when it occurs with が: 誰もが皆来た "Everyone came." It is not clear that this kind of construction is possible with object maker を.)
nothing,	品を何も買わなかった。（何も・なにも）
anything	*I bought nothing. I didn't buy anything.*
	何もない。*I don't have anything. I have nothing.*
	何でもない。（何でも・なんでも）*It is nothing.*
	(in combination with negative predicates)
nowhere	どこもだめだ。（どこも）*Nowhere is good. Everywhere is bad.*
	どこでもだめだ。（どこでも）*It is not good anywhere.*
	(In combination with negative predicates. Again, the combination どこも labels all places as bad, while どこでも implies that taken one at a time, each place is bad.)
never	いつもしないことだ。（いつも）*That is something I don't always do.*
	全然しないことだ。（全然・ぜんぜん）*That is something I never do.*
	決してしないことだ。（決して・けっして）*That is something I never do.*
	(in combination with negative predicates)
no way	どうにもできませんね。（どうにも）*There is nothing we can do. There is no way to proceed.*
no one	どれも安くないみたい。（どれも）*It seems as if none of them is cheap.*
	(in combination with negative predicates)

not many,	いくらも時間がない。（いくらも）*There isn't much time left.*
not much.	箱はいくつも残っていない。（いくつも）*There are only a few boxes left.*
	少ししか残っていない。（少ししか・すこししか）
	There is only a little bit left.
	(in combination with negative predicates)
no number	何人もいない。（何人も・なんにんも）*There are no people here.*
	三人もいない。（三人も・さんにんも）
	Even three people are not here. Only two.

どうも

どうも is clearly related to the word どう meaning *how*.

> どうもすみません。*I am very sorry.*
> どうもありがとう。*Thank you very much.*
> どうもいないようですねえ。*It seem somehow as if they are not here.*
> どうも雨になりそうだ。*Somehow it looks like rain.*

どうも literally means something like *every way* or *however it is*. In actual usage it often has the meaning of *very* or *extremely*. どうも occurs in a number of polite idiomatic expressions (the first two examples). It can also be used to indicate something which cannot be expressed in words, often implying a sense of mystery, confusion, or concern (the second two examples). Sometimes these two usages overlap. An expression like この度は どうも〜 is the most appropriate and sincere thing to say at a funeral, a polite situation where the expression indicates extreme emotion. See page 286.

3.11.2 Classifiers

3.11.2.1 Grammar

Classifiers occur in several grammatical patterns each of which has particular implications.
    三匹の犬 *three dogs* with the general structure Classifier＋の＋Noun implies that you are talking about a set or a complete group (with respect to a salient context).

三匹の犬

three dogs (and no more)
三匹の犬が庭にいた。

Three dogs (and no more) *were in the garden.*
三匹の犬を連れて帰ってきた。

She brought home three dogs (a set of three dogs and no other animals).
その日にいなくなったのは三匹の犬ですか。四匹の犬ですか。

Is it a group of three dogs or a group of four dogs which disappeared on that day?

In contrast, 犬の三匹 *three of the dogs* with the general structure Noun＋の＋Classifier implies that you are talking about a subset of some salient larger group. (This is usually called *partitive*, i.e., part of the whole.)

犬の三匹

three of the dogs

となりの犬の一匹が庭に入ってきた。

One of the dogs came into the garden. (There were more next door.)

会場に入ってきた犬の二匹だけは白かった。

Only two of the dogs which came into the arena were white. (The others were brown.)

犬の何匹を捕まえたの？

*How many of the dogs did you catch? (*And how many got away?)

An expression with the structure 犬を〜三匹 where the classifier follows the particle (and might best be described as an adverb) implies any three dogs, not a particular set of dogs and not necessarily a subset of a larger set. The contrast can be seen in the following pairs of sentences.

三匹の犬を待っています。

I am waiting for (my) *three dogs.* (i.e. a specific group of three dogs)

犬を三匹待っています。

I am waiting for (any) *three dogs* (because I collect animals in sets of three).

三人の天使を探しています。

I am looking for a specific set of three angels (but they are hiding).

秘書を三人探しています。

I am looking to employ (any) *three secretaries.*

An expression such as 犬三匹 is found most commonly in lists which specify the number without making any reference to group membership: 犬三匹と猫二匹が部屋に入ってきた *Three dogs and two cats came into the room.*

3.11.2.2 Examples

The classifiers discussed here should all be easily recognized and used appropriately. A complete list of words used as classifiers would actually number several hundred. The fifteen most frequent expressions are numbered, although 〜人・にん・り and 〜つ are far and away the two most common. Classifiers are grouped here by sound irregularities. Temporal expressions (with classifiers like 〜日・か・にち and 〜月・がつ・げつ) are discussed on pages 206 and 296.

No sound changes

The numbers and classifiers are pronounced with no regular sound changes.

〜台・だい   *vehicles, large machines,* and *appliances* [12th]
(cars, buses, trains, trucks, bicycles; cameras, radios, tape recorders, computers, refrigerators, washing machines, microwave ovens, air conditioners, pianos, etc.)

〜題・だい   *problems, topics, test questions, titles*

〜ページ   *pages*

〜間・ま   *rooms* or *separable spaces* (which may also be temporary)
〜間 are typically created by screens or sliding doors and are measured by the number of tatami mats. They are found in a traditional Japanese setting. 〜間 contrasts with 〜室 which refers to rooms in a building or institution (not specifically Japanese, generally not temporary). See the discussion of 〜坪 on page 294.

〜枚・まい   *flat, thin objects* [5th]
(sheets of paper, cloth, carpets, coats, CDs, panes of glass, futon, towels, shirts, etc.)

〜棟・むね   *buildings*
In contrast to 〜軒, 〜棟 tend to be long and flat or divided into sections like apartment houses, warehouses, tenements, hospitals, etc. They are in general bigger and more substantial and are often more Western.

〜名・めい   *people* (honorific), *guests, customers*

〜面・めん   *flat surfaces, sides* [13th]

〜問・もん   *questions, problems*

〜羽・わ   (typically small) *birds, rabbits* [15th]
Very large, often flightless birds (such as peacocks, flamingos, penguins, etc.) or predatory birds (hawks, eagles, owls, vultures, etc.) might also be counted with 〜匹, the general animal classifier.

Changes with *k*

Classifiers which begin with a *k* sound are pronounced with a double *kk* after numbers 1, 6, 8, 10, and 100. For example, 〜句 for haiku poems:

k to *kk*   一句・いっく *one poem*; 六句・ろっく *six poems*; 八句・はっく *eight poems*; 十句・じゅっく *ten poems*; 百句・ひゃっく *one hundred poems*; etc.

〜株・かぶ   *rooted plants, roots, bulbs*; *shares of stock*
              一株 may be pronounced いっかぶ or ひとかぶ.

〜機・き   *airplanes* (other air vehicles), *machines*

〜曲・きょく   *pieces of music*

〜軒・けん   *buildings*; *establishments, households* (physically and conceptually) [6th]
              Contrasts with 〜戸 just for households, and 〜棟 for buildings which are
              long and flat or divided into sections like apartment houses, warehouses,
              etc.

〜個・こ   *small 3-D objects* [7th]
              (pieces of fruit, drinking glasses, cups, cans, cakes of soap, light bulbs,
              batteries, watches, clocks, eggs, candy, etc.) 〜個 is appropriate only when
              a more specific classifier does not exist.

〜校・こう   *schools*

Classifiers with *s*

Classifiers which begin with an *s* sound are pronounced with a double *ss* after numbers 1,
8, and 10. For example, 〜首 for poems (tanka specifically):

s to *ss*   一首・いっしゅ *one poem*; 八首・はっしゅ *eight poems*; 十首・じゅっしゅ
              ten poems; etc.

〜冊・さつ   *bound volumes* [14th]
              (books, magazines, notebooks, etc.)

〜室・しつ・   When pronounced しつ, *rooms in an institution*; when pronounced へ
へや   や, *rooms in a house or building*
              Note the pronunciation of *one room in a house* (一室) and *two rooms in a
              house* (二室). Compare this with the other mixed numeral classifiers dis-
              cussed beginning on page 258 below. Pronounced either way, 〜室 con-
              trasts with 〜間 which refers to rooms or separable spaces (which may also
              be temporary) in a traditional Japanese setting.

〜食・しょく   *meals*

〜色・しょく   *colors* [8th]

〜隻・せき   *large boats, ships*
              (tankers, cruise ships, etc.) Contrasts with 〜艘 for small boats.

〜艘・そう   *small boats*
(fishing, yachts, row boats, canoes, motor boats, etc.) Contrasts with 〜隻せき for large boats and ships.

〜足・そく   *pairs of footwear*
(socks, sneakers, tabi, etc.)

Classifiers with *h*

The *h* at the beginning of a quantifier typically changes to a *p* after numbers 1, 6, 8, 10, 100, and to a *b* after 3 and the word 何なに. For some, the *h* becomes a *p* after 3 as well. Contrast: 〜匹ひき for animals and 〜泊はく for overnight stays:

h to *p* or *b*   一匹・いっぴき *one animal*; 三匹・さんびき *three animals*; 六匹・ろっぴ き *six animals*; 八匹・はっぴき *eight animals*; 十匹・じゅっぴき *ten animals*; 百匹・ひゃっぴき *one hundred animals*; 何匹・なんびき *how many animals*; etc.

h to *p*   一泊・いっぱく *one night stay*; 三泊・さんぱく *three night stay*; 六泊・ろっ ぱく *six night stay*; 八白・はっぱく *eight night stay*; 十泊・じゅっぱく *ten night stay*; 何泊・なんぱく *how many over night stays*; etc.

〜杯・はい   *containers of a substance* (generally without lids, i.e. not bottles, al- though the substance can be any liquid, any powder, cooked and uncooked rice, sugar, salt, etc.)

The container is often mentioned explicitly since it is a crucial part of the expression. Note the alternation with で.
グラス一杯いっぱいの水みず・グラスで一杯の水 *a glass of water*
バケツの水三杯みずさんばい・バケツで水三杯 *three buckets of water*
盃四杯よんはいの酒 (盃・さかづき) *four (small) cups of sake*
コップ一杯いっぱい *a glass of a liquid*
カップ一杯いっぱい *a cup of a liquid*

〜発・はつ   *outbursts, explosions*

〜匹・ひき   *animals* [3rd]
(including insects but not necessarily including oysters and other sea crea- tures which do not have clear self-propulsion)
Specific animals often have more specific classifiers which are preferred. These include: fish (〜尾び), birds and rabbits (〜羽わ), and larger animals (〜 頭とう) such as cows, horses, sheep, tigers, elephants, etc. There also seems to be a lesser distinction between counting animals in the wild and counting animals which are related to a human activity. For example, *I saw four whales off the coast* (〜匹ひき) versus *Ahab captured three whales* (〜頭とう).

〜本・ほん   *long slender objects* [4th]

(pens, bars, cigarettes, forks, knives, ropes, wires, strand of hair, bottles of beer or sake, cut flowers, bananas, trees, flagpoles, table legs, but also home runs and good hits in cricket (but not foul balls), rolls of film, subway or underground lines, etc.)

Classifiers with *t*

Quantifiers which begin with a *t* sound are pronounced with a double *tt* after numbers 1, 8, and 10. For example, 〜頭 for large animals:

t to *tt*   一頭・いっとう *one large animal*; 八頭・はっとう *eight large animals*; 十頭・じゅっとう *ten large animals* etc.

〜着・ちゃく *major items of clothing, suits*

〜通・つう   *letters, postcards, documents* [11th]

〜滴・てき   *drops of liquid* [10th]

〜点・展・   *points; works of art; items in an inventory*
てん

〜頭・とう   larger animals

(cows, horses, sheep, elephants, tigers, etc. in contrast to 〜匹, which is a general classifier for (smaller) animals)

As discussed under (〜匹), there also seems to be a lesser distinction in usage when counting animals in the wild (〜匹) versus animals which are in some sense related to human activity (〜頭).

Mixed number classifiers

These classifiers are among the most commn and all use at least some of the Japanese names for numbers. Note that the alternative readings for 4 (し・よん) and 7 (しち・なな) come from the Chinese and Japanese readings of the numbers.

一・ひ *one*; 二・ふ *two*; 三・み *three*; 四・よ・よん *four*; 五・いつ *five*; 六・む *six*; 七・なな *seven*; 八・や *eight*; 九・ここ *nine*; 十・とお *ten*

〜つ   *inanimate things, concrete or abstract* [2nd]

This is a general classifier used appropriately only when another more specialized quantifier does not exist. It can never be used for people.

一つ	ひとつ	六つ	むっつ
二つ	ふたつ	七つ	ななつ
三つ	みっつ	八つ	やっつ
四つ	よっつ	九つ	ここのつ
五つ	いつつ	十	とお

Above 10, the number is used without any classifying expression.

百　　ひゃく

いくつ (which can in fact be written 幾つ)

〜粒・つぶ	*small, grain-like objects*

(sand, pachinko balls, small pills, coffee beans, etc.)

一粒　ひとつぶ

二粒　ふたつぶ

三粒　さんつぶ・みつぶ

四粒　よつぶ・よんつぶ etc.

Also

八粒　はっつぶ

十粒　じゅっつぶ

| 〜通り・ | *methods* |
| とおり | |

一通り　ひととおり

二通り　ふたとおり

三通り　さんとおり or みとおり

四通り　よんとおり etc.

Also

十通り　じゅっとおり

| 〜人・り | *people* [1st] |
| ・にん | |

一人　ひとり	六人　ろくにん
二人　ふたり	七人　ななにん・しちにん
三人　さんにん	八人　はちにん
四人　よにん	九人　きゅうにん
五人　ごにん	十人　じゅうにん

Note that 四人 is **not** pronounced よんにん or しにん. Likewise, 九人 is not pronounced くにん. This is the single most common classifier. It is worth getting the pronunciation right!

3.11.2.3 Idioms which include classifiers

The number and nouns in these examples are arbitrary unless stated otherwise. Most of the expressions here apply to people or to intervals of time.

〜置き	一日置き *every other day*
	二日置き *every two days*
	一ヶ月置き *every other month*
〜ごとに	四時間ごとに *at intervals of four hours, every four hours*
	二課ごとに試験がある。 *We have a test every two chapters.*

〜ずつ	一つずつ *one each*
	三枚ずつ *three sheets each*
〜と〜人で	同級生と五人で *with four classmates, the five of us*
	友達と三人で *with two friends, the three of us*

The total number of people (including the speaker) in the last example is three. 一人で means *alone* because the total number of people is one.

〜ども〜	私ども二人 *the two of us; including me, two*
〜とも	二人とも *both of them*
二度とない	二度とない *unrepeatable, never again*
〜人兄弟	三人兄弟 *three siblings*

This expression may also (although not so frequently) be written 三人姉妹 or 三人兄妹 if there is a mixture of brothers and sisters. In all cases it can still be pronounced きょうだい. 兄弟が三人いる means that I have three brothers and sisters (total four children), while a sentence like 家は三人兄弟だ generally means that including myself there are total of three children in my family. A related expression is 五人家族 *a five membered family*.

一人子	一人子 or 一人子 *an only child*
〜人に〜	一人に一つ *one for everyone, one for each person*
	一人にボールペンを四本 *four pens for each person*,
	二人に一つ *one for every two people*
〜ぶりに	五年ぶりに *after five years*
	一ヶ月ぶりに *after a month*, etc.
〜ほど	三人ほど *three people, approximately three people, about three people*
	ボールペンを三本ほど *three pens, as many as three pens*, etc.

ほど is added to classifying expressions to approximate and soften. Thus, the request 鉛筆を百本ほどください is usually interpreted to mean *One hundred pencils please*, although it leaves open the possibility that more or less are okay (if, for example, a store should actually be down to its last ninety-nine pencils). See page 218 for related discussion of ほど.

3.11.3 Other words of quantity and amount

These are words like *few, many*, or *the majority* in expressions like *few people* or the *majority of the students*. While the words here do not agree with their noun like most classifiers, there is a loose agreement with the nature of the noun: can it be conceived of as a countable object (*chairs, doors, computers*, etc.) or as substance of some kind (*air*, water, gold, sand, etc.)? This perception is actually quite flexible in English as well as Japanese. Compare: "I found water" (substance) and "I bought three waters" (bottles of water, types of water). Note also that many abstractions are in fact countable (*ideas, utterances, emotions*, etc.).

幾つか・ いくつか *some, a few*	いくつか質問がある。*I have a few questions.* いくつかの間違い *some errors, a few mistakes* おいくつですか。 *How old are you?* (lit. *How many do you have?*) (for countable nouns)
幾らか・ いくらか *some, a bit*	今日はいくらか気分がよくなってきた。*I feel a bit better today.* いくらか責任がある *have some responsibility, feel some responsibility* (for substance nouns)
少数・ しょうすう *small number*	少数の人々 *a small number of people* 少数の学生の意見 *the opinion of a few students* (For countable nouns; 水の少数 is strange, and can be contrasted with 水 の少量 which refers to a small quantity of water.)
少し・ すこし *little*	水を少し飲んでください。*Have a little water.* 時間が少しかかります。*It will take a little time.* (for substance nouns)
全て・ すべて *all, every*	ここにいる全ての人 *all of the people here, every person here* (for countable nouns)
全部・ ぜんぶ *all*	その皿の全部 *all of those plates* その本を全部読んできた。*I read all of that book.* (for countable nouns)
大部分・ だいぶぶん *most*	大工の大部分 *the majority of carpenters, most of the carpenters* 部屋の大部分はゴミでいっぱいです。*Most of the room is filled with trash.* (for countable nouns)
たくさん *a lot, many*	その森にはシカがたくさんいる。*There are many deer in that forest.* たくさん雪が降った。*A lot of snow has fallen.* 質問をたくさんした。*They asked a lot of questions.* (for both countable and substance nouns)
多数・ たすう *many*	多数の学生がアルバイトをしている。 *A majority of students are working part-time jobs.* (for countable nouns)

半分・	ケーキの半分 *half a cake*
はんぶん	そのポリバケツには水(みず)が半分入っている。
half	*That plastic bucket is half filled with water.*
	8の半分は4である。 *Half of eight is four.*
	(for both countable and substance nouns)
殆ど・	ほとんどの学生は勉強(べんきょう)しない。 *Almost all students don't study.*
ほとんど	山(やま)の木(き)はほとんど枯(か)れてしまった。 *Almost all of the trees are dying.*
almost,	時間(じかん)をほとんど使(つか)ってしまった。 *We have used almost all of our time.*
nearly	(for both countable and substance nouns)
皆・みな・	その鉛筆(えんぴつ)八本(はっぽん)を皆買(か)った。 *I bought all eight pencils.*
みんな	彼(かれ)の言(い)うことは皆本当(ほんとう)ですか。 *Is everything he says true?*
all, every	その水(みず)を皆飲(の)んだ。 *I drank all of that water.*
	(For both countable and substance nouns; 皆(みんな) of course is also a noun which means *everyone*.)

3.12 Onomatopoeia

English onomatopoeia words include expressions such as *bow-wow*, *ding-dong*, or *ka-boom*. They tend to represent actual sounds, and they tend to sound childish. Typical animal noises in Japanese include ワンワン *bow-wow* and コケコッコー *cock-a-doddle-do*. In addition to words mimicking animals, however, Japanese has words which represent feelings, psychological states, and manner (how something is done). There are hundreds of such words in Japanese, and except for simple animal sounds, they are not usually thought of as childish. Further, while these words may sound almost "made-up" to the ears of a native English speaker, all of the words listed here are standard and common enough to be found in almost any Japanese-English dictionary. In traditional Japanese grammar, there are four types of mimetic expressions: (i) those that mimic sounds in nature (擬音語(ぎおんご)), (ii) those that mimic human or animal noises (擬声語(ぎせいご)), (iii) those that describe the manner of an action (擬態語(ぎたいご)), and (iv) those that describe psychological states (擬情語(ぎじょうご)). The second and third types are the most common.

If we compare English and Japanese, we find that English has many verbs which refer to different versions the same action. For example walking:

walk, stride, strut, swagger, lumber, stomp, trudge, ramble, stroll,
amble, saunter, shuffle. toddle, waddle, stagger, perambulate

In contrast, Japanese has relatively fewer different words for different kinds of walking, but a great number of what are normally called sound-symbolic modifiers which produce different versions of the same verb. Again with walking:

どしどし歩く	*walk with a loud noise*	sound
とたどた歩く	*walk noisily and violently*	sound and manner
よろよろ歩く	*wobble*	manner
ぶらぶら歩く	*stroll*	manner
てくてく歩く	*hike*	manner
だらだら歩く	*walk slowly, without enthusiasm*	manner
のろのろ歩く	*walk slowly*	manner
うろうろ歩く	*loiter*	manner

The different onomatopoeia words may represent the sound of walking (for example, どしどし with a loud noise) or the feeling of strolling (ぶらぶら which is easy) or the feeling of hiking (てくてく which is purposeful and more strenuous).

Onomatopoeia expressions occur in the following grammatical patterns, behaving sometimes like adverbs and other times like nouns.

日本語をぺらぺら話す。
He speaks Japanese fluently. (as an adverb)
日本語をぺらぺらと話す。
He speaks Japanese in the manner of someone fluent (as an adverb, with particle と)
日本語がぺらぺらだ。
His Japanese is fluent. (as a noun with だ)
日本語がぺらぺらになった。
His Japanese has become fluent. (as a noun with ～になる)
ぺらぺらの日本語だ。
It is fluent Japanese. (as a noun with の)

A representative list of these expressions is sorted below based on grammatical characteristics: adverb or noun. Some expressions occur in both lists. An entry like がつがつ食べる・と食べる *wolf down* means that がつがつ can occur with or without particle と. Note, however, that words like the following already include と as part of the word: がらっと, きちんと, ぐっと, さっさと, さっと, ざっと, しんと, ちゃんと, ぱっと, むっと, etc. An entry like ふわふわだ・になる *be soft* in the noun list indicates a parallel alternation between ～だ and ～になる. In the examples, any expression with the verb する occurs only (and usually with an idiomatic meaning) with the verb する.

Adverb   あっさり諦らめる・と諦らめる *give up with no regrets*; いらいらする *be irritated*; うきうきする・とする *be buoyant, happy*; うすうす気づいていた・と気づいていた *had noticed*; うっかりする・とする *carelessly, by accident, absentmindedly*; うっとりする・とする *be enchanted*; うとうとする *doze off*; おろおろする *be in a dither*; うんざりする *be fed up with*; がつがつ食べる・と食べる *wolf down*; がっかりする *be disappointed*; がぶがぶ飲む・と飲む *guzzle*; がらっと開ける *open wide*; きちんと *neatly*, tidily; ぎっしり詰まっている・と詰まっている *be densely, tightly, closely packed*; きらきら光る・と光る *sparkle, glitter*; ぎりぎり間に合う *arrive just in time*; くすくす笑う・と笑う *giggle, titter*; ぐっすり眠る・と眠る *sleep like a log*; ぐっと引く *jerk*; くよくよする *worry, fret*; ぐらぐらする *be unsteady, wobbly*; くるくる回る・と回る *go round and round*; こそこそ隠れる・と隠れる *hide secretly, stealthily*; ごたごたしている・ごたごたとしている *be busy, occupied, messy*; こつこつ勉強する・と勉強する *study diligently, step-by-step*; ごろごろ転がる・と転がる *roll, tumble*; さっさと *quickly, promptly*; さっと立ち上がる *stand suddenly*; ざっと *cursorily, quickly*; ざらざらしている・としている *be rough, coarse*; しくしく泣く *weep, sob*; じめじめしている・としている *be damp, wet*; じろじろ見る・と見る *stare*; しんとする *be silent*; ものをずけずけ言う人・と言う人 *a person who speaks his mind*; すやすや眠る・と眠る *sleep calmly, peacefully*; すんなり入る・と入る *go in smoothly, without difficulty*; ぞくぞくする・とする *shiver*; ぞっとする *shiver, tremble*; 風がそよそよと吹く *breeze blows softly, gently*; そわそわする *be restless, fidget*; たらたら流れる・と流れる *drip a stream of blood or sweat*; ちびちび飲む・と飲む *sip*; ちゃくちゃくと進歩する *make steady progress*; ちゃんと座る *sit properly*; ちらちらする *flicker, flutter*; ちらほら見えてくる・と見えてくる *appear and disappear*; つるつるしている *be slippery, silky*; てきぱきと働く *work briskly, actively*; 胸がどきどきする *heart pounds*; とぼとぼ歩く *plod*; にこにこ笑う・と笑う *smile, beam*; にやにやしている・としている *smirk*; ねばねばしている *sticky*; ぱっと暗くなる *suddenly go dark*; 羽をばたばたさせる・とさせる *flap wings*; はらはらする *feel unease*; ばらばらまき散らす・とまき散らす *patter, scatter*; ぴかぴかする *sparkle*; びくびくしながら・としながら *hesitantly*; ひそひそ話す・と話す *whisper*; ひょっこり現れる・と現れる *suddenly appear, appear unexpectedly*; 頭がふらふらする *feel dizzy*; 家でぶらぶらする *be idle at home, sway*; ふわふわしたクッション *soft cushion*; ぺらぺらしゃべる *speak fluently*; ぽかぽかする *be pleasant, spring-like, warm*; ぽっくり死ぬ *die suddenly*; ほっと息をつく *sigh*; 涙がぼろぼろこぼれる・とこぼれる *shed big tears*; むかむかする *feel sick, nauseated*; むっとする *become sullen*; 怒りがむらむら沸いてくる・と沸いてくる *anger boils up*; めそめそ泣く *sob*; もじもじしながら *hesitantly*; よたよた歩く・と歩く *toddle*; わくわくする *be excited, thrilled*

Noun うやむやだ・になる *is unsettled*; うんざりだ *fed up with*; かちかちに凍る *freeze hard*; がっかりだ *disappointed*; ぎっしりだ・になる *be dense, tight, close, packed tightly*; ぎりぎりだ *be just in time*; ぐらぐらだ *unsteady, wobbly*; つるつるだ・になる *slippery, silky*; ごたごただ・になる *busy, occupied, messy*; ざらざらだ・になる *be rough, coarse*; すれすれで間に合

う *be just in time, narrowly, barely, to the top*; ねばねばだ・になる *sticky*; ばらばらだ・になる *pattering, scattered*; ぴかぴかだ・になる *sparkling*; ぴったりだ・になる *sudden, tight, exact*; 頭がふらふらだ・になる *feel dizzy*; ふわふわだ・になる *be soft*; ぺこぺこだ・になる *be famished, very hungry*; へとへとだ・になる *exhausted*; ぺらぺらだ・になる *fluent*; ぽかぽかだ・になる *be warm, pleasant, spring-like*; めちゃくちゃだ・になる *messed up*; よたよただ・になる *toddling*

3.13 Conjunctions

3.13.1 Lists of nouns

A crucial distinction here is whether or not a particular conjunction indicates a complete list or an approximate list.

and   本を三冊と鉛筆を四本買ってきた。（と）

I went and bought three books and four pencils.
本も鉛筆も買ってきた。（〜も〜も）

I went and bought both books and pencils.

and, etc.   学校のために本やノートなどを買ってきた。（〜や〜など）

I went and bought books, notebooks, and other things for school.
本とか鉛筆とかを買ってきた。（〜とか〜とか）

I went and bought books, pencils, and other things.
言語学には統語論や意味論といった分野がある。（〜や〜といった）

In linguistics there are fields such as syntax and semantics.
鉛筆だのノートだのを買ってきた。（〜だの〜だの）

I went and bought a pencil and other stuff.

(This is the equivalent of や when writing in the である style.)

or   ジョンかビルに会ったはずだ。（か）

He should have met with John or Bill.
電話なり手紙なりで答えをお知らせください。（〜なり〜なり）

Please let me know your answer by phone or letter.
これかあるいはそれ〜（あるいは）

this or that 〜
パーティーは明日、それとも明後日なの？（それとも）

Is the party tomorrow? Or the day after?
明日または明後日、パーティーがあるかも知れない。（または）

The party is probably tomorrow or the day after.

not only, but   手だけじゃなくて足も蚊にさされた。（だけじゃなくて）

Not just my hands but also my legs were bitten by mosquitoes.

手のみならず足も蚊にさされた。（のみならず）

Not just my hands but also my legs were bitten.

手といわず足といわず蚊にさされた。（〜といわず〜といわず）

I was bitten by mosquitoes not just on my hands and feet.

(These last two examples are more characteristic of the である style.)

3.13.2 Conjoining sentences

Note from the examples which of these can be used to begin sentences as well. In each set, the different expressions are basically arranged from most to least common (with many of the later examples actually being quite rare).

and,   高いです。それに好きな色がありません。（それに）

in addition,   *They are expensive. And, there is no color I like.*

moreover,   田中さんのアパートはきれいだった。その上交通の便がいいところにあっ

furthermore   た。（その上・そのうえ）*Tanaka's flat is pretty. It is also in a convenient location.* (also その上に・そのうえに)

この町は小さいし、することもないからあまり好きじゃありません。

（〜し〜し）*This town is small and there is nothing to do, so I don't like it very much.*

音楽はクラシックをよく聞く。それとポップスも時々聞く。（それと）

I often listen to classical music. In addition, I sometimes listen to popular music.

田中さんのアパートはとてもきれいだ。さらに交通の便がいいところにあっ

た。（さらに）*Tanaka's flat is pretty, and furthermore, it is in a convenient location.*

彼女はお金持ちでおまけに美人だ。（おまけに）

She is rich, and what is more, she is beautiful as well.

彼は寄付をした、しかも気前よく。（しかも）

He contributed, and very generously.

その計画は複雑だ。そればかりじゃなく、えらくお金がかかる。（そればかりじゃなく）*That plan is very complicated. And not only that it will be very expensive.*

食べたり寝たりしかしなかった。（〜たり〜たり）

All we did was eat and sleep.

or 　　　ここで食べるの？それとも外食をするの？（それとも）

Will you eat here, or will you go out?

ここで食べようか、あるいは外食しようか。（あるいは）

Shall we eat here, or shall we go out?

ここで食べる。または公園に行って食べる（または）

We will eat here, or possibly we will go to the park and eat.

生きるべきか死ぬべきか。それが問題だ。（〜か〜か）

"To be or not to be, that is the question."

行くんですか！行かないんですか！（〜か〜か）

Are you going?! Or are you not going?!

but,　　　中島君は来ましたが、山本さんはまだです。（が）

however,　*Nakajima has come, but Yamamoto hasn't yet.*

although,　（だが or ですが at the beginning of a sentence)

even though,　読んだけどわからなかった。（けど）*I read it, but I didn't understand it.*

nevertheless　(Also けれど and けれども which are increasingly more polite; だけど、で
すけど、けれど、and けれども can also be used at the beginning of a sentence. が is also used between two sentences where the first sentence seems
only to "set up" the second. It is often unnatural to think of it as meaning
but in such cases. Think about the most natural English translations of 失
礼ですがお名前は？ or お店に行きますがついで何か買ってきましょうか.)

一生懸命準備をした。しかしうまく行かなかった。（しかし）

I prepared a great deal. However, things did not go well.

皆に何度もイーメールを出した。それでもだれも来なかった。（それでも）

I sent e-mail to everyone many times. But, no one came. (でも alone as
well)

彼に緊急の電話をした。ところが留守番電話だった。（ところが）

I phoned him with an urgent call, but I got an answering machine.

全部読んだのにわからなかった。(のに or なのに after a noun) *I read it
all, but I didn't understand.* (それなのに at the beginning of a sentence.)

病気にもかかわらず会議に出席した。（にもかかわらず）*Although she
was ill, she attended the meeting.* (それにもかかわらず at the beginning of
a sentence)

ほとんどうまく行きました。ただ後片付けが大変だった。（ただ）

Basically everything went well. But cleaning up was a lot of work.

お金がないくせによく外食する。（くせに）*He eats out a lot even though
he doesn't have any money.* (癖 *habit* on its own refers to what is usually a
bad habit)

小さいながらも両親の気持ちがよくわかる。（〜ながらも）

Even though they are small, they understand the feelings of their parents.

社長でありながら気さくな人だ。（～ながら）

Although he is the company president, he is still friendly.

入院しないまでも家でゆっくり休んだ方がいいですよ。（までも）

Even though you needn't go to the hospital, you should rest at home.

彼は試験に合格したと言った。もっとも後でそれはうそだと分かったが。

（もっとも）*He said he passed the exam. But, we found out later that he was lying.*

お金を持って出かけたところが買いたい物が見付からなかった。（ところが）*I took my money, but I didn't find anything I wanted to buy.*

彼はよく勉強する。それにしてはあまり成績がよくない。（それにしては）

He studies a lot. Nevertheless, his grades are not very good.

思ったより高かったけど、やっぱり買うことにした。（やっぱり）

It was more expensive than I thought, but I bought it nonetheless.

(やっぱり *is a spoken version of* やはり.)

猫がたくさんいるものの行儀のいい猫は一匹もいない。（ものの）

Although we have a lot of cats, none of them are well-behaved.

早く休めばよかったものを無理をして病気になってしまった。（もの）

Although it would have been okay to rest earlier, I worked hard and ended up ill.

新しい車はほしいしお金はないし困りますね。（～し～し）

I want a new car, but I don't have any money. It is a problem.

because, since, so, as a result
高いから、すぐは買わないでしょう。（から）*Because it is expensive, I doubt I will buy it soon.* (だから *or* ですから *at the beginning of a sentence*)

勉強しているので邪魔しないほうがいい。（ので *or* なので *after a noun*)

It is better not to bother him since he is studying.

勉強しなかったため、成績があがらなかった。（ため）

Because I don't study, my grades don't get any better.

(also ために, and そのため or そのために *at the beginning of a sentence*)

学費がまた上がったゆえ、借金がますますかさんできた。（ゆえ）

Tuition has risen again so I'm getting deeper into debt. (also ゆえに, and それゆえ or それゆえに *therefore at the beginning of a sentence*)

学費がまた上がった。従って借金がますますかさんできた。（従って・したがって）*Tuition has risen again. And as such, I'm getting deeper into debt.*

学費がまた上がった。その結果借金がますますかさんできた。（その結果・そのけっか）*Tuition has risen again. As a result, I'm getting deeper into debt.*

これは一人で到底できないと思った。そこで先生におねがいして手伝って
もらった。（そこで）*I didn't think I could possibly do this alone, so I*
asked the teacher for help.

バスが遅れて、おそくなってしまった。（〜て）

The bus was late so I ended up not getting here on time.

バスが遅れた。それでおそくなってしまった。（それで）

The bus was late so I ended up not getting here on time.

安かっただけにたくさん買えた。（だけに）

Since they were cheap, we were able to but a lot.

まだ子どもだもの！（もの）

But he's only a child! It's because he's only a child!

even if   今から準備しても無理かもしれない。（〜ても）*Even if we prepare from*
now, it will probably be impossible. (それにしても *at the beginning of a*

sentence)

安くなったって、絶対に買わない。（って）

Even if it gets cheaper, I will not buy it.

手紙を書いてくれたところで、返事はしないよ。（ところで）

Even if you were to write, there would be no response.

not only, but   電話番号を教えてくれただけじゃなくて携帯電話も貸してくれた。（だけ
じゃなくて）*Not only did she give me the phone number she lent me her*
cell phone.

電話番号を教えてくれた。それのみならず携帯電話も貸してくれた。（そ
れのみならず）*Not only did she give me the phone number she lent me*
her cell phone.

田中さんのアパートは便利なところにあるのみならず家賃もとても安い。

（のみならず）*Not only is Tanaka's apartment convenient, the rent is*
low.

4 Language and everyday life

4.1 Rituals

Each section here contains a fairly exhaustive list of all the ways to perform a certain ritual. The examples range from the most common to both polite and humble expressions. Which expressions are appropriate for which circumstances? And in a particular circumstance, which expressions are more or less polite? Remember that the beginnings and endings of interactions with people (in person, on the phone) are the most ritualistic.

4.1.1 Greetings

Morning (until about 11am)
おはようございます。（お早ようございます）
おはよう。
Good morning.

From about 11am
こんにちは。（今日は）
Good afternoon.

From about dusk
こんばんは。（今晩は）
Good evening.

While all of these expressions can be used with people outside of your immediate family, こんにちは and こんばんは are slightly strange (and distancing) when greeting immediate family members (quite like the English "Good afternoon" actually). It is also possible to use おはようございます the first time you meet someone like a colleague, fellow club member, or co-worker at the beginning of the school, meeting, or work day regardless of the actual time of day.

As a joke, you might hear おそようございます when you have not managed to get out of bed until noon or you are late for work or school. In terms of their grammar, おはよう and おそよう are simply very polite adjectives. Members of clubs, sports teams, etc. generally greet each other with おっす spoken with a long drawn out *s* regardless of the time of day. This is probably more masculine sounding than not, and is rumored to be an abbreviated and highly stylized form of おはようございます.

On greeting people you see regularly, it is quite common to make reference to your last meeting and to acknowledge your on-going obligations. This is particularly true in any kind of a professional context (but is by no means limited to such situations).

この間はどうもありがとうございました。　（間・あいだ）
この間はありがとうございました。
この間はどうも。
この間はお世話様でした。　（お世話様・せわさま）
この間はどうもお世話様でした。
この間は大変お世話様でした。　（大変・たいへん）
先日はどうもありがとうございました。　（先日・せんじつ）
先日はありがとうございました。
先日はどうも。
Thank you for the other day. Thank you (for some specific action).

お世話になります。　（世話・せわ）
またお世話になります。
Thank you for what you will do for me (again).

お世話になっています。　（世話・せわ）
お世話になっております。
いつもお世話になっています。　（いつも）
いつもお世話になっております。
お世話様です。　（お世話様・せわさま）
いつもお世話様です。
Thank you for what you always do for me.

こちらこそ。
いえいえ、こちらこそ。
No, no, it is I who should be thanking you.

Where は occurs, it can be omitted and replaced with a slight pause instead. The expressions in the above list which occur with 先日 are a bit more formal than those with この間. The past tense forms are appropriate when making referring to a specific past event or favor, while those in the future indicate thanks for a specific future event or favor. 〜ている expressions indicate an ongoing sense of obligation to another person (particularly when accompanied with いつも). 世話になる means *to be taken care of* while 世話する means *to take care of.* こちらこそ is a common reply which turns the thanks around. It can be used after any expression of gratitude (to indicate mutual appreciation). こそ itself is a particle which simply emphasizes what has preceded.

今年こそ頑張ります。

I will work hard from this year.

自分自身の子供をもってこそはじめて親の愛情がわかる。

It is not until you have your own children than you can understand the love of a parent.

Less commonly, you might ask after someone's health. These are used most naturally when someone has actually been ill (seriously or not). The first two are often given as translations of English *How are you?* but are in fact not particularly common amongst the Japanese themselves. To the degree that they are used in Japan, they reflect a relatively long time since the last meeting. The expressions with 調子 can be used more broadly to ask about any general condition, e.g. business, study, daily life, etc.

お元気ですか。 （元気・げんき）

元気？

How are you?

お変りありませんか。 （お変り・おかわり）

お変りないですか。

Have there been any changes? How are you?

具合はいかがでございますか。 （具合・ぐあい）

具合はいかがでしょうか。

具合はいかがですか。

具合はどうですか。

お元気になりましたか。 （元気・げんき）

元気が出るようになりましたか。

大分お元気になりましたか。 （大分・だいぶ）

大分元気が出るようになりましたか。

よくなりましたか。

よくなられましたか。

大分よくなりましたか。

大分よくなられましたか。

調子はいかがでございますか。 （調子・ちょうし）

調子はいかがでしょうか。

調子はいかがですか。

調子はどうですか。

Are you well? Are you better now? How are you?

The most polite (and an always appropriate) response to these expressions (particularly those with 元気) is お陰様で which means *Thanks to you*. This is actually a polite response to any greeting along the lines of *How are you? Are you doing well? Is your new job or career going well?* It is particularly appropriate when the person asking you is a teacher or other person who has supported you in some direct or indirect way, thereby contributing to your success. Other more specific responses to the various *How are you?* questions include:

ええ、相変わらず。（相変わらず・あいかわらず）
Yes, things are the same. There have been no changes.

ええ、元気。（元気・げんき）
うん、元気だよ。
うん、元気です。
ええ、元気になりました。ありがとうございます。
ええ、よくなった。
ええ、よくなりました。
Yes, I am fine.

ええ、なんとか。
ええ、まあ。
I manage to get along.

The following expressions are appropriate when greeting someone you have not seen in a very long time:

久しぶり。（久しぶり・ひさしぶり）
久しぶりです。
お久しぶりです。
お久しぶりでございます。
しばらく。
しばらくです。
しばらくでございます。
しばらくでした。
しばらくぶり。
しばらくぶりです。
しばらくぶりでございます。
しばらくぶりでした。
It has been a long time.

しばらく literally refers to a length of time, and it is possible to say something like もうしばらくお待ちください *Please wait a bit longer*. There seems to be weak regional variation as to whether ひさしぶり or しばらく is preferred. Likewise the expression may sound more or less masculine or feminine. Imitate the usage of your favorite native speaker.

Alternatively, the following very polite expressions are appropriate if you have not been in touch with someone in a longer rather than a shorter period of time, and there is some sense that you have been neglectful in maintaining your end of the relationship.

ごぶさたしています。（ご無沙汰・ごぶさた）
ごぶさたしております。
大変ごぶさたしています。（大変・たいへん）
大変ごぶさたしております。
ごぶさたしておりました。
大変ごぶさたしておりました。
I haven't called you in too long.

無沙汰 is a noun meaning *silence* or *neglecting to call.*

4.1.2 Enterings

There are a number of expression appropriate for when you are entering a place. These vary not only in level of politeness, but also in which expression is appropriate for which location (your own home, someone else's home, your own office, someone else's place of business, a place where you are a customer, etc.).

ごめんください。ご免ください。（ご免・ごめん）
Excuse me. Hello!?

This is said loudly to get someone's attention when you are standing at the front of an apparently empty counter (usually in a small family run business), or standing in the entrance hall of someone's house. The entrance hall of a Japanese house (the 玄関), although inside, is still technically outside. If the front door is unlocked, it is more than usual to open it and stick your head in to shout ごめんください. Salespeople do this with particular vigor. This expression should not to be confused with ごめんなさい which is an actual apology.

失礼します。（失礼・しつれい）
失礼いたします。
Excuse me.

おじゃまします。（邪魔する・じゃまする）
おじゃまいたします。
おじゃまさせていただきます。
Excuse me. (lit. *I am about to be a burden.*)

These are said after you have been invited in but before entering someone else's house or office. The third expression (with the causative) is far and away the most polite.

Upon returning to your own home

ただいま。（只今・ただいま）
I'm back.

Upon returning to your office or business after a long business trip or day out

ただいま帰りました。（帰る・かえる）
ただいま戻りました。（戻る・もどる）
I'm back.

Whoever is there to welcome you back says お帰^{かえ}りなさい. ただいま on its own is an adverb means *presently* as in ただいま電車^{でんしゃ}がまいります。 *Presently, the train will arrive* (a common announcement in train stations).

4.1.3 Welcomings

Again, these vary based on the location and who is welcoming whom. Commands ending in 〜ませ are very polite, slightly archaic, and feminine sounding.

どうぞ。
どうぞ入ってください。（入る・はいる）
どうぞお入りください。
どうぞお入りくださいませ。
どうぞご遠慮まく。（遠慮・えんりょ）
Please come in. Please don't hesitate.

Here we have an occurrence of the word 遠慮^{えんりょ} which mean something like *restraint* or *holding back*. Proper restraint is considered a virtue in Japan, and knowing when to exercise 遠慮^{えんりょ} and when it is unnecessary is a key component to any kind of success. Knowing how to get your own way while giving the impression of holding back may be considered an art.

どうぞ。
どうぞ、上がってください。（上がる・あがる）
どうぞお上がりください。
どうぞお上がりくださいませ。
Please come in.

One can invite in with one of two verbs: 入^{はい}る or 上^あがる. 上^あがる is particularly appropriate when a guest must step up from the entrance hall generally into the speaker's home but also into Japanese inns, some restaurants and hotels, potentially anywhere you have to take your shoes off.

よく来てくれました。（来る・くる）
よく来て下さいました。（下さる・くださる）
よくいらっしゃいました。
よく御出でになりました。（御出で・おいで）
よくお越し下さいました。（越す・こす）

Thank you for coming. (literally, *You have come* or *You have crossed over* said generally to someone who has made an effort)

On welcoming someone to your own place of business

いらっしゃいませ。
いらっしゃい！
Please come in. Welcome.

Said to someone returning home by someone already at home. As noted above, the person who is returning responds with ただいま.

おかえり。（帰る・かえる）
おかえりなさい。
おかえりなさいませ。
Welcome back.

Said to someone who is returning to the workplace from some job away from the office.

おつかれさま。（お疲れ様・おつかれさま, 疲れる・つかれる）
おつかれさん。
おつかれさまです。
ごくろうさま。（ご苦労様・ごくろうさま, 苦労・くろう）
ごくろうさん。
ごくろうさまです。
Welcome back. Good job.

These two expressions mean something like *You are a tired person* or *You are a hard working person.* おつかれさま is more appropriate when the person actually looks tired, and it may be rude when said to a superior (since it may be rude to speculate about a superior's physical or mental condition). ごくろうさま does not have this connotation, and simply expresses appreciation for a person's labor. The person who is returning is most likely to respond おかえりなさい. The more informal versions can also be used as a greeting of sorts if you are bringing tea or some kind of refreshment to a person who has been working hard. The people who have been working are most likely to respond ありがとうございます. All of these expressions in the past tense (でした) can be used at the end of the work day, said to those leaving. The person leaving first says お先に, お先に 失礼します, or お先に失礼いたします. Those remaining behind respond: おつかれさまでした.

4.1.4 Taking your leave

そろそろ〜

もうそろそろ〜

もうこんな時間ですか。じゃあ、そろそろ〜

もうこんな時間ですか。じゃあ、あしたはちょっと〜

Well, (it is getting late ～and tomorrow ～)

そろそろ失礼します。（失礼・しつれい）

もうそろそろ失礼します。

もうこんな時間ですか。そろそろ失礼します。

そろそろ失礼いたします。

もうそろそろ失礼いたします。

もうこんな時間ですか。そろそろ失礼いたします。

そろそろ失礼させていただきます。

もうそろそろ失礼させていただきます。

もうこんな時間ですか。そろそろ失礼させていただきます。

お暇させていただきます。（暇・いとま）

そろそろお暇させていただきます。

もうこんな時間ですか。そろそろお暇させていただきます。

Well, it is getting late and I must excuse myself.

In the expressions here, the causative form is the most polite. そろそろ is an onomato-poeic expression which might be thought of as the sound of time passing. While it is part of a larger fixed expression, more often than not it is neither necessary nor particularly elegant to insist on saying the whole expression. In English, you might begin with an apology and an explanation of how you have an early morning, etc. An apology before leaving may also be appropriate in Japanese, but the single word そろそろ (probably preceded with a すみませんが or a mildly surprised もうこんな時間ですか) will convey your desire to leave politely and instantly. As part of the ritual in Japanese, an accommodating but polite host will insist that you stay, perhaps two or three times. If the invitations are sincere, but you really do need to go, you have to manage to refuse each time. In this conversation, the unspoken part is in English in parentheses.

A：もうこんな時間ですか。じゃあ、そろそろ〜 (*I must be getting home.*)

B：そうですか。でも、まだ早いんじゃないですか。

A：でも、あしたちょっと〜 (*I have an early day and things to do.*)

B：ああ、そうですか。せっかくいらっしゃったのに、残念ですね。

A：ええ、でも〜

B：それじゃ、タクシーでもお呼びしましょうか。

A：いいえいいえ、どうぞおかまいなく。

In a business or other more formal situation, your desire to leave may be acknowledged relatively quickly. This is particularly true if your call is more obligatory than social and the person you are visiting is very busy. Self-introductions at the beginning of any new relationship and obligatory visits to colleagues and superiors at certain times of the year are all part of 挨拶, which refers to ritual greetings and acknowledgements of all kinds.

When leaving someone else's home or office (as opposed to your own), a simple *Excuse me* is appropriate.

失礼します。（失礼・しつれい）
失礼いたします。
Excuse me.

Other expressions for good-bye include the following:

さようなら。（左様なら・さようなら）
さよなら。
Good-bye.

While this is thought of as the standard word for *good-bye*, its use is relatively restricted. It is used between teachers and students at the end of class. When it is used in a business or family situation, it sounds as if you will not meet again, at least not for a relatively long time. In general, it seems to indicate not just a farewell, but a conclusion (to the school day, to a period in a relationship). Day-to-day relationships are different because they are built on an ongoing sense of obligation which never concludes (and which is constantly reinforced with repeated 挨拶).

では。
じゃあ。
じゃあね。
それでは。
それじゃあ。
Bye. Ciao.

These are all much less formal. じゃ is a contraction of では wherever you hear it (in particular そうじゃない versus そうではない).

ではまた。（又・また）
じゃまた。
それではまた。
それじゃまた。
See you again.

ではまたあとで。 （後で・あとで）
じゃまたあとで。
ではのちほど。 （後ほど・のちほど）
それではまた後で。
それじゃまた後で。
それではのちほど。
See you again later.

バイバイ。
Bye bye.

This sounds like children speaking, adult speaking to children, or the occasional adult interaction.

お先に。 （先・さき）
お先に失礼します。 （失礼・しつれい）
お先に失礼いたします。
Excuse me (for going ahead of you.)

This can be said if you are leaving first. The people remaining behind will bid you farewell with おつかれさま or ごくろうさま. Likewise, it is appropriate if you are a guest staying overnight and you are allowed to bathe before family members. It can be said before or after your bath. Before bathing お先にお風呂いただきます is also appropriate.

As noted above, さようなら is rather strange when leaving home (unless you are setting off on a long journey or you are actually running away). The standard way to say *good-bye* when you leave for school or work is:

行って来ます。 （行く・いく, 来る・くる）
行ってまいります。
行って来るよ。
I'll be back.

Any person staying behind would respond:

行っていらっしゃいませ。 （行く・いく）
行っていらっしゃい。
行ってらっしゃい。
Come back.

Said before going to bed, but also when leaving very late:

お休み。 （休む・やすむ）
お休みなさい。
Good night.

Said to people who are actually sick, and most commonly heard in doctor's offices:

お大事に。 （大事・だいじ）
Take care of yourself.

This sounds like the person who is leaving lives quite far away or when caution is required (i.e. driving home at night in the rain, walking home drunk, etc.).

気をつけて。 （気・き）
気をつけて帰ってください。
気をつけてお帰りください。
気をつけてお帰りくださいませ。
お気をつけて。
お気をつけてお帰りください。
お気をつけてお帰りくださいませ。
Take care on your way home.

Often said to someone about to take a journey of some kind:

体に気をつけて。 （体・からだ, 気・き）
体に気をつけてください。
Take care of yourself.

This can be said at the end of a cooperative or group effort, although either the speaker or the helper can be leaving. Furthermore, these expressions do not actually require that anyone leave (only that the effort be concluded). Expressions with 世話になる may indicate that you feel as if you have benefited specifically.

ご協力ありがとうございました。 （協力・きょうりょく）
どうもご協力ありがとうございました。
Thank you for your cooperation.

どうもお世話になりました。 （世話・せわ）
どうもいろいろお世話になりました。
どうもお世話様でした。 （世話様・せわさま）
どうもいろいろお世話様でした。
Thank you for your help. I am obliged to you.

4.1.5 Apologizing, getting someone's attention, and prefacing a request

すみません。 （済みません・すみません）
すいません。
すまない。
すまん。
どうもすみません。

どうもすいません。
どうもすまない
どうもすまん。
I am sorry. I am obliged.

すみません is the single most common apology in Japan. It can be used really whenever you have made another person aware of your presence (usually in a small way): when you pass in front of them, when you bump into someone, when someone let's you go ahead of them, when someone holds a door open for you, when someone takes a message for you, when someone lends you a bit of change. It is also used to get the attention of a waiter of a salesperson. If Japanese can be accused of apologizing too much when speaking English, it is because すみません is being translated as *I am sorry.*

ごめんなさい。（ご免・ごめん）
ごめん。
ごめんね。
本当にごめんなさい。（本当・ほんとう）
本当にごめん。
本当にごめんね。
本当にごめんよ。
I am sorry. (sounds more intimate or familiar)

悪い。（悪い・わるい）
悪いね。
悪かった。
本当に悪い。（本当・ほんとう）
本当に悪いね。
本当に悪かった。
I am sorry. It was bad of me. I am bad. (relatively informal)

失礼します。（失礼・しつれい）
失礼いたします。
失礼。
Excuse me.

In general, quite formal, although a simple 失礼 in particular is often used with strangers after sneezing, passing in front of them, lightly touching someone accidentally (not in a crowded train), etc. If you actually push someone, すみません is more appropriate.

申し訳ない。（申し訳・もうしわけ）
申し訳ないです。
申し訳ありません。
申し訳ございません。
大変申し訳ございません。（大変・たいへん）
There is nothing I can say.

Much more formal. You are literally saying there is nothing you can say to excuse your behavior.

おそれいります。（恐れ入ります・おそれいります）
大変おそれいります。（大変・たいへん）
大変恐縮です。（恐縮・きょうしゅく）
大変恐縮でございます。
I apologize. I am very sorry. I am very much obliged.

恐れる is a verb which means to *fear* or *awe*.

Almost all of the above apologies followed by が〜 can be used to get someone's attention or to preface a question or request. Such a sentence is really only the first half of a full sentence, but the specific question or request is not spoken until the accommodating listener has given his or her attnetion. The apology you choose reflects how complicated your subsequent statement or question is going to be, and a difficult or awkward favor will be preceded by a more formal opening gambit. Apologies and requests are softened when they are preceded by a hesitant ちょっと or a more polite お忙しいところ. They can be made more substantive by adding 大変. As in English, you can begin a complicated request with an entire story: ご存じかどうかわかりませんが〜 *I don't know if you have heard about this but 〜*. In addition, more formal (and more sincere) speech is generally pronounced more slowly and more carefully with the proper body language.

Neutral interactions with strangers

すみませんが、今何時ですか。
Excuse me, but do you have the time?
ちょっとすみませんが、ここ開いてますか。
Excuse me, is this seat taken?
すみませんが、明日の会議はどこかちょっと調べていただけますか。
Excuse me, but could you find out the location of tomorrow's meeting?
すみませんが、明日の会議はどこですか、ちょっと調べていただけますか。
Excuse me, but could you possibly find out the location of tomorrow's meeting?

The requests above are neutral, and the relative social status of the two participants is either unknown or not that different.

Much more formal interactions

申し訳ありませんが、席を一つ譲っていただけませんか。

I am terribly sorry, but could I possibly borrow one of these chairs?

遅くなって申し訳ありません。

I am terribly sorry that I am late. There is no excuse for my tardiness.

大変申し訳ございません。鍵をなくしてしまいました。

There is no excuse. I have lost the key.

恐れ入りますが、駅までの道を教えていただけますでしょうか。

I am very sorry, but could you possibly tell me the way to the station?

大変恐縮ですが、明日までお待ち願えないでしょうか。

I am very very sorry, but could we possibly have you wait until tomorrow
    (for what we promised today)?

In these interactions, the speaker is aware of his or her own inferior status: a new employee is speaking to superiors, a younger person is speaking to an older person, an employee is speaking to a customer. Alternatively, the speaker may be apologizing for what is either inexcusable or simply stupid and therefore humiliating behavior.

Asking more personal questions

失礼ですがお名前は？

Excuse me, but may I have you name?

大変失礼ですが、お名前を教えていただけますか。

I am very sorry, but could you tell me your name?

失礼ですが、おいくつでしょうか。

Excuse me, but how old are you?

Questions of a personal nature are usually preceded by 失礼 since it is rude to ask personal questions. Note that ごめん does not generally occur in any of these request patterns.

    These same expressions can be used to begin a more involved request for information or to ask a favor. Quite possibly, a thank you of some kind is appropriate at the end.

ありがとうございます。
ありがとうございました。
教えてくれて、ありがとうございます。（教える・おしえる）
教えてくれて、ありがとうございました。
教えていただき、ありがとうございます。
教えていただき、ありがとうございました。
ご親切に、ありがとうございます。（親切・しんせつ）
ご親切に教えていただき、ありがとうございました。

Thank you. Thank you for explaining it to me. I have been a burden, and I thank you.

If your request requires the listener to make a further effort on your part, some expression with よろしく is necessary and appropriate.

よろしくお願いします。（願う・ねがう）
どうぞよろしくお願いします。
よろしくお願いいたします。
どうぞよろしくお願いいたします。
お手数をかけまして、申し訳ありませんが、どうぞよろしくお願いいたします。（手数・てすう, 申し訳・もうしわけ）*Thank you for your consideration. I apologize for being a burden, but thank you very much for your consideration.*

Note that よろしく is used at the beginning of any kind of relationship between people. It signals an implicit request for ongoing cooperation (establishing a relationship where the expression お世話になります should eventually be appropriate). It is used above to conclude the asking of a favor, signaling the hope that you will be able to grant the favor or fulfill the request. It is used at the end of self-introductions, signaling the hope that the new relationship should go well. It is used at the beginning of the new year to reaffirm an ongoing relationship (今年もよろしくお願いいたします). At the end of any kind of planning meeting or discussion it reflects a group desire that all members of the group will play their parts so that the overall project will be successful.

4.1.6 Expressing thanks

Many of the expressions found here have been discussed already with other uses. In particular, expressions used to end a meeting or to take your leave often include a sense of thanks. The range of forms discussed above applies here as well. All of these expressions may be put into the past tense (ございました) if you have a specific event or moment in mind, although such literalness is not necessary.

ありがとうございます。（有り難う・ありがとう）
どうもありがとうございます。
Thank you.

本当にどうもありがとうございます。（本当に・ほんとうに）
誠にどうもありがとうございます。（誠に・まことに）
心から感謝いたします。（感謝・かんしゃ）
Thank you very much. Thank you from the bottom of my heart. My sincere thanks.

どうもありがとう
ありがとう。
どうも。
Thanks.

毎度ありがとうございます。（毎度・まいど）
毎度どうも。毎度。
Thank you every time. (said to a regular customer)

ご協力ありがとうございます。（協力・きょうりょく）
Thank you for your cooperation.

お世話になりました。（世話・せわ）
I am obliged.

4.1.7 Congratulations

おめでとう。（お目出度う・おめでとう）
おめでとうございます。
Congratulations.

あけまして、おめでとう。（明けまして・あけめして）
あけまして、おめでとうございます。
新年、おめでとう。（新年・しんねん）
新年、おめでとうございます。
新年、あけまして、おめでとう。
新年、あけまして、おめでとうございます。
Happy new year.

卒業、おめでとう。（卒業・そつぎょう）
卒業、おめでとうございます。
ご卒業、おめでとうございます。
Congratulations on your graduation.

大学入学・ご入学〜　（入学・にゅうがく）
Congratulations on entering university. Congratulations on beginning university.

誕生日・お誕生日〜　（誕生日・たんじょうび）
ハッピーバスデー。
Happy birthday.

The entire song *Happy Birthday to you* is sung in Japan in カタカナ English.

結婚・ご結婚〜　（結婚・けっこん）
Congratulations on your marriage.

出産・ご出産〜　（出産・しゅっさん）
Congratulations on the birth of your new child.

4.1.8 Condolences

For obvious reasons, condolences are given in difficult circumstances. While a number of standard expressions exist, a general このたびはどうも〜 *On this occasion* 〜 is considered most natural and most heartfelt. 度 is a word meaning *time* or *occasion* which is more polite than 時. Again there is no need actually to complete the expression to convey your emotion (and the fuller expression may actually ring less true). Other more complete expressions of condolence include:

このたびはどうも御愁傷様です。（御愁傷様・ごしゅうしょうさま）
このたびはどうも御愁傷様でございます。
On this occasion, there is profound grief. (愁傷 = *grief, lamentation, condolence*)

心からお悔やみ申し上げます。（お悔やみ・おくやみ）
From the heart, I express regret. (悔やみ = *regret, repent of, mourn for*)

4.1.9 Telephone conversations

Note the prevalence of honorific and very polite verbs forms in all of these exchanges. There is no need for pronouns because the verb forms (and use of name endings like 〜さん) make it obvious who is talking to whom. Also, the beginning and ending of a telephone conversation are the most ritualized, and the two participants may not actually be responding directly to each other. For example, the person answering the phone may or may not give their name. Regardless, the person who has made the call may confirm (or reconfirm) that they have reached the correct person or household.

もしもし。
Hello.

Used to begin any phone conversation, もしもし is actually a very polite way to get a person's attention, and can be used in face-to-face interactions as well (for example, to call out to someone who is facing away).

The person who has answered the phone will follow one of two basic patterns: home or work. Note the が〜 at the end of many of the phrases below. Something どちら様でしょうか or 何でしょうか has been omitted because it is obvious from the context.

もしもし。
もしもし。中山でございますが。
もしもし。中山ですが。
Hello. This is the Nakayama's (residence).

もしもし。
もしもし。日々新聞の人事課でございますが。
もしもし。日々新聞の山森でございますが
もしもし。人事課の山森でございますが
もしもし。人事課でございますが。お世話になります。
もしもし。日々新聞の人事課でございます。お世話になります。

Hello. This is the personnel department of the Nichinichi Newspaper, Yamamori speaking. Thank you for calling.

When answering the phone in a professional setting, it is normal to give the name of the organization, unless there is an intervening operator, then answer with the name of the department, section, or office. Some people give their own name immediately; others do not. It is also common to begin with お世話になります, even before you know who has called. For people who answer the phone a lot, a greeting such as もしもし。日々新聞の人事課でございます。お世話になります may be spoken very quickly as if it is as a single word. This kind of speech is probably more characteristic of men than women, especially those who are extremely busy (or wish to give that impression).

If the person calling wishes to speak to someone else, ask them to wait.

ちょっと待って。（待つ・まつ）
ちょっと待ってください。
ちょっとお待ちください。
少々お待ちください。（少々・しょうしょう）
少々お待ちくださいませ。
少々お待ちいただけませんか。
お電話代わりますから少々お待ちください。（代わる・かわる）

Just a second. Please wait a moment. I will transfer you, so please wait a moment.

If you want to ask who is calling:

失礼ですが。（失礼・しつれい）
失礼ですが、お名前は。（名前・なまえ）
失礼ですが、どちら様ですか。（どちら様・どちらさま）
失礼ですが、どちら様でいらっしゃいますか。
失礼ですが、どちら様でいらっしゃいますでしょうか。

Excuse me. Excuse me, but may I have your name?

A plain 失礼ですが on the phone is usually a request for your name. The last example here (with both いらっしゃいます and でしょう) is characteristic of the extremely ritualistic speech used almost exclusively on the phone or in extremely polite face-to-face interactions. Such a style is generally professional and should be used sparingly outside of such a context.

Finally, when you answer a phone call which has been transferred to you, it is usual to begin with something like the following:

もしもし。電話代わりました。（代わる・かわる）
Hello. Your call has been transferred.

Or you can simply begin all over again.

The person who has made the telephone call also has a number of choices depending on the nature of the call. Again, there is a major difference between calling a residence and calling a business.

もしもし。
中山さんですか。
中山さんのお宅ですか。（お宅・おたく）
中山さんでいらっしゃいますか。
中山さんのお宅でいらっしゃいますか。
Is this Mr. Nakayama? Is this the Nakayama's residence?

中山さんはいらっしゃいますか。
正弘さんはいらっしゃいますか。
正弘さんはいますか。
正弘君はいる？
中山はおりますか。
Is Mr. Nakayama there? Is Masahiro there?

中山さんですか。
正弘さんですか。
正弘君？
中山君かい。
Is this Mr. Nakayama? Is that Mr. Nakayama? Is this Masahiro?
Is that Masahiro? Masahiro?

Note the usage of the honorific でいらっしゃいます rather than super-polite でございます. If the speaker is related to Nakayama, however, it is more polite to use the humble おります. Finally, the question marker 〜かい is very informal, somewhat masculine sounding. The person making the call knows who is going to answer the phone or recognizes the voice of the person who has answered.

日々新聞ですか。
日々新聞の人事課ですか。
Is this the Nichinichi Newspaper? Is this the personnel department of the Nichinichi Newspaper?

人事課の中山さんお願いできますか。
人事課の中山さんにお願いします。
人事課の中山さんはお願いできますか。
May I speak to Mr. Nakayama in the personnel department?

In addition, a person making a phone may have to introduce him or herself. As noted in Chapter 3 (page 234) personal reference on the phone is highly conventualized. Instead of saying 私, it is normal and polite to refer to oneself as こちら. The person you are addressing is そちら or そちら様. *Who* is どちら or どちら様.

こちらは市役所の岡本でございますが。
市役所の岡本でございますが。
市役所の岡本ですが。
市役所の岡本です。
This is Okamoto from City Hall.

私、岡本と申しますが。 （私・わたくし）
私、市役所の岡本と申しますが。 （私・わたくし）
私、市役所の岡本という者ですが。 （私・わたし）
My name is Okamoto from City Hall.

もしもし。市役所の人事課でございますが。
もしもし。市役所の人事課でございます。私、岡本と申します。 （私・わたくし）
Hello. This is the City Hall personnel department. My name is Okamoto.

In this last example, the person calling gives a clear self-introduction. As you might expect, it is very unlikely that the caller will use familiar Japanese is such a situation.

As with greetings, there are several ways to end a phone call. To some degree, the expressions here can be combined, and something like では、失礼いたします。ごめんください is polite and not at all unusual. If you want to be succinct and polite ごめんください is best.

失礼します。 （失礼・しつれい）
失礼いたします。
I will now be rude (by ending the phone call).

失礼しました。 （失礼・しつれい）
失礼いたしました。
夜分遅く失礼しました。 （夜分遅く・やぶんおそく）
夜分遅く失礼いたしました。
I have committed a rudeness. I have been rude by calling you so late.

ごめんください。
Goodbye.

では。
Well ～

バイバイ。
Bye-bye. (childish)

さようなら。さよなら。
Goodbye. (for a while)

The middle of a phone conversation (like the middle of a letter) is not as ritualistic. While an appropriate level of formality must be maintained, this is not substantially different from face-to-face conversation. It is sometimes observed that many phone conversations actually seem to be more polite than face-to-face interactions (turn to the example on page 28), but this is at least partially related to the fact that speaking on the phone does not allow for visual confirmation. No one wants to insult someone accidentally, so better to be too polite than not polite enough. Related to this lack of visual confirmation, it should be noted that neither person on the phone is actually ever silent for very long. In particular, the listener is expected to acknowledge the progress of the conversation with a string of はい's or grunts. This is called 相づち, and the speaker interprets it to mean that the other person is listening and following along. While the role of 相づち is exaggerated on the telephone, it is actually a crucial part of face-to-face conversation as well. Again, neither person is ever silent for very long, and the listener will acknowledge progress in the discussion with short phrases as well as with nods of the head. (People also nod on the phone, but with little effect!) Intonation breaks and use of particle ね at the end of a phrase signal that the speaker expects some kind of acknowledgement, and a lack of appropriate 相づち is usually understood to mean that the listener is not paying attention or does not understand what is going on. Typical phrases include: はい, ええ, そうですか, なるほど, へえ？, あらまあー, as well as the occasional grunt. All of these are most safely translated into English as "I see" or "Really?" with varying degrees of surprise. They should not on their own be taken to mean "I agree" or "Yes, that is what I think as well." The timing for 相づち is actually quite easy to learn because the intonation signals are very obvious, and many learners of Japanese seem to go through a stage when their 相づち is nearly fluent although they are still very unsure of the content of the conversation.

4.1.10 Introductions

Almost all students of Japanese learn to give self-introductions, and it is guaranteed that if you go to Japan, you will introduce yourself more than you have ever done in your entire life. As with phone calls (and most other ritualistic interactions), it is the beginning and ending which follow set patterns. The first word in a self-introduction is almost always はじめまして.

はじめまして。スミスです。
はじめまして。スミスでございます。
はじめまして。スミスと言います。（言う・いう）
はじめまして。スミスと申します。（申す・もうす）
Hello. My name is Smith.

If you prefer, this can be preceded by the statement that you are about to introduce yourself. The causative form is the most elegant.

自己紹介します。（自己紹介・じこしょうかい）
自己紹介いたします。
自己紹介させていただきます。
I will now introduce myself.

There is one basic way to end. よろしく is the single key word which means you are at the end. If it is omitted and you simply stop talking, your listeners will probably be confused.

よろしく。
どうぞよろしく。
どうぞよろしくお願いします。（願う・ねがう）
どうぞよろしくお願いいたします。
Very please to meet you. May we have a fruitful relationship.

以上。（以上・いじょう）
以上です。
That is all.

It is also possible to conclude with a short 以上^{いじょう}です. In situations where a large group of people are all introducing themselves, this expression may be used instead of something with よろしく. However, this is probably most usual in a group of people who consider themselves all to be of more or less equal status.

While Japanese introduce themselves surname first, and while people normally address each other by their family names, a non-Japanese may choose to introduce him or herself in whatever way is comfortable (first or last name only, both names in either order). Of course, Japanese all know that speakers of English generally use first names, and quite often accommodate themselves to this custom. Nevertheless, while you may always use first names with your Japanese friends, it is much less frequent in a professional context. In a situation where you are the boss or the teacher, it may actually be difficult for your employees or your students to address you by your first name.

4.1.11 At a person's house (and at meals)

What a host might say before serving food:

何^{なに}もないんですが、どうぞ。
何もありませんが、どうぞ。
何もございませんが、どうぞ。
何もございませんが、どうぞご遠慮なく。（遠慮・えんりょ）
This is nothing, but please 〜

少しばかりですが、どうぞ。（少し・すこし）
This is just a small (meal), *but please* 〜

お口^{くち}に合^あうかどうかわかりませんが、どうぞ。
I don't know if you will like this or not, but please 〜

どうぞ。
どうぞ、どうぞ。
Please.

さっ、食^たべなさい。
さっ、食べてください。
どうぞ、食べてください。
どうぞ、召^めし上^あがってください。
Please eat.

どうぞ、ご遠慮なく。（遠慮・えんりょ）
Please, don't hesitate.

The claim that there is nothing to eat often seems a bit comic. As a rule, a formal Japanese meal is a feast which the guests cannot hope to eat. I have known people to say that for a dinner to be a success, half of the food put out should be left over when everyone has finished. With the exception of rice (which should never be left in your bowl uneaten), there is actually little compunction to eat everything which has been put before you. Of course, as a meal becomes less formal, this becomes less and less true. Likewise, in an informal situation, the cook is not likely to encourage you with more than a simple どうぞ.

Whether the situation is formal or not, it should be considered mandatory to say いただきます (lit. *I receive*) before eating or drinking anything. It is also polite when someone gives you any kind of gift.

いただきます。
遠慮なく、いただきます。（遠慮・えんりょ）
I receive. I won't hesitate.

おいしそうですね。
おいしそうでございますね。
It looks wonderful. It looks delicious.

いただいてもよろしいでしょうか。
Is it okay to eat?

At the end of a meal, everyone thanks the cook with some version of ごちそうさまでした、 regardless of the formality of the situation.

ごちそうさん。
ごちそうさま。
ごちそうさまです。
ごちそうさまでした。
It was a feast!

The response from the host or cook is:

おそまつさまでした。 （粗末・そまつ）
It was a scanty meal. It was a poor effort. It was nothing.

The host or cook might also ask if you have had enough.

たくさん？
もうたくさん？
たくさんですか。
もういっぱい？
いっぱいですか。
いい？
いいですか？
もうよろしいですか。
十分召し上がりましたか。 （じゅうぶん）
Have you had enough? Are you full?

Be careful when answering short expressions like いい？ with ええ、いいよ. You may end up saying either that you have had enough or that you would like more. This is actually similar to the English conversation, *Okay? Yeah, okay.* Depending on the intonation this can be interpreted to mean either "Yes I have had enough" or "Yes, I would like some more."

4.2 Japan facts

4.2.1 Measurements

Japan is a metric country using meters (メートル), grams (グラム), and liters (リットル). Standard prefixes include milli- (ミリ), centi- (センチ), and kilo- (キロ). CC (シーシー) stands for cubic centimeter. When the context of use is clear, there is no need to specify the question of length, weight, or volume. If we are both on diets and I ask your weight, an answer of ７０キロ is interpreted as 70 kilograms. If I want to know the distance from Kyoto to Kobe, ７０キロ is interpreted as 70 kilometers. Length or distance (距離) is measured in meters (メートル). Area (面積) is measured in meter^2 (平方メートル). Volume (体積) is measured in meter^3 (立方メートル).

Temperature is measured in centigrade セ氏 = 摂氏. The counter for degree is ～度 and 70 degrees C is written セ氏７０度. Fahrenheit is called カ氏 = 華氏 although Japanese, like most people in the world, have no sense of Fahrenheit temperature.

Japan has a traditional system of measurements, all of which appear in literature, and a few of which are still used in daily life. Complete lists can be found on page 1268 of *The New Nelson Japanese-English Character Dictionary* (Haig 1997). Expressions still encountered on a regular basis include:

一寸法師・いっすんぼうし *Tom Thumb*
(一寸 = 1.19 inches = 3.03 centimeters)

一尺・いっしゃく a traditional measurement for cloth still used in making kimono, etc.
(一尺 = 11.92 inches = 30.32 centimeters)

３０００里・り a general expression for a *great distance*
(一里 = 2.44 miles = 3.93 kilometers)

坪・つぼ area of two tatami mats
(一坪 = 35.57 square feet = 3.30 square meters (平方メートル))
Although the size of tatami mats actually varies somewhat from one part of Japan to the next, the measurement is used when discussing the areas of rooms and small land areas.

一反 or 段・いったん a measurement of land
(一反 = 0.245 acres = 0.992 hectares)

一合・ごう a measurement of raw rice
(一合 = 0.384 pints = 0.18 liters)

一升ビン・いっしょうビン a large bottle of sake
(一升 = 1.92 quarts = 1.8 liters)

4.2.2 Currency and counting

The basic unit of currency is the yen, written ～円 and pronounced えん. Coins come in ¥1 (一円), ¥5 (五円), ¥10 (十円), ¥50 (五十円), ¥100 (百円), and ¥500 (五百円) values; paper currency in ¥500 (五百円), ¥1000 (千円), ¥5000 (五千円), and ¥10,000 (一万円) denominations. ¥100 bills still exist but they are basically collectors items (and are not to be spent lightly). This is more and more true of ¥500 bills as well (which are now out of print). A ¥2000 bill is planned for the year 2000. Coins are called 玉 while bills are called 札.

To avoid unscrupulous money lenders (who have been known to add strokes to change one Chinese character into another), the following numbers can be represented unambiguously (should you happen to fill out a contract written with a brush in Chinese characters):

一 → 壱   (not 二, 三, 五 or 十)
二 → 弐   (not 三 or 五)
三 → 参   (not 五)
五 → 伍
十 → 拾   (not 五)

Numbers in Japanese are usually written in Arabic numerals when written horizontally (as in the examples in this book), and in Chinese characters when written vertically. The names of English numbers are based on 10^3 (thousands) while the names of Japanese numbers are based on 10^4 (ten thousands). To keep the correspondence clear, it is easiest to remember reference points. For example: 1,000,000 = 百万 and 1,000,000,000,000 = 一兆. In spite of the differences in organization, Japanese use comas every three places when writing large Arabic numbers. Note that there are also differences between the names of large numbers in the US and the UK.

一	いち	1 *one*
十	じゅう	10 *ten*
百	ひゃく	100 *one hundred*
千	せん	1,000 *one thousand*
一万	いちまん	10,000 *ten thousand*
十万	じゅうまん	100,000 *one hundred thousand*
百万	ひゃくまん	1,000,000 *one million*
千万	せんまん	10,000,000 *ten million*
一億	いちおく	100,000,000 *one hundred million*
十億	じゅうおく	1,000,000,000 *one billion* (UK *1,000 million*)
百億	ひゃくおく	10,000,000,000 *ten billion* (UK *10,000 million*)
千億	せんおく	100,000,000,000 *one hundred billion* (UK *100,000 million*)
一兆	いっちょう	1,000,000,000,000 *one trillion* (UK *one billion*)

The symbols of mathematics are the same in Japanese and English, but the translations of the symbols are obviously different.

Addition (10+10=20)
To add is 足^たす.
１０足^たす１０は２０だ。１０に１０を足^たすと２０になる。
Ten plus ten is twenty. Adding ten to ten makes twenty.

Subtraction (10–3=7)
To subtract is 引^ひく.
１０引^ひく３は７だ。１０から３を引^ひくと７になる。
Ten minus three is seven. Taking three from ten makes seven.

Multiplication (10×10=100)
To multiply is 掛^かける, and the multiplication table is called the 九々^{くく}.
１０かける１０は１００だ。１０に１０をかけると１００になる。
Ten multiplied by ten is one hundred. Multiplying ten by ten makes one hundred.

Division (10÷5=2)
To divide is 割^わる.
１３を６で割^わると２が立^たって１残^{のこ}る。１０を５で割^わると２が立^たつ。
Dividing thirteen by six is two with one left over. Ten divided by five is two.

Fractions (分数^{ぶんすう}) such as 1/3 are read 三分^{さんぶん}の一^{いち} (and are usually written in the following steps: 3, /3, and 1/3, at least when the writer is thinking in Japanese).

Odd numbers are 奇数^{きすう}. Even numbers are 偶数^{ぐうすう}.

4.2.3 Time and calendars

Units of time from smallest to largest include the following:

ミリ秒	びょう	*millisecond*
秒	びょう	*second*
分	ふん	*minute*
時	じ	*hour*
日	か・にち	*day*
週	しゅう	*week*
月	つき	*month*
か月	かげつ	*month* (also written カ月 or ヶ月)
年	ねん	*year*
十年	じゅうねん	*decade*
世紀	せいき	*century*
千年	せんねん	*millennium*

十分 may be pronounced じゅっぷん or じっぷん. The latter pronunciation is considered archaic by some, elegant by others. 一月 may be pronounced いちがつ *January* or ひとつき *one month*. 一か月 refers to a length of time one month long.

AM is 午前. PM is 午後. Twelve noon is 正午. A time such as 1:30 is pronounced いちじはん or いちじさんじゅっぷん. There are no special terms for fifteen minutes before or after the hour. Trains and other such schedules are written in a 24-hour clock.

The names of the dates of the month are given here. Remember all of the irregularities: (the first, the first ten dates, the twentieth, any date ending in a four).

1日	ついたち	17日	じゅうしちにち
2日	ふつか	18日	じゅうはちにち
3日	みっか	19日	じゅうくにち
4日	よっか	20日	はつか
5日	いつか	21日	にじゅういちにち
6日	むいか	22日	にじゅうににち
7日	なのか	23日	にじゅうさんにち
8日	ようか	24日	にじゅうよっか
9日	ここのか	25日	にじゅうごにち
10日	とおか	26日	にじゅうろくにち
11日	じゅういちにち	27日	にじゅうしちにち
12日	じゅうににち	28日	にじゅうはちにち
13日	じゅうさんにち	29日	にじゅうくにち
14日	じゅうよっか	30日	さんじゅうにち
15日	じゅうごにち	31日	さんじゅういちにち
16日	じゅうろくにち		

As with months, 3日, 4日, 5日, etc. may be pronounced さんにち, よんにち, ごにち, etc. when you are talking about the length of time, i.e. 5日かかった "It took five days" (and not the name of the day). Of course 5日間 is probably more common. A leap year with a February 29th is an 閏年.

In addition to the Western (solar) calendar, each year in Japan is also designated with the name of the emperor and the year of the reign. The current reign is called 平成 which began on the 7th of January 1989. The first year of an new era is known as 元年 rather than 一年, giving for example 平成元年, *the First Year of Heisei*. A list of the reigns and the years of the modern era (usually from Meiji onward) is given here. Japanese began officially to use the Western calendar on the first day of January 1873 (明治6年). As is seen here, the conventional ordering for dates is year/month/day.

めいじ　　　明治　1年　1868　(明治元年)
　　　　　　　　　2年　1869～
　　　　　　明治45年　1912

たいしょう	大正	１年	１９１２年７月３０日（大正元年）
		２年	１９１３〜
	大正１５年		１９２６
しょうわ	昭和	１年	１９２６年１２月２５日（昭和元年）
		２年	１９２７〜
	昭和６３年		１９８８
へいせい	平成	１年	１９８９年１月７日（平成元年）
		２年	１９９０〜
	平成１２年		２０００

The emperor is usually referred to as the 天皇 *The Son of Heaven* while alive. After death, the era name is used. Hirohito (裕仁) is now referred to as the 昭和天皇. The current emperor is Akihito (明仁). His wife is Michiko (美知子), and the crown prince is Naruhito (徳仁).

Japanese talk about both the Chinese zodiac and the Western zodiac. Current years are indicated. Add or subtract twelve to determine earlier and later correspondences.

| Chinese zodiac | 鼠年・ねずみどし・ねどし *rat* (1996); 牛年・うしどし *ox* (1997); 虎年・とらどし *tiger* (1998); 兎・うさぎどし・うどし *rabbit* (1999); 竜年・たつどし *dragon* (2000); 蛇年・へびどし・みどし *snake* (2001); 馬年・うまどし *horse* (2002); 羊年・ひつじどし *sheep* (2003); 猿年・さるどし *monkey* (2004); 鳥年・とりどし *rooster* (2005); 犬年・いぬどし *dog* (2006); 猪年・いのししどし・いどし *boar* (2007) |
| Western zodiac | 山羊座・やぎざ *Capricorn*; 水瓶座・みずがめざ *Aquarius*; 魚座・うおざ *Pisces*; 牡羊座・おひつじざ *Aries*; 雄牛座・おうしざ *Taurus*; 双子座・ふたござ *Gemini*; 蟹座・かにざ *Cancer*; 獅子座・ししざ *Leo*; 乙女座・おとめざ *Virgo*; 天秤座・てんびんざ *Libra*; 蠍座・さそりざ *Scorpio*; 射手座・いてざ *Sagittarius* |

The usually translation of *birthday* is 誕生日. The more technical *date of birth* is 生年月日 which reflects the usual order for writing dates in Japanese.

The Japanese equivalent of *Baby, what's your sign?* is 君、何座？ Such a line is as effective in Japanese as its English equivalent. Japanese are also interested in blood type (血液型) as a reflection of personality. The question here is 君、何型？ While everyone has their own theory, A 型 is serious; B 型 is moody, O 型 is optimistic, and AB 型 is unpredictable. Most Japanese are A 型.

National holidays

Japan has fifteen national holidays. The period from the 29th of April to the 5th of May contains four holidays and usually one weekend, and is known as Golden Week. Periods of social and obligatory gift-giving are in August (お中元) and at the end of the year (おせいぼ). The New Year's holiday is officially one day. Larger stores throughout the country generally re-open for business on the 2nd. Unofficially, many smaller stores are closed (and little work is done) until the 3rd of January or so.

1月　1日	お正月・おしょうがつ, 元旦・がんたん	New Year's Day
1月15日	成人の日・せいじんのひ	Coming of Age Day
2月11日	建国記念日・こくみんきねんび	National Foundation Day
3月22日	春分の日・しゅんぶんのひ	Vernal Equinox Day
	☆ゴールデン・ウィーク	Golden Week
4月29日	☆緑の日・みどりのひ	Green Day (the former Emperor's birthday)
5月　3日	☆憲法記念日・けんぽうきねんび	Constitution Day
5月　4日	☆国民の休日・こくみんのきゅうじつ	Citizen's Day
5月　5日	☆子供の日・こどものひ	Children's Day
7月20日	海の日・うみのひ	Ocean Day
9月15日	敬老の日・けいろうのひ	Respect for the Aged Day
9月23日	秋分の日・しゅうぶんのひ	Autumnal Equinox Day
10月10日	体育の日・たいいくのひ	Sports Day
11月　3日	文化の日・ぶんかのひ	Culture Day
11月23日	勤労感謝の日・きんろうかんしゃのひ	Labor Thanksgiving Day
12月23日	天皇誕生日・てんのうたんじょうび	the Emperor's Birthday

4.2.4 Names

Japanese names (given names in particular) almost all have interesting stories behind them. A common conversation topic is a person's name. When you are first introduced, it is polite to ask how a person writes their name in Chinese characters (それはどの字で〜 or それはどの漢字で〜), which leads naturally to the question of what the character's mean, and on to why those characters were chosen.

Top family names 1994					
	1. 佐　藤	さとう	8. 小　林	こばやし
	2. 鈴　木	すずき	9. 山　本	やまもと
	3. 高　橋	たかはし	10. 加　藤	かとう
	4. 田　中	たなか	11. 吉　田	よしだ
	5. 渡　辺	わたなべ	12. 山　田	やまだ
	6. 伊　藤	いとう	13. 佐々木	ささき
	7. 中　村	なかむら	14. 松　本	まつもと

15. 山 口　やまぐち　　　18. 斎 藤　さいとう
16. 井 上　いのうえ　　　19. 清 水　しみず
17. 木 村　きむら　　　　20.　林　はやし

Top given names	Boys	Girls
	1. 昭二・しょうじ	1. 和子・かずこ
	2. 昭・あきら	2. 昭子・あきこ
1927	3. 和夫・かずお	3. 久子・ひさこ
	4. 清・きよし	4. 照子・てるこ
	5. 昭一・しょういち	5. 幸子・さちこ
	1. 勝・まさる	1. 和子・かずこ
	2. 勇・いさむ	2. 洋子・ようこ
1944	3. 勝利・かつよし	3. 幸子・さちこ
	4. 進・すすむ	4. 節子・せつこ
	5. 勲・いさお	5. 勝子・かつこ
	1. 誠・まこと	1. 由美子・ゆみこ
	2. 浩・ひろし	2. 真由美・まゆみ
1964	3. 修・おさむ	3. 明美・あけみ
	4. 隆・たかし	4. 久美子・くみこ
	5. 達也・たつや	5. 恵子・けいこ
	1. 誠・まこと	1. 久美子・くみこ
	2. 大輔・だいすけ	2. 裕子・ひろこ
1975	3. 学・まなぶ	3. 真由美・まゆみ
	4. 剛・つよし	4. 智子・ともこ
	5. 大介・だいすけ	5. 陽子・ようこ
	1. 翔太・しょうた	1. 愛・あい
	2. 拓也・たくや	2. 彩・あや
1989	3. 健太・けんた	3. 美穂・みほ
	4. 翔・しょう	4. 成美・なるみ
	5. 達也・たつや	5. 沙織・さおり
	1. 拓也・たくや	1. 美咲・みさき
	2. 健太・けんた	2. 愛・あい
1995	3. 翔太・しょうた	3. 遥・はるか
	4. 翼・つばさ	4. 佳奈・かな／舞・まい
	5. 大樹・だいき	5. -------

Source: Meiji Life Insurance, cited in たまごクラブ特別編集まひよ名づけ百科／ベネッセ
コーポレーション1995

4.2.5 Letter writing

As one might expect, Japanese letter writing styles range from the very formal to the very informal. To write letters with confidence, it is probably best to imitate the Japanese themselves and buy a guide book with explicit guidelines and examples of letters for all occasions. Such books are available for Japanese readers as well as for students of the language. In general, however:

Opening and closing words

Instead of expressions such as *Dear*, *To whom it may concern*, or *Yours sincerely*, more formal Japanese letters begin and end with standard pairs of words. These are simply placed at the beginning and end of a letter, and must be chosen to reflect the content, purpose, and formality of the letter. Again, getting a guide book is the best way to be sure.

Opening words	*Closing words*	
拝啓・はいけい	敬具・けいぐ	most common formal, requires both seasonal greetings and expressions of concern about the other person
前略・ぜんりゃく	早々・そうそう	less formal, seasonal greetings are optional although expressions of concern are still required
拝復・はいふく	敬具・けいぐ	for a reply, but not very common

Seasonal greetings

The opening line of a personal letter usually makes some kind of reference to the season or to the weather. There are a whole series of possible openings for formal letters. Less formal letters might say only that it has been hot or cold or rainy.

How are you?

As with an English letter it is standard to express concern about the well being of the other person. This may be a simple "How are you?" One may ask after the health of the reader and their family. Or one may apologize for not writing in a long time.

Closing

Again, it is customary to express concern about the well-being, health, or business of the other person before signing off with the appropriate closing word.

4.2.6 Postal addresses

Japanese political geography is divided into increasingly smaller areas. In cities, except for main thoroughfares, streets themselves rarely have names, and even when they do, they are almost never used in addresses. Addresses reflect increasingly precise area names.

Cities are divided into areas which are then divided into smaller areas and so on until the individual houses are numbered. The numbers on individual houses often look random because the houses are numbered in the order in which they were built (or registered). The number therefore tells you little about location and is often not used. It is quite possible (and in fact very common) to have someone's address and have almost no clue as to where they live.

Below, possible area names are listed from largest to smallest. These are followed by address examples. Note that address elements are ordered from largest to smallest — basically the reverse of what is standard in English. When translating from Japanese into English, it is common to reorder the various elements to conform to the normal English order (i.e. something like smallest to largest).

International subdivisions

| 国 | こく | *country* | 中国・ちゅうごく、英国・えいこく、 |
| | | | アメリカ合衆国・アメリカがっしゅうこく |

National subdivisions

〒	郵便マーク	*post code, zip code*	〒627、〒071-23、
	(ゆうびん)		〒980-0811
都	と	*urban area*	東京都・とうきょうと
道	どう	*province*	北海道・ほっかいどう
府	ふ	*urban prefecture*	京都府・きょうとふ, 大阪府・おおさかふ
県	けん	*prefecture*	長野県・ながのけん, 熊本県・くまもとけん
州	しゅう	*state*	コロラド州、オックスフォード州
		(for US and Australian states, for UK counties)	

State/county subdivisions

市	し	*city*	京都市・きょうとし, 松山市・まつやまし
郡	ぐん	(rural) *district*	東郡・あずまぐん・ひがしぐん
町	まち・ちょう	*town*	東町・あずままち・ひがしちょう・etc.
村	むら	*village*	東村・あずまむら・ひがしむら

City/town subdivisions

区	く	*ward* (in big cities)	新宿区・しんじゅくく
町	まち・ちょう	*town*	青山町・あおやままち・あおやまちょう
条	じょう	*street*	七条・しちじょう
丁目	ちょうめ	*block*	三丁目・さんちょうめ
番地	ばんち	*sub-division*	54番地・ばんち
号室	ごうしつ	*room, apartment*	403号室・ごうしつ

These last four are often written with numbers only. 番街 (ばんがい) or 通り (とお) can be used to translate street names into Japanese, e.g. 5番街 (ばんがい) *Fifth Avenue*, ベーカー通り (どお) *Baker Street*, etc.

The name of the addressee is followed by the character ～様〔さま〕 for personal correspondence while ～殿〔どの〕 is used on official business addressed to an individual. If the addressee is a teacher, ～先生〔せんせい〕 may also be used: 山本正明様〔やまもとまさあきさま〕, 山本正明殿〔やまもとまさあきどの〕, 山本正明先生〔やまもとまさあきせんせい〕. When a letter is addressed to a company, the company name is followed by the characters ～御中〔おんちゅう〕: 東京銀行御中〔とうきょうぎんこうおんちゅう〕. When you are sent (or you send) a self-addressed envelope, it should be labeled with ～行〔ゆき〕: 山本正明行〔やまもとまさあきゆき〕. Before returning this envelope, the ～行〔ゆき〕 is crossed out and replaced with ～様〔さま〕, ～殿〔どの〕, or ～御中〔おんちゅう〕.

4.2.6.1 Examples

Note the conventional ordering (from largest to smallest) of the elements within the address.

〒０７０北海道旭川市末広５条９丁目　山本一明　様

Mr. Kazuaki Yamamoto, Suehiro 5 Jo 9 Chome, Asahikawa-shi, Hokkaido 070

〒０７０北海道旭川市末広５条９丁目　山本一明様方〔かた〕　John Smith 様

Mr. John Smith,　c/o Kazuaki Yamamoto, Suehiro 5 Jo 9 Chome, Asahikawa-shi, Hokkaido 070

〒６０２－０３京都府京都市北区小山東玄似町　中村詩織　様

Ms. Shiroi Nakamura, Higashigen'ni-cho, Koyama, Kita-ku, Kyoto-shi, Kyoto-fu 602-03

〒３６５群馬県前橋市大手町１－１－１　群馬県教育長　坂西哲男　殿

Mr. Tetuo Sakanishi, Superintendent of Schools, Gunma Prefecture, Otemachi 1-1-1 (1 Jo 1 Chome 1 Banchi), Maebashi-shi, Gunma-ken 365

〒１５０東京都渋谷区渋谷３－９－９東京建物渋谷ビル　株式会社エルゴソフト　御中

Ergosoft, Ltd, Tokyo Shibuya Building, Shibuya 3-9-9, Shibuya-ku, Tokyo 150

Note in the above that there are several different styles of romanization. As noted at the end of this chapter, there are actually several different romanized versions of Japanese, but they all have enough in common that this should not cause a great deal of confusion.

4.2.6.2 Japanese prefectures and capital cities (total forty-seven)

Japan has forty-three prefectures (県〔けん〕), two urban prefectures (符〔ふ〕), one ～道 (北海道〔ほっかいどう〕), and one ～都 (東京都〔とうきょうと〕) for a total of forty-seven national subdivisions. The thirteen largest cities by population (as of October 1995) are numbered on the far right. Note that 川崎市〔かわさきし〕 and 北九州市〔きたきゅうしゅうし〕 are not prefectural capitals. The prefectures are sorted into their 地方〔ちほう〕 or *regions* (which are arranged basically from north to south, east to west). (source: Statistics Bureau and Statistics Center, Management and Coordination Agency, Government of Japan)

北 海 道	ほっかいどう	札 幌 市	さっぽろ	[5th]

東 北	とうほく			
青 森 県	あおもり	青 森 市	あおもり	
岩 手 県	いわて	盛 岡 市	もりおか	
宮 城 県	みやぎ	仙 台 市	せんだい	[12th]
秋 田 県	あきた	秋 田 市	あきた	
山 形 県	やまがた	山 形 市	やまがた	
福 島 県	ふくしま	福 島 市	ふくしま	

関 東	かんとう			
茨 城 県	いばらき	水 戸 市	みと	
栃 木 県	とちぎ	宇都宮 市	うつのみや	
群 馬 県	ぐんま	前 橋 市	まえばし	
埼 玉 県	さいたま	大 宮 市	おおみや	
千 葉 県	ちば	千 葉 市	ちば	[13th]
東 京 都	とうきょう			[1st]
神奈川 県	かながわ	横 浜 市	よこはま	[2nd]
神奈川 県	かながわ	川 崎 市	かわさき	[9th]

中 部	ちゅうぶ			
新 潟 県	にいがた	新 潟 市	にいがた	
富 山 県	とやま	富 山 市	とやま	
石 川 県	いしかわ	金 沢 市	かなざわ	
福 井 県	ふくい	福 井 市	ふくい	
山 梨 県	やまなし	甲 府 市	こうふ	
長 野 県	ながの	長 野 市	ながの	
岐 阜 県	ぎふ	岐 阜 市	ぎふ	
静 岡 県	しずおか	静 岡 市	しずおか	
愛 知 県	あいち	名古屋 市	なごや	[4th]

近 畿	きんき			
三 重 県	みえ	津 市	つ	
滋 賀 県	しが	大 津 市	おおつ	
京 都 府	きょうと	京 都 市	きょうと	[6th]
大 阪 府	おおさか	大 阪 市	おおさか	[3rd]
兵 庫 県	ひょうご	神 戸 市	こうべ	[7th]
奈 良 県	なら	奈 良 市	なら	
和歌山 県	わかやま	和歌山 市	わかやま	

中 国	ちゅうごく		
鳥 取 県	とっとり	鳥 取 市	とっとり
島 根 県	しまね	松 江 市	まつえ
岡 山 県	おかやま	岡 山 市	おかやま
広 島 県	ひろしま	広 島 市	ひろしま [10th]
山 口 県	やまぐち	下 関 市	しものせき

四 国	しこく		
徳 島 県	とくしま	徳 島 市	とくしま
香 川 県	かがわ	高 松 市	たかまつ
愛 媛 県	えひめ	松 山 市	まつやま
高 知 県	こうち	高 知 市	こうち

九 州	きゅうしゅう		
福 岡 県	ふくおか	福 岡 市	ふくおか [8th]
福 岡 県	ふくおか	北九州 市	きたきゅうしゅう [11th]
佐 賀 県	さが	佐 賀 市	さが
長 崎 県	ながさき	長 崎 市	ながさき
熊 本 県	くまもと	熊 本 市	くまもと
大 分 県	おおいた	大 分 市	おおいた
宮 崎 県	みやざき	宮 崎 市	みやざき
鹿児島 県	かごしま	鹿児島 市	かごしま

琉 球	りゅうきゅう		
沖 縄 県	おきなわ	那 覇 市	なは

Tokyo itself consists of twenty-three wards (区), twenty-seven cities (市), six towns (町・町), and eight villages (村). The wards (the central part of the city) are listed here.

東 京 都	とうきょうと		
足 立 区	あだち	墨 田 区	すみだ
荒 川 区	あらかわ	世田谷 区	せたがや
板 橋 区	いたばし	台 東 区	たいとう
江戸川 区	えどがわ	中 央 区	ちゅうおう
大 田 区	おおた	千代田 区	ちよだ
葛 飾 区	かつしか	豊 島 区	としま
北 区	きた	中 野 区	なかの
江 東 区	こうとう	練 馬 区	ねりま
品 川 区	しながわ	文 京 区	ぶんきょう
渋 谷 区	しぶや	港 区	みなと
新 宿 区	しんじゅく	目 黒 区	めぐろ
杉 並 区	すぎなみ		

4.2.7 Telephones and telephone numbers

The basic three minute local call is ¥10. Public telephones are 公衆電話. Many Japanese use pre-paid phone cards (テレフォン・カード) which come in denominations ranging from ¥500 to ¥5000. Many public phones will accept only phone cards. Public phones in Japan also vary as to whether international calls are possible are not. As in the rest of the world, cell phones are increasingly common. As part of the new etiquette, it is considered polite (particularly on trains) to use cell phones (携帯電話) away from others (i.e. in the areas at the end of a train car rather than in your seat).

Police emergency calls are 110 (no charge). Fire and ambulance emergency calls are 119 (no charge). Telephone information is 104. Collect calls/reverse charges are made at 106. Time is 117. Weather is 177. An English speaking Nippon Telephone and Telegraph (NTT) operator is found on 0120-364483. An 0120 call is toll free. Cell phone numbers begin with code 090.

All area codes (局番) within Japan begin with a 0 (this 0 is omitted when calling from overseas), although they vary in length. Area codes may be from two to five digits long while the actual phone number may be from four to eight digits long. Tokyo numbers are the longest at ten digits (beginning with code 03). The international dialing code for Japan is 81. The telephone book is a 電話帳. Information/directory assistance is ご案内.

Remember that Japanese has at least two ways of reading the basic numbers.

一	いち・ひ	六	ろく・む
二	に・ふ	七	しち・なな
三	さん・み	八	はち・や
四	し・よ・よん	九	きゅう・く・ここ
五	ご・いつ	十	じゅう・とお

These various names are used to create easy to remember mnemonics for phone numbers, much like 1-800-CALLUSA might stand for 1-800-225-5872 in the US. In the UK, the same affect is achieved with easy to remember number combinations such as 0800-123123 or the ever popular 0800-000000. Japanese examples take the form 0120-262-158 where the sounds of the numbers form a sentence, in this case フロニイコーヤ which means 風呂に行こうや！ " Let's go the bath!". This would be typical for a hotel with a large spa.

4.3 Japanese orthography

The Japanese language is written with a mixture of Chinese characters (漢字), two syllabaries (平仮名 and 片仮名), and a smattering of romanization (ローマ字). The Japanese government has established a list of 1945 characters which may be used in all official documents, including newspapers. These are called the 常用漢字. In addition there is a list of 284 characters for use only in proper names. Chinese characters were borrowed

with sound and meaning from China beginning in the sixth century A.D. As is illustrated below, both かな syllabaries are derived from Chinese characters, although by different
methods. ひらがな are cursive versions of characters with the same sound. カタカナ are
more angular symbols which are parts of the original Chinese characters. They originated
as abbreviations of the more complex characters. Unlike Chinese characters, ひらがな and
カタカナ do not have intrinsic meaning and are therefore more like letters of the English
alphabet (which also represent sound only).

   The Chinese characters listed in these two tables are not the only possible origins although they are one source.

平仮名・ひらがな

あ	安	い	以	う	宇	え	衣	お	於
か	加	き	機	く	久	け	計	こ	己
さ	左	し	之	す	寸	せ	世	そ	曾
た	太	ち	知	つ	川	て	天	と	止
な	奈	に	仁	ぬ	奴	ね	祢	の	乃
は	波	ひ	比	ふ	不	へ	部	ほ	保
ま	末	み	美	む	武	め	女	も	毛
や	也			ゆ	由			よ	与
ら	良	り	利	る	留	れ	礼	ろ	呂
わ	和	ゐ	為			ゑ	恵	を	遠
ん	无								

片仮名・カタカナ

ア	阿	イ	伊	ウ	宇	エ	江	オ	於
カ	加	キ	機	ク	久	ケ	介	コ	己
サ	散	シ	之	ス	須	セ	世	ソ	曾
タ	多	チ	千	ツ	川	テ	天	ト	止
ナ	奈	ニ	仁	ヌ	奴	ネ	祢	ノ	乃
ハ	八	ヒ	比	フ	不	ヘ	部	ホ	保
マ	末	ミ	三	ム	牟	メ	女	モ	毛
ヤ	也			ユ	由			ヨ	興
ラ	良	リ	利	ル	流	レ	礼	ロ	呂
ワ	和	ヰ	井			ヱ	慧	ヲ	乎
ン	尔								

All Chinese characters have both sound and meaning, and in the history of Japanese, かな
developed from specific characters in order to represent the verbal endings of the language
(which have sound but whose parts have no specific meaning). In the modern language
we find 行く, 行かない, 行ける, 行ければ, 行ったら, etc. In writing from the earlier part
of the twentieth century, we find representations such as 行ク, 行カナイ, 行ケル, 行ケレ

バ, 行ッタラ, as well as many more than the 1945 Chinese characters used today. Using characters for sound only remains as a vestige in the representations of some foreign place names. For example, America was originally represented 亜米利加 (アメリカ) while England still is 英国 (えいこく) or イギリス. London once was 倫敦 (リンドン). Since Asia is represented 亜細亜 (アジア) and abbreviated with the character 亜 (ア), the US is generally referred to as 米国 (べいこく). Other common geographic abbreviations include the following. Note that not all of the compounds here even have a Japanese reading. Thus, the compound 蘭国 appears in newspapers and might be read らんこく but this reading is not listed in dictionaries, and the compound is simply read オランダ. Similarly for 仏国・フランス and 伊国・イタリア.

ヨーロッパ	欧州	おおしゅう	Europe
オランダ	蘭国		Holland
ドイツ	独国	どっこく	Germany
フランス	仏国		France
イタリア	伊国		Italy
オーストラリア	豪州	ごうしゅう	Australia
北アメリカ	北米	ほくべい	North America
南アメリカ	南米	なんべい	South America
ロシア	露国	ろこく	Russia
	ソ連	ソれん	Soviet Union
	旧ソ	きゅうソ	former Soviet Union

Of course, the names of most foreign countries are now written in カタカナ, but the Chinese character abbreviations persist in compounds such as 日米 (にちべい) *Japan-US* or 英米 (えいべい) *UK-US* or words such as 来英 (らいえい) *coming to England*. Names in places like China are obviously written in Chinese characters and, as noted on page 115, pronounced as closely as possible to an original Chinese pronunciation.

There are two basic styles of romanization, Hepburn (named after Dr. James Hepburn who used it in his Japanese and English dictionary published in 1867) and Kunrei. Hepburn (ヘボン式 (しき)) is based on the spelling conventions of English and is probably the most common. Kunrei (訓令式 (くんれいしき)) is the official romanization taught in Japanese schools and used in Japan (as well as in this book). The two systems differ primarily in the representation of the し, ち, つ, and ふ sounds (*shi, chi, tsu, fu* versus *si, ti, tu, hu*) as well as in the representation of long vowels (using macrons or writing double vowels). There are also some older and idiosyncratic romanization possibilities, as well as romanization systems based on languages other than English. The very first romanization of Japanese was based on Portuguese (Rodriguez 1604-1608). Some examples of less standard romanization include: 伊藤 (いとう) *Itoh* or ケーキを *keeki-wo*. The sound of an ん changes quality before an *m, b,* or *p*. This is sometimes represented in the romanization: 群馬 (ぐんま) *Gumma* or *Gunma*, 文部省 (もんぶしょう) *Mombusho* or *Monbusho*, 乾杯 (かんぱい) *kampai* or *kanpai*. There are various ways to indicate long vowels such as おう (ō, ô, o, oo, ou, o). The character ん may or may not have a special form, a common way being an apostrophe where ambiguity might result. Compare: 記念 kinen *commemoration* and 禁煙 kin'en *no smoking*.

Vocabulary associated with orthography

清音	せいおん	unvoiced sound (か, さ, た, は, etc.)
濁音	だくおん	voiced sound (が, ざ, だ, ば, etc.)
拗音	ようおん	consonant + *y* + vowel (きゃ, きゅ, etc.)
促音	そくおん	double consonant sound (りっぱ, etc.)
濁り	にごり	the two dots associated with voiced sounds
半濁音	はんだくおん	circle which indicates a *p* (ぱ, ぴ, ぷ etc.)
踊り字	おどりじ	repetition symbols (時々, すゝむ, すゞき)
棒	ぼう	カタカナ symbol for a long vowel (a *stick*)

Punctuation

句点, 丸	くてん・まる	period 。
読点	とうてん	comma 、
	ピリオド	period .
	コンマ	comma ,
疑問符	ぎもんふ	question mark ?
感嘆符	かんたんふ	exclamation point !
中黒, 中点	なかぐろ・なかてん	dot used in lists, between カタカナ words ・
中線	なかせん	dash ―
	スラッシュ	slash ／
点線	てんせん	ellipsis dots ・・・
波形	なみがた	～
かぎ括弧	かぎかっこ	single quotation marks 「 」
二重かぎ括弧	にじゅうかぎかっこ	double quotation marks 『 』
引用符	いんようふ	quotation marks " "
丸括弧	まるかっこ	parentheses ( )

Common symbols and typescript styles

米印	こめじるし	※
郵便マーク	ゆうびんマーク	post office mark 〒
傍点・脇点	ぼうてん・わりてん	dots used to make characters easier to read (to the right of vertical text)
下線	かせん	<u>underline</u>
傍線	ほうせん	sideline (to the right of vertical text)
太字	ふとじ・ボールド	**bold**
斜体	しゃたい・イタリック	*italics*

4.3.1 Ordering Japanese words

The familiar あいうえおか〜 ordering of Japanese words is called the あいうえお順 or the 五十音順 based on the above 五十音図 *Fifty Sound Table* (with ten 行 *rows* and five 段 *columns* of sounds). It is used to organize dictionaries and is the closest Japanese equivalent to English alphabetic order. There is a second, traditional ordering which begins いろはにほへと〜. In its entirety, which includes two obsolete sounds (ゐ *wi* and ゑ *we*) as well as the *wo* reading of を, this ordering forms a Buddhist poem on the transitoriness of life. This translation is taken from page 1248 of *The New Nelson Japanese-English Character Dictionary* (Haig 1997).

いろはにほへと	色はにおいへど	*Colors are fragrant*
ちるぬるを	散りぬるを	*but they fade away.*
わかよたれそ	我世誰ぞ	*In this world of ours*
つねならむ	常ならむ	*none lasts forever.*
うゐのおくやま	有為の奥山	*Today cross a mountain*
けふこえて	今日越えて	*of life's illusions,*
あさきゆめみし	浅き夢見じ	*and there will be no more shallow*
ゑひもせす	酔もせず	*dreaming, no more drunkenness.*

While both orderings developed in the same period of Japanese history, the いろは ordering has fallen into disuse in the last century.

4.3.2 Unexpected spellings

While most Japanese words are written according to well-known rules, there are some apparent irregularities.

おお not おう	多い・おおい *many, frequent, common*; 狼・おおかみ *wolf*; 大きい・おおきい *big*; 氷・こおり *ice*; 氷る・こおる *freeze*; 凍る・こおる; *freeze, congeal*; こおろぎ *cricket* (insect); 十・とお *ten* (things); 遠い・とおい *far*; 通り・とおり *road, manner*; 通る・とおる *go along, commute, travel down*; 透る・とおる *be transparent*; 通す・とおす *hand over, pass by*; 炎・ほのお *flame, flare*; 頬・ほお・ほほ *cheek*

(おお is a reflex of an original おほ representation.)

ええ not えい	お姉さん・おねえさん *older sister*
	ねえ *right?, indeed*

(The two words here are both of Japanese origin; the more common えい indicates words of Chinese origin.)

ぢ not じ   近々・ちかぢか *soon, before long*; 縮・ちぢむ *shrink, contract*; 縮・ちぢ める *shrink, cut short*; 散り散り・ちりぢり *scattered*; 鼻血・はなぢ *nose-bleed*; 間近い・まちがい *near, close at hand*

づ not ず   息づく・いきづく *to live, be alive*; 口付け・くちづけ *a kiss*; 元気づける・ げんきづける *encourage, cheer up*; 言付け・ことづけ *a message*; 近づく・ ちかづく *approach*; 近づける・ちかづける *place near*; 鼻詰まり・はなづ まり *stuffed up nose*; 続く・つづく (something) *continues, goes on*; 続け る・つづける *continue* (something); 綴り・つづり *spelling*; 相づち・あい づち *nod one's head, chime in* (during a conversation); 片付ける・かたづ ける *clean up*

The following in compounds
〜付け・づけ *continue* (something); 〜伝い・づたい *continue* (something); 〜積み・づみ *continue* (something); 〜詰め・づめ   *continue* (something); 〜連れ・づれ

(There is no difference in the pronunciation of ぢ and じ. Likewise for づ and ず.)

Selected references
参考文献・さんこうぶんけん

The works listed here were consulted (in ways large and small) during the writing of this book. While all entries contain the information usually found in an English bibliography, the language of the entry reflects the language of the book. English and Japanese titles are mixed, and ordered in English alphabetic order.

Akiyama, Nobuo and Carol Akiyama. 1994. *Japanese for the Business Traveler*. Barron's Educational Series, Hauppauge, New York.

Akiyama, Nobuo and Carol Akiyama. 1995. *Master the Basics: Japanese*. Barron's Educational Series, Hauppauge, New York.

Akiyama, Nobuo and Carol Akiyama. 1996. *2001 Japanese and English Idioms. 2001日本語慣用句・英語イディオム*. Barron's Educational Series, Hauppauge, New York.

Ashby, Janet. 1994. *Read Real Japanese*. Kodansha International, Tokyo.

Bachnik, Jane M. and Charles J. Quinn. 1994. *Situated Meaning: Inside and Outside in Japanese Self, Society, and Language*. Princeton University Press, Princeton, New Jersey.

Batchelor, R. E. and M. H. Offord. 1982, 1993. *Using French: A Guide to Contemporary Usage*. Cambridge University Press, Cambridge.

Batchelor, R. E. and C. J. Pountain. 1992. *Using Spanish: A Guide to Contemporary Usage*. Cambridge University Press, Cambridge.

Bowring, Richard and Haruko Uryu Laurie. 1992. *An Introduction to Modern Japanese. Book One: Grammar Lessons*. Cambridge University Press, Cambridge.

Chaplin, Hamako Ito and Samuel E. Martin. 1967. *A Manual of Japanese Writing 2*. Yale University Press, New Haven, Connecticut.

Comrie, Bernard. 1976. *Aspect*. Cambridge University Press, Cambridge.

Comrie, Bernard. 1985. *Tense*. Cambridge University Press, Cambridge.

Corwin, Charles (ed.). 1968. *A Dictionary of Japanese and English Idiomatic Equivalents. 和英熟語慣用句辞典*. Kodansha International, Tokyo.

Daniels, F. J. 1967. Japanese. In *Word Classes*. North-Holland Publishing Company, Amsterdam. 57-87. (Reprinted from *Lingua* 17).

Di Sciullo, Anna-Maria and Edwin Williams. 1987. *On the Definition of Word*. The MIT Press, Cambridge.

Drohan, Francis G. 1991. *A Handbook of Japanese Usage*. Charles E. Tuttle Company, Routledge, Vermont and Tokyo, Japan.

Downing, Pamela. 1996. *Numeral Classifier Systems: The Case of Japanese*. John Benjamins Publishing Company, Amsterdam and Philadelphia.

Durrell, Martin. 1992. *Using German: A Guide to Contemporary Usage*. Cambridge University Press, Cambridge.

Flexner, Stuart Berg (ed.). 1987. *The Random House Dictionary of the English Language, Second Edition*. Random House, New York.

藤原与一・磯貝英夫・室山敏昭. 1985. *表現類語辞典*. 東京堂出版, 東京.

Hadamitzky, Wolfgang and Mark Spahn. 1997. *Kanji & Kana* (revised edition). Charles E. Tuttle Company, Routledge, Vermont and Tokyo, Japan.

Haig, John H. (ed.). 1997. *The New Nelson Japanese-English Character Dictionary*. Charles E. Tuttle Company, Routledge, Vermont and Tokyo, Japan. Revised edition of the Classic Edition by Andrew N. Nelson, 1974.

Halle, Morris and G. N. Clements. 1983. *Problem Book in Phonology*. The MIT Press, Cambridge.

Hamano, Shoko. 1998. *The Sound-Symbolic System of Japanese*. CSLI Publications, Center for the Study of Language and Information, Stanford, California and Kurosio Publishers, Toyko.

Hatasa, Yukiko Abe, Kazumi Hatasa, and Seiichi Makino. 2000. *Nakama 2: Japanese Communication, Culture, Context*. Houghton Mifflin, Boston.

Hepburn, James Curtis. 1983. *A Japanese and English Dictionary with an English and Japanese Index*. Charles E. Tuttle Company, Routledge, Vermont and Tokyo, Japan. First published in 1867.

Hiroo Japanese Center. 1989. *The Complete Japanese Verb Guide*. Charles E. Tuttle Company, Routledge, Vermont and Tokyo, Japan.

堀内克明／監修. 1996. *カタカナ外来語／略語辞典*. 自由国民社, 東京.

Horvat, Andrew. 2000. *Japanese Beyond Words: How to Walk and Talk Like a Native Speaker*. Stone Bridge Press, Berkeley, California.

Ide, Sachiko and Naomi Hanaoka McGloin (eds.). 1990. *Aspects of Japanese Women's Language*. Kurosio Publishers, Tokyo.

Iida, Masayo. 1996. *Context and Binding in Japanese*. CSLI Publications. Center for the Study of Language and Information, Stanford, California.

Jacobsen, Wesley, M. 1992. *The Transitive Structure of Events in Japanese*. Kurosio Publishers, Tokyo.

Jansen, Marius B. (ed.) 1988. *Japanese Studies in the United States: Part I, History and Present Condition.* Japanese Studies Series XVII. The Japan Foundation. Available from the Association for Asian Studies, Ann Arbor.

Japanese-English Picture Dictionary. 1990. Éditions Rényi, Toronto.

The Japan Foundation Japanese Language Institute. 1986. *Basic Japanese-English Dictionary.* 基礎日本語学習辞典. Oxford University Press, Oxford.

Japan Foundation. 1993. 海外び日本語教育の現況. *Survey Report on Japanese-Language Education Abroad.* The Japan Foundation, Tokyo.

Japan Foundation. 1998. Japanese Language Statistics in 1998. *Breeze.* Fall 1999 Quarterly. The Japan Foundation, Tokyo.

Japan Foundation. 1998. 海外び日本語教育の現況. *Survey Report on Japanese-Language Education Abroad.* The Japan Foundation, Tokyo.

Jorden, Eleanor Harz. 1987, 1988, and 1990. *Japanese: The Spoken Language*, Parts I, II, and III. Yale University Press, New Haven, Connecticut.

Jorden, Eleanor Harz and Hamako Ito Chaplin. 1976. *Reading Japanese.* Yale University Press, New Haven, Connecticut.

Kaiser, Stephen. 1993. *Japanese Language Teaching in the Nineties.* Japan Library, Sandgate, Folkestone, Kent.

Kamiya, Taeko. 1997. *Japanese Particle Workbook.* Weatherhill, New York and Tokyo.

Kaneko, Anne. 1990. *Japanese for All Occasions.* Charles E. Tuttle Company, Routledge, Vermont and Tokyo, Japan.

Kawashima, Sue A. 1999. *A Dictionary of Japanese Particles.* Kodansha International, Tokyo.

木原研三・福村虎治郎・小西友七／編者. 1997. *新グローバル＆ニューセンチュリー英和・和英辞典CR-ROM.* 三省堂, 東京.

Kindaichi, Haruhiko. 1978. *The Japanese Language* (translated by Umeyo Hirano). Charles E. Tuttle Company, Routledge, Vermont and Tokyo, Japan. Originally published as 日本語 by Iwanami Shoten (1957).

金田一春彦・林大・柴田武／編者. 1988. 日本語百科大辞典. *An Encyclopaedia of the Japanese Language.* 大修館書店, 東京.

小泉 保・船城道雄・本田晶治・仁田義雄・塚本秀樹. 1989. 日本語基本動詞用法辞典. 大修館書, 店東京.

Koine, Yoshio (ed.). 1980. *Kenkyusha's New English Japanese Dictionary.* 新英和大辞典. Kenkyusha, Toyko.

広辞苑・第四版. 1991. 岩波書店, 東京.

広辞苑・CD-ROMマルチメディア版. 1996. 岩波書店, 東京.

Kuno, Susumu. 1973. *The Structure of the Japanese Language.* The MIT Press, Cambridge.

Lampkin, Rita L. 1995. *Japanese Verbs and Essentials of Grammar.* NTC Publishing Group, Chicago, Illinois.

Levin, Beth and Malka Rappaport Hovav. 1995. *Unaccusativity*. The MIT Press, Cambridge.

Loveday, Leo J. 1996. *Language Contact in Japan*. Oxford University Press, Oxford.

Machida, Nanako. 1998. On the null beneficiary in benefactive constructions in Japanese. In Akatsuka, Noriko et al. eds., *Japanese Korean Linguistics* , Vol. 7. 409- 425.

Makino, Seiichi and Michio Tsutsui. 1986. *A Dictionary of Basic Japanese Grammar*. 日本語基本文法辞典. The Japan Times, Tokyo.

Makino, Seiichi and Michio Tsutsui. 1995. *A Dictionary of Intermediate Japanese Grammar*. 日本語文法辞典 *(中級編)*. The Japan Times, Tokyo.

Makino, Seiichi, Yukiko Abe Hatasa, and Kazumi Hatasa. 1998. *Nakama 1: Japanese Communication, Culture, Context*. Houghton Mifflin, Boston.

Makkai, Adam, Mazine T. Boatner, and John E. Gates. 1984, 1991, 1995. *Handbook of Commonly Used American Idioms*. Barron's Educational Series, Hauppauge, New York.

Martin, Samuel E. 1952. Morphophonemics of standard colloquial Japanese. *Language* 28.3 (part 2). Supplement: Language Dissertation No. 47.

Martin, Samuel E. 1988. *A Reference Grammar of Japanese*. Charles E. Tuttle Company, Routledge, Vermont and Tokyo, Japan. First published by Yale University Press in 1975.

Masuda, Koh (ed.). 1974. *Kenkyusha's New Japanese-English Dictionary*. Kenkyusha, Tokyo.

松村明／編. 1988. *大辞林*. 三省堂, 東京.

Maynard, Senko K. 1990. *An Introduction to Japanese Grammar and Communication Strategies*. The Japan Times, Tokyo.

Maynard, Senko K. 1998. *Principles of Japanese Discourse*. Cambridge University Press, Cambridge.

三上章. 1960. *象は鼻が長い*. くろしお出版, 東京.

Miller, Roy Andrew. 1962. *A Japanese Reader: Graded Lesson for Mastering the Written Language*. Charles E. Tuttle Company, Routledge, Vermont and Tokyo, Japan.

Miura, Akira. 1983. *Japanese Words & Their Uses*. Charles E. Tuttle Company, Routledge, Vermont and Tokyo, Japan.

Miura, Akira. 1993. *English in Japanese: A Selection of Useful Loanwords*. Weatherhill, New York and Tokyo.

Miura, Akira and Naomi Hanaoka McGloin. 1994. *An Integrated Approach to Intermediate Japanese*. 中級の日本語. The Japan Times, Tokyo.

Miyamoto, Akito (Japanese) and E. C. Parnwell (English). 1989. *オックスフォード米語イラスト辞典*. *The New Oxford Picture Dictionary*. Oxford University Press, Oxford.

Mizutani, Osamu. 1981. *Japanese: The Spoken Language in Japanese Life* (translated by Janet Ashby). The Japan Times, Tokyo.

Mizutani, Osamu and Nobuko Mizutani. 1987. *How to be Polite in Japanese.* 日本語の 敬語. The Japan Times, Tokyo.

Mori, Junko. 1999. *Negotiating Agreement and Disagreement in Japanese.* John Benjamin Publishing Company, Amsterdam and Philadelphia.

Naganuma, Naoe. 1951. *Grammar and Glossary* (accompanying *Naganuma's Basic Japanese Course*). Tokyo, Japan.

Nakao, Seigo (ed.). 1995. *Random House Japanese-English English-Japanese Dictionary.* Random House, New York.

Niyekawa, Agnes M. 1991. *Minimum Essential Politeness in Japanese: A Guide to the Honorific Language.* Kodansha International, Tokyo.

Olshtain, Elite and Andrew D. Cohen. 1989. Apology: A Speech-Act Set. In Shoshana Blum-Kulka, Juliane House, and Gabriele Kasper (eds.), *Cross-cultural Pragmatics: Requests and Apologies.* Ablex Publishing, Norwood, New Jersey. 18–35.

O'Neill, P. G. 1972. *Japanese Names.* Weatherhill, New York and Tokyo.

Oxford-Duden Pictorial Japanese and English Dictionary. 1983. Oxford University Press, Oxford.

Palmer, F. R. 1986. *Mood and Modality.* Cambridge University Press, Cambridge.

Rodriguez, João. 1604–8 *Arte de Lingoa de Iapam.*

Rubin, Jay. 1998. *Making Sense of Japanese: What the Textbooks Don't Tell You.* Kodansha International, Tokyo.

Sansom, G. B. 1995. *An Historical Grammar of Japanese.* Curzon Press, London. First published by Oxford University Press in 1928.

Sasaki, Mizue. 1997. *Speak Japanese Naturally.* The Hokuseido Press, Tokyo.

Shibamoto, Janet S. 1985. *Japanese Women's Language.* Academic Press, Orlando, Florida.

Shibatani, Masayoshi. 1990. *The Languages of Japan.* Cambridge University Press, Cambridge.

Sherard, Michael, L. 1986. *Escape from Katakana English.* NHK Bunka Koza, Japan Broadcasting Corporation.

The Society of Writers, Editors and Translators, Tokyo, Japan. 1998. *Japan Style Sheet: The SWET Guide for Writers, Editors, and Translators.* Revised edition. Stone Bridge Press, Berkeley, California.

Stein, Jeff (ed.). 1979. *The Random House College Dictionary.* Revised Edition. Random House, New York.

Sugawara, Makoto. 1985. *Nihongo: A Japanese Approach to Japanese.* The East Publications, Tokyo.

杉本つとむ・岩淵　匡／編. 1994. 日本語学辞典. *New Japanese Linguistic Dictionary.* おうふう, 東京.

Tagashira, Yoshiko and Jean Hoff. 1986. *Handbook of Japanese Compound Verbs.* The Hokuseido Press, Tokyo.

武部良明. 1976. 漢字の用法. 角川書店, 東京.

Tatematsu, Kikuko, Yoko Tateoka, Takashi Matsumoto, and Tsukasa Sato (Inter-University Center for Japanese Language Studies). 1992. *Writing Letters in Japanese.* The Japan Times, Tokyo.

田宮規雄／監修. 1995. たまごクラブ特別編集たまひよ名づけ百科. ベネッセコーポレーション, 東京.

Tanimori, Masahiro. 1994. *Handbook of Japanese Grammar.* Charles E. Tuttle Company, Routledge, Vermont and Tokyo, Japan.

寺村秀夫. 1982, 1984, and 1991. 日本語シンタクスと意味 I, II, III. くろしお出版, 東京.

Tsujimura, Natsuko. 1996. *An Introduction to Japanese Linguistics.* Blackwell Publishers, Cambridge, Massachusetts and Oxford, England.

Tsujimura, Natsuko and Takako Aikawa. 1999. Two types of *zi*-verbs in Japanese. *Journal of the Association of the Teachers of Japanese.* 33.1. 26–43,

梅棹忠男・金田一春彦・坂倉篤義／編. 1997. 日本語大辞典・第二版. 講談社, 東京.

Unger, J. Marshall. 1996. *Literacy and Script Reform in Occupation Japan.* Oxford University Press, Oxford.

謡口明. 1989. 間違えやすい漢字の使い分け: これだけ知っていれば十分. 日本実業出版社, 東京.

Uwate, Aiko Nishi. 1982. 名: *Japanese Names for Babies.* Los Angeles, California.

Vance, Timothy J. 1987. *An Introduction to Japanese Phonology.* State University of New York Press, Albany, New York.

Vance, Timothy J. 1993. *Kodansha's Romanized Japanese-English Dictionary.* Kodansha International, Tokyo.

Watt, Yasuko Ito and Richard Rubinger. 1998. *Readers Guide to Intermediate Japanese.* University of Hawai'i Press. Honolulu, Hawai'i.

English index

This index lists both English words (found in discussions) and subject topics.

Japanese index
索引・さくいん

This index lists all the Japanese words (prefixes, suffixes, etc.) which are found in discussions or are used to make a particular point. Specific words found in the longer lists of examples are not included. Words are listed in the あいうえお〜 order. A "〜" generally indicates that a word is a prefix, a suffix, or part of a compound. Topics which have Japanese names are found romanized in the English index.

MORRIS AUTOMATED INFORMATION NETWORK

0 1004 0274004 5

DATE DUE

JAN - - 2013